SMART PORTFOLIOS

Robert Carver is an independent investor, trader and writer. He spent over a decade working in the City of London before retiring from the industry in 2013. Robert initially traded exotic derivative products for Barclays Investment Bank and then worked as a portfolio manager for AHL – one of the world's largest hedge funds – before, during and after the global financial meltdown of 2008. He was responsible for the creation of AHL's fundamental global macro strategy, and then managed the fund's multi-billion dollar fixed income portfolio.

Robert has Bachelors and Masters degrees in Economics. His first book *Systematic Trading: A unique new method for designing trading and investing systems* was published in 2015. Robert manages his own portfolio of equities, funds and futures using the methods you can find in his books.

SMART PORTFOLIOS

A practical guide to building and maintaining
intelligent investment portfolios

Robert Carver

Hh

Hh Harriman House

HARRIMAN HOUSE LTD
18 College Street
Petersfield
Hampshire
GU31 4AD
GREAT BRITAIN
Tel: +44 (0)1730 233870
Email: enquiries@harriman-house.com
Website: www.harriman-house.com

First published in Great Britain in 2017
Copyright © Robert Carver

Hardback ISBN: 978-0-85719-531-9
eBook ISBN: 978-0-85719-572-2

British Library Cataloguing in Publication Data
A CIP catalogue record for this book can be obtained from the British Library.

"Apportion what you have into seven, or even eight parts, because you do not know what disaster might befall the land."

— Ecclesiastes 11:2 (New Standard Version)

"I only have one piece of advice. Diversify.

"And if I had to offer a second piece of advice, it would be: Remember that the future will not necessarily be like the past. Therefore we should diversify."

— Harry Markowitz, pioneer of portfolio theory

"Fund consultants like to require style boxes such as 'long-short,' 'macro,' 'international equities.' At Berkshire our only style box is '**smart**.'"

— Warren Buffett, Annual letter to
Berkshire Hathaway shareholders, February 2011

Contents

Part Two: Creating Smart Portfolios

Part Three: Predicting Returns

Part Four: Smart Rebalancing

Preface

This book is about answering three deceptively simple questions:

1. **What** should you invest in?

2. **How much** of your money should you put into each investment?

3. Should you subsequently make **changes** to your investments through further buying or selling?

All these questions involve **trade-offs**: the world of investment is a place without free lunches, and where you can't eat all your cake and expect to have leftovers.

For example: should you invest in the portfolio with the highest return, the lowest risk, or some mixture of the two? Is buying a couple of investment funds sufficient, or is it worth creating a highly diversified portfolio, splitting your cash between dozens or even hundreds of funds and individual shares? Do you need to constantly buy and sell to make the highest returns, or should you save on brokerage costs and do nothing? Are the higher costs of actively managed funds justified by higher returns?

Making smart investment decisions also means worrying about **uncertainty**. Those who regard themselves as financial experts – such as journalists, economists and fund managers – continuously make highly confident predictions about what will happen in financial markets tomorrow, next week, or next year. But in reality the future is unclear and forecasting incredibly hard.

Life would be very easy if you knew with 100% certainty that bonds will definitely do better than stocks next year. But what should you do if there is only a 55% chance of bonds outperforming – and how do you calculate that probability?

My aim in this book is to provide an accessible and practical guide to creating and managing smart portfolios which can deal with the trade-offs and uncertainties of the real world. There are no fancy equations, and no prior knowledge of financial theory or statistics is required. Constructing and managing portfolios doesn't have to be rocket science – you just need to be a bit **smarter**.

I will show you simple methods to create the portfolio that suits you best – regardless of how comfortable you are with risk, how much money you have to invest, what funds and equities you can buy, and how predictable future returns are.

The world of investment is more diverse than ever, but also more complicated. This book will help you navigate that world.

Who should read this book

The general principles in the book should be applicable to investors in most countries. The examples are drawn from the US and the UK because of the wide range of Exchange Traded Funds[1] (ETFs) that are available in these countries, and because of my own personal experience. Nevertheless all the techniques I describe can be easily adapted for use elsewhere.

This book is primarily intended for professionals who are paid to manage other people's money, from financial advisors (who could be managing relatively small accounts of tens of thousands of dollars or pounds), private bankers and wealth managers; right through to institutional funds (which I would define as managing at least ten million dollars or pounds). In addition, experienced private investors should find much of value in the approaches I describe here.

I believe it is useful for all investors to understand the difference between managing small portfolios and large ones, and for this reason the example portfolios I use start at a few hundred dollars and pounds, and go up to one billion dollars. Throughout the book I'll explain the different implications of paying retail brokerage costs or managing huge institutional funds.

The book is intended for experienced investors, so I don't cover the detailed mechanics of how shares are purchased, or how ETFs and other kinds of funds work. If this is an area where you need to do some background reading then Appendix A contains a selection of books that will help fill any gaps in your knowledge.

Even experts in portfolio construction techniques should find this book worthwhile. I think we all need reminding that the models used in finance are based on assumptions that are usually wrong, and often dangerous.[2]

Finally, the methods in this book can be applied to any type of portfolio, containing one or more different kinds of asset.[3] In particular, I show you how to invest in collective

---

1.   An ETF is a kind of investment fund which can be traded and owned like a normal equity. Normally ETFs are used for straightforward investments like tracking stock market indices, and are relatively cheap to own.

2.   There are also a number of technical footnotes sprinkled throughout the book to keep more knowledgeable readers interested.

3.   Technical note: So in principle specialist institutional managers can use it to create single country equity portfolios or allocate across global equities. However the methods are most valuable when

funds like ETFs, but also directly in individual equities. I also explain how and when it makes sense to combine these approaches.

Finding your way around

Although I've tried to use a minimum of jargon it's impossible to avoid completely. Often it's easier to use a short phrase containing one or two words rather than writing long complicated sentences. I have defined any technical terms at the point of first use. There is also a glossary at the end of the book in case you miss, or forget, those definitions.

Some key concepts will need more than just a footnote or glossary entry to explain. For those I'll use **concept boxes**, like the one you can see below.

CONCEPT: THIS IS AN EXAMPLE OF A CONCEPT BOX

These boxes contain very important concepts which you need to understand.

It's vital that you understand everything inside a concept box. The same cannot be said of **digression boxes**, like this one:

DIGRESSION: THIS IS AN EXAMPLE OF A DIGRESSION BOX

These boxes contain material that is interesting and will be useful for some readers, but they are not essential reading if you're short of time.

What's in this book

This book is divided into four parts. The first part covers the essential **theory**. Don't panic: I have included the absolute minimum of theoretical mumbo jumbo as my intention is to give you an intuitive understanding rather than bombarding you with dozens of equations. But it's important to understand the basics of why certain portfolios are better than others, what effect uncertainty has on the choice of the best portfolio, and how costs affect these decisions.

Part two is about applying that theory to create portfolios using a **top-down** process.

---

applied in a top level asset allocation problem where you start with a clean slate, and then allocate the portfolio amongst asset classes, and then within them.

A top-down process involves starting with the big decisions before moving on to smaller ones. The biggest investment decision is which **asset classes** you want to own, such as bonds and equities, and how to divide your portfolio between them. Then you should look at how the equity part of your portfolio should be carved up, and the same for bonds. As I'll explain later in the book, the top-down approach is the best way of getting the most diversified portfolio for the amount of capital you have.

In the first two parts of the book I assume that future returns can't be predicted and will be identical for all the assets in your portfolio.[4] But in part three I discuss what you should do with your portfolio if you think you or others can **predict future returns** to some degree.

I explain some forecasting models I use to predict returns and demonstrate their use, as well as how to safely incorporate your own judgment into portfolio selection. I show you how you can evaluate actively managed[5] mutual funds and unit trusts, and decide if they are worthy of inclusion in your investment shopping basket. By the end of part three you'll also know some jargon: you'll understand what **smart beta** is, what constitutes **robo advice**, and be able to evaluate these fashionable new trends in investment.

In part four I look at what you should do after you've built your portfolio. It would be nice if you could just sit back and watch your investments grow, but in practice life isn't that straightforward. Some trading is occasionally necessary to keep your portfolio on an even keel and to stop it becoming unbalanced. Part four explains how to do this **rebalancing** without it costing you a fortune in brokerage commissions and other costs. I also show you how to minimise your tax bill.

Appendix A points you towards some useful resources, including other books and websites that might be worth reading, and several data sources. Appendix B lists the assumptions I use in the book about costs and the behavior of different kinds of assets. Appendix C contains technical details for the skilled enthusiasts who want to go beyond the basic techniques I present in the main body of the book.

At the end of the book is a short reference section which contains copies of useful tables and other information.

There is also a website for this book: www.systematicmoney.org/smart. This contains links to spreadsheets with further example portfolios, other sheets to help you build your own portfolios, and some to help you implement the techniques in Appendix C.

---

4.   Technical note: Actually I assume that risk-adjusted returns are identical. You will understand the distinction after reading chapter three.

5.   An example of a passive investment is an ETF that just invests in an index like the S&P 500 or FTSE 100. These are normally relatively cheap, with low annual management fees. An active fund manager will buy a different portfolio and try to outperform the index. This normally costs more.

Introduction

Investing today

ONE OF MY FAVORITE BOOKS ON INVESTMENT IS TITLED *SIMPLE But Not Easy* by Richard Oldfield. Investment has never been easy, but it used to be much simpler.

Twenty-five years ago investors had few options. Most people relied on professional fund managers to look after their money and these managers charged fat fees for their expertise. But with high equity returns this didn't matter so much. If you were earning 10% a year on your investments, paying 2% to an expert manager seemed reasonable.

Braver souls went out on their own and invested directly into portfolios of shares. With wide spreads and chunky brokerage commissions this wasn't a cheap option either, especially if you churned your portfolio with frequent buying and selling. Fortunately the extra costs of frequent trading were masked by the upward march of the stock market; just like fund management charges were.

Most investors stuck to firms listed in their domestic market: much easier than trying to buy equities listed in a foreign country, and the fantastic returns available locally were more than enough. Academic researchers call this effect **home bias**.

Widows, orphans and others of a nervous disposition preferred to own bonds. Their pedestrian returns were scoffed at by the brainwashed disciples of the cult of equities. Few embraced the mixed portfolios of bonds and stocks that academic researchers advocated. As the brokers and fund managers might have asked, when did you last see a professor of economics driving a Porsche?

As for more esoteric investments like hedge funds, these were the exclusive domain of the rich and well connected.

Things have certainly moved on since then. What if we could acquire a time machine and spirit an investor off the sidewalk of Wall Street or the pavement of the City of London forward to the present day? What changes would they notice, apart from a few new skyscrapers and a less formal dress code?

Firstly, it is a lot **cheaper** to invest. Thanks to technological innovation and fierce competition, brokerage charges are much lower, especially in the US. However, these apparently great deals can be dangerous. The constant jabbering of market commentators and slick advertising of online stockbrokers is a toxic combination, which can easily lure you into unnecessary buying and selling. Ironically, lower commissions have resulted in most people trading far too much: just like half-price deals in the supermarket encourage shoppers to fill their trolleys to the brim.

In principle though lower costs are a good thing. The fees charged by fund managers are also considerably lower these days. Investors can now choose from a wide range of cheap **passive funds** that follow a particular index like the S&P 500 or FTSE 100. Competition from passive managers has also helped drive down the fees of active management.

That is the good news. The bad news is that **expected returns have become a lot lower and more unpredictable**. So although **absolute** costs are lower, they're still **relatively** high once lower expected returns are taken into account.

Why have expected returns fallen? Well, inflation has fallen off a cliff. This is good news in theory, but high past inflation fooled investors into thinking healthy returns were their birthright. It's no longer safe to assume asset prices will steadily increase year after year.

Indeed a quarter century of steadily rising share prices has been sharply interrupted twice; once in the tech crash of 1999 and then again in 2008. In contrast, bonds have performed incredibly well in the last couple of decades, especially once we account for their lower risk. But this great track record probably won't last. As I'm writing this book, many bonds have very low or even negative yields, and the fear of inevitable interest rate increases spooks the market.

It was never easy to predict financial market movements; but now the future is more uncertain than ever.

Still, thanks to good bond performance, investing across a **diversified** portfolio of bonds and stocks has been a very successful strategy over the last 25 years. It is easier than ever to buy such a portfolio because there are far more investment options in the market. Specifically, an exciting new type of passive investment fund appeared in 1993: **Exchange Traded Funds** (ETFs).

Exchange Traded Funds give easy to access stocks, bonds and many other asset classes that the average investor of 25 years ago would have been completely unaware of.

Passive ETFs are much cheaper than the actively managed funds whose performance has rarely justified their heftier fees. Our time traveller from the past might be surprised to find that active funds have not gone away. Perhaps they would have expected a few superstar fund managers to survive the onslaught of passive indexing, but they'd be shocked to find that active managers still control over 70% of the market. The active fund management industry continues to befuddle and bedazzle investors who cannot work out whether promises of higher returns can really justify such premium prices.

ETFs also make it much easier to get exposure to different countries, so in theory at least home bias should be a thing of the past. In practice many people still prefer the comforting familiarity of stocks listed in their home country, or funds covering the same space.

Although I am a big fan of ETFs, most of them have one crucial disadvantage. They give you exposure to a specific index (like the S&P 500 or FTSE 100), made up of fixed weightings in particular securities. These indices are normally weighted by **market capitalisation (market cap)**: the more valuable the firm, the larger the weight. There is fierce debate amongst academic researchers and industry insiders as to whether this is the best possible weighting scheme.

There are other ways of weighting firms in indices and recently ETFs have appeared to implement them. For example, in many countries you can opt for an **equally weighted** fund where each firm in an index has the same weight, regardless of size.

Plenty of fund managers now also offer something called **smart beta**. The more complex flavors of smart beta sit somewhere between active management and passively tracking the performance of a particular index to get **beta**; the finance industry's fancy term for market capitalization-weighted exposure. I'll talk about smart beta much more in part three.

There are also currency hedged ETFs, leveraged ETFs, inverse ETFs, target retirement ETFs, long:short ETFs, commodity ETFs, and volatility ETFs. I probably missed some. No doubt there will be a few more kinds of ETFs out by the time you read this.

All this choice is a good thing, but our investor from the past will be frozen into inaction by the sheer variety of what is now on offer in the investment marketplace. Indeed, any thoughtful investor of the present day should feel exactly the same way.

A highly diversified portfolio of stocks and bonds, spread across many countries, is more accessible than before. But what is the best way of achieving it? Funds or individual shares? Active funds or passive ETFs? Passive market cap indexing, or one of the numerous alternatives? Should we buy and hold forever, or actively trade?

Also, what exactly does a highly diversified portfolio look like? What proportion of stocks, bonds and other kinds of assets should it contain? How much should you allocate to each country or industry? Should you try to pick individual stocks? All these options involve different trade-offs between costs and benefits. Which is best?

Finally, without the comfort blanket of a permanent bull market, future returns seem more uncertain than ever. How should you adapt your portfolio to reflect this uncertainty?

Their head spinning with confusion, our visitor from the past runs back into their time machine and slams the door; desperate to return to the comforting simplicity of the past.

Why this book?

Numerous books have been written in the last 20 years to help investors make sense of the changing and ever more complex number of investment options. Why have I written another one – and why should you read it?

Smart: not highly technical or overly simplistic

Many books promote one of two extreme views about portfolio building: it's either a black art requiring advanced mathematics to grasp, or a trivial problem requiring you to buy a small portfolio of ETFs regardless of how much you have to invest. The truth is more nuanced.

The standard method for finding the best portfolio is indeed relatively complex, but it isn't necessary to use it, and it may even be dangerous to do so. On the other hand, a portfolio comprised of a small number of ETFs is fine if you have just a few hundred dollars or pounds, but investors with more money can do better.

In contrast to those two polar approaches, this book is about being **smart**: not overly technical, and not too simplistic. It's smart to have an intuitive understanding of the relevant financial theory, and in part one I explain that theory in an accessible way. It's smart to use straightforward methods that are consistent with the right theory, and it's smart to use simple rules of thumb to help you make decisions. This book is full of methods, and rules of thumb; all fully explained with examples.

I give you smart techniques to build your portfolio, but also to rebalance it in the most efficient fashion. You'll understand why all investors should own some equities, but why a portfolio with 100% equities is never justified. I also explain thoroughly why diversification is the most important attribute in a smart portfolio, and the best way to achieve it.

A single integrated approach to building your portfolio

There are many great books on investing in shares, deciding your asset allocation, investing in ETFs, and on picking active fund managers. However, I think what an investor really needs is a single integrated approach with a framework that works for their entire portfolio. This book describes such an approach – which UK and US based investors can use to build multi-asset portfolios. These portfolios can consist of ETFs, active funds and equities; or a combination of all three.

I give you simple rules to determine whether you should be investing directly in shares, or in ETFs, and how many funds or shares you should buy. Plus I explain how you can compare cheaper passive ETFs and more expensive actively managed funds.

I address important questions including: how should you select the best ETF? How should you compare the costs and other features of different ETFs? Are new fangled smart beta ETFs worth buying? What are the hidden pitfalls of inverse ETFs, leveraged ETFs, commodity ETFs, and currency hedged ETFs? Is robo investing worth paying for? How many shares do you need to buy for adequate diversification? How should you select those shares? Should you invest in alternative assets, and if so how?

Finally I explain how to blend assets with different levels of risk, and how to construct portfolios that suit the level of risk that the investor can cope with.

Uncertainty

There is one key factor which is almost completely overlooked in most books on investment: **uncertainty**. Predicting the future is much harder than most people think. Historical data on returns contains much less useful data than you might expect. In this book I discuss the reasons why forecasting returns is so difficult. I also explain the importance of slow moving economic trends such as the multi-decade fall in inflation, and how this makes the past less relevant today.

Only once you are used to thinking about the world in uncertain terms can you start making the right decisions. For example, an active fund is outperforming its passive benchmark, despite charging considerably more. But is that down to luck, or is it skill? I provide you with tools to answer this and other similar questions.

Although the future is uncertain there are important degrees of uncertainty. Some properties of future returns are more predictable than others: how risky different assets are, and how similar they are likely to perform. I show you how to use these more reliable kinds of information when you're constructing your own portfolios. Finally, I also cover the use of systematic forecasting algorithms, and plain old human gut feel, when trying to predict the future.

Costs

Until quite recently most investors ignored costs, preferring to focus on increasing returns. However, many people are now realising that costs are very important; unlike uncertain returns they are highly predictable, and lowering costs is the easiest way to increase the returns on your portfolio. Mostly the advice given to investors keen on paying less for their investment is to stick to passive ETFs.

This is pretty good advice, but there is much more to using costs to make the right investment decisions. First of all you need the right data, so I show you how to calculate the true costs of your investments to a high degree of accuracy, including invisible costs that are usually ignored or hidden from view. Secondly you need to understand how costs affect small retail and large institutional investors differently. Thirdly you need to think about **trade-offs** between costs and potential benefits, many of which are uncertain.

Important trade-offs that I discuss include: the cost and benefits of diversification, whether smart beta funds and active funds are worth buying given their higher charges, and how many funds or shares you should buy given the size of your investment portfolio.

I also explain how you can reduce your trading costs through smart rebalancing strategies to reduce the volume of trades you need to do, and smart execution tactics to reduce the costs of each of those trades.

Is this book still relevant?

I finished writing this book in the summer of 2017. Most of what I say here will hopefully still be useful in 2027, 2037, and beyond – assuming it stays in print that long! For example, I make some assumptions about future returns in different asset classes, but these are just arbitrary figures which make the results I show you easier to interpret:[6] my findings aren't affected if you use different assumptions.

However, there are some details which won't age so well. For example, I name specific ETFs; in the future these could close down, or better funds could turn up. To help you out I'll explain how you should research new ETFs and what features you should be looking for. There is detailed advice given throughout on selecting ETFs, with a summary on page 513.

Also, many of the decisions in this book are based on cost figures, which will be different if you use a more expensive broker than I do, or if brokerage charges change in the future. I'll explain how you should adapt my findings to reflect different levels of commissions.

---

6.   Technical note: Relative returns adjusted for risk are what is important, and I usually assume these can't be predicted, and are identical across different assets.

Prologue: What do we know?

INVESTMENT IS A RISKY BUSINESS: IT INVOLVES MAKING DECISIONS that will expose our hard earned wealth to an uncertain future. Before making these decisions it's worth thinking about how much we know, or don't know, about what will happen in the future.

What we *probably don't know*: future average returns

Typical conversation between me and a new acquaintance at a wedding, party, baptism or bar mitzvah:

Them: "So what do you do?"

Me: "Well I used to work for a hedge fund. Now I trade my own money, write books and do some consultancy."

Them: "So you're an expert on finance! Do you mind if ..."

Me: (hastily interrupting) "I wouldn't say I was an expert exactly..."

Them: (not listening) "... I ask you for some advice?"

Here are some genuine questions I've had from friends, relatives, and random people I have met at social events:

- "What is going to happen in Greece? Will the bond market rebound?"
- "Now then, what do you think about Japan? Should I sell my Japanese investment trusts?"
- "Do you think I should invest in bamboo?" (I wish I was making this one up.)

All these people are assuming that an expert should be able to give them expert advice. I usually politely refuse, which causes surprise and sometimes offends.

This is a common problem. Here is a quote from philosopher-trader Nassim Taleb's book *Fooled by Randomness*:

"One day a friend of my father… called me during his New York visit… he wanted to pick my brain on the state of a collection of financial markets… I was not interested in markets ('yes, I am a trader') and did not make predictions, period… it almost damaged the relationship… for the gentleman called him with the following grievance 'When I ask a lawyer a legal question, he answers me with courtesy and precision. When I ask a doctor a medical question, he gives me his opinion… Your indolent and conceited 29-year-old son is playing prima donna and refuses to answer me about the direction of the market!' "

Why do Nassim and myself refuse to give our 'expert' opinion? Let's look again at the list of questions above and I will rephrase them slightly:

- "Predict what is going to happen to the price of Greek bonds in the future."
- "Predict what will happen to the price of Japanese investment trusts in the future."
- "Predict what will happen to the price of bamboo in the future."

In order to give my expert opinion I have to predict the future of asset prices. This is difficult. It's much more difficult to predict the future of market prices or economic data than it is to solve a legal or medical problem.

In fact the state of economic and financial prediction in the 21st century is similar to that of medicine in the 18th century. Doctors bled the patient with leeches[7] and if they recovered doctors claimed all the credit. But if they died it was just 'bad luck' or 'unforeseeable circumstances'.

Similarly, present day market pundits will gracefully take plaudits when they are right, but rarely admit mistakes. Unforeseeable circumstances is no longer an acceptable medical excuse, but economic forecasters still use it frequently. Some will get it right more often than not, but with enough people trying, the laws of probability will always grant a select few a run of good luck they can attribute to their own skill.

Unlike medicine, financial forecasting has hardly progressed during the 240 years that have passed since economist Adam Smith wrote *The Wealth of Nations*, and effectively founded modern economics whilst his medical contemporaries were busy bleeding their patients.

Here is a selection of particularly poor forecasts over the years:

"Stocks have reached what looks like a permanently high plateau."

— Irving Fisher, Professor of Economics at Yale, three days before Black Thursday in 1929, the most devastating stock market crash in US history.

---

7.   I understand that leeches might be making a comeback in medicine, which isn't something that I'm personally comfortable with.

"Stocks are now in the midst of a one-time-only rise to much higher ground–to the neighborhood of 36,000 on the Dow Jones industrial average."

— James Glassman and Kevin Hassett writing in 1999. Shortly afterwards the Dow peaked at just under 11,500 before falling to 7600.

"It is hard for us, without being flippant, to even see a scenario within any kind of realm of reason that would see us losing one dollar in any of these transactions."

— Joseph Cassano, head of US insurance giant AIG's financial product division, speaking in 2007. One year later AIG was bankrupt and had to be rescued by the US government in a $180 billion bailout.

"The Federal Reserve is not currently forecasting a recession."

— Ben Bernanke, head of the US Federal Reserve, and supposedly the most knowledgeable economist in the world, speaking on 10 January 2008. A few months later the US National Bureau of Economic Research declared that the US was already in recession when this speech was made.

I think financial and economic forecasting will never reach the accuracy of medical diagnosis. But why is forecasting prices so hard?

Firstly, because financial markets are **complex**. Of course both doctors and economists study complex systems made up of large numbers of individual elements – organs and cells in medicines; firms and individuals in economics. The difference is that the billions of humans who make up the economy have their own free will, and as a result their behaviour and resulting interactions are extremely unpredictable.

The various parts of the human body mindlessly do the same thing day after day. The body automatically fights off nearly all infections, with only relatively serious diseases or old age requiring external medical intervention. An engineer would describe the body as a **stable and self correcting system**.

In contrast, as you can see from the quotes above, financial markets are often **highly unstable**. They have a tendency to try to commit suicide, frequently veering off into huge bubbles followed by deep collapses, which require massive government bailouts to alleviate any effect on the real economy.[8]

---

8. In one respect things have improved: the response of global governments to the 2008 crash wasn't perfect, but it was undoubtedly much better than the feeble efforts of 1929 onwards. But what hasn't

Secondly, forecasting prices is difficult because not only do you have to predict the future, **you need to predict the future better than anyone else**. Current market prices already reflect the collective estimate of every investor in the world based on all the information that is currently available.[9]

You might think that shares in Samsung should be cheap because one of their smart phones has an unfortunate habit of spontaneously combusting. But everyone else knows that too and the price of Samsung shares will reflect that information. Without access to inside information that is unknown to others, you can't accurately predict where prices will go next.

Perhaps you think you can predict what will happen to asset prices if a particular event happens in the future, such as Britain leaving the European Union or Donald J. Trump becoming US President. But unless you can calculate the chance of this event happening better than everyone else, this isn't going to be a route to instant riches.

As a result it's very difficult indeed to know what will happen to the price of Greek bonds, Japanese investment trusts, bamboo, or any other financial asset.[10] Smart investors are aware of the terrible track record that humans have of forecasting the market, and are highly sceptical of anyone who claims otherwise. I'll play it safe and in the first two parts of this book I assume that **we can't predict future returns**.[11]

What we *probably know*: similarity and risk

All investors know they shouldn't put all their eggs into one basket. Buying just one type of asset means you'll be exposed to the risk that it will fall dramatically. Rather than sinking your entire capital into bamboo, Japanese investment trusts, or Greek bonds, you should **diversify** and buy a **portfolio** of investments.

Ideally these investments should be **as different as possible**. A portfolio containing shares in 20 companies might seem highly diversified. But if all those companies are UK clothing retailers you will still be dangerously exposed to a downturn in the British apparel market. You need to spread your money more widely.

Fortunately assets which have had similar returns in the past tend to carry on doing so in the future: **similarity is a relatively predictable attribute of prices in financial markets**.

---

changed is that (virtually) nobody saw it coming. Sticking with the medical analogy, economists are like doctors who can now recognise when a patient is about to die, and have worked out how to use a defibrillator to restart their heart, but who were completely oblivious of anything going wrong until the patient was almost on the verge of death.

9. Technical note: You may recognise this as one of the flavours of the efficient market hypothesis.
10. I am generally sceptical of financial experts having some special insight into future price movements but there are some systematic ways to predict prices which may have some value. I talk about these shortly.
11. Technical note: To be pedantic I assume that risk-adjusted returns are identical for all assets.

We also know that some investments tend to be **riskier** than others. For example, lending money to the Norwegian government for 12 months, by buying a one-year bond, is incredibly safe. The Norwegian economy is underpinned by huge petroleum reserves and is more than capable of supporting its relatively small population even when oil prices are depressed. The chance of not being paid back in full is negligible. Furthermore, Norwegian interest rates, which will also affect the bond price, aren't likely to change very much over the course of a year.

Now consider a highly speculative internet start-up, which consists of a few people in a rented office (none of whom have run a business before), a poorly written business plan, and a website address (gr8tplacetobuy5tereo.or.tv) which is hard to type and even harder to remember. Buying shares in this venture would be incredibly risky. There is an infinitesimal chance it will become the next Facebook or Amazon, and a much larger chance you will lose your entire investment.

If you had a $2000 to invest, how much would you put into Norwegian bonds, and what would you invest in gr8tplace? Unless you have a gambling problem you wouldn't put all your money into gr8tplace. Even someone with a very high tolerance for risk shouldn't put half into gr8tplace; you're almost guaranteed to lose 50% of your overall wealth. You'd probably want to have much more than half your investment in safe Norwegian bonds.

Like similarity, risk is relatively predictable – certainly much more predictable than average returns. Whatever happens in the future, bonds issued by stable governments will never be riskier than speculative internet stocks.

Smart investors are happy to assume they can predict the similarity and risk of future returns. In this book I'll show you how to use these two factors – the things you **probably** know – to decide which portfolio to invest in.

What we *definitely know*: costs

In introductory finance courses around the world, students are taught about a theoretical portfolio which contains every tradeable asset in the world:[12] every stock, every bond and every fund... all of which should be traded throughout the day, every day of the year! In reality it's impossible to own this perfect portfolio. Out in the real world we have to face up to paying **costs** every time we buy or sell.

Many costs are **fixed**, regardless of the size of the transaction. In the UK it currently costs me £6 in commission to buy one share in supermarket Marks & Spencer. Buying just one share in each of the 2400 firms currently listed on the London Stock Exchange would cost over £14,000 in brokerage fees – more than the shares themselves are worth. Trading them every day would cost hundreds of thousands of pounds a year! All this is before we consider investing in multiple countries, or in other asset classes.

---

12.   Technical note: This is the market portfolio of the Capital Asset Pricing Model.

Fixed costs make it prohibitively expensive to have portfolios with hundreds of shares. So rather than buying individual shares most investors should buy **funds**: mutual funds, unit trusts, investment trusts or Exchange Traded Funds (ETFs).[13] My terminology for these is **collective funds** because they allow a group of investors to collectively buy small shares of a large portfolio.

However this isn't ideal. A fund won't necessarily buy the individual shares in the same proportions as you would if you could buy them directly. The fund managers probably won't trade the shares in the fund the way that you'd want to. So in chapter six of this book I will show you how to weigh up the costs and benefits of investing directly in the underlying assets, versus investing in funds.

Fixed costs are less of a problem as you get wealthier and can invest in larger amounts. A grandmother with a few thousand dollars can only buy a few funds; a large pension fund with a few hundred million dollars can easily invest in thousands of individual stocks. I'll show you examples of how to find the right portfolio at different levels of wealth, from a few hundred dollars or pounds, up to a billion dollars.

Like I said above; asset returns, risk and similarity can't be predicted with complete certainty. Smart investors know that costs are relatively easy to forecast, and that minimising costs should be a major part of any decision about investment.

What we might, *perhaps know*: forecasting returns

I am pretty pessimistic about my own ability to predict returns. I don't believe most other people are very good at it either. But there are some exceptions. Part three of this book will explain how to adjust your portfolio choices when future returns have some predictability.

Some of this predictability comes from well known financial market anomalies. For example, small firms have consistently outperformed larger firms in the past. Stocks which have gone up in price over the last 12 months often continue to outperform. Firms with lower PE ratios or higher dividend yields do better than those in the opposing camps. Researchers in academic finance call these additional sources of return **risk factors**. In their opinion, if you're getting extra profits it must be at the cost of extra risk.

These factors can be exploited in a couple of different ways. Firstly you can use **systematic forecasting models** to improve your prediction of future returns. I'll show you how to use these rules to adjust your portfolio weights and pick certain stocks.

Alternatively you can get someone else to do the work for you. **Smart beta** funds try to capture additional returns from risk factors. These fashionable funds are a little more expensive than run of the mill passive index funds, but cheaper than actively managed funds. I'll help you evaluate if they're worth bothering with.

---

13.   I go into more detail about the difference between these later.

You may still be convinced you can beat the market without taking on extra risk and no amount of scepticism from me will change your mind. I'll show you how to adjust portfolio weights given an opinion on what prices are going to do, and more importantly by **how much** it's safe to change them. I will also explain how you can use any stock picking skill you have to include your favourite firms without messing up the rest of the beautifully constructed portfolio you will own after reading part two.

Finally, you might believe you can't personally beat the market, but that professional fund managers can: by **actively** buying and selling stocks. I'll help you decide what is more important: the uncertain extra return an active manager **might** give you, or the higher costs they **definitely** charge.

PART ONE

Theory

of

Smart Portfolios

Part One: Theory of Smart Portfolios

"It is tough to make predictions, especially about the future."

— Yogi Berra, baseball coach

In part one I describe some concepts, techniques and insights that will be used in the rest of the book.

The first chapter addresses a deceptively simple question: What is the best portfolio? The second chapter discusses the uncertainty of future returns. Then in chapter three I explain the problems created by uncertainty when you're trying to find the best portfolio. Chapter four introduces the practical methods I'm going to use for building portfolios that solve these problems.

Chapter five introduces costs; both the charges which you pay for buying and selling investments, and also holding costs such as the annual management fees of collective investment funds like Exchange Traded Funds (ETFs). Finally in chapter six I show how to evaluate the benefits of diversifying your portfolio against the costs of doing so.

I show how to use all of these methods to create smart portfolios in part two.

CHAPTER ONE

What is the Best Portfolio?

BUILDING A PORTFOLIO INVOLVES DECIDING WHICH ASSETS TO include and how much of your capital to allocate to each of them: the **portfolio weights**. But what exactly is the **best** set of portfolio weights?

If you have a complicated product then defining what is best isn't always easy. Cars are pretty complicated. Is the best car the one with the highest fuel efficiency? The automobile that goes the fastest? The vehicle with the largest number of mechanical horses in its engine? Is it the best looking, or the cheapest? The answer depends on what you personally are looking for in a car. Portfolios are no different; a set of investments that suit one person will be completely inappropriate for another.

Chapter overview

I define the best portfolio as:

The highest expected real after costs total geometric absolute return, for a given level of risk and time horizon, in a particular investment currency.

That is quite a mouthful. Let me break it down and explain each part in turn.

Geometric mean return	The type of averaging to use when evaluating levels of future and past returns.
Expectations	Investment is about what we expect to happen in the future. How do we assess what outcomes are likely?
Risk and time horizon	The best portfolio will depend on your tolerance for **risk**: to what degree you can cope with potential losses over different time periods.
Total return and dividends	Does it matter whether you get your return from price rises, dividends, or both?

After costs	All investments involve paying costs of various kinds; you need to take these into account when evaluating different investments.
Real returns	It's important to think about the effect of inflation: **real** returns are returns with inflation deducted.
Currency	The point of investment is to provide an income stream or capital for future expenditure. Therefore you need to worry about portfolio growth in the currency in which you will spend money in the future. But the best portfolios are widely diversified, and you can't get international diversification without exposing your portfolio to movements in foreign exchange rates. Should you protect yourself against adverse currency movements?
Absolute returns versus embarrassment and relative returns	Many investors are concerned about their performance relative to others. The potential embarrassment from doing something different to the consensus and getting it wrong is hard to ignore.
Non-financial considerations	All of these are purely financial considerations, however modern day investors are increasingly thinking about the moral and ethical consequences of their investment decisions as well.

The rest of this chapter goes into more detail about each of these different aspects.

Geometric mean return

When thinking about the average of past and future returns I use the **geometric mean** rather than the more common **arithmetic mean**. The geometric mean better reflects what you will actually earn over time.

To understand this better let's look at an example. Consider an investment in which you invest $100 and earn 30%, 30% and –30% over the next three years of returns. The arithmetic mean is the sum of annual returns: 30% + 30% – 30% = **30%**, divided by the number of years (3), which equals **10%**. Therefore you might expect to have an extra $30 after three years, probably more thanks to the magic of compound interest.

But how much have you actually made? Look at table 1. After three years you have just **$118.30**: much less than expected. Compound interest is a wonderful thing, but it magnifies losses as well as gains.

TABLE 1: LUMPY RETURNS

	Year one	**Year two**	**Year three**
Account value start of year	$100	$130	$169
Arithmetic return	30%	30%	–30%
Dollar return	$100 × 30% = $30	$130 × 30% = $39	$169 × -30% = –$50.70
Account value end of year	$100 + $30 = $130	$130 + $39 = $169	$169 – $50.70 = **$118.30**

Now look at table 2. Notice that the annual return here is much lower, just **5.76%** a year, but it's consistent. The final account value after three years is exactly the same as in table 1: $118.30. **The geometric mean of a series of returns is the consistent return that gives the same final account value.**[14] So the geometric mean of 30%, 30% and –30% is 5.76% a year.

TABLE 2: CONSISTENT RETURNS

	Year one	**Year two**	**Year three**
Account value start of year	$100	$105.80	$111.85
Arithmetic return	5.76%	5.76%	5.76%
Dollar return	$100 × 5.76% = $5.76	$105.80 × 5.76% = $6.09	$111.85 × 5.76% = $6.45
Account value end of year	$100 + $5.76 = $105.76	$105.76 + $6.09 = $111.85	$111.85 + $6.45 = **$118.30**

I explain in chapter two how you can use arithmetic means to calculate the geometric mean of returns.

Geometric returns give a more realistic picture than mean returns. To take an extreme example, consider the following series of returns: 200%, 200%, –99%. The arithmetic return is 100%; what a fantastic investment! But the geometric mean is much lower, and significantly negative: –55.2%. What is more you will have virtually nothing left after three years have passed: less than a tenth of your initial investment.[15]

---

14.   Technical note: More precise definitions can be found in Appendix C, page 491.
15.   Starting with $100 after the first year of a 200% return you will have $300, then after the second

The geometric mean is always lower than the arithmetic mean, unless all annual returns are identical. The difference between the two measures is larger for more volatile assets.[16] For example, figure 1 shows that the average real return (after inflation) of S&P 500 equities in the US from 1928–2016 was 8.2% and for 10 year bonds it was 2.2%. However, the geometric means were 6.2% (equities) and 1.8% (bonds) respectively.

FIGURE 1: ARITHMETIC AND GEOMETRIC MEANS FOR US STOCKS AND BONDS

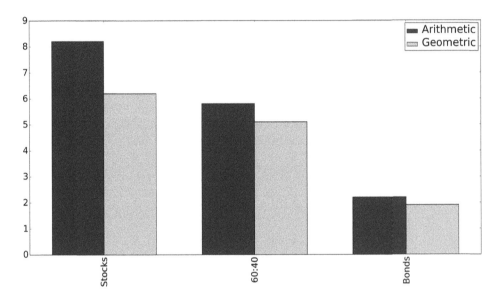

Based on annual returns from 1928–2016. 60:40 portfolio contains 60% equities and 40% bonds.

For the riskier US stock market the geometric return is a quarter lower than the arithmetic return; for relatively safe US bonds it is just one eighth less. Similarly, for a portfolio of 60% equities and 40% bonds[17] the average return was 5.8%; almost a third lower than for equities alone (6.2%). But the geometric mean of 5.1% was only 18% lower. Using the geometric return makes pure equity portfolios less attractive than more diversified alternatives.

---

year $900. The 99% loss in the third year leaves you with just $9. With a consistent annual loss of 55.2%: after one year you have $44.80, after two years $20.07, and after three years $9.

16. Technical note: A good approximation is that the geometric mean is equal to the arithmetic mean, minus half the variance of returns. The variance is the standard deviation squared. I introduce this approximation in the next chapter.

17. Technical note: With annual rebalancing.

It's worth emphasising this: the benefits of diversification are greater when average returns are measured with geometric means.[18]

Expectations

A central theme in this book is that nobody has a crystal ball. You can't see into the future. All you can do is make the best decision based on the information and **expectations** that you have available now. Expectations are usually derived from what has happened in the past.

An expectation can be a **fixed point**, for example: "UK equity returns after inflation have averaged 5% since 1900.[19] Therefore they will be **exactly 5%** next year." This sounds absurd but many people make fixed point market predictions without any indication of how uncertain they are. This is about as futile as predicting that the next toss of a coin will definitely turn up heads. There is a 50% chance your prediction will be wrong.

Alternatively you can specify an expectation in terms of a **statistical model** which specifies a **range of outcomes**. An accurate statistical model for coin tossing would be "I expect to get heads 50% of the time, and tails 50% of the time." Interestingly, few market pundits make predictions which contain meaningful indications of how uncertain the future is, as they prefer people to think they are infallible.

How would you build a model for expected UK equity returns based on historic data? Since 1900 equities have returned around 5% annually[20] after inflation. In 90% of calendar years annual returns were between -16% and +40%.

If you assume the future is like the past then you have your statistical model: "Future real UK equity returns will average 5% annually after inflation (with 90% of annual returns between -16% and +40%)". The model includes an expected **average return** (+5%) and the **expected variation** or **risk** around that average (90% of outcomes fall between -16% and +40%).

In the jargon of statisticians these numeric values are the **parameters** of the model. As you'll see in later chapters, models of statistical expectation are a key input when trying to work out which is the best portfolio.

However, this is just a model: **there is no guarantee that it will be correct**. Firstly it might be the **wrong model**. It could be too simplistic, ignoring as it does the very worst and very best returns, and not specifying the rest in much detail.

---

18.   Technical note: There is some disagreement about whether it is correct to maximise geometric returns, and whether the diversification benefits produced can be used to pay higher costs. This problem goes away if you use the median rather than the mean to evaluate the distribution of expectations of future portfolio values. See Appendix C, page 491.

19.   Source: 2016 Barclays Equity Gilt Study.

20.   For now I'm using the traditional arithmetic mean as the difference is irrelevant in this simple example.

Secondly, although I've written down the model parameters as precise numbers, they are also subject to variation: this is known as **parameter uncertainty**. I'd get quite a different average return if I looked at the worst ten years (1905–1915 with an average stock market fall of 0.2% a year) or the best (1975–1985 with a rise of +11% a year).

Finally, **the future might be very different from the past**, with the parameters or the model itself needing to change to reflect the new reality. In the next chapter I'll explain how you can incorporate these different kinds of **model uncertainty** into your expectations.

Risk and investment horizon

Risk is a slippery concept. It is relatively easy to write down a definition:

Risk is the possibility of losing money.

But that still leaves us with two major problems. Firstly, there are numerous ways of **measuring** it. Secondly, there is no consensus on what is a **tolerable level of risk**, as everyone has their own preference.

I deal with the measurement problem by using my own preferred measure of risk,[21] which I introduce in chapter two. I also show how that translates into likely outcomes over different time periods, to allow you to calibrate your own perception of risk against the metric I'm using.

However, I can't just set a specific level of risk tolerance. You might prefer riskier portfolios, if you can get a higher expected return. Or perhaps you would rather put up with lower returns and less risk. I explain how to adapt your portfolio to different levels of risk tolerance in chapter four.

In the first two parts of this book I assume that you are focused on **total return**: price appreciation plus income. This will simplify my explanations and calculations considerably. This won't suit everyone, so in part three I explain how to design portfolios with higher yields for investors who would prefer to take their profits in dividend income rather than rising prices.

---

21.   If you're curious it's the expected geometric standard deviation of returns. I explain this properly in chapter two.

CONCEPT: ACCUMULATING AND DISTRIBUTING FUNDS

One very simple way to tweak your portfolio to suit your preferences for income or total returns is by using **accumulating** and **distributing** funds. Many **collective funds** are available in both these flavours.

Accumulating funds do not pay dividends; any dividends or bond coupons earned by their underlying shares or bonds are kept inside the fund and used to buy more assets. This means their price will rise faster. There will be no dividend tax payable, but when you come to sell you will pay larger capital gains taxes. Of course you can determine when you sell, potentially timing your sale to minimise tax. I discuss this much more in part four.

Distributing funds pay out all the income that their underlying assets earn. They are more suitable for investors who need an income You will have to pay tax on your dividend income. But because they will appreciate less in price they won't be as exposed to potential capital gains tax when you sell.

Caution: be careful when looking at past returns of funds. Do not compare accumulating and distributing funds based purely on how their prices have changed. This is unfair on distributing funds. You need to add back the dividends earned for a fair comparison.

Costs

In chapters two, three and four I talk about a magical theoretical world where there are no costs involved in investment. Sadly this is a fantasy. In the real world you have to pay costs every time you buy or sell. Even if you adopt an idealised Warren Buffett like approach and never sell,[22] you still have to stump up for the costs of making the initial investment, and there are usually management or custody fees to pay, as well as dividends to reinvest.

As with returns, you should use **expected** costs. Fortunately costs are much easier to forecast than returns. Some costs are highly **visible** and are known precisely, such as fund management fees and brokerage commissions. Other costs are harder to see, hidden and practically **invisible**; but it is still important to estimate their effect on returns. I go into more detail about these different kinds of costs in chapter five.

---

22.   Of course in the real world Warren Buffett does sell stocks. For example during 2016 he sold over 50 million shares in Wal-Mart. Even Buffett doesn't slavishly follow the idealised Buffett approach.

Real returns

Investment is not an activity you do for its own sake, even if you are a nerdy type like myself who enjoys the number crunching that is involved. The point of it is to produce a capital sum, or a stream of income, which will be used to purchase goods in the future. Hence you need to worry about changes in the future price of those goods: **inflation**.

It is not enough to use **nominal** returns from which inflation hasn't been deducted. Instead you should use **real** returns that have been adjusted for expected inflation.

Inflation is as unpredictable as asset returns, perhaps more so. Unless you buy inflation-linked bonds you cannot know in advance what your real returns will be. Such bonds are not available for every country and tend be expensive, implying very poor returns. [23]

Predicting inflation is really hard; but don't panic, you don't need to accurately forecast inflation or real returns – in fact I don't try to predict returns at all in the first two parts of this book.

There is another implication of inflation which is worth remembering. **Because we care about real returns there is no truly 'risk free' investment.** Leave your money in cash or in a bank account and it will almost certainly be depleted by inflation. [24] Because of inflation, holding on to un-invested 'safe' cash is actually a very risky decision with an uncertain outcome.

Embarrassment: absolute returns versus relative returns

So far in this chapter I've assumed that you don't care about other people's returns, only your own. In the jargon of finance this is a preference of **absolute** returns and a disregard for **relative returns**. However, relative returns can undeniably be important when they are **embarrassing**. Underperforming the general market is embarrassing. Even if nobody else knows about it you will probably feel regret at your own apparent stupidity.

This embarrassment outweighs the positive feeling you get when you are profitable despite the general market falling. If you were to follow the crowd and lose money along with every other investor, you would not feel so bad.

This is doubly true for institutional investors. There used to be a saying amongst corporate purchasers of computing equipment: "Nobody ever got fired for buying IBM." Sticking

---

23.   As I'm writing this (in early 2017) yields on 20 year UK inflation linked government bonds are around -0.9% compared to 2.1% for the non-inflation linked alternative. For these bonds to be fairly priced, future inflation needs to be around 3%; well above the current rate of 0.5% and even higher than the Bank of England's target of 2%.

24.   At the time of writing (early 2017) inflation is close to zero in many major economies, but sustained periods of deflation (negative inflation) still seem unlikely. If they occur it is likely that banks will start charging negative interest rates and governments will take action to prevent people from storing large amounts of cash: this could even mean a complete ban on the use of physical cash.

with the status quo is always safer than going out on a limb. It is relatively easy to explain to clients that you have lost money when the whole market has fallen. It's much more painful if the market has gone up and your fund hasn't.

Institutional investors should formally quantify their capacity for embarrassment by comparing their returns to a **benchmark**. Differences between your return and a benchmark are known as **tracking errors**. It's nice when tracking errors are positive on average, since you are outperforming, but tracking errors that are large in magnitude (whether positive or negative) mean you are deviating too much from your benchmark.

It's important to specify exactly what size of tracking error you are comfortable with, and how you're going to measure it.[25]

I've pointed out already that people have different tolerances for risk. They also have different tolerances for embarrassment. Those who can cope with being embarrassed can afford to deviate more from the norm. I discuss how to factor these preferences into your portfolio choice in chapter four.

Currency

I said above that the point of investment is to provide an income stream or capital for future expenditure. This means you need to measure your expected portfolio growth in the currency in which you will do your future spending.

I'm a firm believer in diversified investing: across different asset classes and different countries. But spreading your portfolio over multiple countries will mean you are exposed to changes in foreign exchange rates. If your own currency appreciates versus that of a country you are investing in, then your returns will be hurt. Conversely, a relative depreciation in your currency will unexpectedly boost your returns.

It's possible to eliminate this risk by **currency hedging**, or using funds that do this hedging for you. For example, suppose you're a US investor looking to invest in the Korean KOSPI equity market index using Exchange Traded Funds (ETFs). One of the cheapest unhedged ETFs is HKOR. Alternatively you can buy a currency hedged alternative, DBKO.

If the Korean won falls against the dollar, but the KOSPI stock index remains at the same level, you'd be protected from any losses in the hedged product DBKO while the unhedged fund would lose money. This financial engineering is achieved by the fund manager trading currency derivatives to hedge their exposure. However, if the Korean won rises against the dollar you won't see any benefit in a hedged ETF.

---

25.   Technical note: A simple measure of tracking error is the standard deviation of relative returns between your portfolio and the benchmark. For more on this complex subject I'd recommend reading *Portfolio Performance Measurement and Benchmarking* by Jon Christopherson, David Carino and Wayne Ferson.

In a real-life example, on the day that the UK voted to leave the European Union in June 2016, virtually all my unhedged foreign equity ETFs increased in value in British pound terms, despite all of them falling in price, because the pound collapsed. If I'd opted for currency hedging I would have felt the full weight of the price falls.

Many investors like currency hedging. They are confident that they can predict returns but are not sure about currency movements. To them it makes sense to remove currency from the equation by hedging. Hedging also reduces embarrassment. It is embarrassing to admit you got your market call correct, but ended up losing money because of currency losses.

Personally, I'm extremely sceptical about the need for currency hedging, for a number of reasons. Firstly, hedging doesn't improve pre-cost returns. Over time currency returns are fairly random so hedging won't systematically gain or lose anything. Hedging also reduces the diversification benefit of having a portfolio of assets spread over multiple currencies, by making them more correlated with each other.

Then there are the costs. Some of these are very obvious: currency hedged funds usually have higher management fees than unhedged alternatives. The Korean equity funds I mentioned above are typical: HKOR (unhedged), has an 0.38% annual management fee[26] and DBKO (hedged) a much higher 0.58% fee.

In addition to this there are also **invisible costs** associated with currency hedging which don't appear in the expense ratios but still detract from performance: **rolling** and **carry** costs.

Rolling costs come from the regular trading of currency hedging positions needed to keep the hedge in place. Carrying costs happen because hedgers have to pay the difference in interest rates between the hedging and investing currencies. These are particularly expensive in emerging markets, which usually have much higher interest rates. For example, my broker currently[27] charges me 0.4% to borrow money in the US, and 1.25% in Korea. So a fund invested in the Korean market, but hedged into US dollars, will lose 1.25% – 0.4% = **0.85%** of performance a year in carrying costs.

Overall, hedging is an expensive alternative without any clear advantages. I recommend that you steer clear of currency hedged products unless there is no alternative[28], or you absolutely have to hedge.

---

26.   This is the explicit annual fee charged by the fund manager. There are other costs associated with holding ETFs which I discuss in chapter five.
27.   I also have to pay an additional spread on top of these interest rates which would make hedging even more expensive, though these would be relatively low for an ETF manager. Rates correct as of February 2017.
28.   Technical note: Sophisticated institutional investors can hedge their exposures cheaply themselves using futures contracts or currency forwards. Still I'd recommend only doing so when the carrying costs are in your favour, and if you understand the risks involved.

A purely financial judgement

It might seem obvious that the best portfolio will give you the highest **financial** return, albeit with added qualifications such as those I've discussed above. However, this is increasingly not true. Many investors are looking beyond pure profits and want to *do the right thing*. Ethical and environmental considerations are becoming increasingly important.

Take Norway's sovereign wealth fund, the largest in the world. In 2015 it sold shares in firms related to the palm oil and coal industries and it has refused to invest in US retailer Walmart due to ethical concerns.

Taking decisions based on these non-financial factors is a complicated subject and beyond the scope of this book. However, in chapter eleven I consider the monetary effect of excluding certain stocks from your investment portfolio. This will allow you to quantify the possible downside of doing the right thing.

Of course it can also make financial sense to move beyond narrow self interest and invest in a portfolio which is better for society as a whole. Firms excluded from ethical portfolios will probably be bad investments in the long run, such as those which rely on depleting stocks of non-renewable energy, or companies that have reputational risk which could lead to customers deserting them.

Key points

Use the right kind of average	The correct way to measure average returns is with **geometric means**. The benefits of safer, more diversified portfolios are higher when measured using geometric means.
We can't see into the future	There is no guarantee that the past will repeat itself, but to make decisions you need to have expectations about the future. Using a **statistical model** to describe your expectations is better than making fixed point forecasts. Models may not reflect reality so it's important to be aware of their flaws.
Can you handle the risk?	It is vital to make an honest assessment of your own tolerance for losses or shortfalls in returns, so that you can build a portfolio you'll be comfortable with.
Costs are important	Costs are the elephant in the corner of the investment room; often ignored and overlooked but incredibly important, and unlike future returns they are easy to forecast. Every investment decision you make should include an assessment of likely costs.

There is no such thing as a safe, risk free, investment	Once you consider inflation, even cash isn't safe. Inflation-linked bonds issued by stable governments come closest to being risk free for long-term investors, but buying these will usually lock in a guaranteed negative return.
Can you handle the embarrassment?	You need to be honest about your capacity for embarrassment if you deviate from the consensus and then underperform. This will influence how brave you can be when choosing your portfolio.
Avoid currency hedging	It costs too much and is unlikely to give you any benefits. Only hedge if you have no choice or are likely to be embarrassed by the impact of not doing so.

CHAPTER TWO

Uncertainty and Investment

INVESTMENT IS A RISKY BUSINESS. THERE IS HUGE UNCERTAINTY about what will happen in the future, and how it will affect the shares and funds that we are thinking of buying. Just how predictable is the future? How can you use what happened in the past to help you make predictions? This chapter does not explain how to build a foolproof crystal ball. But it will give you a better understanding of how uncertain the world is and how you can deal with that uncertainty in a smarter way.

Chapter overview

The investment game	**The investment game** is a simple game which is very difficult to play. Learning this game will help you think about the uncertainty of future returns when investing in the real world.
Statistical modelling	I show you how to use statistical models to successfully play the investment game; analysing past data and using it to make predictions about the future.
The uncertain past	Statistical models have a significant flaw: they rely on an **uncertain past**. I explain this concept in the last part of the chapter, and tell you what you should do about it.

The investment game

Gambling and investing are very similar activities. Both involve exposing your money to an uncertain outcome.[29] Take Edward 'Ed' Thorp: a famous gambler who in the early 1960s was probably the first person to beat the casino at Blackjack by card counting.

---

29. Some people think that *gambling* is bad, and *investing* is good, with *trading* perhaps somewhere

Imagine you could watch Ed playing Blackjack. When he sits down at a casino table he has a great deal of information. He knows that there are a certain number of packs of cards in the deck[30] and that each pack contains four aces, four kings and so on.[31] For example, with a four-pack deck there are $(4 \times 4) = 16$ aces out of $(4 \times 52) = 208$ cards. It's trivial to work out the probability of an ace being dealt as the first card: $16 \div 208 = 7.6\%$

Even if Ed plays perfectly[32] the casino has a small house edge. A rational player would not play Blackjack in the first hand of a fresh deck, since they would expect to lose on average. In Blackjack you don't have the option of not playing certain hands; but you can participate relatively cheaply by only betting small stakes.[33] Whilst Ed is playing these initial hands he is watching every card as it is dealt. From these he can deduce which cards are left in the deck and thus how the probability of getting a particular card is changing.

Ed has to do this all in his head without attracting the attention of casino employees, so rather than count every card he uses a counting system that keeps track of important cards. We have no such restriction so we can look at the entire **distribution** of all the cards that have been dealt. I've shown the first 32 cards dealt in an imaginary game in figure 2, ordered and stacked up to show clearly how many of each there are. (Because a card's suit is irrelevant in Blackjack, I ignore it; all cards are shown as spades for convenience.)

There are $(4 \times 4) - 1 = 15$ aces remaining out of $(4 \times 52) - 32 = 176$ cards. The probability of receiving an ace has risen to $15 \div 176 = 8.5\%$. The more cards that appear, the more certainty about what is left in the pack and the easier it is for card counters to beat the casino.[34]

As Ed gets more information about the remaining cards in the deck he will start to vary his betting to take advantage of hands which he expects to be profitable. Being able to accurately count transforms the house edge in Blackjack into a narrow advantage for Ed.

---

in the middle. I disagree. All involve putting money at risk, with an uncertain outcome. What is bad is when someone is betting when they are guaranteed to lose on average, or when they put too much of their capital into a particular bet, or both. This sort of behaviour is rare amongst professional poker players, but is common amongst amateur gamblers and traders alike. There is nothing wrong with gambling, investing, or trading; as long as you know what you are doing and never bet or invest when the odds are against you.

30.   Prior to 1961, Las Vegas casinos used a deck with just a single pack of cards. This made card counting relatively straightforward. Since then decks with multiple packs have become almost ubiquitous, and it's common to see decks with six, seven or even eight packs.

31.   I'm assuming here for simplicity that this is a fresh deck which has just been shuffled.

32.   So called 'basic strategy'. See *Beat the Dealer* by Ed Thorp, or any of the numerous other blackjack books published in the last 50 years.

33.   Most casinos would be unhappy about someone hanging around a table, watching the cards being dealt and waiting for the deck to become favourable before sitting down to play.

34.   In Blackjack, players play against the dealer. The dealer has to use a pre-determined strategy and so cannot benefit from knowing what cards are left in the pack.

FIGURE 2: STACKING CARDS MAKES THEIR DISTRIBUTION EASIER TO VISUALISE

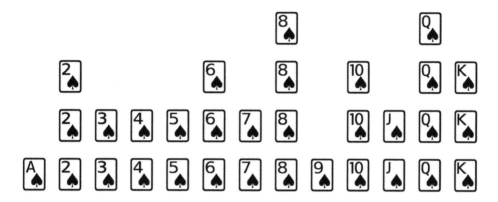

First 32 cards dealt from a four pack deck.

Introducing the investment game

After making a small fortune in Blackjack, Ed publicised his method by writing the book *Beat the Dealer*. Casinos responded by changing the rules to making counting harder and banning known card counters from their casinos, including Ed.

But Ed was off to greener pastures. He set up a hedge fund, Princeton Newport partners, and made a very large fortune from that, and his subsequent fund Edward Thorp and Associates. The techniques that Ed used to decide how much to bet, given the risk and returns available, were exactly the same in both his early gambling days and his hedge fund career. Clearly playing games of chance, and making investment decisions, are more similar than you might think.

To illustrate this, let me introduce you to a card game of my own invention: **the investment game**. Although the game is apparently simple to play it will help you learn how to make real-world investing decisions in a smarter way. The game begins with an extremely large undealt deck of cards whose contents are a secret and consists of a number of rounds. In each round you have to decide whether to gamble, or not to play, and how much to bet.

Regardless of your decision, a card is then dealt which determines how your bet would have performed if you had gambled. Then follows a second round, where again you have to choose between playing and sitting out. The game continues in this way indefinitely.

For example, suppose that you decided to gamble $100 in the first round. You are then dealt a card like this:

+6.1%

This means that you will receive back your $100 bet, plus another 6.1%, or $106.10. Of course there are also negative value cards. So you could have had this:

-2.0%

If you were dealt this card after betting $100 you'd only get back $98.

So, how much should you gamble? Indeed should you gamble anything at all? To answer this question you need to **predict** what the next card you receive is likely to be, just as in Blackjack. For example if you knew with certainty the next card would be +100% then you should bet your entire stake!

This would be a **fixed point** forecast, a term we looked at in chapter one. There is absolutely no uncertainty, just a precise prediction of what will happen next. Without being able to see the next card in advance you'd be crazy to make forecasts like this. However, you can also make forecasts based on a **statistical model**. Remember from chapter one: a model includes both an expected **average**, but also an idea of the **variation** in outcome.

For example, suppose there was a deck of 100 cards in the investment game, and you'd managed to sneak a look at them before the game whilst the dealer's back was turned. You notice that 51 of the cards have a value of -1%, and 49 have a value of +1%.

The dealer then shuffles the cards, so you don't know which card is coming up first. You should not place a bet in the initial round since you're slightly more likely to lose than win. The first card laid will have an **expected average value** of [(49 × 1%) + (51 × -1%)] ÷ 100 = **-0.02%**. Statistical models also provide some idea of the **variation** in outcome, or **risk**, but I will return to that later.

Unlike in Blackjack, it is possible in the investment game to watch the cards that have been played without placing a bet. After all you can easily download a history of stock prices in the real world, even if you've never invested a dollar in that stock. So there is no need to place small bets to see the first few cards.

Suppose the first three cards that were laid all had a value of -1%. You now know that there are 51 - 3 = 48 of the -1% cards remaining, and all 49 of the original +1% cards. The new expected average is [(49 × 1%) + (48 × -1%)] ÷ 97 = **+0.01%**. Playing the fourth round would now make sense, since you're slightly more likely to get a positive return. This is quite a small advantage, so you probably won't want to place an especially large bet, but I'll discuss the question of how much to bet in due course.

Just like in Blackjack, unless you are an outright cheat who has marked the cards you won't know with complete certainty what the next card is. But cheating just a little so you know what cards were in the deck initially, and can work out what is left, is enough to give a small advantage.

This is the key difference between Blackjack and the investment game: without cheating **you do not know what cards were in the deck to begin with**. This means you can't infer what cards are left after some have been dealt.

BLACKJACK

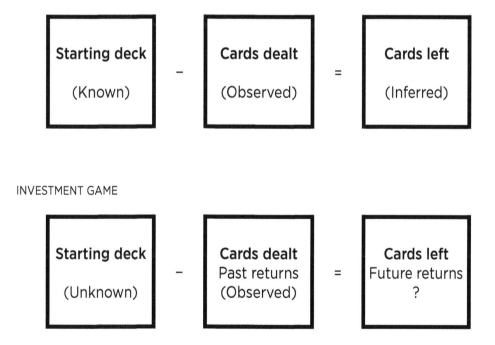

INVESTMENT GAME

Unlike in Blackjack, card counting appears to be a waste of time in the investment game. To put it another way, examining patterns of past returns will give you no information about the future. You would have no way of knowing if it was worth playing a particular hand. As Nassim Taleb wrote in *The Black Swan*, "The casino is the only human venture I know where the probabilities are known... and almost computable... In real life you do not know the odds, you need to discover them... "

How do you get round this seemingly intractable problem? There are a number of options you could consider, but the most common approach used in real life investment is to **assume that history repeats itself**. This means that you are expecting the pattern of cards dealt in the future to be similar to what has already been dealt. For this to be true **the cards that have been dealt must be representative of the cards remaining in the deck**. If the starting deck is extremely large, the undealt deck is going to look almost exactly like the starting deck, no matter how many cards have already been dealt.

This leads to a completely different strategy than what you'd use if you were playing Blackjack, or indeed any game where you know exactly what the starting deck of cards looks like. More aces dealt in Blackjack means an ace is **less likely** to be dealt next. But in the investment game if many positive cards are dealt it means that positive returns are **more likely** in the future.

INVESTMENT GAME WITH AN ASSUMPTION

Starting deck (Unknown) Same pattern as cards dealt	**Cards dealt** Past returns (Observed) Representative of starting deck	**Cards left** Future returns (Expectation) Almost identical to starting deck: Same pattern as cards dealt

Assuming the cards dealt are representative of the starting deck; hence future cards will look like past cards.

In real-world investment, this assumption translates to this: **future returns are expected to look like past returns**. This is the implicit presumption made by almost all investors and everyone working in the financial industry despite legal and regulatory disclaimers urging caution.

We know this assumption is widespread just by looking at the behaviour of investors. Fund manager track records are pored over by financial journalists and assumed to have prophetic power. The historical returns of different assets are measured to one, two or even three decimal places; an utterly pointless exercise unless they provide a meaningful guide to the future. Mathematically skilled investment experts compete to find the largest historic dataset on which to perform complex tricks of statistical analysis.

Clearly almost everyone involved in the markets has their eyes fixed firmly on the rear-view mirror.

Statistical modelling

We now have a smart strategy for how to play the investment game:

1. Analyse the cards that have been dealt (past returns).

2. Assume these will have a similar pattern to the starting deck.

3. Create expectations about the undealt cards using a statistical model based on an analysis of dealt cards (past returns).

4. Decide whether to bet, and how much to bet, based on a statistical model for undealt cards (future returns).

Let's imagine you have started playing the investment game, a few cards have been dealt and you've ordered and stacked them to illustrate the distribution, as I did for Ed's game of Blackjack in figure 2. These are shown in figure 3.

FIGURE 3: DISTRIBUTION OF CARDS WHICH HAVE BEEN DEALT AFTER 35 ROUNDS OF THE INVESTMENT GAME

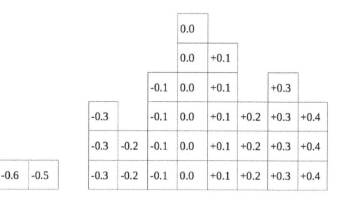

Returns shown are percentages (0.1 is 0.1%).

Notice that some cards (–0.4, +0.5 and +0.6) haven't yet been dealt. A more convenient way of visualising this information is to use a **histogram**, as in figure 4. This shows the same information but without needing to display the individual cards. The pattern of returns in a histogram is also called a **distribution**.

FIGURE 4: HISTOGRAMS ARE A MORE CONVENIENT WAY OF VISUALISING THE DISTRIBUTION OF PAST RETURNS

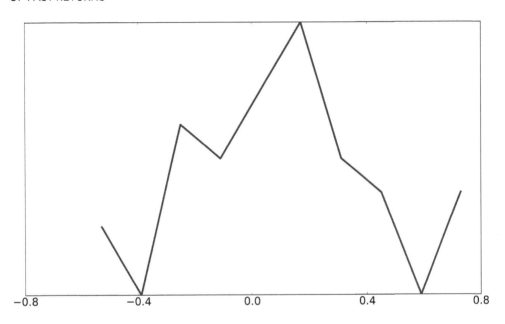

To think about the chances of getting any particular card is quite a complex exercise. Instead you're going to **summarise** the distribution with **estimates** of various **parameters**. These will become the parameters of your **statistical model**, which you'll then use to forecast future returns.

What sort of parameters should you use? Well, you need to work out: (a) whether it is worth playing the next round, and (b) how much to bet.

Firstly, to decide whether to play you need to know your expected **average** mean return. If the average was negative there would be no point participating: you should watch and wait until the expected average has gone above zero. In the distribution in figure 4, the mean return is positive: **0.08571%**. The geometric mean is slightly lower: **0.08521%**. As this is positive it's worth playing the next round.

Secondly, the correct size of your bet depends on the expected **variation** in returns. You might be expecting a positive return on average, but you could be unlucky and get an exceptionally poor card. You wouldn't want to bet very much if you are pretty likely to turn over a bad −0.5% card, or even a horrible −1% card. How can you measure the **risk** of these different outcomes?

There are many ways of doing this but I prefer to use **standard deviation**[35]: the average deviation from the mean return. The standard deviation of the returns shown in figure 4 is **0.3220%**.

CONCEPT: STANDARD DEVIATION

The **standard deviation** is a measure of how dispersed some data is around its average; so for asset returns it's a measure of how risky the asset is. I often use the term **volatility** as shorthand for the standard deviation of returns.

Individual equities have a standard deviation of around 25% to 30% a year (a little more in emerging markets, a little less in more developed markets). Bonds tend to be safer, depending on their maturity. A typical two-year bond issued by a safe government has an annual volatility of around 1.5% a year, and a ten-year bond would be more like 8%.

Most readers won't need to estimate their own values for standard deviations since you can use the typical values I've included in Appendix B (page 485). For the technically minded, the precise formula for calculating volatility is in Appendix C (page 489), but you don't need to know this since you can use a spreadsheet to calculate it. I explain how in Appendix C.

Standard deviation can seem like a very abstract way to measure risk. In chapter four I'll show how different portfolio standard deviations give rise to different expected portfolio performance. This will allow you to work out what kind of standard deviation you are comfortable with.

As I use geometric means, I'll also be using geometric standard deviations. However it's usually safe to assume the two versions are equal. For example, the geometric standard deviation of the returns in figure 4 is 0.3219%, which is virtually identical to the arithmetic version: 0.3220%. Throughout the rest of the book I don't distinguish between the two different types, instead I just refer to a generic standard deviation.

---

35. Technical note: Standard deviation has the advantage that it is calculated using all the returns, which makes it a more robust statistic than say maximum loss (also called maximum drawdown), or Value At Risk, which focuses on the tail. However its main advantage is simplicity.

CONCEPT: APPROXIMATING GEOMETRIC MEAN

There is a useful formula for finding the approximate geometric mean, given the arithmetic mean and the standard deviation.

The formula is:

geometric mean = arithmetic mean − 0.5 × (standard deviation)^2

For example, if you take the values in figure 4, which have an arithmetic mean of 0.08571% and a standard deviation of 0.3220%:

geometric mean = 0.08571 − 0.5 × (0.3220)^2 = 0.08520

This is virtually the same as the correct value (0.08521%). As you can see this approximation is close enough for all practical purposes. I use it throughout the book.

Returning to the game, remember you are trying to work out what the chances of a particularly poor card are. Looking at figure 3, the chance of a 0.5% loss or greater is around 6% (there are two cards out of 35 where this occurs). However, what are the chances of a 1% loss? Since it's never happened, is it zero?

To answer this, you need to add a missing element to your statistical model of expected future returns. You need to assume your returns have a particular type of statistical **distribution**. A commonly used distribution is the **Gaussian normal distribution**, also known as the Bell Curve because of its shape.

A Gaussian distribution with the same mean and standard deviation as figure 4 is shown in figure 5, overlaid on top of the original distribution. You can see that it is a reasonably good match.

If your returns are Gaussian normal, then the mean and standard deviation alone are sufficient to say how likely certain returns will be. Referring to table 3, you will see values one standard deviation or less around the average 68.2% of the time, and returns two standard deviations or less about 95.4% of the time. In 2.3% of periods you'd see a change two standard deviations better than the average. You'd also see a return which is two standard deviations worse than the average 2.3% of the time, because the Gaussian distribution is **symmetric**.

FIGURE 5: THE ORIGINAL DISTRIBUTION FROM THE GAME PLUS A MATCHING GAUSSIAN DISTRIBUTION

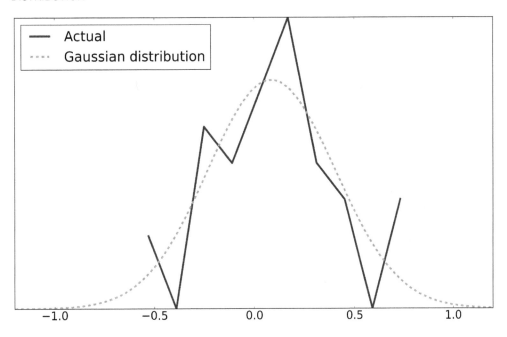

TABLE 3: THE GAUSSIAN DISTRIBUTION

	Probability of lower value	Probability of higher value	Value in example
+2 standard deviations	97.7%	2.3%	0.72%
+1 standard deviations	84.1%	15.9%	0.41%
Mean	50%	50%	0.09%
−1 standard deviations	15.9%	84.1%	−0.24%
−2 standard deviations	2.3%	91.7%	−0.56%

'Value in example' column based on an arithmetic mean of 0.0857% and standard deviation of 0.322%

In concrete terms, suppose you are dealt 1,000 cards from a deck with an arithmetic mean of 0.0857% and a standard deviation of 0.322%. You would expect 682 (68.2% of

1000) of those cards to be within one standard deviation: between –0.24% and 0.41%[36]. Around 23 (2.3% of 1000) of those cards would be above 0.72% (two standard deviations better than the average). And around 23 cards would have values of –0.56% or lower[37] (two standard deviations below the average).

You can now work out the chances of a 0.5% loss in the investment game, based on the statistical model of returns shown in figure 5. A 0.5% loss is 0.5857% below the average of 0.0857%, because 0.0875% – (–0.5%) = 0.5857%. So a loss of 0.5% is 0.5857% ÷ 0.322% = 1.82 standard deviations below the average. The chance of this happening with the normal distribution are **3.4%**.[38] Out of every 1000 cards dealt in the future you would expect 34 to have a value of –0.5% or worse.

Notice this is slightly different from what actually happened in the cards dealt for the investment game example. Two out of 34 cards had a loss of 0.5% upwards, equivalent to 5.9% of the time (or 59 cards out of every 1000). There is a difference between the **actual past** returns (figures 3 or 4, or the solid line in figure 5) and the **statistical model** of past returns (the dotted line in figure 5). Although they have the same mean and standard deviation, they have different distributions. **The distribution shown with a dotted line in figure 5 is Gaussian; but the actual distribution shown with a solid line in figure 5 isn't.**

It's also possible to work out the chances of a more severe 1% loss, something you couldn't do with the actual returns in figure 3. First find the difference between minus 1% and the average of 0.0857%: 0.0875% – (–1%) = 1.0857%. That represents 1.0857% ÷ 0.322% = 3.37 standard deviations. The chance of this occurring with the normal distribution are tiny: **0.04%**. Out of every 10,000 cards dealt in the future you would expect just four to have a return of 1% or lower.

Be careful: these results come with a **very** big health warning. Gaussian models are notoriously bad at modelling extreme returns in financial markets. With a Gaussian distribution you'd get a 4 standard deviation fall on only 1 out of 31,500 days (roughly once every century). But from 1914 to 2014 the Dow Jones Index had a 4 standard deviation fall on more than 30 occasions!

Using a statistical model with a Gaussian distribution makes your life much easier since you only need to estimate two parameters: the mean and the standard deviation. But you should never forget that it is not a complete and accurate representation of reality.[39]

---

36. 0.0857% – 0.3220% = –0.2363% and 0.0857% + 0.3220% = 0.4077%
37. 0.0857% + [2 × 0.3220%] = 0.7297% and 0.0857% – [2 × 0.3220%] = –0.5583%
38. I explain in Appendix C on page 493 how to use a spreadsheet function to reproduce these calculations.
39. Technical note: It's possible to use more complex distributions, which incorporate higher moments such as skew and kurtosis. However this approach is no panacea. Firstly, the estimation error in higher moments is considerable, and can be badly affected by one or two outliers. Secondly, and more importantly, highly complex models usually lead to a false sense of security. No matter how complex your model, it can never capture the possibility of an unforeseen extreme *Black Swan* event (from

The uncertain past

Statistical modeling of past returns is very useful, but it also has serious flaws. There is also **model uncertainty**.

You don't know if (a) your assumption about the shape of the distribution is correct – whether it is really Gaussian, or (b) if the estimates of expected mean and standard deviation are wrong, or (c) if the cards dealt so far are really representative of the undealt deck.

In real life you also don't know if the distribution or its parameters will change over time. This would be like the dealer in the investment game replacing the remaining undealt cards in the deck with a completely different deck, without telling anyone. At least in Blackjack you know when the dealer is reshuffling!

To summarise: the statistical model tells you how much **predictable** asset return volatility to expect, but there is also **unpredictable** variation coming from the fact you can't completely trust the model.

Mostly you just have to shrug your shoulders and live with these unpredictable risks. It's important to keep them in the back of your mind, but it's difficult to deal with them in a systematic way.[40] However, there is one notable exception. It's relatively easy to quantify how **uncertain the parameter estimates in the statistical model are**. I call this the **uncertainty of the past**, because these estimates are derived from past data.

CONCEPT: THE UNCERTAINTY OF THE PAST

"… economic forecasts are better than nothing, but their origin lies in extrapolation from a *partially known past* through an unknown present to an unknown future…" (my emphasis)

– Denis Healey, UK Chancellor of the Exchequer 1974–9

You know the future is uncertain. But the past also contains uncertainty.

Of course you can see what cards have already been laid in the investment game: there is no uncertainty about that. But you can't see **everything** in the past: you didn't see the starting pack that the cards were drawn from, and never will. Instead the best you can do is try and infer what the initial pack looked like.

---

the book of the same name, by Nassim Taleb). Personally I prefer to use a simple risk model whose shortcomings are very obvious.

40. Technical note: At least we can't deal with them without using relatively complicated techniques – complex distributions with more parameters for higher moments, multiple state models with different distributions, and Bayesian methods to judge whether a small sample is representative given a prior opinion on the larger population. However, the element of unpredictable risk created by parameter uncertainty has by far the biggest effect on forecast uncertainty, which is why I've chosen to focus on it here.

Similarly in real life you can easily download a history of stock prices; no uncertainty there either. But to make investment decisions you're going to need to assume that these stock prices were generated by a statistical model with some parameters: a mean and a standard deviation.

Unfortunately there are numerous sets of parameters that could possibly have generated the historical returns that you've observed. You'll never be entirely sure exactly which set of parameters to use. All you can do is look at the possible range of parameter values and work out which are the most plausible candidates given the historical data. You can never say with 100% confidence which exact parameter values produced the historic data.

This isn't just uncertainty about the future, it's **uncertainty about the past**. But since we assume the future will look like the past this will affect how confidently we can forecast the future.

Let's return to this question: Should you play the next round of the investment game, given the 35 cards that have been dealt in figure 3? Clearly you should play if you are reasonably confident that the average value of the cards remaining in the deck is positive. But remember that the deck is very large, so that the cards left in the deck will be virtually the same as the pattern of cards in the starting deck before the game began.

So we can ask this question instead: How likely is it that the average return of the cards in the deck at the start of the investment game was positive, given the cards that have already been dealt?

To answer this you need to estimate the expected average of the original deck. That's easy, it's the same as the arithmetic or geometric mean of the cards you've already seen. But you also need to know **how uncertain you are about that estimate**.

CONCEPT: ESTIMATING THE UNCERTAINTY OF AN AVERAGE

It's easy to estimate the expected average return, if you have some historical data which you assume is representative. But how certain can you be about that estimate?

To work this out I used a statistical technique called **bootstrapping**. First of all I took the historical data, which in this case are the returns in figures 3 and 4. I then created a series of 'alternative histories' by randomly selecting returns from the data. Each alternative history has the same number of returns as the historical data – 35 in this case.

To make one version of history I randomly chose a series of 35 returns from the data set. Each time I chose a return I replaced it, so it can be chosen again (otherwise

I'd end up with exactly the same returns in each of the alternative histories). I then measured the mean return in the alternative history.[41]

This process was repeated many thousands of times. This gave me a **distribution of mean estimates**, shown in figure 6.

Figure 6 shows the likely distribution of the average return in the starting deck, given you've been dealt the 35 cards in figure 3. This is **not** the same as the past distribution of dealt cards dealt in figure 4. It is **not** the expected Gaussian normal distribution of future cards from the statistical model, overlaid on top of the actual distribution in figure 5. Instead it shows the **uncertainty of one of the parameters** (the mean) in the statistical model.

FIGURE 6: WHAT DO WE EXPECT THE AVERAGE VALUE IN THE ENTIRE STARTING DECK TO BE, GIVEN THE 35 CARDS ALREADY DEALT?

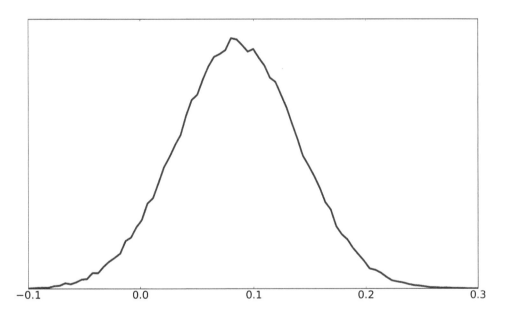

As you would expect, the mean of this distribution is the same as the arithmetic mean of the cards that have been dealt: 0.0857%. In half the alternative histories the mean is

---

41.   Technical note: As you'll see later I can also measure other statistics, such as the risk and Sharpe Ratio. If I have returns from multiple sources I can also measure correlation, and the average difference in returns. There is more information about this in Appendix C, page 493.

higher than this, in the other half lower. It also turns out that there is a 95% chance[42] that the arithmetic mean of the starting deck was between -0.023% and 0.195%.[43]

That is quite a wide range, which reflects the fact that you've only seen 35 cards, and so can't be especially confident about what the starting deck looked like. Remember it's not telling you that there is a 95% chance of the next card having a value between -0.023% and 0.195%. Instead it means there was a 95% chance that the average value of the starting pack was in this range. Because of our assumptions this implies there is also a 95% chance that the **average value of all the cards you're going to be dealt in the future** is in this range.

Returning to the original question we're trying to answer, according to my calculations there is a 94.2% chance that the average of the starting pack was above zero.[44] This is pretty high; if I was you I'd happily start to play this game.

Incidentally it's also possible to work out the **uncertainty of our estimate of the standard deviation of returns**. There is a 95% chance that the standard deviation of the original pack is between 0.24% and 0.40%.[45] There is considerably more certainty about the standard deviation than the mean.

To put it another way, **you can make better predictions about risk than return.**

These findings will be very useful in the next chapter when we consider how informative historical asset returns are in practice.

---

42.   For a Gaussian distribution this is roughly a range of minus two to plus two standard deviations. For this reason it's a commonly used statistic.

43.   If you want to know the maths: the standard deviation of the distribution of means is the standard deviation of the cards we've been dealt, 0.322%, divided by the square root of the number of cards (35), which is 0.0544%. Two standard deviations is 0.109%; which around the average of 0.0857% gives a 95% confidence range of –0.0232% to 0.1946%.

44.   If you want to know how I work this out see Appendix C, page 494.

45.   Technical note: The standard deviation of the sampling distribution of standard deviations (what a mouthful!) is approximately 0.72 multiplied by the standard deviation of the original data, 0.322%, divided by the square root of the number of values in the original data (35), which is 0.0392%. This approximation is fine for a large enough sample. The 95% range is given by the standard deviation of the dealt cards, 0.322% plus or minus two standard deviations of the estimate: 0.322% + (2 × 0.0392%) = 0.40% and 0.322% – (2 × 0.0392%) = 0.24%.

Key points

The market is no casino	It's worse than a casino! At least in a casino the odds are known precisely before you play.
The future is not the past	It's common to assume that future returns will be similar to what happened in the past. But you cannot extrapolate history to the point where you know for sure what will happen next year.
Statistical models based on the past are useful	These models can give you an idea of future average returns and their likely variation (standard deviation), assuming the patterns of the past repeat in the future.
But the past is uncertain	Past data is much murkier than the parameters of neat statistical models suggest. To make smart decisions you need to quantity how confident you are in the predictions of your models, by measuring how much uncertainty there was in the past.

CHAPTER THREE
Trying to Find the Best Portfolio

YOU'VE ALREADY SEEN IN THE LAST CHAPTER THAT YOU CAN USE historical returns to build **statistical models** to try and forecast the patterns of future returns. In this chapter I'll explain how these allow you to use standard optimisation techniques to find the best portfolio weights. But I'll also show you that these techniques are tricky to use correctly, often come out with crazy recommendations, and don't deal with the problem of **uncertainty of the past** that is inherent in statistical modeling.

Chapter overview

Portfolio optimisation, made simple	The intuition behind the standard techniques for deciding portfolio weights, explained with a minimum of theory.
Uncertain returns and unstable portfolios	The effect that the uncertainty of the past has when you're trying to find the best portfolio weights.
Why the future won't be like the past	Why it is smarter to use realistic expectations of future returns.

In this chapter I point out the problems and difficulties of portfolio optimisation. The next chapter discusses some practical solutions.

Portfolio optimisation, made simple

My aim here is **not** to teach you how to do portfolio optimisation using the standard methods: there are plenty of books out there that do that,[46] and I think it's unnecessary and even dangerous for most investors to use these techniques.

Instead I want to extract some useful insights from the optimisation process, which I will then use in chapter four to create a method for constructing portfolios in a simpler and more reliable way. You'll get an intuitive feel for how the standard model works and what the pitfalls are.

Optimisation in practice

To do a portfolio optimisation you start with a list of possible assets to include in your portfolio, and some **expectations** of future asset returns. You then consider different portfolio **weights**, and look for the portfolio that is expected to be the best.

Remember from chapter one that the best portfolio will have the highest expected **geometric mean** return for some level of expected **risk**. I defined risk as the **standard deviation** of returns in chapter two. Our expectations of geometric mean and standard deviation will come from a **statistical model**, of the kind you saw in chapter two.

Let's look at a concrete example. Suppose you are trying to optimise a portfolio with a choice of just two assets: the US S&P 500 equity index, and an index of US ten year government bond prices. If you want you can assume that you're getting exposure to these assets via ETFs, although it makes no practical difference.

I have nearly 100 years of historical data which I'm going to analyse to produce estimates of the parameters for my statistical model. My estimates of geometric mean and standard deviation from real historical total returns are shown in table 4.

TABLE 4: HISTORIC ANNUALISED AVERAGE AND STANDARD DEVIATION OF REAL RETURNS FOR US ASSETS

	Arithmetic mean	Geometric mean	Standard deviation
US 10 year bond	2.20%	1.86%	8.27%
S&P 500 equities	8.20%	6.23%	19.80%

Based on annual returns from 1928–2016

---

46. For example, *Robust Portfolio Optimization and Management* by Frank Fabozzi.

What is the best portfolio? The best portfolio will have a large proportion of assets with higher expected returns: so clearly more equities. But reducing the risk of a portfolio will also make it more attractive, making bonds look like a better option.

These two goals are clearly contradictory. It would be nice to have assets that offered both high return and low risk, but real life is rarely so generous.

To find the best weights for each asset you need to find the portfolio with the best **expected return adjusted for risk**. There are many ways of calculating this, but I will be using one of the simplest: the **Sharpe Ratio**.

CONCEPT: SHARPE RATIO (SR)

The Sharpe Ratio (SR) measures the risk-adjusted returns of an asset. Higher Sharpe Ratios are better, as they mean that returns are expected to be higher, or risk is expected to be lower.

Formally it is the expected average return over a particular time period divided by the **standard deviation** of returns for the same time period. So the annual SR would be the average annual return, divided by the standard deviation of annual returns. So for arithmetic returns:

arithmetic SR = arithmetic mean ÷ standard deviation

Strictly speaking you should deduct the risk free rate from returns before calculating the Sharpe Ratio. I do not do this. This simplifies the book, and with the low levels of interest rates prevailing as I write this in early 2017, there is no meaningful difference.[47]

From table 4 the Sharpe Ratio of US bonds is the average return of 2.20% divided by the standard deviation of 8.27%, or 0.266.

I use geometric returns for the Sharpe Ratios in this book.

geometric SR = geometric mean ÷ standard deviation

Again from table 4 the Geometric Sharpe Ratio for bonds is the geometric return of 1.86% divided by the standard deviation[48] of 8.27%, or 0.225. Geometric Sharpe Ratios are usually lower than the arithmetic version, mainly because geometric means are always lower than arithmetic means.[49]

---

47.   Technical note: It also has no effect on my results since in the first two parts of the book I mostly assume Sharpe Ratios are identical for all assets, and in part three I only worry about relative Sharpe Ratios.

48.   Remember from the previous chapter that the arithmetic and geometric standard deviation are virtually identical.

49.   Technical note: This isn't true for arithmetic Sharpe Ratios above around 0.70; but this is much higher than I assume is likely.

There are a couple of reasons why the Sharpe Ratio is not perfect. Firstly it is based on an imperfect risk measure: the **standard deviation**. This assumes symmetric gains and losses, which is pretty unrealistic. The standard deviation measure also implies that very large rises and falls in prices should be relatively rare. In reality they are much more common. The 1987 stock market crash was a 20 standard deviation event. To get a rough idea of how unlikely that was, a 7 standard deviation event should only happen every 3 billion years or so.

Secondly the Sharpe Ratio will not suit the risk preferences of every investor. The Sharpe Ratio assumes that a 2% increase in return would exactly balance a 2% increase in risk. But this higher risk level will make some investors nervous, and this wouldn't be a trade-off they would be happy with. I'll return to this problem in the next chapter.

Despite these imperfections the Sharpe Ratio has the advantage of being relatively simple to calculate and understand, which is why I use it throughout the book.

TABLE 5: HISTORIC SHARPE RATIOS FOR US ASSETS

	Geometric mean	Standard deviation	Sharpe Ratio
US 10 year bond	1.86%	8.27%	0.225
S&P 500 equities	6.23%	19.80%	0.315

Based on annual returns from 1928–2016. Sharpe Ratio is geometric mean divided by arithmetic standard deviation. The latter will be very close to the geometric standard deviation.

Table 5 shows the Sharpe Ratio for both the assets in our simple example. It looks like equities have the highest Sharpe Ratio as well as the highest geometric mean. Does this mean that the best portfolio should be entirely in equities? Are the next few hundred pages of this book a waste of time? No. If you put 100% into equities you will be missing out on **diversification**, and diversification lowers risk. Diversifying your portfolio is one of the smartest things you can do.

Let me explain. Obviously the risk of a portfolio will depend on the risk of the underlying assets. A lower proportion allocated to riskier assets will make the portfolio safer, and vice versa. However portfolio risk also depends on how **similar** the returns of each asset are.

If the assets in your portfolio are very similar then it will be riskier. A portfolio consisting entirely of US car manufacturers would be highly exposed to a downturn in the American automobile market. Conversely more diversified portfolios with dissimilar assets will have lower risk. If you have exposure to lots of different asset classes and countries then you won't be badly affected if US car owners suddenly decide to start driving Toyotas.

Because the geometric mean increases when risk falls (as explained in chapter one), it will also be slightly higher for more diversified portfolios; assuming of course that arithmetic returns do not fall too much at the same time.

To capture this effect of return similarity among different assets we need to add an additional parameter to the statistical model to measure it: **correlation**.

CONCEPT: CORRELATION

Correlation is a way of measuring the similarity of returns for two assets.[50] Correlations are always between −1 and +1, and are standardised so they can be calculated and compared even when assets have different risk.

For example, suppose we have the following series of fictional returns:

	Monday	**Tuesday**	**Wednesday**
Microsoft	5%	−2.5%	3%
Apple	10%	−5%	6%
General Motors (GM)	−5%	2.5%	−3%

A correlation of plus one indicates that the asset returns will move perfectly in sync, even if their magnitude is different. The daily return of Microsoft is always exactly half that of Apple, so the stocks would be perfectly correlated with a correlation of +1, although the risk of Apple is twice that of Microsoft.

A correlation of minus one implies that returns will always move against each other. The returns of General Motors are exactly the opposite of those in Microsoft. They are also always half, and the opposite, of the returns in Apple. GM will have a correlation of minus one with both these firms.

Zero correlation implies there is no linear relationship between two assets.

You can summarise correlations in a **correlation matrix**, like table 6.

---

50.   For information, see Appendix C, page 493.

TABLE 6: HIGHLY UNREALISTIC EXAMPLE OF A CORRELATION MATRIX

	Microsoft	**Apple**	**General Motors**
Microsoft	1	*1*	*−1*
Apple	1	1	*−1*
General Motors	−1	−1	1

Notice that assets always have a correlation of 1.0 with themselves, shown by the values in bold along the diagonal. Also notice the symmetrical nature of correlation matrices; the values are reflected on either side of the diagonal. In the rest of the book I include only half the correlations, excluding those shown here in italics from the top-right diagonal section of each matrix.

In practice you will not see such extreme correlations in the real world. However assets that are similar, such as the equity of firms trading in the same country and industry like Microsoft and Apple, will have high positive correlations. If assets have less in common, not being from the same asset class, country, or industry, then their correlations will be much lower.

You probably won't need to measure correlations yourself: the method for building portfolios I introduce later doesn't require explicit correlation estimates. But if you're interested Appendix C (page 493) explains how to calculate correlations using a spreadsheet package.

Table 7 shows my estimates of correlation for the two US assets we're using.

TABLE 7: CORRELATIONS OF RETURNS FOR EXAMPLE OPTIMISATION

	Bond	**S&P**
US 10 year bond	1	
S&P 500	0.05	1

Based on annual returns from 1928–2016

We can now start to explore what effect changing the weights of a portfolio has on its risk and return. To do this I'll be using some standard formulas for calculating the risk and return of a portfolio. You don't need to know the precise maths I'm using here but if you're interested the relevant formulas are in Appendix C, page 495. At this stage we're only concerned with pre-cost returns. Costs, and after cost returns, are considered later in chapters five and six.

Figure 7 shows the geometric mean return of all the possible portfolios of equities and bonds. The next few plots all have the same format: the x-axis shows the proportion of bonds increasing from left to right, from zero to 100%. As we have only two assets the proportion in equities will also change from 100% (left-hand side) to 0% (extreme right). For now I'm ignoring the option of putting cash into the portfolio; I'll return to this in the next chapter.

Since the S&P is expected to give the highest geometric return the best portfolio allocation is 100% in equities (extreme left of the plot).

FIGURE 7: GEOMETRIC RETURN REDUCES AS MORE BONDS ARE ADDED

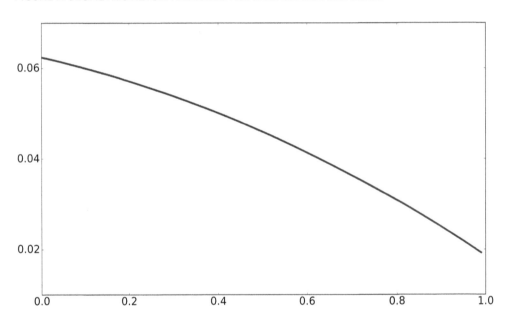

Y-axis shows geometric return of an equity/bond portfolio. X-axis shows allocation to bonds, remainder is in equities. 0= 100% in equities. 1.0 = 100% in bonds.

Figure 8 shows the **risk** of each combination of portfolio weights, using my preferred measure of annual standard deviation. Up to a point substituting bonds for equities reduces risk. Interestingly I don't get the very lowest risk with the entire portfolio in bonds. Keeping a modest amount of equities in the portfolio actually reduces risk. Even though equities are more volatile they provide some diversification, which reduces the overall risk of the portfolio.

FIGURE 8: RISK REDUCES AS BONDS ARE ADDED; BUT SAFEST PORTFOLIO HAS SOME EQUITIES

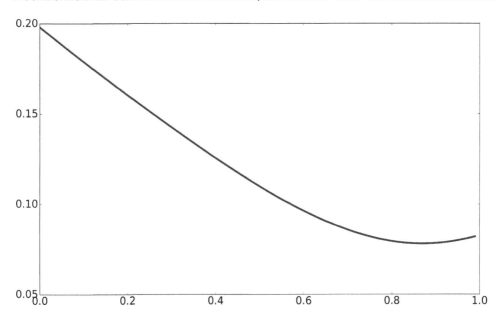

Y-axis shows standard deviation of an equity/bond portfolio. X-axis shows allocation to bonds, remainder is in equities. 0= 100% in equities. 1.0 = 100% in bonds.

Finally figure 9 shows the Sharpe Ratio: the geometric return divided by the standard deviation. This shows an interesting pattern as we go from left (all equities) to right (all bonds). Initially as I add bonds to the portfolio the reductions in risk outweigh lower average returns, and the Sharpe Ratio rises. At some point however risk isn't going down fast enough, and the Sharpe Ratio gets harmed by substantially lower geometric returns.

FIGURE 9: SHARPE RATIO IS MAXIMUM WITH A BLEND OF BONDS AND EQUITIES

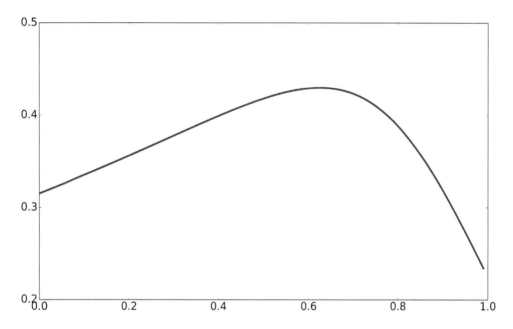

Y-axis shows geometric Sharpe Ratio of a bond/equity portfolio. X-axis shows allocation to bonds, remainder is in equities. 0= 100% in equities. 1.0 = 100% in bonds.

The allocation with the highest Sharpe Ratio is around 60% in bonds and 40% in equities. However the expected geometric return of this portfolio (4.1%) is around a third less of the all-equity option (6.2%).

Figure 10 shows this visually. The best portfolio is in the top left-hand corner; it has maximum return and minimum risk. Unfortunately it isn't possible to reach this point with the two assets we have. The worst portfolio is in the bottom right. Our two assets sit in opposing corners, bonds with relatively low return and low-risk asset; and the S&P 500 with higher returns but also more risk.

FIGURE 10: NOT OBVIOUS WHAT THE BEST PORTFOLIO IS

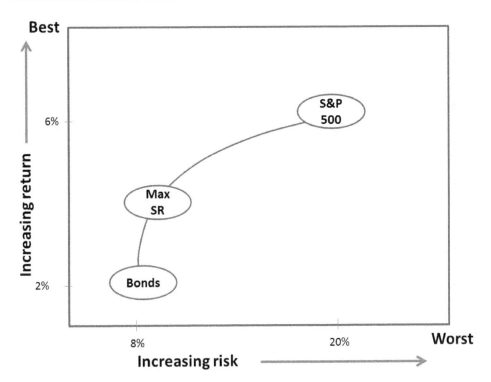

Max SR is maximum Sharpe Ratio portfolio.

The curved line between the two assets shows all the possible portfolios we can invest in. The line is curved because of diversification. If bonds and the S&P 500 had a correlation of +1 then it would be a straight line.

It isn't obvious whereabouts on the curved line you want to be. The maximum Sharpe Ratio (SR) portfolio is just one possible compromise between equities and bonds. We still haven't addressed the difficult question of whether you should go for the highest Sharpe Ratio, or a portfolio with higher returns but also more risk, or another option entirely. For now I'll assume you want to maximise Sharpe Ratio, but I will return to this important issue in the next chapter.

Some simple portfolios

I'm now going to show you a few very simple portfolios to give you some intuition about how the standard portfolio optimisation process works and what its flaws are. I'll set up a statistical model for each portfolio, push them through the optimising process, and examine the weights that come out. To reiterate: I don't use formal optimisation in the book and I won't explain the process in any detail – I just show the results it produces.

These portfolios all contain three completely imaginary assets, which go by the rather dull names of A, B and C. Each of these portfolio tables has the same format, showing a correlation matrix, the estimated arithmetic mean and standard deviation of returns, and the resulting optimal portfolio weights. The optimal weights are those that give the highest geometric Sharpe Ratio.

Let's begin with portfolio 1 which has highly correlated assets, such as equities in the same industry and country, like Apple, Google and Microsoft which are all US tech stocks. All the assets have the same average return and the same standard deviation. Unsurprisingly the optimal weights are all identical, with one third of the portfolio in each asset.[51]

PORTFOLIO 1: EXAMPLE: HIGHLY CORRELATED, SAME MEAN AND STANDARD DEVIATION

Correlations

	A	B	C			Avg.	Std. dev.
A	1				A	4%	8%
B	0.9	1			B	4%	8%
C	0.9	0.9	1		C	4%	8%

Optimisation

	Weight
A	33%
B	33%
C	33%

Correlation matrix, arithmetic average and standard deviation of returns, and resulting optimal weights (maximum geometric Sharpe Ratio).

I get exactly the same weights in portfolio 2 where the assets are completely unrelated, with zero correlation. The conclusion you should draw from these first two portfolios is this: if correlations, expected average returns and standard deviations are identical then you should split your portfolio evenly. This is true for both high and low correlations, as long as they're the same across all pairs of assets.

---

51.   In this and subsequent results there is some rounding, so weights may not add up to 100%.

This is an important result which I'll use in the next chapter when I explain **handcrafting** – my own preferred method for determining portfolio weights.

PORTFOLIO 2: EXAMPLE: NO CORRELATION, SAME MEAN AND STANDARD DEVIATION

Correlations

	A	B	C
A	1		
B	0.0	1	
C	0.0	0.0	1

	Avg.	Std. dev.
A	4%	8%
B	4%	8%
C	4%	8%

Optimisation

	Weight
A	33%
B	33%
C	33%

Correlation matrix, arithmetic average and standard deviation of returns, and resulting optimal weights (maximum geometric Sharpe Ratio).

Now I show you what happens if we change the correlation matrix, so we have one asset that is unrelated to the others (C), and two assets that are very similar (A and B). In portfolio 3 you can see that the unrelated asset (C) is picking up almost half the portfolio allocation, with the rest split between the similar assets (A and B).

PORTFOLIO 3: EXAMPLE: VARYING CORRELATION, SAME MEAN AND STANDARD DEVIATION

Correlations

	A	B	C			Avg.	Std. dev.
A	1				A	4%	8%
B	0.7	1			B	4%	8%
C	0.0	0.0	1		C	4%	8%

Optimisation

	Weight
A	27%
B	27%
C	46%

Correlation matrix, arithmetic average and standard deviation of returns, and resulting optimal weights (maximum geometric Sharpe Ratio).

Portfolio 4 shows the result of changing standard deviation when I have uncorrelated assets. One asset (C) is riskier than the others. As a result I needed less of it in the portfolio. It's very hard to see how the optimiser comes up with the precise weight it does. For this reason I prefer to use a portfolio construction method which uses **risk-adjusted weightings**. I explain what this involves in chapter four.

PORTFOLIO 4: EXAMPLE: VARYING STANDARD DEVIATION, NO CORRELATION AND SAME MEAN

Correlations

	A	B	C
A	1		
B	0.0	1	
C	0.0	0.0	1

	Avg.	Std. dev.
A	4%	8%
B	4%	8%
C	4%	12%

Optimisation

	Weight
A	40%
B	40%
C	18%

Correlation matrix, arithmetic average and standard deviation of returns, and resulting optimal weights (maximum geometric Sharpe Ratio).

Portfolio 5 brings us back to highly correlated assets, but now C is only a tiny bit riskier than the others. This small additional risk is enough to remove this asset completely from the portfolio! In portfolios where correlations are high it only takes small differences in expected standard deviation to produce very extreme weights.

PORTFOLIO 5: EXAMPLE: VARYING STANDARD DEVIATION, HIGHLY CORRELATED AND SAME MEAN

Correlations

	A	B	C			Avg.	Std. dev.
A	1				A	4%	8.0%
B	0.9	1			B	4%	8.0%
C	0.9	0.9	1		C	4%	8.5%

Optimisation

	Weight
A	50%
B	50%
C	0%

Correlation matrix, arithmetic average and standard deviation of returns, and resulting optimal weights (maximum geometric Sharpe Ratio).

I got exactly the same problem in portfolio 6, but this time it is a tiny difference in means that gives asset C all the allocation. Generally portfolio optimisation is **unstable** – it often produces extreme weights with only small differences in the inputs; especially when assets are highly correlated. I explain the implications of this in more depth later in the chapter.

PORTFOLIO 6: EXAMPLE: VARYING MEAN, HIGHLY CORRELATED AND SAME STANDARD DEVIATION

Correlations

	A	B	C
A	1		
B	0.9	1	
C	0.9	0.9	1

	Avg.	Std. dev.
A	4.0%	8%
B	4.0%	8%
C	4.5%	8%

Optimisation

	Weight
A	0%
B	0%
C	100%

Correlation matrix, arithmetic average and standard deviation of returns, and resulting optimal weights (maximum geometric Sharpe Ratio).

Portfolio 7 shows that the instability caused by slightly different means isn't as strong where assets are uncorrelated. A much better performing asset, C, gets a slightly higher weight but doesn't crowd out the rest of the portfolio entirely as in portfolio 6.

PORTFOLIO 7: EXAMPLE: VARYING MEAN, NO CORRELATION AND SAME STANDARD DEVIATION

Correlations

	A	B	C			Avg.	Std. dev.
A	1				A	4%	8%
B	0.0	1			B	4%	8%
C	0.0	0.0	1		C	6%	8%

Optimisation

	Weight
A	26%
B	26%
C	47%

Correlation matrix, arithmetic average and standard deviation of returns, and resulting optimal weights (maximum geometric Sharpe Ratio).

Summary

This section has been a little dense, so let me summarise the key points.

Small differences in expected means and standard deviations can produce extreme weights when correlations are high. In the second part of this chapter, 'Uncertain returns and unstable portfolios', I explain why this is a serious problem.

The best portfolio has **the maximum return for some level of risk**, but what level of risk? Is maximising Sharpe Ratio the most appropriate goal for every investor? I explore some smart solutions to this problem in chapter four.

Riskier assets with higher standard deviation of returns should get lower weights, but the resulting weights are hard to interpret. Chapter four also introduces a smarter method for dealing with this: **risk weighting**.

If means and standard deviations are equal then the portfolio weights I get with identical correlations are very neat, with an equal split across assets. If correlations are a little different there is also a nice intuitive pattern, with similar assets seeing their share of the portfolio split between them. I use these results in chapter four when I explain the **handcrafting** method I use to decide portfolio weights.

Uncertain returns and unstable portfolios

So far in this chapter I've used statistical models based on past data whilst ignoring the **uncertainty of the past** problem I discussed at the end of chapter two. But in reality we can never say exactly what the parameters of these statistical models should be.

What impact does this have on the ability of the standard optimisation model to find the right portfolio? As you saw earlier in portfolios 5 and 6, very small differences in expected returns and standard deviations can cause portfolio weights to become extreme, especially when correlations are high. A modest 0.5% difference in expected standard deviations in portfolio 5, and a 0.5% difference in expected geometric means in portfolio 6, was enough for the optimiser to give one or two assets an allocation of zero.

But using such extreme weights and putting all your eggs in a relatively small number of baskets is inherently dangerous. What if you allocate your entire portfolio to an asset whose price ends up falling precipitously? If your forecasts aren't precise enough then using the weights produced by a portfolio optimiser could end up losing you a lot of money.

Do we really know the geometric mean and standard deviation of typical financial assets to an accuracy of 0.5% or less? Let's find out.

Remember from the concept box on page 44 that you can work out from historical data the amount of uncertainty in a statistical parameter estimate, like the geometric mean. To do this you generate numerous alternative histories from the data, then measure the geometric mean of each. The distribution of these measurements shows how much variation there is in the estimate of geometric mean used in your statistical models. It's also possible to do a similar exercise for other statistics, such as the standard deviation, correlation and Sharpe Ratio.

Figure 11 shows the variation in the estimate of geometric mean of the S&P 500 and US bonds, using the same historical data I've used throughout the chapter.

From table 4, the average geometric mean of equities is 6.23% and for bonds it is 1.86%. But how confident can we be in those estimates? Not very. The mean for equities could plausibly be well above 10%, or slightly negative. The mean for bonds has a slightly narrower range, because it's a safer asset. But the uncertainty is still many times larger than the 0.5% difference in means that we know can produce extreme portfolio weights.

FIGURE 11: SOME DIFFERENCE IN ESTIMATES OF GEOMETRIC MEANS

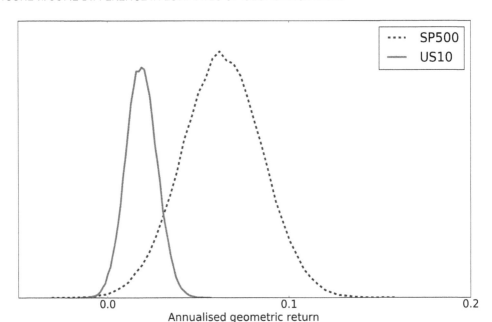

Now let us turn to risk. Have a look at figure 12. This shows the distribution of standard deviations of both assets.

This confirms that stocks are much riskier than bonds, but we already knew that. There is another feature of figure 12 that is worth noticing: there is less uncertainty in standard deviations than in geometric means. Even accounting for past uncertainty we can be in no doubt that equities were a riskier asset than bonds, as their distributions don't overlap at all.

Remember that the best portfolio has the highest **risk-adjusted return**. We now know that stocks are definitely **riskier** than bonds. But is the distinct advantage of higher geometric returns in figure 11 enough to overcome the greater volatility of stocks?

Fortunately we already have a method for calculating risk-adjusted returns: the **Sharpe Ratio**. Figure 13 shows the distribution of Sharpe Ratios for stocks and bonds. Notice any difference between this and figure 11? Once I've accounted for risk by calculating the Sharpe Ratio there is no significant difference between stocks and bonds; stocks have a slightly higher expected Sharpe but the distributions virtually overlap. **It's impossible to distinguish between historic Sharpe Ratios**.

It's also clear that estimates of Sharpe Ratios have considerable uncertainty: this comes mainly from the huge uncertainty of estimates of geometric mean.

FIGURE 12: ACROSS ASSET CLASSES STANDARD DEVIATIONS CAN BE MEANINGFULLY DIFFERENT

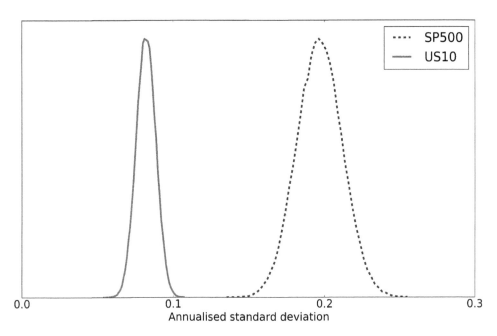

FIGURE 13: IT'S ALMOST IMPOSSIBLE TO DETERMINE IF SHARPE RATIOS ARE DIFFERENT

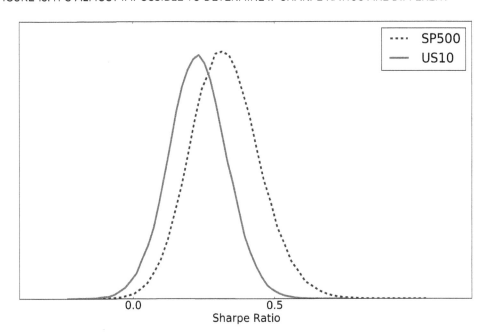

Figure 14 reinforces this: it shows the distribution of the **difference** in Sharpe Ratios. In this figure a positive number means stocks outperform bonds on a risk-adjusted basis. Again there is significant uncertainty. It isn't possible to say with any degree of confidence which asset had historically higher risk-adjusted returns.

FIGURE 14: DISTRIBUTION OF DIFFERENCE IN SHARPE RATIOS

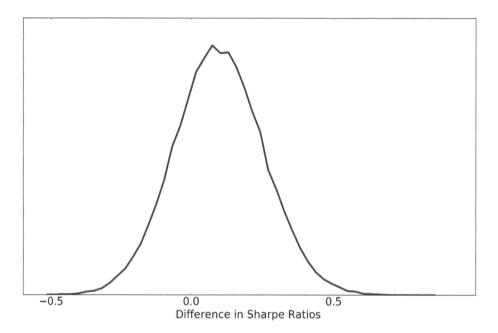

Difference in Sharpe Ratios

To wrap up this analysis, figure 15 shows the distribution of estimates for correlations. Like volatility these also have less uncertainty than expected returns.

FIGURE 15: DISTRIBUTION OF CORRELATION ESTIMATES

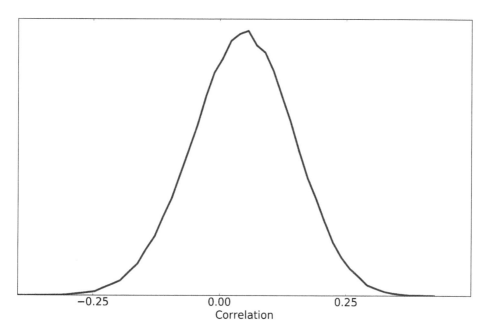

Let's summarise what have we learned so far:

Risk-adjusted returns	The **uncertainty of the past** is largest for risk-adjusted returns. We can be 95% confident that the estimated relative Sharpe Ratio (SR) of the two assets was within a range of around 0.5 SR units.* For US stocks and bonds this uncertainty range is –0.16 to 0.36. This is a huge degree of estimation error: our estimates of Sharpe Ratio are effectively worthless.
Standard deviations	The uncertainty of standard deviation estimates is much lower than for the Sharpe Ratio. It also depends on how risky the asset is. For bonds the 95% range of confidence is in a range of around 2% annual standard deviation (actual range 7.1% to 9.2%). For equities the range is around 5% (actual range 17.2% to 22.2%).
Correlations	In typical financial data estimates of bond and equity correlations are 95% likely to be within a range of around one-third (actual range –0.12 to 0.21).

* Technical note: The confidence interval will be narrower with assets that are more highly correlated. However with higher correlations the optimisation process is more likely to produce extreme weights. So my broad findings would be similar.

What effect does all this uncertainty have on the portfolio weights produced by the standard optimiser? To find out I ran three sets of experiments. In each experiment I kept the characteristics of the original data, but changed one parameter at a time: either the relative Sharpe Ratio (for which I tweaked the arithmetic mean of equities to produce the right values), the standard deviations (where I changed the volatility of equities as this has the larger range), or the correlation.

Then for each type of parameter I produced portfolios consistent with the extreme upper end and extreme lower end of the 95% confidence interval of my estimates of each parameter.

The results are shown in table 8. Strikingly, the effect of past uncertainty of relative Sharpe Ratios on optimal portfolio weights is enormous: we can be 95% confident that past data implies a weight to equities of between 8% and 56% of the portfolio – a huge range of outcomes. Uncertainty in standard deviations and correlations also produces different portfolio weights, but with a much smaller range of possibilities.

TABLE 8: PORTFOLIO WEIGHTS ARE QUITE DIFFERENT DEPENDING ON WHICH PARAMETER ESTIMATES ARE USED

		Bonds	Stocks
No change	As per tables 4 and 7	60%	40%
High relative stock SR	Stock SR = 0.57	44%	56%
Low relative stock SR	Stock SR = 0.05	92%	8%
High stock std. dev.	Stock std. dev. 22.2%	68%	32%
Low stock std. dev.	Stock std. dev. 17.2%	55%	45%
High correlation	Correlation 0.21	56%	44%
Low correlation	Correlation –0.12	63%	37%

Based on annual returns from 1928-2016 with parameter estimates as per tables 4 and 7, except for the changes shown in each row. Portfolio weights chosen are those that maximise geometric Sharpe Ratio (SR). Std. dev. is the annual standard deviation of asset returns.

This is actually a fairly benign scenario, because bonds and equities have a relatively low correlation. If these assets had a higher correlation then the portfolio weights produced by small differences in Sharpe Ratios and standard deviations would be even more extreme, as attested by portfolios 5 and 6 above.

It's worth reiterating that these results only account for parameter uncertainty. We're not accounting for any other kinds of model uncertainty, like using the wrong statistical model or the parameters changing in the future. So even the wide variations shown in portfolio weights above make very optimistic assumptions about the future predictability of returns.

There are three smart strategies I am going to use to cope with these problems. Firstly to produce portfolio weights that are sensible for assets with different volatility I am going to use a method called **risk weighting**. The second strategy is a technique called **handcrafting** to build robust portfolios which use information about correlations in a sensible way. Both risk weighting and handcrafting are explained in chapter four.

Finally, and very importantly: **I assume risk-adjusted returns are identical for all assets**. Look again at figure 13 (page 67). You can't separate the two distributions of Sharpe Ratios. Historical estimates of risk-adjusted returns contain no meaningful information about future risk-adjusted returns. Smart investors know that we have no crystal ball.[52]

Why the future won't be like the past

The problem of uncertainty of the past isn't the only issue involved with using statistical models based on past data. Another good reason not to blindly extrapolate past data is that future returns of most asset classes are likely to be considerably lower than they were in the past.

CONCEPT: REALISTIC EXPECTATIONS OF FUTURE RETURNS

A report[53] published in 2016 surveyed 400 large institutional investors and discovered that they expected to earn 5.5% from their bond portfolios, 10% from equities, 10.9% from real estate and 10.9% from their overall portfolio. All these figures were for the arithmetic mean of nominal returns, including inflation. These numbers reveal some worrying truths about the people who are paid to look after clients' money.

---

52. This assumption will hold for the rest of part one and also for part two. However in part three I explain how you might be able to forecast risk-adjusted returns and the implications of this for portfolio weighting.

53. 'Building Bridges', State Street Global Advisors and *Financial Times*, 2016. www.ssga.com/investment-topics/asset-allocation/2016/ft-remark-survey-us-building-bridges.pdf

Firstly it's mathematically impossible to earn 10.9% on your portfolio given these assumptions; unless you put everything you have into a single asset class – real estate – or use leverage. It's deeply concerning that many institutional investors don't understand the basic maths behind portfolio theory.

Secondly these figures look very optimistic. Look back at table 4, on page 49. Historic real returns for US bonds and equities came in at just over 2% and 8% respectively. To get the kind of returns in the survey will require inflation of around 3%. As I write this in 2017, the average of UK and the US inflation is running at less than 1%. Future expectations of US inflation are around 1.7%.[54]

What's happened here is that investors have looked backwards at nominal returns before inflation. Because inflation was higher in the past their return expectations remain anchored at these higher levels. If the real returns in table 4 are repeated with inflation at 1.7% then nominal returns will be below the expectations in the survey.

But even that is optimistic! Expecting the real returns in table 4 is very unrealistic. The fantastic real returns in stocks and bonds over the last 40 years or so were driven by macroeconomic trends that are unlikely to repeat themselves. In particular, asset values were uplifted by a large fall in inflation, which in turn reduced interest rates and increased stock price-to-earnings (PE) ratios. For example the PE ratio on the S&P 500 has risen from around 7 in early 1980 to around 26 now, in early 2017. That rise in PE ratio has added about 3.5% to average annual returns over the last 36 years.

With inflation between zero and 1% in most developed countries there is limited scope for this repricing to continue. Indeed if inflation rises then returns will probably be dragged down by a reverse repricing which will cause PE ratios to fall (and so reduce stock prices), and bond yields to rise (causing bond prices to plummet).

There are several reasons why it's smart to have realistic expectations of future returns:

- With lower expectations of returns, costs become much more important. If you expect a 5% return then the difference between paying 0.5% and 1% in costs is significant: 0.5% in extra costs will destroy one tenth of your future returns. If you assume the high returns of the past will persist then costs won't seem so important.

- Unrealistic expectations can lead to over trading. If you think you should be getting 10% in your portfolio and you're only getting 5%, then it's tempting to start trading too often or take on more risk to chase higher returns.

---

54. St Louis Fed 5-Year, 5-Year Forward Inflation Expectation Rate, September 2016.

- If you think there is a bull run in share prices coming you might be tempted to load up on equities and forget about diversification.

To deal with this problem I adjusted the historical data of US equity and bond returns I've been using to reflect more realistic expectations, but also my assumption that all assets will have the same geometric Sharpe Ratio.[55] The adjusted values for means, standard deviations and Sharpe Ratios are shown in table 9.

Notice that:

- Geometric returns are lower than in table 4 (page 49), reflecting more realistic expectations.

- The geometric Sharpe Ratios are now the same for both assets.

- The adjustment process has left the standard deviations identical to the original data in table 4. These adjustments also leave the correlation unchanged at 0.05.

TABLE 9: EXPECTED FUTURE REAL RETURNS FOR US EQUITIES AND BONDS

	Arithmetic mean	Geometric mean	Standard deviation	Sharpe Ratio
US 10 year bond	1.6%	1.3%	8.27%	0.15
S&P 500 equities	5.0%	3.0%	19.80%	0.15

Based on annual returns from 1928–2015; but adjusted to reflect more realistic expectations and identical geometric Sharpe Ratios. Sharpe Ratio is geometric mean divided by standard deviation.

The maximum Sharpe Ratio portfolio is now 68% in bonds and 32% in equities. This is less in equities than when I used the original historical estimates, since equities now have the same geometric Sharpe Ratio as bonds (before equities had a slightly higher Sharpe). This portfolio has an expected geometric return of 2.31% and a standard deviation of 8.7%. The geometric Sharpe Ratio is 0.266.

---

55.   Technical note: First I calculated some arithmetic means for each asset which I think are more likely, given current valuations and likely future inflation. I tweaked these until the geometric Sharpe Ratio of both assets was identical. I then worked out the difference between these new arithmetic means, and those in the original data. Then I subtracted the difference in means from each historic return.

I will use these adjusted statistical parameters in the next chapter,[56] when I discuss how to find the best portfolio using methods that are simpler and more robust than the standard optimisation technique.

Key points

	The techniques of portfolio optimisation have a bad name; to most people they are impenetrable mumbo jumbo and skilled experts know they often produce dangerously wrong results.
Portfolio optimisation is dangerous in the wrong hands. Keep it in the laboratory.	Specifically, small differences in inputs into the optimisation model can produce extreme portfolio weights. These will only make sense if you have very accurate predictions of future returns, which you don't.
	But you shouldn't ignore these techniques entirely. Experimenting with these models gives us useful insights that can be used to build portfolios in smarter and safer ways.
	On closer examination, the data we have on movements of financial markets is very noisy. This is dangerous as small differences in the **statistical model** of returns can produce large differences in portfolio weights.
The past isn't certain	In particular it's extremely difficult to predict risk-adjusted returns. Statistical distributions of past Sharpe Ratios are almost indistinguishable from one another.
	You should assume risk-adjusted returns are identical (at least until part three).
	In contrast to returns, the risk of different assets, their volatility, is relatively predictable.* Similarly correlation, how asset returns co-move, is also more predictable than returns.** In the next chapter I explain how to use these relatively predictable attributes of different assets to find the best portfolio.

* Volatility does of course vary over time; increasing dramatically in crisis, such as 2008. However, it's relative volatility that's important when constructing portfolios. Usually stocks are riskier than bonds, longer maturity bonds are riskier than their shorter maturity cousins, emerging markets more than developed markets; and these relationships are unlikely to change much in the future. Unless you're leveraging your portfolio, short-term changes in the absolute level of volatility are unimportant.

56.   After reading part two you will end up owning diversified portfolios of equities and bonds which are likely to have lower risk than those just for the US. This means the figures here are not consistent with the standard deviations I use later in the book in chapter eight where I discuss asset allocation. However it's always better to have more conservative forecasts, so it's no bad thing to frame your expectations based purely on US returns which are likely to have higher risk than a globally diversified portfolio.

** Correlations do change over time; the correlation between US bonds and equities has changed sign several times over the past 100 years, and in the 2008 financial crisis many uncorrelated assets became closely linked. However, as with volatility it's relative correlations that are more important, and these are relatively predictable. Apple and IBM stock will always be more correlated than Apple stock and Korean three-year government bonds, even if the Apple / IBM correlation varies over time.

CHAPTER FOUR

Simple, Smart, and Safe Methods to find the Best Portfolio (Without Costs)

I N THE LAST CHAPTER I SHOWED THAT THE STANDARD METHOD for finding the best portfolio is deeply flawed. It has unrealistically high expectations of how precise your estimates of asset returns need to be. It can't cope with slight differences in asset volatility when correlations are high. It assumes a trade-off between risk and return that won't suit everybody.

So far I've only come up with one solution: **use equal expected risk-adjusted returns for all assets**. This will help but is by no means sufficient to deal with all the issues portfolio optimisation throws up. In this chapter I explain some other smart methods to help you find the best portfolio.

Chapter overview

Dealing with different risk appetites	Building portfolios that suit your own tolerance for risk.
Risk weighting	How to include assets with different degrees of volatility in the same portfolio.
The handcrafting method	The simple and safe method I use for building portfolios in this book.
Some practical issues	Adapting my portfolio optimisation techniques to cope with some real world problems.

Everything in this chapter ignores a really important issue – costs. I come to look at those in the next chapter.[57]

Dealing with different risk appetites

This book would have been a lot easier to write if everyone had the same tolerance for risk. There would be a single best portfolio that was right for each and every reader. Unfortunately this isn't the case. Some people need, or want, to get much higher returns and can cope with the resulting risk. Others wish to protect their capital at all costs.

To get around this problem I'm first going to define three kinds of portfolio. I'll use these three portfolios throughout the book. Later in the chapter I explain how these can be adapted to suit your own personal level of risk preference.

Maximum Geometric Return	This is the portfolio for someone with a high tolerance for risk. This portfolio will contain more equities and fewer bonds. It will have a lower expected Sharpe Ratio, but the highest possible geometric mean.
	An example of a maximum geometric return portfolio would be: **20% allocated to bonds and 80% in the S&P 500**. Using the more realistic forward looking expectations I derived at the end of the last chapter (in table 9), I'd expect: geometric return 3.0%, standard deviation 16.0%, Sharpe Ratio 0.190.
	I explain later in the chapter why it's never necessary to hold a portfolio with 100% allocated to equities.
Maximum Sharpe Ratio	This is the portfolio with the highest expected Sharpe Ratio. To achieve this requires allocating a higher proportion to low-risk assets like bonds. It will have a lower geometric mean than the high-risk portfolio.
	The maximum Sharpe Ratio portfolio using my more realistic estimates for returns is: **68% bonds, 32% S&P 500**. Expected geometric return: 2.3%, standard deviation 8.7%, Sharpe Ratio 0.266.
	As I explain later in the chapter it isn't necessary to hold portfolios which contain more bonds if you need less risk than this: the best approach is to split your money between the maximum Sharpe Ratio portfolio and cash.

---

57.   I'm also ignoring the process that you should use to keep your portfolio weights close to their initial level: **rebalancing**. I return to this in part four.

Compromise	Any portfolio that falls between the two extremes above is a **compromise**. An example of a compromise portfolio would be **40% bonds and 60% in S&P 500**. Expected geometric return: 2.9%, standard deviation 12.5%, Sharpe Ratio 0.229.

Figure 16 shows these three portfolios visually.

FIGURE 16: MIX AND MATCH FOR DIFFERENT PORTFOLIO RISK LEVELS

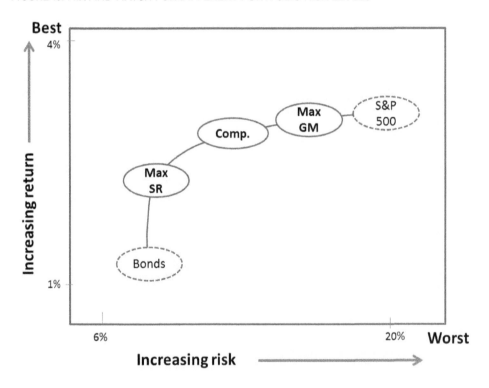

Comp.: the compromise portfolio. Max SR is maximum Sharpe Ratio. Max GM is the maximum geometric mean portfolio.

Which portfolio will suit a specific investor?

It's not easy to work out which of these portfolios would suit a specific investor best, because annual standard deviation of returns is a very abstract way of thinking about risk. It's more natural to worry about how likely you are to lose money over a given time period. Or how much you could lose if you were really unlucky. You need to work out how likely it is that a given portfolio will perform well or lose money.

CONCEPT: ESTIMATING THE UNCERTAINTY OF PORTFOLIO RETURNS

You will remember from the previous two chapters that I used a statistical technique called **bootstrapping** to find the amount of uncertainty of parameter estimates in a statistical model of returns. I can also use this method with a given set of portfolio weights to quantify the **uncertainty of portfolio returns**.

First of all I take the historical data: annual returns of US stocks and bonds from 1928 to 2016 (adjusted so they have the more realistic characteristics shown in table 9). I then create a series of **alternative histories** by randomly selecting returns from the data. Each history is the same length: either 5 years or 20 years depending on the scenario I am analysing.

To make one history I randomly choose a series of years from the data set, and find the returns for bonds and stocks in each of those years. So, for example, if I selected 1987 then I'd use the adjusted stock return (–1.1%), and bond return (–8.9%) for that year. Each time I choose a year I replace it, so it can be chosen again. I then use the appropriate portfolio weights to calculate the average geometric mean of each portfolio for the alternative history.[58]

I then repeat this process many thousands of times. This gives me a **distribution of portfolio geometric means**

Now have a look at figure 17 and table 10.

Figure 17 shows the possible distribution of average annual geometric returns over a 20-year period, calculated for four portfolios: All equities, Maximum Geometric Mean (80% equities), Compromise (60% equities), and Maximum Sharpe Ratio (32% equities).

It is based on the historical returns for US bonds and stocks since 1928, adjusted so that the Sharpe Ratios are identical and more realistic (as summarised in table 9, page 73). The grey area in each distribution shows the proportion of the time that the average return is negative after 20 years. Each portfolio also has a dotted line showing the median geometric return. Table 10 gives some key statistics for these distributions.

---

58.   There is more about this in Appendix C.

FIGURE 17: LIKELY DISTRIBUTION OF GEOMETRIC RETURNS OVER A 20-YEAR PERIOD

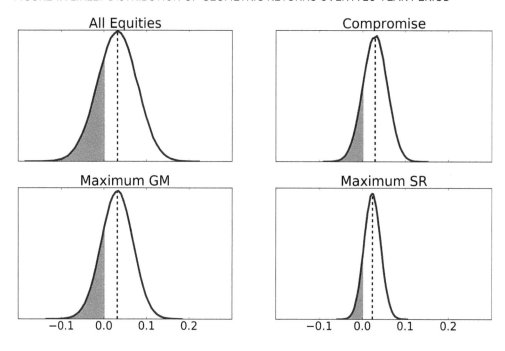

TABLE 10: CHARACTERISTICS OF GEOMETRIC MEAN DISTRIBUTION FOR DIFFERENT PORTFOLIOS, 20-YEAR RETURNS

	Median	Worst 5%	Probability <0%
All equities	3.1%	−4.5%	24.7%
Maximum geometric mean	3.1%	−2.9%	20.0%
Compromise	2.9%	−1.7%	15.0%
Maximum Sharpe	2.3%	−0.8%	11.0%

Based on bootstrapping annual returns of US stocks and bonds from 1928–2016. First column: the average geometric mean across all alternative histories. Second column: the geometric mean at the point of the distribution where only 5% of 20-year returns are worse. Third column: The proportion of the time that a portfolio loses money over 20 years.

Take for example the all equity portfolio. It has the highest average geometric return (3.1%), but 5% of the time it's average return over 20 years is worse than −4.47%. The expected probability of losing money if you hold an all equity portfolio for 20 years is around a quarter.

By comparison the maximum geometric mean portfolio has exactly the same geometric mean, but its worst losses are not as bad, and you have less chance of losing money. You can see why I don't advocate an all equities portfolio – when using geometric mean it has no benefit over the maximum geometric mean portfolio, but has higher risk and a worse potential downside.

Figure 18 explains why this happens. The figure shows the change in geometric mean as we go from 0% in bonds (left-hand side) to 100% in bonds (right-hand side). This is similar to the earlier figure 7 except that I'm now using the modified data with identical Sharpe Ratios. This time round, adding bonds to an all equity portfolio has no effect[59] on geometric mean, until around 20% of the portfolio is in bonds. This is the **maximum geometric mean portfolio**: it has the same geometric mean as a pure equity portfolio, but with lower risk. There is no point reducing the bond allocation further as it has no perceptible effect on the geometric mean.

Portfolios with 100% equities are pointlessly risky: allocating a little to bonds reduces risk with no effect on geometric returns.

The maximum Sharpe Ratio portfolio is even safer with a narrower range of outcomes, but has a lower average return. There is only an 11% chance it will have lost money over 20 years.

---

59.   If you are sharp eyed you will see that the actual maximum geometric mean occurs at a bond allocation of around 10%. But remember from the previous chapter that estimates of geometric mean are very uncertain – we don't know with much precision exactly where this maximum will be. In practice we can treat all portfolios with bond allocations of between 0% and 20% as having identical geometric means. It is better to be safer and opt for the least volatile of these options: a 20% bond allocation. Allocating more than 20% to bonds causes the geometric mean to fall meaningfully.

FIGURE 18: GEOMETRIC MEAN IS HARDLY AFFECTED WHEN SOME BONDS ARE ADDED TO THE PORTFOLIO

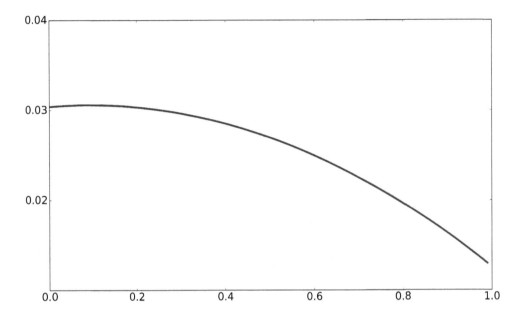

Not everyone can wait 20 years to see what happens. In my experience many people say they have a long investment horizon, but they will still look at their portfolios more frequently. The results are quite different if I repeat the exercise with five year returns as figure 19 and table 11 show.

FIGURE 19: DISTRIBUTION OF PORTFOLIO GEOMETRIC RETURNS OVER FIVE YEARS

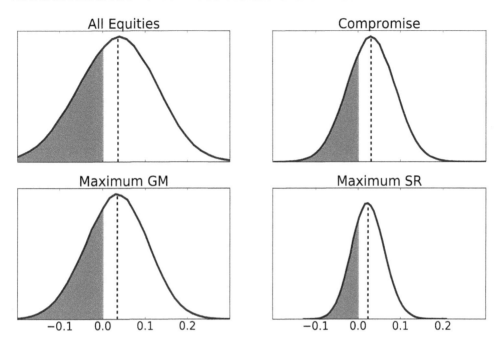

TABLE 11: CHARACTERISTICS OF GEOMETRIC MEAN DISTRIBUTION FOR DIFFERENT PORTFOLIOS, FIVE YEAR RETURNS

	Median	Worst 5%	Probability <0%
All equities	3.4%	−11.9%	35.1%
Maximum geometric return	3.4%	−8.82%	32.4%
Compromise	3.03%	−6.24%	29.6%
Maximum Sharpe	2.33%	−3.82%	27.2%

Based on bootstrapping annual returns of US stocks and bonds from 1928–2016. First column: Average geometric return. Second column: the geometric mean at the point of the distribution where only 5% of five year returns are worse. Third column: The proportion of the time that a portfolio loses money over five years.

The main takeaway here is that portfolio returns will be more erratic if you aren't investing for the long haul. The longer your time horizon, the more risk you should be able to take:

at least in theory.[60] Another way of looking at this is to see how the expected distribution of account values evolves as time passes.

Check out figure 20. This shows what I'd expect to happen to an investment of $1,000 in the high risk portfolio (20% bonds, 80% equities), which was made at the start of 2017. This is constructed using the same bootstrapping method I've used so far, except now I am showing the results for a single portfolio over different periods of time.

FIGURE 20: EVOLUTION OF DISTRIBUTION OF MAXIMUM GEOMETRIC MEAN PORTFOLIO VALUE OVER TIME

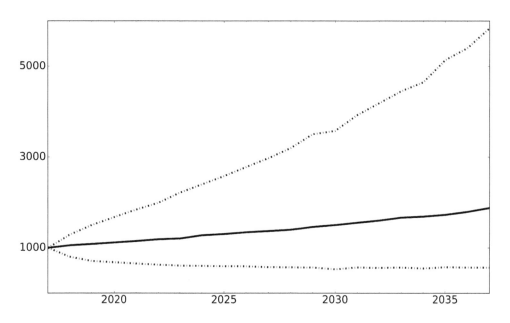

Investment begins in 2017. Solid line shows median expected value of $1,000 throughout time, when invested in the maximum geometric mean portfolio. The dotted lines show the lowest 5% of values and highest 5% of values in each time period.

The solid line shows how the expected average portfolio value changes: remember it's an average across many alternative histories. You wouldn't have such smooth returns in reality: in practice your portfolio would be a lot more volatile. The dotted lines show the worst 5% and best 5% portfolios in the distribution at each time point.

---

60.   Things are complicated if for example you need to withdraw a certain amount each month to fund your living expenses: you'll need to take less risk if this is the case. Arguably you should also reduce the amount of risk you're taking as you approach your retirement date if you intend to convert your investments into an annuity.

For example, the median outcome after 20 years is that the portfolio has grown to about $1,850. But there is a 5% chance that the portfolio will be worth $520 – much less than you started with. On the other hand there is also a 5% chance that it will be worth more than $5,650.

Figure 21 is the same picture for the maximum Sharpe Ratio portfolio, where on average I'd expect it to grow to around $1,600. There's clearly less chance of losing money, although obviously the upside is limited.

FIGURE 21: EVOLUTION OF DISTRIBUTION OF MAXIMUM SHARPE RATIO PORTFOLIO VALUE OVER TIME

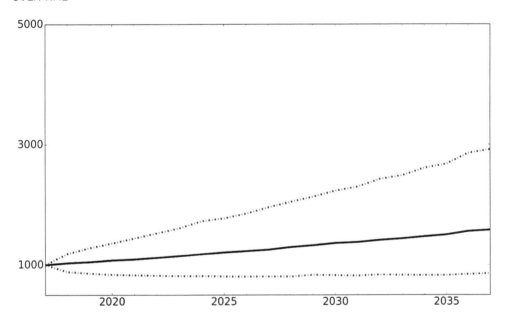

Investment begins in 2017. Solid line shows median expected value of $1,000 throughout time, when invested in the maximum Sharpe Ratio portfolio. The dotted lines show the lowest 5% of values and highest 5% of values in each time period.

As the famous saying goes, investment decisions come down to **fear and greed**. Which portfolio is right for each investor depends on whether it is the thought of losing money or the lust for higher returns that is uppermost in their mind. Hopefully this section has helped you to decide what kind of portfolio you should buy for some given preferences of return and risk.

Different investor types

Will the three portfolios I've presented cover every possible level of risk tolerance? Unfortunately not. In this section I'm going to explain the smart way to adapt these three portfolios depending on individual risk preference.

Ultra safe	Risk tolerance: Very low. No access to leverage.
	Example: Closed pension plan with a high proportion of retired investors.
Careful	Risk tolerance: Low. No access to leverage.
	Example: Elderly retiree supplementing a modest pension.
Average	Risk tolerance: Medium. No access to leverage.
	Example: Middle-aged worker close to retirement with inadequate pension provision.
Brave	Risk tolerance: High. No access to leverage.
	Example: Relatively young and well-paid investor with no financial commitments or dependents.
Borrower	Risk tolerance: Medium to high. Can use leverage.
	Example: Relatively young, well paid and financially sophisticated investor; like a banker or stockbroker.

Ultra safe

An ultra safe investor finds even the maximum Sharpe Ratio portfolio too racy. If you looked at the last few plots I've shown in this chapter and had to lie down afterwards, then you have an ultra safe disposition. What should you do? Perhaps you should put your entire investment into low-risk bonds; maybe even keep some in cash if you are really terrified.

Actually there is a better option which will give you a higher return with the same risk. You should put **some of your portfolio in cash and the remainder in the maximum Sharpe Ratio portfolio**.

Don't believe me? Suppose for example that you are targeting volatility of 6% a year. The first row of table 12 shows how you could get a standard deviation of 6% by investing partly in bonds (8.3% risk) and putting 28% of your portfolio in cash (assumed to be zero risk – I return to that assumption shortly; I also assume that the real return on cash is zero although this doesn't affect the results much).

However you can do better than that. The second row of table 12 shows that putting 69% of your portfolio in the maximum Sharpe Ratio portfolio and 31% in cash will give you exactly the same standard deviation. But the return on this portfolio is significantly higher. There is no reason to prefer a mixture of bonds and cash.

To be clear this means that 22% (32% of 69%) of your assets will be in stocks, 47% (68% of 69%) in bonds, and the remaining 31% in cash. **Even investors who are terrified of risk should have some exposure to equities**.

TABLE 12: TWO DIFFERENT WAYS TO ACHIEVE A 6% RISK TARGET

	Portfolio weight		Portfolio			Proportion in		Final	
	Bond	S&P	R_g	Std dev	Cash return	Portfolio	Cash	R_g	Std dev
Cash & bonds	100%	0%	1.26%	8.3%	0%	72%	28%	0.97%	6.0%
Cash & Max SR	68%	32%	2.31%	8.7%	0%	69%	31%	1.68%	6.0%

R_g is expected geometric mean return. Std dev is expected standard deviation of returns. Max SR is the maximum Sharpe Ratio portfolio. Uses the asset characteristics described in tables 7 and 9 (realistic future expectations). Assumes the real return on cash is zero.

Figure 22 shows the portfolios in table 12.

There is one important caveat: **cash does not have zero risk**, as I pointed out in chapter one. Future inflation isn't known with certainty so once you start measuring performance with real returns there are **no risk free assets**.

What effect does this have on the return and risk of an ultra safe investors portfolio? To answer this I used some historic data for the real returns of US treasury bills, which are a good proxy for cash. Their returns have some risk (standard deviation about 3.7%), are correlated with bonds (correlation about 0.49) but not with equities (correlation about 0.08), but also have a modest real return (arithmetic mean return of 0.4%, after adjusting them to be more realistic as I did with the other assets at the end of chapter three).

FIGURE 22: ULTRA SAFE INVESTORS SHOULD MIX CASH AND THE LOW-RISK PORTFOLIO

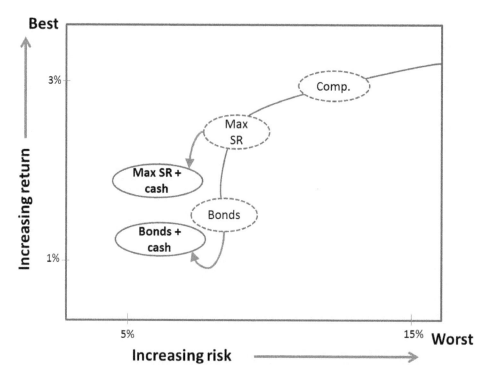

'Bonds + Cash' is a portfolio containing 72% Bonds and 28% Cash. 'Max SR + Cash' is invested 69% in the Maximum Sharpe Ratio portfolio, and 31% in Cash. Both portfolios have the same risk. 'Comp' is the compromise portfolio. The maximum geometric mean portfolio is not shown: it is off the scale of this graph. Cash is assumed to earn no real return and have zero risk.

If I replace safe cash (zero risk, zero return) with treasury bills then I will get the results in table 13.

The first row of table 13 is just a copy of my earlier portfolio targeting 6% annual volatility by blending safe cash and the maximum Sharpe Ratio portfolio. The second row shows what happens if I replace theoretically safe cash with realistically risky cash. To get down to the same level of risk I have to put more cash in. Although cash now has a positive return this slightly reduces the return of the portfolio.

The third row of the table shows the safest possible portfolio that you can hold and even with everything in cash the risk is still quite high: 3.7%. So investors who are terrified of losing money should bear in mind that **they cannot escape risk entirely**: there really is no place to hide.

Of course if your investment horizon is relatively short you should certainly keep a significant proportion of your net worth in safer assets: paper currency, coins, savings accounts and treasury bills. But over longer periods you can't assume that money held in these forms will hold its value. Putting large chunks of your portfolio into cash will be a losing proposition if inflation heats up in the future.

TABLE 13: THE EFFECT OF MAKING CASH RISKY

	Portfolio		Cash		Proportion in		Final	
	R_g	Std dev	R_g	Std dev	Portfolio	Cash	R_g	Std dev
Safe cash & Max SR	2.31%	8.7%	0%	0%	69%	31%	1.68%	6.0%
Risky cash & Max SR	2.31%	8.7%	0.33%	3.7%	61%	39%	1.62%	6.0%
Safest possible	N/A	N/A	0.33%	3.7%	0%	100%	0.33%	3.7%

First row: assumes the real return on cash is zero and risk is zero. Second and third rows: assume cash has a positive real return and some risk. Second row: Match risk of first row. Third row: 100% in risky cash. Rg is expected geometric mean return. Std dev is expected standard deviation of returns. Max SR is the maximum Sharpe Ratio portfolio. Uses the assets characteristics described in tables 7 and 9 (realistic future expectations).

Careful

A careful person is happier to take on more risk. A careful investor will be fully invested in the **maximum Sharpe Ratio** portfolio. Given a typical mixture of safer assets like bonds, and higher risk equities, this usually produces a portfolio with a standard deviation a little above that of bonds but with much better returns. Using the realistic future expectations of returns in tables 7 and 9 the maximum Sharpe Ratio portfolio has a standard deviation of 8.7% (versus 8.3% for bonds), and geometric returns of 2.3% (1.3% for bonds).

Average

An investor with average tolerance for risk will be fully invested in a **compromise** portfolio. This has more invested in equities than the maximum Sharpe Ratio portfolio, but less than the maximum geometric mean portfolio. This investor will get a higher return than a careful investor, but at the cost of more risk (and a lower Sharpe Ratio). Although there are many possible compromise portfolios I will be using a version with an allocation of 40% to bonds and 60% to equities.

Brave

A brave investor will be fully invested in the **maximum geometric mean** portfolio. This investor will get a higher return than the careful and average investors, but with more risk, and their Sharpe Ratio will also be lower. Even the maximum geometric mean portfolio will contain some bonds: I will be using an allocation of 20%.

I've already mentioned this but it's worth repeating: **nobody should invest entirely in equities**. This has higher risk than the maximum geometric mean portfolio, but is unlikely to deliver an improvement in expected geometric returns. Table 14 shows this in stark detail.

TABLE 14: MOVING FROM MAXIMUM GEOMETRIC MEAN PORTFOLIO TO ALL EQUITY INCREASES VOLATILITY AND HAS NO BENEFIT FOR RETURNS

| | Portfolio weight | | Portfolio | |
	Bond	S&P	R_g	Std dev
Maximum GM	20%	80%	3.04%	16.0%
All Equity	0%	100%	3.04%	19.8%

Maximum GM is the portfolio with the maximum geometric mean. Rg is expected geometric mean return, Std dev is expected standard deviation of returns. Uses the assets characteristics described in tables 7 and 9 (realistic future expectations).

Borrower

This is someone who can use leverage in their portfolio[61] and can tolerate more risk than the low-risk portfolio. This kind of investor should borrow money and then invest it in the **maximum Sharpe Ratio** portfolio. Because the maximum Sharpe Ratio portfolio has the best trade-off between risk and return, this will produce a higher expected geometric mean than the maximum geometric mean portfolio, but with the same standard deviation of returns. You can see this in table 15 and figure 23.

I have assumed that money can be borrowed at a real interest rate of zero. This is unrealistic, but borrowing will still make sense given the returns shown here as long as the real interest rate is less than 0.75%.

---

61.   Methods for getting leverage include: portfolio margin (borrowing against the value of the portfolio), UK spread bets, futures, contracts for difference, and buying internally leveraged collective investments (as discussed later in the chapter).

TABLE 15: TWO DIFFERENT WAYS TO ACHIEVE A HIGH RISK TARGET

	Portfolio weight		Portfolio			Proportion in		Final	
	Bond	S&P	R_g	Std dev	Borrow	Portfolio	Borrow	R_g	Std dev
Maximum geometric mean	20%	80%	3.04%	16%	N/a	100%	0%	3.04%	16%
Maximum SR leveraged	68%	32%	2.31%	8.7%	0%	184%	−84%	3.67%	16%

R_g is expected geometric mean return. Std dev is expected standard deviation of returns. Uses the assets characteristics described in tables 7 and 9 (realistic future expectations). Leveraged portfolio assumes we borrow an additional 84% of our capital at 0%. This is then invested in the maximum Sharpe Ratio (SR) portfolio.

FIGURE 23: INVESTORS WITH HIGH RISK TOLERANCE SHOULD LEVERAGE THE MAXIMUM SHARPE RATIO PORTFOLIO

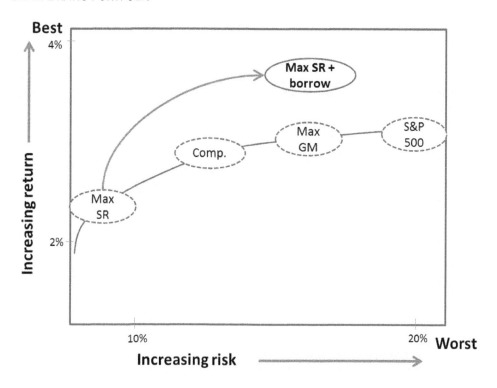

'Max SR + borrow' is the maximum Sharpe Ratio (SR) portfolio with leverage. Comp: Compromise portfolio. Max GM: Maximum geometric mean portfolio. Bonds are not shown: they would be off the scale of this graph.

Unfortunately most investors cannot, or are unwilling, to borrow to invest or to use derivatives. Running a leveraged portfolio requires great care as positions must be reduced appropriately when losses are made.[62] I do not discuss leveraged portfolios in this book.

The danger of safe assets

Before moving on to the next section, there is a quirk of portfolio maths that is worth understanding.

Table 16 is a copy of table 9 which shows my expectations of future returns in the US. To this I've added a new asset: safer bond.

TABLE 16: EXPECTED FUTURE REAL RETURNS FOR US EQUITIES AND BONDS

	Arithmetic mean	Geometric mean	Standard deviation	Sharpe Ratio
US 10 year bond	1.6%	1.30%	8.27%	0.15
Safer bond	0.4%	0.38%	2.07%	0.18
S&P 500 equities	5.0%	3.00%	19.80%	0.15

Copy of table 9. I've added an additional asset, safer bond.

I am now going to make you an offer that you should refuse.

My offer is **to exchange the 10 year bond we've been using for this new, safer bond.** The safer bond has a quarter of the risk of the original bond. Even better, it has a higher geometric Sharpe Ratio! Lower risk and better Sharpe Ratio – surely this is an unmissable, once in a lifetime opportunity?

The answer depends on your risk preference. An **ultra careful investor** should definitely take this offer, as should a leveraged investor who is willing to **borrow**. However if you are investing in the **compromise** or **maximum geometric mean** portfolio then this is a very bad idea: the lower returns make the safer bond less attractive even with a higher Sharpe.

However, what if you are an investor who is investing in the **maximum Sharpe Ratio portfolio**? Surely improving the Sharpe Ratio of one asset is an unequivocally good thing? Actually, the smartest thing to do is to refuse this offer.

---

62.   This is discussed in chapter nine of my first book, *Systematic Trading*.

The first row of table 17 repeats the highest Sharpe Ratio portfolio using the original bond. Thereafter I replace it with the new safer bond. The second row, 'Safer bond (max SR)', shows the optimal, maximum Sharpe Ratio portfolio with the safer bond.

TABLE 17: AN ASSET WITH LOW RISK DRAGS DOWN PORTFOLIO RISK WHEN USING MAXIMUM SHARPE RATIO

	Portfolio weight		Portfolio	
	Bond	S&P	R_g	Std dev
Original bond	68%	32%	2.31%	8.7%
Safer bond (max SR)	89%	11%	0.86%	2.9%
Safer bond (match return)	46%	54%	2.31%	10.8%
Safer bond (match risk)	57%	43%	2.00%	8.7%

R_g is expected geometric mean of returns. Std dev is expected standard deviation of returns, based on data in table 16. First row uses the original bond to find the maximum Sharpe Ratio (SR) portfolio. The remaining rows use the new, safer bond. Second row 'Safer bond (max SR)' is maximum SR. Third row 'Safer bond (match return)' matches return of the first row. Fourth row 'Safer bond (match risk)' matches the risk of the first row.

There is good news and bad news. Good news first: the Sharpe Ratio is higher with the safer bond (0.295 versus 0.266 with the original bond). The extremely bad news is that the geometric return on this portfolio has completely collapsed (0.86% versus 2.31%).

No problem; you decide you are not wedded to the idea of a maximum Sharpe Ratio. Suddenly a **compromise** portfolio looks very attractive. You would rather have an expected geometric return of 2.3% than stick to an ideologically pure position with respect to the best portfolio.

The third row of the table, 'Safer bond (match return)', shows that this is possible if you bump up the equity allocation, but at a cost: the risk of this portfolio is now higher than with the original bond (10.8% versus 8.7%). Paradoxically you have made your portfolio safer (by replacing the original bond with a less volatile alternative), but to get the same return as before you need to take more risk.

You have one final attempt to get this right. Instead of trying to match the return of the first row, you instead shuffle the weights around to match the risk. This gives you the figures in the final row of the table, 'Safer bond (match risk)'. The risk is spot on, but there is now a shortfall on the geometric return. The Sharpe Ratio (SR) of this portfolio is also lower (0.232 compared to 0.266 with the original bond). Another paradox: adding a safer asset with a higher SR reduces the Sharpe of a portfolio given the same risk level.

Taking this *great* deal was a mistake: **low-risk, low-return, assets should be avoided by Sharpe Ratio maximising investors who can't use leverage.**[63] This is because you have limited cash: investing in safer assets that have lower returns is a poor use of that cash.

There are a number of possible solutions to this problem. I list them below, with my favourite solution first.

Avoid low-risk assets (recommended)	**The smartest option is to avoid assets which have very low risk.** So, for example, bonds with a shorter maturity tend to have less risk than those with a longer maturity. Given the choice I'd only allocate to longer bonds: with at least five years, and ideally longer, before their term finishes.
	Also corporate bonds and emerging market bonds are relatively risky. Including those in your portfolio alongside safer government bonds will push up the average standard deviation of your bond allocation.
Increase the proportion of risky assets	If you stick with very low-risk assets then you could try moving away from the optimal SR (low risk) portfolio towards something with more equities to keep your return higher. This is row 3 of table 17, 'Safer bond (match return)'. However you're now taking on too much risk.
	I would avoid this option.
Obtain leverage through collective funds	An alternative is to use collective funds to access leverage, for example leveraged ETFs, mutual funds or UK investment trusts with internal leverage, or perhaps even hedge funds. (I discuss hedge fund allocations in chapter seven.) This way you can invest in low volatility assets like short maturity bonds, but at a higher risk.
	Using leveraged funds is superficially appealing, but they also have inherent dangers. See the digression box below for an explanation.
	I'd definitely avoid leveraged ETFs as they aren't suitable for long-term investments, only for taking short-term tactical bets.

---

63.   Technical note: This is different from the assumptions of the classical Capital Asset Pricing Model (CAPM), which assumes leverage is freely available at the risk free rate. In the theoretical idyll of CAPM an asset like the lower risk bond with a higher Sharpe Ratio would be welcomed into your portfolio with open arms. But in the real world investors who can't borrow to invest need to worry about their absolute level of returns, not just the trade-off between risk and return.

| **Do your own leveraging** | You can use leverage to increase the return and risk on the portfolio to more suitable levels. |
| | This is the **borrower** option described above and **is only suitable for skilled and experienced investors** who can use leverage. |

DIGRESSION: LEVERAGED ETFS

Leveraged funds give you twice, or even three times, the return you'd get from the underlying asset. For example SSO is a US ETF offered by ProShares which gives you twice the return of the S&P 500. Leveraged funds are quite popular: SSO alone has about $1.5 billion under management.[64] They're also dangerous and toxic; let me explain why.

Firstly they're leveraged, which makes them naturally riskier. If you borrow money to invest then your portfolio becomes more sensitive to price movements, and there is a higher risk of a total loss.

Secondly there is a hidden attribute of leveraged funds which means you can end up losing money even if the underlying price hasn't gone anywhere: the **daily reset**. For example if the S&P 500 goes from $100 to $105, and then back down to $100, a vanilla S&P tracker would have an unchanged price. But a twice leveraged version would have lost 0.5%.[65] This doesn't sound much, but over a long sequence of highly volatile days a leveraged fund will significantly underperform an unleveraged competitor.

Also leveraged funds are very expensive. For example the expense ratio on the leveraged SSO is 0.92% compared to the cheapest unleveraged S&P 500 ETFs at less than 0.1%. There is also an interest cost to actually borrow the money needed to invest.[66]

Finally these funds don't actually own anything. Some use listed derivatives like futures, but others get their exposure via contracts with banks. This creates counterparty risk and liquidity risk.

If you're smart you'll avoid investing in leveraged ETFs.

---

64. There are also short or inverse leveraged funds that bet on prices falling. Normally these wouldn't make sense; I assume throughout this book that asset prices go up in the long run. However I briefly discuss a specific type of short volatility fund in chapter seven, which is about alternative assets.
65. The first 5% rise is doubled to become a 10% rise, so $100 becomes $110. The second loss of 4.76% is doubled to become a 9.52% loss, so $110 becomes $99.52.
66. Technical note: If the fund uses derivatives like futures the funding cost is implicit in the derivatives price, but it will still drag down returns.

Risk weighting

Here is a reminder of the troubling discoveries we made in chapter three about using **standard deviation** as an input into portfolio optimisation:

Hard to interpret	Riskier assets with higher standard deviation of returns get lower weights, but the resulting weights are hard to interpret.
Dangers of the optimiser	When correlations are high, small differences in expected standard deviations will produce extreme weights.
The uncertainty of the past	You can't be certain what your standard deviation estimates should be. The degree of uncertainty depends on how risky the asset is: for equities there is more uncertainty about the volatility parameter estimate than there is for bonds.

To deal with this set of problems I'm going to introduce a new technique for deciding portfolio weights: **risk weighting**. Let's start by looking at a simple example: portfolio 8. Here there are three arbitrary assets which are uncorrelated with identical geometric Sharpe Ratios, but asset C has more risk.

PORTFOLIO 8: EXAMPLE: VARYING STANDARD DEVIATION, NO CORRELATION AND SAME GEOMETRIC SHARPE RATIO

Correlations

	A	B	C
A	1		
B	0.0	1	
C	0.0	0.0	1

	Avg.	Std. dev.	Sharpe Ratio
A	4.00%	8%	0.46
B	4.00%	8%	0.46
C	6.25%	12%	0.46

Optimisation

	Weight
A	37.3%
B	37.3%
C	25.4%

Correlation matrix, arithmetic average and standard deviation of returns, and resulting optimal weights (maximum geometric Sharpe Ratio).

So far we have used **cash weightings** in our portfolios. The cash weighting to an asset is literally the amount of cash invested in each asset. So a 60% cash weight of a $10,000 portfolio means you buy $6,000 worth of stocks, bonds or funds. Instead, I'm now going to use **risk weightings**. The risk weighting is the weighting in the portfolio normalised by the amount of risk each asset has.

To calculate risk weightings in this example I first had to normalise all the returns for every asset so they have **the same standard deviation, but without changing their geometric Sharpe Ratio.** Table 18 shows the results. In this simple example I only needed to alter asset C.

The calculation involved isn't always straightforward, because of the non-linear relationship between arithmetic means and geometric Sharpe Ratios, but you won't need to do this yourself, so relax. Although in this simple example all the Sharpe Ratios are the same, that doesn't have to be the case for this method to work.

TABLE 18: RE-NORMALISING RETURNS SO THEY HAVE THE SAME STANDARD DEVIATION BUT WITHOUT AFFECTING SHARPE RATIO

	R_a A	Std. Dev B	Sharpe Ratio $[A - 0.5B^2] \div B$	Target Std. Dev D	New R_a E	New Sharpe Ratio $[E - 0.5D^2] \div D$
A	4.00%	8%	0.46	8%	4%	0.46
B	4.00%	8%	0.46	8%	4%	0.46
C	6.25%	12%	0.46	8%	4%	0.46

R_a: Arithmetic average return. Std Dev: Standard deviation. I recalculate the average return so that the Sharpe Ratio of asset C is unchanged when the standard deviation changes. The calculation shown for Sharpe Ratio uses the approximation of geometric means, divided by standard deviation.

I now have a portfolio with equal geometric means, equal standard deviations and identical correlations. We already know what the optimiser will do with this (remember portfolio 1, page 58; and portfolio 2, page 59). It will produce **equal weights.**

However these portfolio weights are optimal **risk weights**, because I calculated them after changing the volatility of each asset so they were equal. Risk weights don't tell us how much of each asset we actually need to buy. For that I have to convert **risk weights back into cash weights,** as table 19 shows.

TABLE 19: FROM RISK WEIGHTINGS STRAIGHT TO CASH WEIGHTINGS, PORTFOLIO 8

	Std. Dev B	Target F	Ratio G = F ÷ B	Risk weight H	Approx. cash weight J = H × G	Total approx weight K = Sum(J)	Normalising factor L = 100% ÷ K	Final Cash weight J × L
A	8%	8%	1	33.3%	33.3%	88.9%	1.12	37.5%
B	8%	8%	1	33.3%	33.3%	88.9%	1.12	37.5%
C	12%	8%	0.66	33.3%	22.2%	88.9%	1.12	25.0%

You can use any arbitrary target standard deviation (F). The normalising factor ensures the final cash weights add up to 100%. There is some rounding.

You've probably noticed that the cash weights in the final column are almost identical to those in portfolio 8. For correlations which aren't too high the risk weighting method will produce very similar weights to those you'd get from optimising cash weights. But it's much smarter, easier and more intuitive to work out the right risk weights, and then translate them back into cash weights.

Risk weightings are also **safer** when correlations are high. Remember portfolio 5 (page 62)? There we saw extreme weights with only a small difference in volatility; something that wouldn't happen using the risk weighting method.

Mostly in this book I calculate risk weightings and then convert them into cash weightings, so it's important to understand how this process works:

Calculate risk weights	In the first stage of the process you ignore standard deviations, and pretend that all assets have the same volatility. With that in mind work out which **risk weights** will give you the best portfolio. Remember risk weights are weights calculated assuming that all assets are equally risky.
	Later in the chapter I explain the **handcrafting** method which can be used to find risk weights directly.

Calculate asset volatility	Now in the second stage of the process we account for different asset volatility.
	Estimate the standard deviation of every asset in your portfolio based on historic data using the formulas in Appendix C, page 489; or use the rule of thumb standard deviations in Appendix B, page 485.
	If the assets are similar enough you can assume they have the same volatility; which means that cash weightings and risk weightings will be identical. I discuss this possibility later in the chapter.
Set a target volatility	The **target volatility** will be the same for all assets and can be any arbitrary number; it doesn't matter what because the final stage in the process will ensure you always end up with weights which add up to 100%.
	Suggested values to use are: the average volatility across assets, the highest volatility or the lowest volatility.
Calculate the volatility ratio	The volatility ratio is the **volatility target** divided by the **volatility estimate** for each asset.
Find the approximate cash weights	Multiply the **risk weighting** of each asset by the appropriate **volatility ratio**. This will give you an **approximate cash weight** for each asset. These weights aren't guaranteed to add up to 100%.
Calculate the normalising factor	Add up the **approximate cash weights** and divide 100% by their total. So for example if your approximate cash weights add up to 25% then your normalising factor will be 100% ÷ 25% = 4. If they sum up to 250% the normalising factor is 100% ÷ 250% = 0.4.
Normalise the risk weights	Multiply each **approximate cash weight** by the **normalising factor**. That will give you the **final cash weights**. These will always add up to 100%.

The handcrafting method

Assuming **equal risk-adjusted returns** (as we saw in chapter three) and **using risk weighting** (as in the previous section of this chapter) are a big help in getting better weights out of portfolio optimisations, but by themselves they still don't guarantee consistently sensible results as it's still possible for the standard portfolio optimisation method to produce extreme portfolio weights.

There are a few different ways of solving this conundrum,[67] but my personal preference is to use a very simple technique which involves abandoning formal portfolio optimisation entirely whilst still producing very credible portfolio weights.

To corral wild herds of assets into well organised portfolios I will be using a **top-down** method, which I like to call **handcrafting**.

Top-down handcrafting

Prior to leaving the finance industry in 2013 I had little free time to organise my own portfolio. For many years I had stuck with UK equities. I did not want the hassle of researching and buying individual equities overseas, and the UK retail market for individual bonds was very undeveloped (and still is). My strategy was seriously unsystematic, and I bought into every fad and fashion that came along. At one point I had well over 100 companies in my portfolio.

Then ETFs arrived in the UK and I started dabbling with those. Again I didn't have a clear plan. If I saw a piece of research suggesting corporate bonds were undervalued, then I went ahead and bought a corporate bond ETF. Soon I had a large and chaotic ETF portfolio to go alongside my scattered mess of UK equities.

My portfolio was in chaos which was particularly embarrassing for someone with expertise in quantitative finance; I really ought to have known better. I made a number of mistakes but the biggest was building my portfolio from the **bottom up**. My exposure to asset classes and to different countries wasn't the result of deliberate decisions, but a consequence of what I'd already decided to buy.

In this book I advocate the opposite strategy: **top-down**. Here is an example of a simple top-down allocation. First decide your allocation to **asset classes**, like equities and bonds. Then determine the allocation to each **country**: US, UK, Japan and so on. Decide what the allocation should be to equities within the same country but in different **industries**: how much in US Technology stocks, and how much in US Utilities, and so on. Finally work out the weights for the equities that make up a particular industry in a given country; so within US Technology what proportion in Google, Apple and so on.[68]

At each stage in the process you decide how you should get the exposure you need; through collective funds like ETFs or buying individual stocks. This ensures you will get a portfolio with the best possible trade-off between diversification and costs.

---

67.   Technical note: The two main respectable alternatives are bootstrapping, where we optimise on repeated samples of past data, and shrinkage, where we change the inputs of the optimisation so they produce a better result. I briefly describe these methods in Appendix C on page 496. They are much more complicated than handcrafting and my research shows they struggle to do significantly better.
68.   As you'll see in part two, the allocation process will usually be more complicated than this, but the basic top-down principle still holds.

I've named the portfolio construction method I use **handcrafting**. It's not the result of a blind use of dangerous portfolio optimisation software, or scribbling down weights based on gut feeling, but a simple process based on my own systematic research into the best way to use portfolio optimisation techniques. There is a certain process you should follow, but also room for human judgment.

Building portfolios using gut feeling makes me think of a gnarled artisan using a blunt chisel to carve a wobbly stool. A true expert might produce a beautiful piece of furniture, but most of us can't hope to emulate that. A portfolio created entirely by a computer algorithm is something like a piece of cheap mass-produced furniture: it may not suit you and could have hidden weaknesses making it too fragile to sit on.

But a handcrafted portfolio should make you think of a skilled craftsman wielding modern power tools to create a bespoke chair that is robust, well designed and built to suit your exact requirements.

The method

The handcrafting method is easier to explain with an example. Think back to the two assets I've used in the last couple of chapters: US equities and US Bonds. To make things interesting lets add a third asset: UK equities.

First I'm going to use standard optimisation to find the best portfolio, plus the tricks I've already shown you in this chapter. I'm going to calculate some correlation estimates using historic data, utilise **risk weighting** which means that the assets will have the same standard deviation in my optimisation, and equalise the geometric Sharpe Ratios for the reasons I've mentioned numerous times before.

The results, and the weights I get from optimisation, are shown in portfolio 9. This should look familiar – the weights are identical to those in portfolio 3 (page 60).

PORTFOLIO 9: USING RISK WEIGHTING IN THE THREE ASSET EXAMPLE WITH EQUALISED SHARPE RATIOS

Correlations

	A	B	C
A	1		
B	0.68	1	
C	0.00	0.00	1

	Avg.	Std. dev.
A	4%	8%
B	4%	8%
C	4%	8%

Optimisation

	Weight
A	27%
B	27%
C	46%

Correlation matrix, arithmetic average and standard deviation of returns, and resulting optimal weights (maximum geometric Sharpe Ratio).

Now here's how I used the handcrafting method to optimise this portfolio.

Group similar assets together	I grouped assets which are similar together; those with the highest correlations. I created two groups: 1. An equity group (US and UK equities) 2. A bond group (just one asset: US 10 year bonds)
Equal weights for each group	I gave the equity group a 50% weight and the bond group a 50% weight.
Allocate within group weights equally	Within the equity group I gave US equities 50% and the UK 50%. The bond group has only one asset, which receives 100% within the group.

Calculate asset weights	Each asset weight is a product of the **within group weight** and the **weight of the group**. So for the two equities the weights were 50% (group weight for equities) multiplied by 50% (within group weight). For bonds the weight was 50% (group weight for bonds) multiplied by 100% (within group weight). This gives:
	• UK equities 25%
	• US equities 25%
	• US bonds 50%

The resulting weights are extremely close to those in portfolio 9. In this example my smart yet simple method produces weights that are as good as those from a 'proper' optimisation. Although they aren't identical, the expected Sharpe Ratios from the handcrafted and the properly optimised weights will be extremely similar; 0.713 for the optimised weights and 0.710 for the handcrafted version. There is always some uncertainty about correlation estimates,[69] so the handcrafted method provides weights that in practical terms are as good as the properly optimised maximum Sharpe Ratio portfolio weights.[70]

Remember that these are risk weightings and I'd need to convert them into cash weightings before they were used.

Advantages of the handcrafted method

Produces the maximum Sharpe Ratio portfolio

The handcrafted method sets **equal portfolio weights within each group**. Remember from the previous chapter that the equal weight portfolio will be optimal (highest Sharpe Ratio) if the geometric means, standard deviations and correlations within a group are equal[71] (portfolios 1 and 2). It's worth understanding exactly why the equal weight portfolio has the highest Sharpe Ratio.

The geometric mean is the arithmetic mean with a correction for risk. So if all assets have the same standard deviation (because of risk weightings) and equal geometric means (because of my assumptions) then this implies that **all assets have the same arithmetic mean**. The arithmetic mean of a portfolio is just the weighted average of the arithmetic

---

69.   Because geometric Sharpe Ratios are equal, and standard deviations are identical (risk weighting), the correlation alone determines the optimal portfolio weights.

70.   Incidentally the handcrafted and properly optimised weights would be identical if the two equity markets had a correlation of 1.0.

71.   It's possible to use a more complicated version of the handcrafting method when correlations are not equal within each group. This is described in chapter four of my book *Systematic Trading*.

means of its assets, so **all possible combinations of assets in the portfolio will have an identical arithmetic mean**.

Therefore the **Sharpe Ratio of the portfolio will only be affected by its risk**. In fact lower risk will increase both the portfolio's geometric mean (numerator of the Sharpe Ratio) and reduce its standard deviation (denominator of the Sharpe Ratio). Because all assets have the same standard deviation the risk of a portfolio will be driven entirely by how diversified it is. More diversification implies lower risk, which means higher Sharpe Ratio.

Because all correlations are identical the equal weight portfolio is also the most diversified. Therefore given the assumptions we've made, the equal weight portfolio has the maximum Sharpe Ratio.[72]

But are these assumptions realistic?

Equal standard deviations	We're using **risk weightings** in the handcrafting method, so all assets automatically have identical expected standard deviations.
	Standard deviation estimates have relatively low uncertainty, so they are relatively predictable.
Equal geometric means (equal Sharpe Ratios)	Because standard deviations are equal the geometric means will also be equal if Sharpe Ratios are the same. I've already explained at length why I'm assuming assets have identical Sharpe Ratios.*
Equal correlations	This assumption is reasonable as long as our groups are of similar assets. This is true when the assets in a group are highly correlated, like equities from the same industry – but also when they are equally unrelated, perhaps because they're from different asset classes.
	The assumption is unrealistic if you have a mixture of highly correlated and uncorrelated assets in a group, which shouldn't happen if you've done your grouping properly.

* If you're still convinced that you can predict what an asset's Sharpe Ratio is likely to be have another look at figure 12 in chapter three. And figure 13. If that doesn't work, reread the whole book so far.

---

72.   Technical note: This is true for weights within groups. However, there is a subtle problem with weights across groups, if the groups are of radically different size. In this case a group with more assets should get more weight than a group with fewer constituents. That is why the optimal Sharpe Ratio weighting for bonds (with only one asset, rather than the two in the equities group) is slightly lower (46%) than the handcrafted weight of 50% (see the discussion on page 111). There is a similar issue when some groups have lower correlations inside the group than others. Both effects are minimal; but I explain on page 497 how to formally correct for this.

Hopefully that will dissuade you from trying to predict Sharpe Ratios (at least for now: I discuss how you can predict Sharpe Ratios in part three, and explain how to adapt handcrafted weights accordingly).

No data is harmed in the making of this portfolio

The handcrafting method doesn't use estimates of performance. It isn't sensitive to small differences in expected average returns, correlations or standard deviations. It isn't unduly bothered by the **uncertainty of the past.** It won't make radical changes to the portfolio every few months when new data is used to re-estimate parameters.

It requires no sophisticated computer software,[73] and can be implemented using only a pencil and paper, though using a spreadsheet is quicker.

Not easily shocked

It's well known that in a market crisis like 2008 almost all assets fall in price,[74] correlations get closer to 1, and diversification seems to vanish into thin air. But the handcrafted method relies on assets being undiversified in a predictable way – is this a problem?

Correlations rising in a crisis is only a serious issue if you've leveraged up your portfolio on the assumption of low correlations (see the digression box below). Then when diversification vanishes you could face a potential total loss that you won't be able to recover from. For most investors it's **average** correlation over time that matters. Without leverage you can survive a temporary correlation storm without being forced to sell off your portfolio after heavy losses, and then benefit from diversification once things return to normal.

The handcrafted portfolio is also less susceptible to getting correlation estimates wrong than a normal optimisation. An unrealistically high correlation estimate won't lead to extreme weights like it does in standard optimisation.

---

73. Though you'll probably be pleased to know that I have tested the handcrafting method using sophisticated computer software. If you're interested in the technical details: I use a clustering algorithm to form the groups automatically, using only past data on an expanding backtesting window. The method has similar out of sample performance to more sophisticated techniques, and shows minimal degradation in performance when moving from in sample to out of sample data.
74. In chapter nine, I examine alternative assets that will hopefully remain genuinely undiversified even in a crisis.

DIGRESSION: RISK PARITY FUNDS

Risk parity funds are very fashionable right now. A risk parity fund allocates risk rather than capital so that all assets in the portfolio have an equal contribution to the risk of the portfolio.

If you go about constructing a handcrafted portfolio using risk weightings, you'll end up with something that is pretty similar to a risk parity fund.[75] A typical risk parity fund has an equal risk weighting of stocks and bonds, with a higher cash weighting to bonds to compensate for the lower risk. An important difference is that risk parity funds are usually **leveraged** to compensate for their low risk.

In the last few years there has been considerable criticism about risk parity funds, some of which arguably also applies to the kind of portfolios in this book. But much of this criticism is unfair.

Yes, leveraged risk parity funds are vulnerable to correlations rising and diversification disappearing, but this is true of any leveraged fund. Indeed most hedge fund strategies need substantially more leverage than risk parity does. As long as assets aren't perfectly correlated there will always be a benefit from diversification. Most people using the handcrafted method will not be leveraging anyway, except for those who fit the **borrower** investor profile I mentioned earlier.

Another criticism is that risk parity funds and maximum Sharpe Ratio portfolios have a higher cash weight to bonds than most people use. Some people argued this is crazy "at the end of a thirty year bull run on bonds."[76]

But if an asset has lower risk it ought to have a higher cash weight. It's reasonable to give a higher risk weight to equities if you want a higher return (the **compromise** and **maximum geometric mean** portfolios), but you should properly understand the additional risk it will give you.

Nevertheless as I am writing this in early 2017 there is widespread fear that rising interest rates will hurt bond performance. Of course if you are sceptical and think it is impossible to forecast risk-adjusted returns then this is a concern you can safely ignore. But if you are still worried, don't panic. In part three I show how to use systematic models to adjust portfolio weights using information about interest rate changes and levels.

---

75.   Technical note: To be pedantic, using risk weightings gives you a volatility parity portfolio, which is close to but not exactly the same as risk parity. Risk parity also ensures that the proportion of total risk in the portfolio coming from each asset class is equal, accounting for internal diversification within each asset class.

76.   (*Financial Times*, 2012). Interestingly, as I write this bond yields are virtually unchanged in the five years that have passed since that article was published. Even the *FT* can't predict the future perfectly.

Multiple levels are possible

The original example I showed for handcrafting was for a portfolio with two levels. I divided the assets into groups (asset classes), then decided what the allocation should be across groups (first level) and within each group (second level). However with a larger portfolio you can extend this to further levels. This means you can construct portfolios of any size in a **top-down** fashion. This is exactly what I demonstrate throughout part two.

Here is an example of a four level allocation. First decide your allocation to **asset classes**, like equities and bonds (first level). Then within asset classes you determine the allocation to each **country** (second level). The next step is to decide within each country what the allocation should be to equities within the same **industry sector** (third level). Finally it's a question of determining the weights for the **individual equities** that make up a particular industry in a given country (fourth level).[77]

Constraints can be built in

Equal weights aren't always appropriate, because you might have **constraints** on the allocations of your portfolio. Fortunately the top-down handcrafted approach can easily be adapted to cope.

For example suppose you wanted to limit your risk-weighted exposure to emerging market equities to 25%. First within the overall equity asset class group you would create two groups: one for emerging and another for developed markets. You'd then have given the emerging market group a 25% weight which reflects your constraint, with developed equities getting the remaining 75%. Finally you'd now allocate normally within the two groups.

How do we calculate portfolios with different levels of risk?

The handcrafted method finds the portfolio with the maximum Sharpe Ratio, given some assumptions. But that portfolio won't suit everybody.

Earlier in the chapter I recommended using either a **maximum Sharpe Ratio** portfolio (highest Sharpe Ratio, but not the highest return), a **maximum geometric mean** portfolio (higher return, lower Sharpe Ratio), or opting for a **compromise** (somewhere between the two). The right portfolio will depend on the investor's tolerance for risk.

The handcrafting method maximises Sharpe Ratio automatically; but how do you get the maximum geometric mean and compromise versions? You can do this with portfolio **constraints**.

---

77. As you'll see in part two, the allocation process will usually be more complicated than this, but the basic top-down principle still holds.

Follow this procedure:

Group low-risk assets together	The top level grouping in your portfolio should collect all the low-risk assets together, with another group for high-risk assets. For example, if you're using bonds and equities as your top level groups* then you naturally have a low-risk group (bonds) and a higher-risk one (equities).**
Set an appropriate weight to the low-risk group(s)	**Maximum geometric mean portfolio:** Give the low-risk group a 10% allocation. This might seem very low, but remember these are **risk weights**. Once translated into **cash weights** the low-risk group will have around 20% of the portfolio.*** **Compromise portfolio:** Give the low risk group a 30% allocation in risk-weighted terms. You can adjust this figure to shift the portfolio volatility up or down to match an investor's specific tolerance for risk. **Maximum Sharpe Ratio portfolio:** Stick to the default handcrafting method and give each group a 50% allocation in risk-weighted terms.
Continue as usual	You should now continue to allocate portfolio weights within the two groups.

* In chapter eight I explain how you can extend this method to include other asset classes at the top level of your portfolio.

** Of course this is a simplification; some blue chip equities will be less risky than a high yield emerging market corporate bond with a maturity date that is decades in future. But this simplification makes life much easier and has virtually no bearing on the final portfolio weights.

*** I derived the 20% cash weight earlier in the chapter. Remember: a higher allocation to bonds will reduce geometric returns, but a lower allocation results in a portfolio with unnecessary risk.

I give more detail on this in chapter eight when I talk about finding portfolio weights for asset classes.

Some practical issues with portfolio allocation

The handcrafting method combined with risk weighting is a relatively simple method that produces robust portfolio weights. However in practice there are some difficulties you may encounter when trying to use it. I discuss these problems, and some smart solutions, in this section.

Do I really need to use full risk weighting?

The formal risk weighting method requires you to calculate the standard deviation of every asset in your portfolio, so you can translate risk weights into cash weights. That might seem like a lot of work. There are three possible approaches you can use:

Full risk weighting with estimated volatility	Estimate the standard deviation of every asset in your portfolio using the formulas in Appendix C, page 489, then use these to go from risk weights to cash weights.
	These risk weights can be fixed, or re-estimated periodically. I discuss these two options in the next section of the chapter.
Risk weighting with rule of thumb volatility	Use the rule of thumb standard deviations in Appendix B, page 485. These risk weights will remain fixed.
Do not use risk weighting	If you think your asset standard deviations are similar enough then you do not need to make any adjustments and can just use your risk weights as cash weights.

You should always use estimated or rule of thumb volatility to adjust weights when the assets in a group are likely to have very different risk, such as across asset classes, or between developed and emerging markets, or bonds issued by borrowers with different levels of creditworthiness.

But things are different at more granular levels of your portfolio where assets are very similar, such as for equities within the same country and industry, i.e. German utility companies. Here it is reasonably safe to assume that everything has identical volatility, which means risk weights are equal to cash weights.

What if volatility changes?

If you have ever estimated your own standard deviations then you will have noticed that volatility changes from time to time. For example in the early 1980s US 10 year bond returns had a standard deviation of nearly 20% a year. From the mid-1990s onwards their volatility had fallen to around 7%.

In theory it is optimal to adjust your portfolio weights as volatility moves around. However this will incur additional trading costs. I explore whether this is worth doing in part four of the book, which is about rebalancing your portfolio.

What if correlation changes?

Correlations don't remain static either. For example US bonds and equities had a positive correlation for much of the 20th century because they were both exposed to high inflation. In the late 1990s, after inflation became less important, US bonds started to behave like a **safe haven asset** and their correlation with equities turned negative.

In theory you should do something about changing correlations and if necessary move assets into different groups; changing your handcrafted weights and reallocating your portfolio accordingly.

But here is a cautionary tale. After the Euro currency was introduced in 1999 its member countries became progressively more integrated, resulting in rising correlations between European asset returns. This was particularly noticeable in the bond market. After 1999 Italian bonds went from being relatively uncorrelated with German bonds to moving in almost perfect lockstep.

Should you have changed your asset grouping to reflect this? In hindsight this would have been pretty stupid. When the financial crisis began in 2008 Italian bonds were suddenly risky again whilst Germany was very much a safe haven. The high positive correlation turned negative rapidly.

The smart option is to avoid moving assets between groups of a portfolio. Because the grouping in the handcrafted method is done on a partly subjective basis this can lead to over trading and destroy the benefits of sticking to a well thought out portfolio allocation.[78]

Alternatives to handcrafting

More sophisticated readers of this book might be very disdainful of simplistic handcrafting. You would prefer a fancier method which sounds more respectable. Although I would never recommend using the standard optimisation model there are some other alternatives that make things safer. I discuss these briefly in Appendix C, on page 496.

Should you always use equal weights within groups?

The handcrafting method recommends weighting equally between assets once you've grouped them. However you'll notice later in the book that I don't always stick blindly to this rule.

---

78.   Technical note: If you're not using the handcrafting method, and doing a formal portfolio optimisation, then you should be adjusting your correlations over time, as long as your method reflects the uncertainty of your estimates, and accounts for trading costs. I discuss this more in part four.

There are four scenarios where equal weights don't make sense:

1. When there is a large mismatch between group sizes.

2. When equal weights deviate too far from the market capitalisation weighted consensus, causing potential embarrassment.

3. When some assets are going to be more expensive to trade or hold than others.

4. When you have assets in your portfolio with risky risk.

Different group sizes

Consider the simple three asset portfolio I used when I introduced the handcrafting method: UK equities, US bonds, and US equities. The grouped weights of this portfolio that maximise Sharpe Ratio are 50% in US bonds, 25% in UK equities, and 25% in US equities. These are all risk weightings which assume the volatility of each asset is identical.

Now suppose I do something stupid and add another 20 developed equity markets to the menu: Germany, Canada, Japan… and so on. This doesn't sound too idiotic, but I'm also not going to add any more bond markets, sticking with just US bonds. *Now* it's a crazy idea.

Using the handcrafted method I still have one huge group for equities with a 50% weight, or 2.27% for each of the 22 countries. The other group for bonds still has just one asset, US bonds, with 50% weight in the overall portfolio.

Would you be comfortable with that? I wouldn't be; I'd feel dangerously exposed to an event which specifically affected US interest rates, like an unexpected result in a US presidential election.

Having half my portfolio in a single bond market is uncomfortable but it is also theoretically incorrect. I can demonstrate this by examining the bond and equity sub-portfolios. Because the equity sub-portfolio has a large number of countries which aren't perfectly correlated, it will be less risky than any individual country.

The bond sub-portfolio however has only one asset inside it: its risk will be the same as for each individual equity country (as we're using risk weightings). So the equity sub-portfolio has slightly less risk, and because I assume all assets have the same arithmetic mean of returns it also has a slightly higher geometric return and better Sharpe Ratio. **I can improve on equal weights in an unbalanced portfolio by increasing the weight on the larger group of assets**.

Of course in practice I wouldn't actually construct a portfolio with a single bond market and 22 equity markets. Usually I'll be trying to keep groups similar in size, but this isn't always possible. So in part two I occasionally recommend a departure from equal weights when there is a substantial difference in group sizes.[79]

79.　Technical note: There is also a theoretical formula for dealing with this problem which is in Appendix C (page 497).

Embarrassment

Later in the book I discuss allocating to the Developed North American equity markets. Developed North America is a particularly boring geographic region because it only contains two countries: the US and Canada. How much should we allocate to each country? The consensus method for allocating portfolios is by **market capitalisation weighting**. On that basis you should put 94% of your investments into the US, with just 6% in Canada. Using handcrafting you'd put 50% into each.

That's a substantial difference. Such a large departure from the consensus of market cap weighting will be a painful and **embarrassing** experience during periods when Canada underperforms the US. If you were using a formal measure of embarrassment like **tracking error**, you'd see a large difference to your benchmark.

How large is your embarrassment likely to be in a real life portfolio setting; i.e. how different are returns from a market cap and a handcrafted portfolio likely to be?

To answer this question I ran an experiment using 22 developed equity markets (to keep things simple I didn't include bonds or emerging equity markets in this study). I tried four different kinds of weighting: fully optimised (the method that I've criticised so much), handcrafted, equal weighted (every country has exactly the same weight – there are no groups), and market cap weighted.

The returns of each portfolio are shown in figure 24.

Notice that the optimised portfolio seriously underperforms, with a geometric mean that is at least 2.5% a year lower than the alternatives. Worse still, the final optimised portfolio weights are crazy; 15 countries had no weighting all, there were non-zero allocations in only seven countries, and a massive 26% just in Finland. Apologies to Finnish readers, but with 21 other countries to choose from that's far too much. This is another nail in the coffin for the idea that historical estimates of returns can be trusted enough to use in a naive optimisation.

The other three portfolios are very similar, with geometric means of between 7.3% and 8.1% a year, and very similar Sharpe Ratios ranging from 0.44 to 0.55. These are not variations in performance that are significantly different (remember from the previous chapter that the uncertainty of past Sharpe Ratios is much higher than these differences). The advantage of handcrafting over market cap weighting, and ungrouped equal weights, is quite slim and is difficult to assess using only historical evidence, as I explain in chapter six.

FIGURE 24: DIFFERENT WEIGHTING SCHEMES DON'T MATTER SO MUCH WITH 22 DEVELOPED COUNTRY STOCK MARKETS

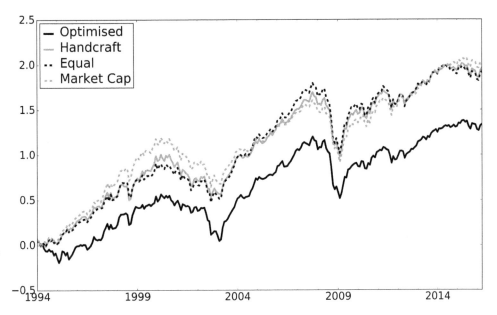

Y-axis shows cumulated returns on a log scale where 1.0 is a 100% return.

It's hard to gauge from this plot how much embarrassment you'd feel from using handcrafting rather than market cap weightings. What happens if we look specifically at the difference between the returns of handcrafted and market cap weighted portfolios?

Figure 25 shows the answer. The mostly rising line in the plot shows how handcrafting with groups outperforms market cap weighting over the time period shown. However, embarrassment is only a problem when you underperform the consensus: during the periods when the line is falling. For example, from mid-2000 coming out of the tech boom the handcrafted portfolio lags market cap weighting by around 15% over the course of 12 months.

You need to be confident you can cope with this kind of temporary humiliation. If you can't then you need to adjust your weights to be closer to the market cap weighted consensus.[80]

---

80.   There is often a conflict between these two considerations: accounting for different group size, and minimising embarrassment. The North American developed equity region is a perfect example. With just two countries it should arguably have a lower weight than the developed European region which has 16. But in market cap weighted terms it has a weight of 56%. As I explain later, I ended up giving the North American region the same weight as Europe: it's my opinion that the issues of different group size (justifying a higher European weight) and minimising embarrassment (justifying a higher

FIGURE 25: COMPARING OPTIMISATION METHODS – TRACKING ERROR

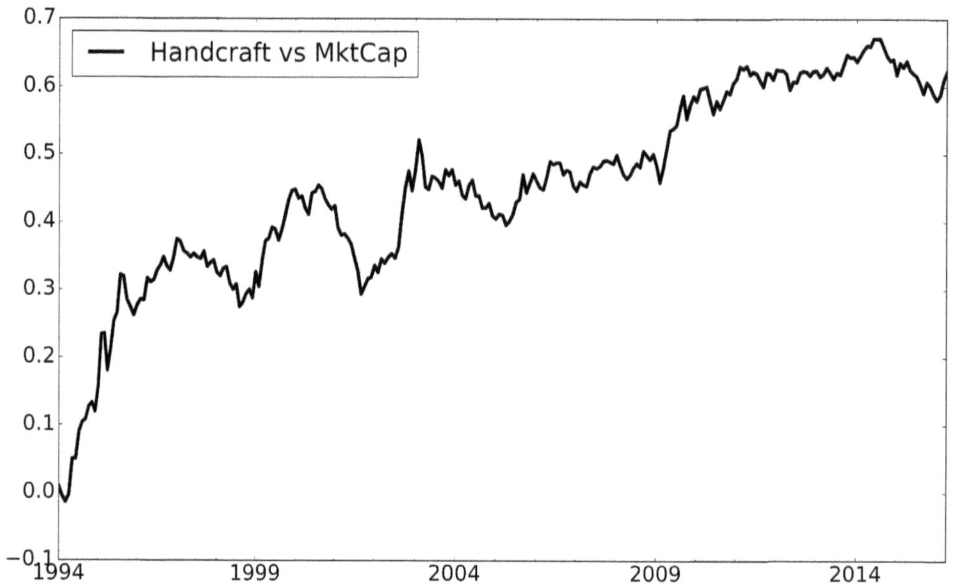

Y-axis shows the difference in cumulated returns on a log scale; e.g. 0.2 implies a 20% total difference in performance over the period.

Expensive assets

I'm assuming that you can't forecast pre-cost risk-adjusted returns. However as I discuss at great length in chapter five, you can forecast costs. This means that you'd expect assets which are expensive to do worse on a post-cost basis.

Some types of asset just cost more to buy or own, and there isn't much we can do about that. ETFs which cover emerging markets and alternative asset classes have much heftier price tags than index trackers for giant liquid markets like the S&P 500. This justifies a lower allocation than the equal weighting they'd have with the same costs. I look at costs in more detail in the next chapter.

Risky risk

Using **risk weighting** implicitly assumes that all risk is predictable and adequately captured by the standard deviation measure that I've been using. Sadly risk isn't perfectly predictable and standard deviation certainly doesn't explain all risk.

North American weight) cancel each other out.

Some assets have less predictable risk than others. Emerging markets, thrilling tech and biotech stocks, and certain types of alternative assets are amongst the worst offenders, along with high yield junk bonds. These toxic assets tend to have long periods of relatively subdued risk, but then their returns suddenly become much more volatile; often almost overnight and without warning.[81]

As well as being unpredictable, the risk profile of these assets isn't pleasant. They don't have the nice symmetric **Gaussian normal distribution** of returns that I introduced back in chapter two. Instead they have evil distributions where steep falls in price are much more common than a Gaussian distribution would expect.[82] A simple symmetric measure of risk like **standard deviation** doesn't adequately capture the inherent nastiness of these assets.

So I'd allocate less to these unpleasant assets than I would if their risk was more predictable and benign.

Be flexible when setting weights: be consistent afterwards

In reality I have no idea whether the optimal weight to Canada within North America is 6%, 40% or 50%; and neither do you. Although we have relatively good statistical estimates of historic correlations (compared to Sharpe Ratios) they are never sufficient to pin down precisely what the optimal weight should have been in the past (remember table 8 from the previous chapter, on page 70). We certainly don't know what correlations or the optimal weight will be in the future.

Different people can use the handcrafting method and legitimately get different results. There is always some subjectivity as to exactly how the grouping is done when handcrafting. Sticking religiously to equal weights within each group is also a matter of judgment, as I discussed above.

You should be fairly relaxed about using the handcrafting method in any sensible way. Use my suggested groups and weightings, or choose your own. Do not get stressed about getting the grouping or weights 'correct': there is no single correct solution. Feel free to move away from strict equal weighting within groups if you feel it is justified. I do exactly that in several of the portfolios I present in part two.

The handcrafting process is not there so you can blindly copy my suggested portfolio weights, but to give you a logical and systematic framework to build portfolios whilst incorporating your own views and opinions. It is unimportant exactly what weights you use in your smart portfolio, as long as you have weights that **you** are happy with. You

---

81.   Incidentally, using an estimate of volatility that varies can be especially dangerous with these types of assets. You will tend to increase cash weights, and thus position size, when volatility is falling. When it rises sharply you will then be more heavily exposed than if you'd kept your estimate of risk constant.

82.   Technical note: They have negative skew, and a high kurtosis (*fat tails*).

need to be happy with them, because the most important consideration above everything else is that you **stick to your portfolio weights once you have chosen them**.

I'll leave the final word on this subject to Harry Markowitz, the inventor of modern portfolio theory, and someone you'd expect to use sophisticated portfolio optimisation techniques:

> "I should have computed the historical co-variances of the asset classes and drawn an efficient frontier *(the standard optimisation method)*. Instead I visualised my grief *(or embarrassment)* if the stock market went way up and I wasn't in it – or if it went way down and I was completely in it. My intention was to minimise my future regret *(or embarrassment)*. So I split my contributions 50/50 between bonds and equities." [My comments in italics.]
>
> — Harry Markowitz, quoted in *The Intelligent Investor* by Jason Zweig

Key points

Risk weighting	Risk weighting is a safe and intuitive way to create portfolio weights. It means that small differences in estimated volatilities won't translate into extreme weights.
Handcrafting: Top-down, equal weighting	Because it is relatively predictable, correlation should be the main focus when allocating portfolio weights, with a correction for different levels of expected volatility (by using risk weighting). In other words portfolios should be as diversified as possible.
	Constructing a portfolio in a top-down fashion is the best way to achieve diversification. This can be achieved by **handcrafting**: grouping assets together and then allocating equally within groups. You should begin first at the asset class level, and then work your way down to allocate to countries, and then finally within countries.

This means you need to decide how much risk you are comfortable with, have realistic expectations for returns, and construct your portfolio appropriately.

One trade-off between return and risk is the **maximum Sharpe Ratio portfolio** with 50% risk weighting in bonds. Sharpe Ratio maximising investors should steer clear of low-risk, low-return assets which are an inefficient use of their cash.

The holy grail of high returns and low risk isn't achievable

Nobody should invest entirely in equities. A maximum geometric mean portfolio which has 10% risk weighting in bonds is safer, and gives you the same expected return. A **compromise** portfolio with 30% risk weighting in bonds is a little safer.

Everyone should invest something in equities. Rather than invest solely in bonds it is better to buy the maximum Sharpe Ratio portfolio and dilute it with cash to make it safer. Warning: there is no such thing as safe cash when we have inflation. Ultra cautious investors who are terrified of losing money should bear this in mind.

Be flexible, then be consistent

Equal weights within the groups of handcrafted portfolios are theoretically the best, but might not always make sense if (a) it causes embarrassment, (b) groups are of different sizes, (c) some assets are more expensive, or (d) you have assets that have unpleasant and relatively unpredictable risk.

There are no "perfect" portfolio weights but you must be consistent with the weights you choose.

CHAPTER FIVE

Smart Thinking About Costs

MOST BOOKS ON INVESTMENT HAVE A FEW WORDS TO SAY ON costs. "Stick to funds with lower charges" is one truism, often found in volumes focusing on passive investing. You won't be surprised to hear that I saw, "Don't be afraid of paying more for better managers" in a guide promoting active fund management. "Avoid trading too often" is good enough advice from a book on trading in individual shares.

This advice all sounds sensible, but it's somewhat superficial and incredibly vague. How should you measure and compare fund charges? Is it really possible to identify better managers and quantify their excellence? What exactly is trading *too often*?

You should also be able to answer other questions which are equally important, but rarely asked: is it worth diversifying and buying more funds if that means paying higher costs on smaller investments? Do you have enough money to invest in individual shares, or should you stick to collective funds like Exchange Traded Funds (ETFs)?

In this chapter I first address the question of how costs should be measured and the smartest way to compare the cost of different investment options. The next chapter shows how to weigh up the possible benefits of diversification against the higher costs of owning smaller positions in funds or individual equities.[83]

Chapter overview

Why costs are important	Why it's worth reading a whole chapter on this subject.

---

83. In part three I discuss how to evaluate other trade-offs between returns and costs, including how to evaluate active fund managers. I show you how much trading you should do in your portfolio in part four.

Cost measurement	What costs are involved in investing and how do we measure them?
How to compare the costs of different ETFs?	Does the headline annual management fee tell you everything you need to know about ETF costs?
How much does it cost to diversify an ETF portfolio?	For example, what is the cost difference between buying a single global equity fund and funds for each individual country?
A warning about cost comparisons	Some cautionary thoughts to consider when comparing the cost of different investment options.
Cost reduction strategies	Some suggestions to keep costs as low as possible.

Why costs are important

Costs are extremely important in investing. Here's why:

1. The **visible** management fee of an investment fund is only a proportion of what it costs. As you'll discover in the rest of this chapter, there are also **invisible costs**.

2. Although not always straightforward to measure, **costs are relatively predictable**; certainly much more predictable than returns (reread chapters two and three if you don't believe me). You cannot be certain that an active manager charging 1% more than a cheap passive indexing fund will make higher returns. But you know for sure that will have to pay a 1% extra fee.[84] Controlling costs is much easier than seeking higher returns.

3. Quoting costs as a proportion of assets managed is very misleading. You should think about costs as a proportion of your likely returns. If you are making 10% a year then a 2% charge equates to 20% of your profits: a much scarier figure.

4. Arguably paying 2% in costs was acceptable in the 1980s and 1990s when equity returns were consistently above 10%. But as I discussed at the end of chapter three, future returns are likely to be much lower. If your pre-cost annual return is only 5% then a 2% management fee means you're giving up 40% of your profits every year!

5. Even small increases in costs can have a dramatic effect in the long run, because of the effect of compounding. Many investors will have to start saving earlier and for longer because life expectancy is increasing.

On those third and fourth points, consider figure 26.

---

84. I explore this trade-off between predictable costs and uncertain returns in the next chapter

FIGURE 26: EFFECT OF DIFFERENT COSTS OVER TIME ON AN INVESTMENT OF $100

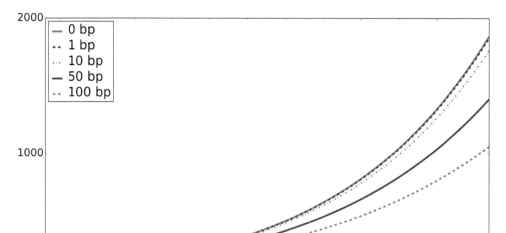

Each line shows what an investor will earn with consistent returns of 5%. The top line is zero cost. Other lines show the cumulative returns earned with costs of 0.01% a year (1 bp, or basis points), 0.1% (10bp), 0.5% (50bp) and 1% (100bp).

The topmost solid line shows what an investor will earn with consistent real returns of 5% and zero costs, if they started when this book was written at the age of 21 and continued until the age of 81; roughly the current average life expectancy in the UK or US. Subsequent lines show the effect of applying higher levels of costs.

A relatively modest 0.10% (in the jargon 10 **basis points** or 10bp on the graph) reduces the final value of the portfolio by over 6%. Half a percent (50bp) drops it by a quarter. Finally an extra 1% (100bp) of costs nearly halves the final portfolio value!

Later in this chapter I calculate costs down to the last 0.01%: a single basis point. Even an extra cost of 1bp will reduce the final portfolio value after six decades by 0.6%, which could be thousands of pounds or dollars on a large retail portfolio. Some institutional investors such as university endowments will have much longer horizons than the 60 years shown here. For them costs are even more important.

Smart investors spend at least as much time thinking about costs as about returns.

Cost measurement

Before you can compare costs you first need to measure them. In this chapter I focus on measuring the costs of (a) directly buying shares in individual equities, and (b) investing in passive index tracking ETFs. Passive ETFs are usually the cheapest way to get market exposure, so we won't look at other kinds of funds like unit trusts or mutual funds, which are relatively expensive and **actively managed** (rather than being passive trackers of indices).[85]

Visible and invisible costs

Part of the reason why investors don't take costs seriously enough is that most of them badly underestimate them. How much do your investments cost you? What costs are you paying and to whom? Do you really know **all** your costs?

Here is a list of costs that are obvious and readily disclosed. I call these **visible costs**.

Brokerage fees	These are paid to stockbrokers whenever a trade is done to cover exchange costs and other costs involved with the mechanics of trading.
	Commissions are charged on purchases and sales of individual shares, ETFs, and other stock exchanged traded vehicles like UK investment trusts and Real Estate Investment Trusts (REITs).
	For smaller purchases these are a fixed minimum fee; typically between $1 and $15 in the US, and £6 and £20 in the UK. Larger trades are usually charged as a fee per share or as a percentage of value.
Taxes	Paid to the government on each trade. Examples include UK stamp duty which is 0.5% paid only on purchases, or the proposed European Financial Transaction Tax which if implemented will be 0.1%.*
Annual management fees	This is the headline annual cost of collective funds like ETFs (officially described as the annual expense ratio in the US, or the ongoing charges figure in the UK). It may include some of the 'other fund management' fees listed below.
	These are usually paid daily out of the assets of the fund or subtracted from any dividend payments, and go to the fund management firm to cover the costs of managing each fund.
	Management fees range from the ultra low – 0.03% per year for the cheapest passive index funds – up to 2% or more for the most expensive actively managed funds.**

---

85. The question of whether active management is worth paying for is something I consider in part three.

Other fund management fees	Administration, custody fees and marketing costs of collective funds.
	These are usually paid out by the fund as and when expenses are incurred to external administrators: banks and lawyers. Marketing costs are paid to the fund manager. These fees are usually less than 0.1% a year although marketing costs can be significantly higher.

* Dividends may be taxed, and capital gains tax may also be payable when investments are held or sold, but I don't cover these taxes here (I look at this in part four).

** Some funds also charge performance fees; if they are profitable the fund managers take a proportion of the profits in addition to the management fee. Performance fees are usually 10% to 20% of any profits earned.

Some of the costs in the list above are murky rather than transparently visible; they are buried in the small print, but at least they are printed somewhere. The same can't be said of **invisible costs**. These are the costs you may not realise you're paying. They are unlikely to be disclosed by fund managers and at best you can only make a rough estimate of them.

Execution costs	These are additional costs you have to pay when buying or selling shares and ETFs. You pay these because the market will **charge you more to buy and pay you less when you sell**. They aren't explicit charges you have to hand over when you trade, but they do reduce your returns.
	Execution costs are most significant for institutional investors, since they are bigger when trading in larger size. They are also larger for all investors when buying relatively illiquid assets such as smaller firms, emerging market equities and thinly traded bonds.
Trading costs inside funds	Collective funds also buy and sell individual shares and bonds inside their funds, and therefore have to pay brokerage commissions and taxes, plus execution costs.
	These costs will be highest for actively managed funds which tend to do a lot of buying and selling, and relatively low for passive index tracking funds.
	Funds rarely disclose the total commissions they pay and may not even measure their execution costs. They are never included in the management fee.

As I discuss later in the chapter, these invisible costs can be substantial and can dwarf the more obvious visible costs.

Initial, holding and rebalancing costs

There are differences in the type and scale of costs, depending on whether you purchase equities directly or via collective funds. If you buy the individual constituents of the DAX-30 German stock index directly then you'll need to pay commissions on your **initial** purchase. Once you've bought shares they will cost you nothing until you decide to sell them[86] (which I will come back to in part four). But in theory if you want to match the DAX-30 exactly you'll have to pay **rebalancing** costs for buying and selling to keep your portfolio weights matching the index.

Alternatively you could buy a DAX-30 tracking fund, which follows the German stock market. You'll incur initial costs on the fund purchase and also have to pay **holding costs** in the form of an **annual management fee**. However there will also be **trading costs inside the fund**, as its managers buy and sell to track the index. These are effectively **holding costs** for you as an investor, since you have no control over them and they will occur regularly.

In summary we have three types of cost:

Initial costs	The costs of setting up your portfolio. Payable on all types of investments. Examples: commissions, initial charges, taxes (all visible), and execution costs (invisible)
Holding costs	Ongoing portfolio charges. These costs have to be paid regularly whilst you hold your position regardless of whether you do any further trading. Examples: annual management fees (visible) and trading costs inside ETFs (invisible).
Rebalancing costs	Costs incurred from any buying and selling you do in your portfolio after it's been set up. Examples: commissions, fund switching charges, taxes (all visible), and execution costs (invisible)

---

86.   Some brokerage accounts charge regular platform fees regardless of whether you are trading or not. But as long as these are the same regardless of what you are holding there is no need to factor them into any decision making.

CONCEPT: THE RULE OF 20

It's not straightforward to compare costs when you have some that only occur once (initial), and others that are ongoing (holding costs and possibly trading costs).

Fortunately financial mathematics has an answer to this problem. Mathematically the future payments of costs are exactly like a bond which pays out annual coupons, but has no final redemption value: this stream of future payments is known as an **annuity**.

You can assign a current value to this ongoing annual charge using a technique called discounted cash flow valuation. This adjusts your future payments so that they have a lower (discounted) value in present day terms.[87] The current value will depend on the level of interest rates: higher interest rates mean future fees are worth less now. It will also depend on the length of time before the investment matures: longer investment horizons mean higher total present values.

For example a $100 annual fee over five years with interest rates at 4% will have an upfront present value of $445, but $100 a year for ten years with the same interest rate is worth almost twice as much: $811. With an 8% interest rate $100 over five years has a present value of $399.

It is difficult to know exactly which interest rate to use as it depends on a number of different factors which are too dull to discuss here. It doesn't help that interest rates are always changing and forecasting future interest rates isn't easy. However at the time of writing US 30 year government nominal bond yields are around 3% which doesn't seem unreasonable as a long-term interest rate.

The length of investment horizon has a more significant effect on the valuation. It's hard to think of a single one size fits all value here, but the average investor in the US or UK is around 50 years old, and can expect to live for another 30 years, so I will use a 30-year horizon.

A $100 annual holding charge discounted at 3% over 30 years has an upfront present day value of just under $2000. So to convert annual costs into a single current value you can multiply by 20.[88] This also happens to be a pleasingly round number, hence I frequently use the phrase: **the rule of 20**. Investors who have a shorter investment horizon can use a different multiplier: for 20 years use a multiplier of 15, for ten years use 8.5, and for five years use 4.5.

---

87. Technical note: You can reproduce these calculations using the Excel bond pricing function.
88. Changing the horizon or interest rate doesn't affect the results as much as you might think. With a 20 year horizon the correct multiplying factor is 14.9, with 40 years it is 23.1. If I keep the horizon at 30 years but change the interest rate then the factor could be as low as 9.4 (10% interest rate) or as high as 27.8 (0.5% interest rate).

Personally I find it more convenient to convert initial costs into an annual charge (which involves **dividing** by 20).[89] This can then be added to the yearly holding costs to get a total annual cost.

total annual cost = (initial cost ÷ 20) + holding cost

Small investors: The effect of minimum fees

Small positions in ETFs or individual equities are expensive to buy. This is because of the tyranny of minimum brokerage commissions.

The broker I use for most of my trading is amongst the cheapest in the world. Nevertheless it still charges £6 per trade for all UK trades under £50,000 and a minimum of $1 per trade in the US. For small investors these minimum fees dwarf all other initial costs.

CONCEPT: BROKERAGE COMMISSIONS AND TAXES

Visible trading costs fall into two main categories:

1. Brokerage commissions

2. Taxes

Commissions are calculated in several different ways. There could be a flat rate per trade, regardless of size (up to some upper limit). This is common amongst retail brokers. Some brokers charge fees for each share traded or a percentage of trade value, again with minimum charges.

Examples of **taxes** include UK stamp duty (0.5%) and the proposed European financial transactions tax, which are both charged as a percentage rate. Flat taxes are less common, but they do exist – the UK PTM levy[90] being an example.

Table 20 shows the costs I pay myself when buying US stocks directly and ETFs, both of which attract the same brokerage charges. By the way, some US ETFs can be bought without commission at certain brokers.

---

89.   If you're familiar with accounting conventions this is equivalent to depreciating the initial trading cost over 20 years using a flat depreciation rate.
90.   The PTM levy partly funds the work of the takeover panel, which regulates mergers and takeovers in the City of London. At the time of writing the fee is £1 for all trades over £10,000 in value.

TABLE 20: INITIAL BROKERAGE COST PER TRADE FOR US EQUITY INVESTORS IN LARGE CAP SHARES OR ETFS

Investment amount	Direct	Direct %	ETF	ETF %
$100	$1	1.00%	$1	1.00%
$500	$1	0.20%	$1	0.20%
$1,000	$1	0.10%	$1	0.10%
$2,000	$1	0.05%	$1	0.05%
$5,000	$1	0.02%	$1	0.02%
$10,000	$1	0.01%	$1	0.01%
$100,000	$10	0.01%	$10	0.01%

Total initial cost for type of investment (columns) for an amount of investment (rows). Uses my assumptions about trading costs in Appendix B, page 480.

Table 21 shows the cost and taxes payable in the UK. Because ETFs do not attract a 0.5% stamp duty tax on purchase they are significantly cheaper.

TABLE 21: INITIAL BROKERAGE AND TAX COST PER TRADE FOR UK EQUITY INVESTORS IN LARGE CAP SHARES AND ETFS

Investment amount	Direct	Direct %	ETF	ETF %
£100	£6.50	6.5%	£6	6%
£500	£8.50	1.7%	£6	1.2%
£1,000	£11	1.1%	£6	0.6%
£2,000	£16	0.8%	£6	0.3%
£5,000	£31	0.62%	£6	0.12%
£10,000	£56	0.56%	£6	0.06%
£100,000	£530	0.53%	£29	0.03%

Total initial cost for type of investment (columns) for an amount of investment (rows). Uses my assumptions about trading costs in Appendix B, page 480.

In percentage terms it's much more expensive for smaller investors in both countries. The UK is pricier because of higher minimum fees, and individual stocks are costlier than ETFs because of stamp duty.

Of course all these figures are broker specific. Later in the book I explain how to adapt my results and recommendations according to the specific fees you pay when you make investments.

Impacting the market

Large institutional investors don't have to worry so much about visible trading costs like commissions, for which they get discounted rates. However invisible **execution costs** are a serious problem for investors buying big quantities of shares.

CONCEPT: INVISIBLE TRADING COSTS

As well as visible brokerage charges and tax, anyone trading in a market will face invisible costs whenever they **execute** any trades. This isn't an explicit charge, but reflects the fact that the market will make you pay more to buy than it will offer you when you are selling. Your returns will be reduced, hence this is effectively a cost even if it isn't obvious or visible.

Consider the following imaginary order book showing the best bids (to buy) and offers (to sell) in the market:

TABLE 22: AN IMAGINARY EQUITY ORDER BOOK

Bid price	Size	Offer price	Size
$1.50	50	$1.51	25
$1.49	100	$1.52	50
$1.48	75	$1.53	200

The mid-price is the average of the **inside spread**, halfway between the best bid of 1.50 and the best offer of 1.51: I make that 1.50 ½. However it's unlikely that you'll be able to buy at 1.50 ½. If you're buying 25 or fewer shares, you'll have to pay 1.51. Selling 50 shares would get you 1.50. The half a cent difference between the mid price and what you actually pay when buying, or receive when selling, is the **bid-ask spread cost**.

However what if you wanted to buy or sell 200 shares? Buying 200 shares will cost $1.52 ½.[91] That's 2 cents higher than the mid-price. A sale of 200 shares would net $1.49;[92] 1.5 cents lower than the mid. On average someone trading in 200 shares will get 1.75[93] cents worse than the mid; of which 0.5 cents comes from the bid-ask spread, and the other 1.25 cents from trading in larger size. This additional 1.25 cent cost is called **market impact**.

If I add up the bid-ask spread cost (0.5 cents) and market impact for trading 200 shares (average of 1.25 cents) then I get the average **total execution cost** (1.75 cents). Because order books are constantly changing it's not possible to predict execution costs exactly for every possible trade, but by monitoring the market regularly we can get pretty good estimates.

Larger trades will have bigger market impact. This is why institutional traders have to worry more about execution costs than retail traders. In table 22 trades of less than 20 shares will have zero market impact and the cost will just be half the bid-ask spread. I assume that retail traders only pay the bid-ask spread when they trade.

To give you an idea of the magnitude of execution costs let's suppose that you are buying a large block of shares in a large cap, highly liquid US share that is in the S&P 500, such as General Electric. The bid-ask spread is likely to be around 0.05%. However, according to my research the market impact of a sufficiently large trade will be around 0.3%.[94]

For an institutional investor the commission on that trade would be tiny at just 0.01% of the value. This means the total execution cost of around 0.35% (bid-ask spread of 0.05% + market impact of 0.3%) will be the lion's share of the total cost of 0.36%. These figures are for a highly liquid US stock. Buying shares in small firms or those traded in other countries, especially emerging markets, will cost institutional investors even more.

As a comparison, I assume a US investor buying $1,000 of stocks will pay a $1 commission which works out to 0.1% of the value, but because they have no market impact they will only pay the bid-ask spread of 0.05%. Their execution cost comes out at just a third of the total cost of 0.15%, with two-thirds coming from commissions.

Conclusion: Large investors should worry about market impact; for small investors minimum commissions are more important.

---

91. 25 × $1.51 + 50×$1.52 + 125×$1.53 = $305. Average for 200 shares is $305 ÷ 200 = $1.52 ½.
92. 50 × $1.50 + 100×$1.49 + 50×$1.48 = $298. Average for 200 shares is $298 ÷ 200 = $1.49.
93. The average of 1.5 cents and 2.0 cents.
94. Appendix B, page 481, explains where these figures come from.

Holding costs for ETFs: Invisible trading costs inside funds

Here is a puzzle for you. Suppose you buy two investment funds that have just launched. Each is run separately by one of a pair of fund managers who used to work together: *Chris The Churner* and *Steady Eddie*. Each uses the same advisory service, *Crystal-Ball Partners*, that updates them daily on what is expected to go up or down in price. Chris and Eddie base all their trading decisions on this advice.

Naturally Chris and Eddie buy the same initial set of stocks. After the first year they send out their annual statements: as you would expect both funds still have the same current holdings, though these aren't the same as they started with. The two funds charge the same management fee. But when you look at their performance Chris has done much worse than Eddie. How is this possible?

The answer is that Chris The Churner has done more **trading**. Every day he has churned his portfolio, buying and selling large chunks of his positions based on the advice he received that morning from Crystal-Ball. But Steady Eddie had a serious illness just after buying his initial positions and ended up in hospital for most of the year. In fact Eddie barely had time to do just one set of trades on the last trading day of the year, replacing last years stocks with Crystal-Ball's current favorites; which is why his holdings end up matching with Chris' on 1 January.

Many of the trades that Eddie did were at worse prices than if he'd done them earlier in the year. But overall the effect of additional commissions and invisible execution costs completely wipes out Chris' profits.

Trading costs inside collective funds are an insidious invisible cost which most investors are blissfully unaware of. Fortunately there isn't too much trading inside passive index tracking funds, at least compared to actively managed funds like Chris and Eddie's. But there is some.

These costs are not usually disclosed. Some funds reveal the commissions and taxes they have paid to trade, as is recommended under the UK regulator's enhanced disclosure regime. But execution costs are rarely, if ever, revealed; some managers are unaware they exist and many others don't bother to estimate them even for internal reporting purposes.

In Appendix B (page 483) I explain how I researched and calculated some figures for turnover within funds. I assume a passive index fund will turn over around 10% of its portfolio in a year. If it is tracking large cap US equities then this will cost roughly 0.04% a year, whereas in the UK it will be around 0.1% because of stamp duty and higher **market impact** costs. Emerging market and small cap funds will have even higher invisible trading costs.

It's possible to get a more precise estimate of trading costs for a specific fund by comparing it with its benchmark and deducting the annual management fee (AER in the US, OCF in the UK). Any remaining difference is mostly because of trading costs:[95]

ETF performance = benchmark return − (expense ratio + trading costs)

trading costs = benchmark return − ETF performance − expense ratio

Bear in mind that funds frequently modify their management fees and sometimes even change their benchmark. If this has happened you will need to calculate the trading cost figure independently for different years and then take an average. Also funds and benchmark returns need to be comparable. They must be in the same currency, and you must make sure that both benchmark and fund performance figures are for total returns including dividends.[96]

DIGRESSION: SYNTHETIC FUNDS

A certain type of ETF manager might appear to have zero trading costs in their funds. They do not own any actual equities or bonds; instead they use something called synthetic replication (these are often described as ETNs: Exchange Traded Notes). The fund makes an agreement, called a swap, with a bank. Under the terms of the agreement the bank will pay the fund the value of the relevant index. No trading costs: what's the catch?

In fact swaps do incur costs: both fees and swap spreads (analogous to the bid-ask spread in equities). There are advantages and disadvantages to this approach, but if a physical fund would have incurred high dealing costs then its synthetic cousin will also be equally costly. The bank will still have to do all the relevant trading to hedge its exposure and will recover its costs through the swap.

The exotic world of synthetic replication is usually no cheaper than actually owning the relevant shares, and may even be more expensive unless the bank can achieve extra economies of scale in trading which outweigh the profit margin they'll include in the swap fees.[97]

---

95.   There will also be minor differences if there are other costs not included in the expense ratio, and because ETFs earn money from lending out their securities in the market. But these pale into significance against trading costs.
96.   Don't use price returns excluding dividends, as some funds deduct their management fee from the dividends they pay out.
97.   ETFs that track commodity prices can also use a kind of synthetic replication using listed derivatives like futures contracts. This doesn't have serious cost implications but it's still important to understand it. I discuss this in part two (chapter nine).

Costs and investment size

You're probably realising that comparing the costs of different funds and shares is a complicated business, mainly because different investors will face higher or lower costs depending on the size of the investments they're making. To illustrate this I'm going to slice the various kinds of costs yet another way, into **fixed percentage costs** which don't change with investment size, and **variable percentage costs** that do change.

Fixed percentage costs are those that remain the same, regardless of whether you put $100 or $1 million into an investment when measured as a percentage. Something that is $1 when you invest $100 (1%), and $10,000 on a $1 million purchase (also 1%) is a fixed percentage cost.

On the other hand if you have to pay $1 for a $100 investment (1%) and $100 on $1 million (0.01%) then it must be a variable percentage cost.

Here is a reminder of the costs that you face as an investor and how I categorise them:

Variable percentage costs	**Initial costs** to set up portfolio: • Minimum brokerage commissions on smaller purchases (visible). • Fixed taxes, e.g. UK PTM Levy (visible).
Fixed percentage costs	**Initial costs:** • Percentage or per share brokerage commissions on sufficiently large purchases (visible). • Percentage based taxes, e.g. UK stamp duty (visible). • Bid-ask spread cost (invisible). • Market impact for large investors (invisible). **Holding costs:** • Annual management fees (visible). • Trading costs inside collective funds (invisible).

Notice I'm assuming that **holding costs do not change with investment size**. Sometimes very large institutional investors can negotiate down expense ratios on certain types of fund, or access cheaper funds that aren't open to the public. But generally an ETF manager isn't going to charge different expense ratios to customers depending on the size of their investment. And they certainly can't preferentially allocate the invisible trading costs they're paying to favour larger investors.

Let's look at an example of how fixed and variable percentage costs interact on a specific ETF. Table 23 shows the costs of buying the FTSE 100 tracker, ISF. You will be seeing a few more of these tables in the rest of this chapter so it's worth spending a moment or two understanding the format.

TABLE 23: EXAMPLE OF COST CALCULATION TABLE: FTSE 100 ETF

	Holding costs			Initial costs						All
	Annual fee A	Trading in fund B	Holding Sub Total C = A+B	Tax D	Cmn. E	Bid-Ask F	Market impact G	Initial Sub Total H = SUM (D:G)	Initial As Annual J = H÷20	Annual total K = C+J
£500					1.2%			1.25%	0.06%	0.23%
£1,000					0.6%			0.65%	0.03%	0.20%
£2,000					0.3%		0%	0.35%	0.02%	0.19%
£5,000	0.07%	0.1%	0.17%	0%	0.12%	0.05%		0.17%	0.01%	0.18%
£10,000					0.06%			0.11%	0.01%	0.18%
£100,000					0.03%			0.08%	0%	0.17%
Institutional					0.01%		0.05%	0.11%	0%	0.17%

All assumptions about costs as per Appendix B. 'Cmn.': Commission

Each row of the table shows the cost of investing a different amount in the ETF, with the final row reserved for very large institutional trades. From left to right, the first three columns show the **holding costs**: annual management fee (column A), invisible trading cost inside fund (B), and the subtotal (C). These are all **fixed percentage costs**. Notice that fixed percentage costs are shown with a single value that is shared across every row.

The next four columns show specific **initial** costs: tax (fixed, column D), brokerage commission ('Cmn.', variable cost, E), bid-ask spread (fixed, F) and market impact (zero for retail investors, but with a fixed value for institutional investors in column G).

If I add up these four columns I get the total initial cost in column H. To make this an annual cost and comparable with the holding costs I use the **rule of 20**, and divide the initial cost by 20, giving me column J. Adding up the subtotal of holding costs (column C) and the subtotal for initial costs (J) gives the grand total cost per year, which is in the rightmost column K. Remember:

total annual cost = (initial cost ÷ 20) + holding cost

These tables are very detailed but they do allow you to easily compare the costs of different funds, shares, or portfolios; regardless of the size of your investment. You just need to find the row of the table which best represents the amount you are putting into the relevant portfolio and then compare this to the same row in an alternative option. In the next chapter I show how to incorporate **expected returns** into these tables. This will allow you to analyse the trade-off between the costs and benefit of diversifying your portfolio.

Meanwhile, the rest of this chapter will show you how to use these tables to compare the costs of some specific different investment options.

How to compare the costs of different ETFs

There are a dozen ETFs listed in the UK tracking the S&P 500, plus another dozen following the almost identical MSCI USA Index. Which should you pick? Clearly where any two products are perfect substitutes for each other you should use the **cheapest one**.

The good news is you don't need to calculate every single tiny part of the total cost when comparing two funds with the same benchmark. Remember:

ETF cost = (initial cost ÷ 20) + management fee + trading cost inside fund

The initial cost is likely to be very similar for both funds. Certainly the commissions should be the same,[98] whilst **bid-ask spreads** and **market impact** (for larger traders) probably aren't that different. In any case small differences in initial costs of ETFs aren't a significant component of overall costs once you've applied **the rule of 20** to convert them into annual terms.

The **trading cost inside the fund** should also be similar unless one fund manager, or their execution trader, is completely incompetent.

For collective investment funds which are similar enough the **difference in management fee** will account for the vast majority of any variation in total cost. Of course if the indices have the same benchmark then it's straightforward to compare their performance, since any difference will be due to total holding costs (trading costs inside the fund plus management fee):

ETF holding costs = benchmark - (management fee + trading cost inside fund)

This also means you can compare the after-cost performance of ETFs with the same benchmark and the **best performer will also be the cheapest**. Just remember to account for any changes in expense ratios or ETF benchmark in the past so you get an accurate figure for expected future holding costs.

---

98.   Unless you're lucky enough to be buying one ETF commission free. But the initial commission is usually a tiny fraction of overall costs.

You need to use the total return including any dividend payments and after deducting any costs that don't appear in published performance figures. Also, to make sure the funds are comparable they should also be in the same currency.

How much does it cost to diversify an ETF portfolio?

Suppose you are a small investor thinking of buying a single global market capitalisation weighted equity ETF. You disagree with the market cap weights and think there is an advantage to investing in separate **diversifying** ETFs, one for developed and another for emerging markets. This is a very important topic which I explore in the next chapter, and many of the decisions we look at in part two of the book involve this kind of problem. But for the moment let's understand how this decision will affect your costs.

Obviously there will be a difference in annual **ETF holding costs** if the management fees of the two diversifying ETFs are larger or smaller than those of the original all encompassing global ETF. It's also likely that emerging markets with less liquid markets will have higher invisible **internal trading costs** inside the relevant ETF. Plus they might have larger bid-ask spreads, so their **initial costs** could be larger.

But more importantly, if you buy multiple funds there will be higher **brokerage fees**. Rather than investing $1,000 or £1,000 into a single ETF you'll be investing a few hundred dollars or pounds into two different ETFs. Because of minimum commissions this will cost twice as much in brokerage charges. Not such a big deal with two ETFs, but what if you want to own an ETF for every country in the global equity index? That's over 40 different funds! For a small initial investment those minimum charges will soon add up.

Let's look at a real example. Table 24 shows my cost calculation for VWRL, a UK-listed ETF for global market cap weighted equities. (I apologise for the UK-centric examples in this chapter, but the significantly higher trading costs in the UK make the results much more interesting.) This has about 93% in developed equity markets and just 7% in emerging markets.

TABLE 24: COST CALCULATIONS FOR FTSE ALL-WORLD ETF (VWRL)

	Holding costs			Initial costs						All
	Annual fee A	Trading in fund B	Holding Sub Total C = A+B	Tax D	Cmn. E	Bid-Ask F	Market impact G	Initial Sub Total H = SUM (D:G)	Initial As Annual J = H÷20	Annual total K = C+J
£100					6.0%			6.08%	0.30%	0.61%
£500					1.2%			1.28%	0.06%	0.37%
£1,000					0.6%			0.68%	0.03%	0.34%
£2,000	0.25%	0.06%	0.31%	0%	0.3%	0.08%	0%	0.38%	0.02%	**0.33%**
£5,000					0.12%			0.20%	0.01%	0.32%
£10,000					0.06%			0.14%	0.01%	0.32%
£100,000					0.03%			0.11%	0.01%	0.32%
Institutional					0.01%		0.05%	0.14%	0.01%	0.32%

All cost assumptions as per Appendix B. 'Cmn.': Commission

Now is it worth diversifying this fund by buying two funds instead, one for developed and one for emerging markets? For reasons that I explain in part two, my preferred cash weights would be 83% in developed equities and 17% in emerging markets.

Table 25 shows the cost of buying this portfolio of two ETFs. Each of the costs shown is the weighted average[99] of the cost for each of the two individual funds I'm using: VEVE (developed) and AUEUM (emerging).

---

99.   The weights in the weighted average are the cash weights. So, for example, to find the weighted average of annual management fee, we take the average of the VEVE fee 0.18% (developed markets 83% weight) and AUEM fee 0.2% (emerging markets, 17% weight): (0.18% × 0.83) + (0.2% × 0.17) = 0.1834%.

TABLE 25: COST CALCULATION TABLE: 83% IN DEVELOPED MARKET EQUITY ETF VEVE, 17% IN EMERGING MARKET EQUITY AUEM

	Holding costs			Initial costs						All
	Annual fee A	Trading in fund B	Holding Sub Total C = A+B	Tax D	Cmn. E	Bid-Ask F	Market impact G	Initial Sub Total H = SUM (D:G)	Initial As Annual J = H÷20	Annual total K = C+J
£100					12.00%			12.14%	0.61%	0.90%
£500					2.40%			2.54%	0.13%	0.42%
£1,000					1.20%			1.34%	0.07%	0.36%
£2,000	0.183%	0.11%	0.29%	0%	0.60%	0.14%	0%	0.74%	0.04%	**0.33%**
£5,000					0.24%			0.38%	0.02%	0.31%
£10,000					0.12%			0.26%	0.01%	0.30%
£100,000					0.02%			0.16%	0.01%	0.30%
Institutional					0.01%		0.07%	0.21%	0.01%	0.30%

VEVE fee 0.18%, trading inside fund 0.05%, bid ask 0.11%. AUEM fee 0.2%, trading inside fund 0.4%, bid ask 0.28%. All other assumptions as per Appendix B. 'Cmn.': Commission

Interestingly this particular diversifying portfolio is actually cheaper than the single fund when it comes to **holding costs** thanks to a slightly lower average management fee. However, the initial costs are much higher, mainly due to the effect of paying two lots of minimum commission at £6 each.

I've highlighted in bold the total cost value for an investment of £2,000 in both tables because this is the **breakeven** value. For smaller investments the single global fund VWRL is cheaper. But if you are investing more than £2,000 then it's worth diversifying and buying two separate funds. **Because of minimum commissions diversification usually costs more for small accounts.**

A warning about cost comparisons

Do not take my cost estimates as gospel, or as any kind of holy writ. In particular any **invisible costs** (execution cost, market impact, and trading costs inside funds) might turn out quite differently from the estimates I'm using. In this chapter, and the next, I use costs to make investment decisions between several options. When I'm doing this please bear in mind that costs could easily be a few basis points (multiples of 0.01%) higher or lower.

This means you should think carefully about a tight decision between two alternatives with very similar cost levels. With slightly different assumptions it could easily go the other way.

Smart tactics for reducing costs

A lot of the material in this chapter is less relevant for the largest institutions. Institutional investors can probably afford to invest directly in shares, although they need not bother if they can find a cheap enough ETF. They will have no problems whatsoever diversifying their ETF portfolio. Minimum brokerage commissions are irrelevant given their mighty position sizes.

However, being a large investor has one major downside: larger **execution costs**. Institutions pay such low commissions that **bid-ask spread** forms a big proportion of their initial purchase costs. Most retail traders can happily live their life in blissful ignorance of **market impact**, but this should be a serious concern for institutional investors.

Below are a couple of different tactics for reducing the execution costs of trading at larger sizes. These can also be used by experienced retail traders, especially those buying less liquid stocks such as those of smaller firms.

Get paid the spread

When you are making larger investments the bid-ask spread cost can form a large part of your costs, particularly on less liquid stocks such as small cap equities and those in emerging markets. How can you reduce this cost? Is it possible to earn the bid-ask spread cost, rather than paying it?

Today most investors are able to access stock exchanges directly and place limit orders to buy or sell at a specific price, rather than merely taking the best price available in the market. Suppose a small cap is priced at $10.00 bid and $10.10 offer; so the mid-price is $10.05. If you are buying and paid the offer at $10.10 then it would cost you $0.05 in bid-ask spread costs, which is a chunky 0.5% of the share price.

Instead why not put your own bid into the market with a limit of $10.00? If you get lucky then your order will be filled there. You'll have a **negative** execution cost of 5 cents per share! Of course you might be unlucky. The price could ramp up after you put in your bid, so your order isn't filled. You'd have to put a new limit order in, which again in turn may not be executed. Eventually your order will be filled, but at a higher price than if you'd just paid the original offer price of $10.10. Does this mean limit orders are a waste of time?

Well, let's pretend that you have access to a magic algorithm that can predict share price movements perfectly and that it's forecasting a gradual 10% rise over the next 12 months. That works out to 0.04% a day; a daily rise of just under 0.4 cents. Suppose you're fantastically unlucky and your order remains unfilled for 20 working days in a row, after which the price will have risen around 8 cents. **On average** you'd expect to pay $10.08: but this is still better than if you'd taken the starting offer of $10.10.

So even if we had access to an infallible crystal ball it would still make sense to submit limit orders. Since we don't have such perfect forecasting algorithms in the real world, paying the spread will, on average, be considerably worse than using limit orders.

Although using limit orders is better on average there is a potential for **embarrassment** if you delay your trades to save money. You will get blamed, or blame yourself, on the occasions when the share price drifts upwards away from the initial price and you end up paying more. The longer you delay your trade, the bigger the likely move away from where it was initially.

To save face and limit the damage you can determine the highest price you'd pay. For example, suppose you set a 20 cent limit. If the price moves from $10.00 bid – $10.10 offer, all the way up to $10.20 bid – $10.30 offer, you should then cut your losses and accept the offer to purchase at $10.30.

Nevertheless if you can stomach the risk I'd strongly advocate a strategy of placing limit orders into the market. As not everyone will be comfortable with this I've assumed that you are paying the spread in the calculations I've used in the rest of the book.

Trade more slowly

Getting paid the spread is much harder for large retail traders in illiquid small caps and institutional traders, for whom the main cost is **market impact**.

Cast your mind back to the order book in table 22 (page 127). The inside spread showed a bid of 50 shares at $1.50, and an offer of 25 shares at $1.51. Now imagine that you're a large trader who follows my advice above and submits a buy order for 10,000 shares at the current bid price of $1.50. This will result in the order book shown in table 26.

TABLE 26: AN IMAGINARY EQUITY ORDER BOOK AFTER A VERY LARGE TRADER HAS JOINED THE BID

Bid price	Size	Offer price	Size
$1.50	10,050	$1.51	25
$1.49	100	$1.52	50
$1.48	75	$1.53	200

Clearly your chances of being paid the spread are slim. There is a very remote chance a large seller will come along at exactly this moment and hit your bid. It's much more likely that other traders in the market, or the computer trading algorithms they're using, will immediately mark up the price leaving your order unfilled. Alternatively if you placed 10,000 shares at the offer then the first 25 shares would be filled immediately, but subsequently the price would again jump in response, leaving you stuck with another 9,975 shares to buy at a much higher market price.

The solution is to break up your order into smaller chunks and execute it more gradually. The slower you execute, and the smaller the size of each order, the lower the market impact of each trade. This is known as **order smoothing** or **order splitting**.

Most institutional investors do some smoothing, or use brokers who provide this service. Otherwise the market impact costs I've used in this book would be considerably higher. Nevertheless, in my experience even relatively sophisticated institutional investors[100] often give themselves quite short periods of time to complete trades, relative to their average holding period. Would it be so bad if a portfolio rebalancing took several weeks or even months to complete, rather than the single day that is usually allowed?[101]

Retail traders who trade in the shares of small firms (small cap) should also smooth their orders. Suppose that you want to buy £10,000 of a very illiquid small cap firm where the bid-ask spread is 1% of the price. If you tried to execute this in one chunk it would cost 0.5% in bid-ask spread costs, plus plenty of market impact. Instead you should split the order for £10,000 into ten separate limit orders, which you put into the market over a period of two weeks. Because each individual order is quite small you end up being paid the spread on each of these orders.

Your commission will be 0.06% on a £10,000 order and 0.60% in total on ten £1,000 orders due to the impact of fixed minimum costs; an extra 0.54% in brokerage commission. You might also end up paying a few basis points more on average by delaying your purchase. But you'd save 1% in costs by being paid the spread at 0.5% rather than having to pay it at 0.5%, plus an additional saving on the market impact costs of doing one big trade. In total you'd save at least 1 – 0.54% = 0.46% and probably more.

For the calculations in the book I've assumed that institutions do some order smoothing in line with current industry averages, and so end up paying for a typical level of market impact as well as the spread. I assume that retail traders do no smoothing and have zero

---

100. There are some exceptions. Very smart investors do focus on keeping costs low by smart trading. For example, in the paper 'Trading Costs of Asset Pricing Anomalies' several researchers who work for a very smart hedge fund AQR use total cost estimates including market impact which are significantly lower than the institutional averages I use in this book.

101. One of the few downsides of passive index funds is that their rebalances have to be done fairly quickly to minimise tracking error to the index. Nevertheless the total trading costs of passive investing are still considerably lower than the active alternatives.

market impact even in small cap stocks. But all kinds of larger traders in less liquid stocks should think seriously about splitting their orders up.

Key points

Small differences in costs matter	With low expectations of future returns, and longer investment horizons, adding just 0.1% to your costs can seriously damage your returns.
Know how much you're paying	Calculating the true total cost of investment and trading can be difficult because of the presence of **invisible** costs. But costs are still easier to forecast than returns.
The costs of diversification	Diversification is undoubtedly a good thing, but it can be more expensive especially for smaller investors. I'll discuss quantifying the benefits of diversification more in the next chapter.
Shop around	Don't pay premium prices for a product you can pick up more cheaply elsewhere. Go for ETFs with the lowest total cost: including both management fees and invisible trading costs.
Trade smart	Submitting limit orders and splitting your orders up can reduce trading costs considerably, especially for larger investors and those buying small cap stocks.

CHAPTER SIX

The Unknown Benefits and Known Costs of Diversification

THE PREVIOUS CHAPTER WAS ALL ABOUT COMPARING THE COSTS of different investment products. This is pretty straightforward, as with some work it's easy to estimate and calculate costs. But many portfolio decisions involve weighing up **highly uncertain benefits against relatively predictable costs**.

In particular, more **diversified** portfolios will probably do better than holding a single share or fund, but you'll need to hold smaller positions, which given minimum fees could cost more. Is it still worth diversifying?

How much money do you need to justify holding individual equities rather than ETFs? Are funds that offer **equal weighting** of stocks worth buying? Can you get round the problem of having small positions in many stocks by only buying a **selection** of stocks in the index?

In this chapter I explain the smart techniques I use for thinking about these questions. I show how these techniques can be used to address the vital question of how much diversification makes sense and to find the most cost-effective way to get exposure to different markets.

Chapter overview

Diversification: What is it good for?	The benefits of diversification.
Should you diversify?	Is it worth diversifying your portfolio if it will cost you more? How do we weigh up the costs and benefits?

Handcrafting, equal weighting, or market cap weighting?	What are the relative benefits and costs of each of these alternative ways of getting exposure to a market?
Buy the whole index, or just part of it?	Can you save on costs by buying only a selection of a market index, whilst not losing too much diversification?
How to invest in a given country	Should you buy a fund, or individual shares? Which shares should you buy? How many of each?
Diversifying over multiple funds	How can you calculate if it's worth diversifying over multiple funds?

This is the final chapter of part one. In part two I show you how to actually create portfolios using all the techniques I've shown you so far.

Diversification: What is it good for?

"Diversification is the only free lunch in finance."

— Attributed to Harry Markowitz, the academic who
founded modern portfolio theory

"There is no such thing as a free lunch."

— Origin unknown

As you learned in the last chapter, diversification isn't entirely free. It will probably cost more in brokerage commissions if you have a modest portfolio. But it does have considerable benefits: it will improve your returns without you needing to do something really hard, like predict risk-adjusted returns.

Before considering whether these benefits outweigh the costs, we need to quantify the size of the benefits. What advantages does a diversified portfolio have?

In the first few chapters I pointed out some interesting facts about portfolio risk and return:

Use expected geometric mean of returns	The geometric return of a portfolio depends on both the arithmetic return and its risk. The approximation I've been using is this:
	geometric mean = arithmetic mean − 0.5 × (standard deviation)^2
	A lower risk equates to a higher geometric mean.

Similar assets have similar risk	If assets are similar enough, like firms in the same country and industry, then it's safe to assume they have identical volatility.
You can't predict the future	Specifically, **risk-adjusted returns** are extremely hard to forecast. I measure risk-adjusted return using the **Sharpe Ratio**: geometric mean divided by standard deviation. Throughout the first two parts of this book I assume that **geometric Sharpe Ratios** are identical for all assets in a portfolio.

If I put these findings together then I get an interesting result: If all assets have the same risk-adjusted return (Sharpe Ratio), and the same risk, then they must have the **same geometric mean** of returns. If all assets in a portfolio have the same geometric mean, and the same risk, then they must also have the **same arithmetic mean**.

Any extra stocks you add to your portfolio will have the same expected returns as the shares you already own. Given these assumptions, increasing the number of assets in a portfolio will have absolutely no effect on arithmetic average returns.[102]

But adding more stocks to your portfolio definitely **reduces your expected risk**, assuming the additional stocks are not perfectly correlated (correlation less than 1). With constant arithmetic returns and falling volatility your geometric mean will gradually increase as your portfolio includes more assets, and your Sharpe Ratio will go up by even more.

Remember from chapter four that some investors will want the maximum Sharpe Ratio, others the highest geometric return, and the remainder will seek a compromise between these two extremes. But both geometric mean and Sharpe Ratio increase with diversification: everyone should be happier with a more diversified portfolio.[103]

Another important point is this: if you assume that risk-adjusted returns can't be forecasted then **diversifying is the only way to improve the geometric returns and Sharpe Ratio of your portfolio**. Picking stocks is a waste of time, because a highly concentrated group of 'high conviction' bets will do worse than a larger diversified portfolio. Diversification is not just a free lunch, it's the only thing on the menu!

The precise benefit you get from diversifying **depends on the average correlation between assets in the portfolio and the number of assets**. The largest improvement will come when assets have very low correlations. More assets are always better, but there are

---

102. For all these calculations I'm utilising the standard portfolio optimisation calculations to calculate expected returns and risk given some portfolio weights and correlations; and assuming equal risk and risk-adjusted return. See Appendix C, page 495, for more.

103. Although of course diversification always improves Sharpe Ratio by more than geometric mean returns. Technical note: There is some disagreement about whether it is correct to maximise geometric returns, and whether the diversification benefits produced can be used to pay higher costs. This problem goes away if you use the median rather than the mean to evaluate the distribution of expectations of future portfolio values. See Appendix C, page 491.

diminishing returns with each asset you add. Five stocks are a lot better than one. Ten stocks are only a little better than five.

Figure 27 shows the increase in geometric mean as assets are added to a portfolio. Each line shows the improvement for a given correlation. Notice that the lines for lower correlation values are truncated. This is because it's difficult to find large numbers of assets in the world with very low correlations. Figure 28 shows what happens to Sharpe Ratios.

FIGURE 27: GEOMETRIC MEAN RETURN IS INCREASED THROUGH DIVERSIFICATION

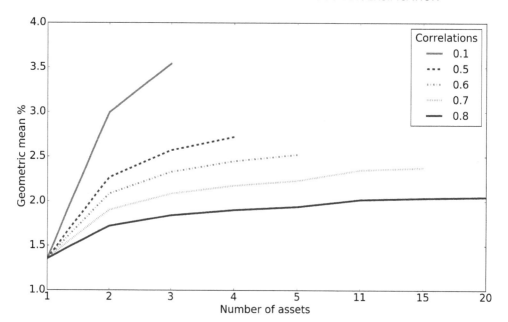

Assumes that a single asset has an arithmetic mean real return of 5% and standard deviation of 27%.

To find the lowest correlations you need to look across **asset classes**, where I assume returns are uncorrelated: a correlation of zero. This is a conservative assumption given that the correlations between bonds and equities has been negative for most of recent history. In my opinion there are probably only three truly distinct asset classes: bonds, equities, and **alternatives**.[104]

---

104. Alternatives are non-standard investments like hedge funds, property and commodities. As I discuss in chapter nine many alternatives are actually fairly similar to bonds and equities. There are, however, genuine alternatives for which an average correlation of 0 with the two main asset classes is reasonable.

At the other end of the spectrum, stocks in the same country and industry, like Google and Facebook (both in the US tech sector), are highly correlated and the lines in figures 27 and 28 labelled with a correlation of 0.8 are most relevant. There is limited benefit to adding more than ten stocks to your portfolio with such high correlation, although there are usually dozens of potential candidates.

All this supports my preferred **handcrafting** methodology of creating top-down portfolios where you allocate to asset classes to get the maximum diversification first, then countries, followed by industries and individual stocks.

FIGURE 28: SHARPE RATIO BENEFITS EVEN MORE FROM DIVERSIFICATION

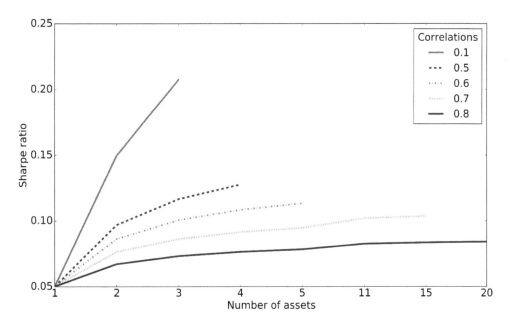

Assumes that a single asset has an arithmetic mean real return of 5% and standard deviation of 27%.

Figures 29 (for geometric mean) and 30 (for Sharpe Ratio) show how an all-equity portfolio would benefit from additional diversification as it grows, starting from a single stock.

FIGURE 29: HIGHER GEOMETRIC MEAN THROUGH CONTINUED DIVERSIFICATION

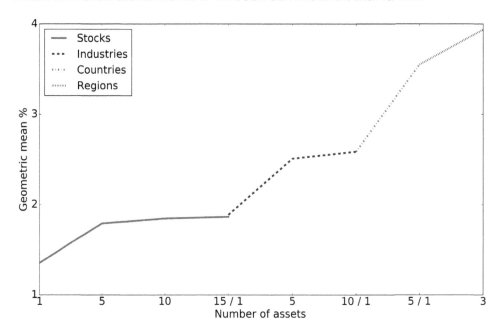

FIGURE 30: IMPROVEMENT IN SHARPE RATIO THROUGH WIDER DIVERSIFICATION

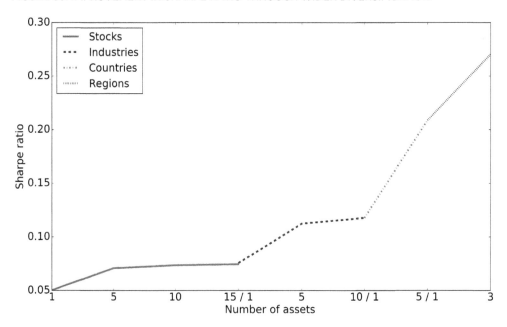

At the extreme left of each figure a single stock has an arithmetic mean of 5% and a geometric mean of just over 1.3%, which translates to a Sharpe Ratio of around 0.05 if I assume a volatility of 27%. I then added four more stocks from the same industry and country. These have the same **arithmetic mean**, but because this lowers the risk of the portfolio the geometric mean rises to 1.8% and the Sharpe Ratio to 0.071.

Continuing along the solid line adding more than ten stocks in the same industry has limited benefit, due to their high correlation (I'm using an average correlation of 0.85, based on my own research). To do better I need to add new industries to the portfolio.

The left-hand point of the dotted line that comes next shows the return of owning a large number of stocks in a single industry and country – the most diversification we can get without adding extra industries. Adding another four industries and moving along the dotted line boosts performance considerably as inter-industry correlations are lower than intra-industry (I use 0.75 for average inter-industry correlation). However it's unrealistic to assume there are more than 10 or 11 distinct industries to allocate to.[105]

Further diversification can then be obtained by allocating across countries within a geographic region (for example within Europe), and across developed market regions (I use three: America, Europe, and Asia).

Should you diversify?

I've shown that diversification is useful, but now for the bad news: it usually isn't a free lunch. Putting your money into a wider range of assets is good in theory, but will probably increase your costs, mainly because of minimum brokerage fees. Is diversification still the smart thing to do?

Diversification costs and benefits

As an illustration, let's try to answer the following specific question: Should a UK investor[106] with £1,100 to invest in UK large cap equities buy a single share from a single industry (as we assume in this part of the book that we can't predict returns it doesn't matter which one), or put £100 into each of 11 shares, picked from each of 11 distinct industries?

First let's calculate the different **costs**. From the last chapter we know that the initial cost of buying individual shares is made up of **tax** (UK stamp duty at 0.5%), **brokerage fees** (I assume a minimum fee of £6 per trade), and invisible **bid-ask spread costs** (I assume

---

105. The most widely used GICS® industry classification system uses 11 top level groupings. I talk about this more in chapter ten.
106. Once again I apologise for using a UK example, but the trading costs in the US are far too reasonable to make this an interesting exercise.

0.05%). With trades this size we don't need to worry about **market impact**. For now I'm going to assume that there are no **rebalancing costs**, to keep the arithmetic simpler.

For the single £1,100 trade the brokerage fee will be 0.55% (£6 ÷ £1,100); adding up all the other costs we get 0.55% + 0.5% stamp duty + 0.05% bid ask cost = **1.1%**. For 11 trades of £100 the commission will be 6% (£6 × 11 ÷ £1,100) giving total initial costs of 6% + 0.5% + 0.05% = **6.55%**. I then need to apply the rule of 20 and divide the initial cost by 20 to get an annual cost. For a single share that gives me 1.1% ÷ 20 = **0.06%**, and for 11 shares 6.55% ÷ 20 = **0.33%**. All together diversifying costs an extra 0.33% – 0.06% = **0.27% a year**.

What about the benefits? Based on my research I estimated that the correlation of shares within the same country but from different sectors is 0.75; and that it is safe to assume that all shares have the same volatility of returns. After doing the calculations I found that going from 1 share to 11 will boost your geometric returns from around 1.36% to 2.18% a year. That is a benefit of 2.18% – 1.36% = **0.82%** versus extra costs of **0.27%**; a net improvement of more than half a percent. In this particular example diversification is definitely worth doing.

Uncertainty of returns when making decisions

The figures above don't tell the whole story. You can be very confident that buying 11 shares will cost you more. But how confident can you be that they will deliver extra returns through diversification?

We had this debate about the trade-off between returns and costs at AHL, the quantitative hedge fund where I used to work. You're probably imagining that we developed a highly sophisticated formula to give us the precise answer. In fact for several years we used a variation of the old proverb, "A bird in the hand is worth two in the bush."[107]

Our version of the proverb was that a more expensive trading system needed to earn twice as much more in pre-cost returns than the extra costs it attracted. In the simple example above we had nearly three *birds in the bush* (0.82% better pre-cost returns) for each *one in the hand* (0.27% worse cost). The precise ratio of birds in bushes, to birds in hands, is 0.82 ÷ 0.27 = 3.03. This is significantly more than two, suggesting the diversification is well worth doing. Though this comparison might seem simplistic, the basic idea that uncertain benefits have less value than certain costs is still valid.

Think back to the concept of **uncertainty of the past** which I introduced in chapter two. I said that we could never be completely confident about our statistical estimates of parameters like average return, risk and correlations; but we could **quantify that uncertainty**. In particular back in chapter three (figure 15 on page 69), I showed

---

107. You will be reassured to know that this was subsequently replaced by a much more complicated method.

there was considerable **past uncertainty** of correlation estimates in real data (although of course correlations are still a lot more predictable than average returns).

I've plotted the uncertainty in the correlation estimate I used for the 11 stock example in figure 31.

FIGURE 31: UNCERTAINTY IN CORRELATION ESTIMATE MEANS WE CAN'T BE SURE ABOUT DIVERSIFICATION BENEFITS

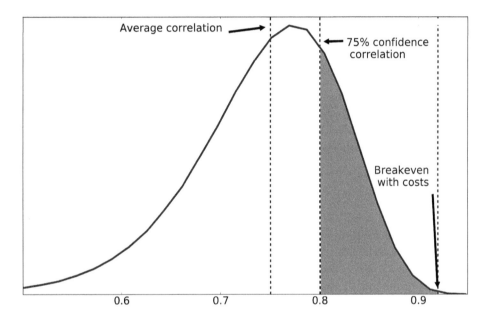

Uncertainty of correlation estimate for stocks in same country and different industries. The average is the expected correlation, 0.75. We can be 75% confident that the correlation is lower than 0.8. The breakeven point at which diversification still makes sense after costs for this example with £1,100 invested is 0.92.

The plot shows the **uncertainty of the past** using a distribution of possible correlation values. I estimated that the average correlation between stocks in different industries is 0.75,[108] but in practice I don't know precisely what the right figure is. However I am 75% confident that the correlation is less than 0.8; only a quarter of the distribution is to the right of this point (shaded in).

---

108. Technical note: For high average correlations the distribution becomes negatively skewed as correlations above 1.0 are not possible. Thus the mean correlation of 0.75 will not correspond to the median (a little higher at around 0.76), or the mode (which is clearly also higher than the mean).

At what level of correlation would diversification no longer make sense, given the costs we are facing in the eleven stock UK example? I calculated that the break-even correlation is 0.915 when maximising geometric mean, and 0.925 when going for the highest Sharpe Ratio. These break-evens are very similar, so at least with this particular example the different preferences of investors don't matter very much.

Clearly the breakeven correlation of around 0.92 is very extreme; there is almost no chance that the past correlation was actually higher than this. In this particular example we can be extremely confident that diversifying was the right thing to do.

Throughout this book I've checked that I can be pretty confident about the results of my analysis, even after accounting for the inherent uncertainty in correlation estimates.[109]

The effect of portfolio size on decisions

Now what if the UK investor has £500 instead of £1,100? What difference will this make to the results? Clearly the effect of minimum brokerage fees will make it costlier to hold smaller positions, but will this entirely overwhelm the benefits of diversifying? At what portfolio size does diversification become uneconomic?

To work this out we need to use the cost calculation tables I introduced in the previous chapter. First let's analyse the costs for different investments in a single share. These are shown in table 27.

Notice there are no holding costs for individual shares. You can see how the brokerage fees fall as a percentage when the purchase size gets larger. All other costs are fixed; the pre-cost geometric return is also constant at 1.36% (the same value I used earlier). The final row corresponds to the calculations I've already shown for a value of £1,100.

---

109. Technical note: I do this with correlations calculated using a 75% confidence interval. This is lower than the 95% usually used in statistical testing, as I want to be "pretty confident" not "nearly absolutely sure".

TABLE 27: COST CALCULATION TABLE – BUYING A SINGLE UK SHARE

Holding costs	Initial costs						All			
	Tax	Cmn.	Bid-Ask	Market impact	Initial Sub Total	Initial As Annual	Annual total	Pre-cost Geo. Return	Net Geo. Return	Net Sharpe Ratio
C	D	E	F	G	H = SUM (D:G)	J = H÷20	K = C+J	P	R = P - K	
£300		2.00%			2.55%	0.13%	0.13%		1.23%	0.0456
£309		1.90%			2.49%	0.12%	0.12%		1.24%	**0.0458**
£365	0%	0.5%	1.60%	0.05%	0%	2.19%	0.11%	0.11%	1.36%	**1.25%**	0.0463
£400		1.50%			2.05%	0.10%	0.10%		1.26%	0.0466
£1,100		0.55%			1.10%	0.06%	0.06%		1.31%	0.0483

Cost assumptions as per Appendix B. Geo. Return is the expected geometric return. Assumes one share has standard deviation of 27%.

Table 28 has the same calculations for a purchase of 11 shares. The pre-cost geometric return is higher because of diversification, but the initial costs are much greater for small portfolio values.

I've highlighted a figure in bold in the penultimate column of each table; this shows that the net geometric return after costs are identical at 1.25% when we have a portfolio value of £365. This is the **breakeven value** at which the portfolio of 11 stocks becomes more attractive than the single stock portfolio. With less than £365 to invest you should stick to one stock.

You can also see that the breakeven point is slightly lower if you focus on Sharpe Ratio rather than geometric mean: the Sharpe Ratio breakeven is shown in bold in the final column of each table, at a portfolio value of around £309.[110]

---

110.   These values are theoretical since in reality investing £309 or £365 in 11 stocks would leave you holding just £28 or £33 in each company. But in practice that wouldn't be enough to buy even a single share in many firms, like UK pharmaceutical firm AstraZeneca where one share currently costs £49.

TABLE 28: COST CALCULATION TABLE – BUYING 11 UK SHARES, ONE FROM EACH SECTOR

Holding costs	Initial costs						All			
	Tax	Cmn.	Bid-Ask	Market impact	Initial Sub Total	Initial As Annual	Annual total	Pre-cost Geo. Return	Net Geo. Return	Net Sharpe Ratio
C	D	E	F	G	H= SUM (D:G)	J= H÷20	K = C+J	P	R = P - K	
£300			22%		22.60%	1.13%	1.13%		1.05%	0.0443
£309			21%		21.90%	1.10%	1.10%		1.08%	**0.0458**
£365	0%	0.5%	19%	0.05%	19.40%	0.97%	0.97%	2.18%	**1.25%**	0.0463
£400			16%		17.10%	0.85%	0.85%		1.33%	0.0561
£1,100			6%		6.55%	0.33%	0.33%		1.85%	0.0781

Cost assumptions as per Appendix B. 'Geo. Return' is the expected geometric return. Breakeven values shown in bold. Assumes one share has standard deviation of 27% and correlation between shares is 0.75.

Risk or return?

Remember in chapter four I said there were two main types of investment portfolios:[111] lower risk, optimised for **maximum Sharpe Ratio**; and **maximum geometric mean portfolios** for investors who are gunning for a higher geometric return. Because of this different investors may choose different options when considering cost-benefit trade-offs, depending on their preferences.

For example, consider the following hypothetical example. Suppose you're considering a diversifying improvement to your portfolio. This increases the Sharpe Ratio by reducing volatility, but attracts a higher cost. Let's use some specific, though imaginary, numbers for the starting benchmark portfolio: initial arithmetic return 8%, volatility 20%, costs 1%, post-cost geometric return 5%, Sharpe Ratio 0.25. These figures are shown in the first row of table 29.

---

111. As well as a compromise portfolio which falls somewhere between the two.

TABLE 29: A HYPOTHETICAL EXAMPLE OF SOME CLOSE ALTERNATIVES

	Pre-cost arithmetic mean	Volatility	Pre-cost geometric mean	Cost	After-cost geometric mean	After-cost Sharpe Ratio
Benchmark	8%	20%	6%	1%	5%	0.25
More diversifying	8%	15%	6.9%	3%	3.9%	0.26

The diversifying option, shown in the second row of the table, has the same pre-cost arithmetic mean but costs 3% a year. However, I'm confident that the volatility will go down to 15%. As the second row of the table shows, the after-cost Sharpe will go up slightly to 0.26, but the after cost geometric return will fall to 3.9%.

Obviously it makes no sense at all for a return maximising investor to do this. But in theory an investor who wants the highest Sharpe Ratio would happily take this option. However, most investors will baulk at reducing their returns by more than a fifth (from 5% to 3.9%), for such a tiny improvement in Sharpe (from 0.25 to 0.26). Although I've chosen these figures deliberately for dramatic effect, this is still a problem you will encounter when making investment decisions in more realistic situations. How do we solve this conundrum?

In practice the main difference between Sharpe Ratio maximisers and geometric mean investors will be their asset allocation. The former will have more safe bonds, and the latter a larger proportion of riskier equities, as I already discussed in chapter four. But once the asset allocation has been done, and we're making decisions within asset classes, I am not going to differentiate between the two types of investors.

I will assume that anyone with a maximum Sharpe Ratio portfolio will be comfortable with the risk implied by their asset allocation, and will not want to give up yet more of their depleted geometric return for a slight improvement in Sharpe Ratio.

This means that throughout the rest of the book I'm going to **maximise geometric mean returns** when comparing portfolios,[112] except when I'm considering asset allocation. This means that I don't need to present every calculation twice for different investors.[113]

---

112. Technical note: In practice then I'm going to be using slightly larger and more conservative portfolio breakeven values than if I was catering to an orthodox Sharpe Ratio maximiser.
113. The results are usually pretty similar anyway. Remember in the simple example for UK investors considering buying 11 shares the breakeven correlation was 0.915 when maximising geometric mean, and 0.925 when going for the highest Sharpe Ratio.

The different costs of ETFs and individual shares

I'm now going to look at a specific application of the diversification benefits versus costs problem: What is the best way to get exposure to an equity market index like the US S&P 500?

There are two main alternatives: you can either **directly invest** in the individual shares that make up the index, or buy a passive **collective fund** that will track the index for you, such as an ETF.[114]

The advantage of direct investment is that you can choose your own weightings, and buy as much or as little of each share as you like. This means you can buy a more diversified portfolio than you'd get if you bought an index fund. In the next section I'll talk about different kinds of portfolio weighting and what advantages they might have. But before that we need to spend some time understanding the different cost structures of shares and ETFs.

Up front purchase costs

Individual shares

Although direct ownership in equities has no ongoing holding cost, it will definitely hurt more than ETFs in initial purchase costs. Partly this is because there is no stamp duty on ETFs in the UK, and in the US you can sometimes buy ETFs for zero commission. But mainly it is because a sizeable purchase of a single ETF tracker can only be replicated by buying 100 (for the FTSE 100) or 500 (for the S&P 500) individual shares, which means paying 100 or 500 sets of brokerage charges.

What about execution costs: market impact and bid-ask spread? Suppose you are putting $2,000,000 into the S&P 500. As I'm writing this you will be buying just over $62,000 of Apple Inc (just over 3% of the index), and just $31 of Lamb Weston holdings[115] (who apparently manufacture frozen potatoes and are 0.001545% of the index), plus positions in 498 other firms.[116]

---

114. I'm ignoring the possibility of using fancier kinds of passive funds, or actively managed funds, both of which I discuss in part three.

115. When I wrote this Lamb Weston were trading at $31: with a total investment in the S&P 500 of $2 million you can buy just a single share of Lamb Weston. So another problem is that you can only buy the entire index if you have an extremely large portfolio. With a smaller portfolio there will be large swathes of the index which you can't buy at all, or because you can't buy fractional shares you will have the wrong weight (even with $3 million you'd want $46 worth of Lamb Weston but you can only buy one share or two; giving you either $31 or $62 worth). This increases tracking error and thus embarrassment.

116. To be pedantic there are slightly more than 500 stocks in the S&P 500 because it contains some multiple share classes for certain firms.

As the largest trade ($62,000) is relatively puny there won't be any **market impact**. Instead it's safe to assume that the hidden execution costs will consist only of a bid-ask spread cost, which for US large cap stocks I assume to be 0.05%.

Up front cost of buying ETFs

Remember that the up front costs of a trade include the **visible** commissions, plus the invisible **execution cost**: bid-ask spread, and market impact on larger trades.

It's straightforward to work out the commission on a single ETF purchase. On small investments this will be the minimum brokerage charge. The bid-ask spread on liquid ETFs covering developed market indices like the S&P 500 is similar to the underlying shares or even tighter; I assume 0.05%.

On a trade of a couple of million you ought to be able to get institutional levels of commissions – perhaps 0.01% – with the same level of bid-ask spread cost. But for trades of this size market impact is more of a concern. If you look at the order book on a typical day it appears that the ETF market hasn't got anywhere near enough liquidity to do trades this size.

In practice large investors can work with ETF market makers to **create** new ETF units. Because this involves going out and buying the individual shares it is safe to assume that this will have a similar market impact to direct investment.

DIGRESSION: ETF CREATION AND REDEMPTION

Many moons ago there were only two types of collective investment fund: open ended and closed ended. US mutual funds and UK unit trusts were **open ended**; whilst UK investment trusts were **closed ended**, as were appropriately named US close ended funds.

Suppose an investor wanted to put more money into an open ended fund. They handed it to the manager, who went and bought the underlying shares to put inside the fund. When investors withdrew money the opposite happened. The fund itself couldn't be traded on a stock market like normal shares could. This made the pricing and fee structure more opaque (as I'll discuss in part three). However fund values tracked the value of the underlying shares very closely.

In contrast someone who wanted to invest in a closed ended fund went to the stock market and bought the fund off someone who already owned it. The underlying stocks in the fund weren't affected when this happened. This did mean that closed end funds often traded at a premium or a discount to the value of the investments inside them.

ETFs are a hybrid of open and closed ended funds. Normally they behave like closed ended funds; you buy and sell them on the stock market. Nothing happens to the underlying shares inside the fund when you trade the ETF.

However let's suppose you wanted to do a huge purchase of an ETF. You'd probably struggle to find liquidity in the market; it's unlikely there would be a seller wanting to do the opposite trade.

Instead you would go to the ETF market maker (these are called authorised participants) and new shares would be purchased to put inside the ETF. This **creates** new units in the ETF. The ETF market cap would increase in line with the additional money put inside. It's price would reflect the value of the underlying shares. Conversely a large sale would create a **redemption** of units.

This process is described in more detail in *The ETF Handbook* by Dave Abner.

The upshot of this is that for very large trades the market impact of an ETF purchase will be the same as buying the individual shares.

As I said above, a couple of million dollars invested in the S&P 500 implies the largest purchase will only be $62,000 in Apple, or roughly 500 shares at current prices. There won't be any noticeable market impact for a trade this size.

Holding costs

You have to pay **holding costs** when you own an ETF; visible management fees and invisible trading costs inside the fund. Once you've bought an individual share then it costs you nothing until you decide to sell it.

If you buy an ETF then the fund manager will take care of any **rebalancing** trades needed as stocks move in and out of the index. Strictly speaking for a fair comparison you should include the cost of replicating this activity if you opt for owning individual firms.[117] Based on my research, which is discussed in Appendix B, I assume this leads to portfolio turnover of around 10% a year,[118] i.e. with a million dollars in shares you'd be doing $100,000 of trading a year.

Conclusion

It's crazy to think that an investor can replicate what an ETF manager does more cheaply if they're trying to do **exactly** what they are doing: buying the same shares and then doing

---

117. However, unlike a passive fund manager you have a choice about doing these trades. I explain how you can reduce your rebalancing costs in part four.

118. I explain in Appendix B (page 483) how I calculated this number based on available research.

the same trades. Running large passive index trackers is a mechanistic process with mostly fixed costs which becomes much cheaper if you're doing it at a very large scale. Only if the manager is charging an excessively high annual fee might it make sense to try and outdo the ETF manager at their own game.

Instead, in the next part of the chapter I'll show you how to invest smartly in individual stocks without paying excessive costs by using **different** portfolio weights; a strategy the ETF manager can't copy as they have to stick slavishly to the index they're tracking.

DIGRESSION: ADMINISTRATION COSTS

There is an important caveat here. The costs I've calculated for direct investment exclude the extra **administration** costs that are involved. It might in theory be cheaper to invest directly in every stock in the S&P 500 rather than in a single ETF, but keeping track of 500 positions with assorted corporate actions and takeovers is a lot of work which an institutional manager will have to pay someone to do.

It's hard to quantify this cost but you shouldn't ignore it. If you're going to follow the index precisely by periodically rebalancing this will require further time and effort.

Theoretically very large-scale direct investment should be cheaper than any collective fund as most passive managers have to make a profit,[119] as well as pay regulatory and other frictional costs which only arise when you're dealing with other people's money. But the rock bottom, sub-0.10% fees, charged by the largest passive index managers like Vanguard and BlackRock on their cheapest products, will be hard to beat. These behemoth-sized managers are benefiting from considerable economies of scale in administration costs.

Retail investors who do their own administration should also consider what economists call the **opportunity cost** of their time. For example, suppose you earn $200 a day, and spend the equivalent of two days a year extra on your investment portfolio[120] because you've opted for direct investment rather than collective funds. Then on a $100,000 portfolio you're effectively paying $400 annually, or 0.4% a year in administration costs.

---

119. Vanguard is owned by the investors in their funds and so are effectively a non-profit organisation. This, plus their sheer size, is why they are so cheap.

120. If you get a financial advisor or accountant to do this for you you'll probably end up paying even more. US financial advisors cost upwards of $250, and in the UK financial advisers charge an average of £150 an hour.

Handcrafting, equal weighting, or market cap weighting?

Index funds will usually work out cheaper but there is an advantage to building your own portfolios of individual equities, which is that you can choose the **weightings**. When you buy an index fund you're stuck with the index weights, which for most indices are normally **market capitalisation**.[121]

Owning a market cap weighted portfolio makes sense if all the investors in the world have collectively come to the right decision about the value of each and every company.[122] But why should this automatically be the best way to weight, and select, a portfolio?

Does it seem reasonable that giant UK bank HSBC should have a much larger weight in the FTSE 100 index (5.5%) than its competitor Royal Bank of Scotland (RBS), with just 0.3% of the index? Some of the higher weight to HSBC can be justified by the lower volatility of it's share price in recent years, but even if I correct for that then the equivalent **risk weightings**[123] of the market cap portfolio still give HSBC ten times the weight of RBS.

Naturally it seems logical that larger companies, with higher earnings, should be worth more.[124] HSBC currently makes nearly £6 billion in annual profits, whilst RBS barely survived the financial crisis.

Looking at this from another perspective however, **a market cap portfolio assumes that investments in larger firms are expected to return more than those in smaller companies**. Otherwise there would be no reason to substantially up-weight HSBC versus RBS.

Now I don't expect RBS to outperform HSBC and start making bigger profits, but that doesn't mean that HSBC shares will massively outperform RBS on a risk-adjusted basis. The known bad news for RBS is already factored into its rock bottom price, as is the relatively rosy picture for HSBC. As I've already discussed, many, many times, **predicting future risk-adjusted returns is very difficult**. It's safest to assume that **risk-adjusted returns are identical**.

---

121. The vast majority of equity indices are market cap weighted; the Dow Jones and Nikkei 225 being the main exceptions. These are price weighted; but since price is proportional to market capitalisation they have similar properties to market cap indices.

122. Technical note: This is the key assumption of the Capital Asset Pricing Model.

123. Remember from chapter four that the risk weighting of a portfolio corrects for different assets having different levels of return volatility. Cash weightings will then be higher for safer assets and lower for riskier assets.

124. Actually company valuations are the product of the size of their earnings and the valuation that the market puts upon those earnings (price-to-earnings ratio). It's less obvious that companies with higher valuation ratios should be worth more. Facebook is currently forecast to earn about $7 billion in profits in 2017, whilst General Electric is expected to pull in over $10 billion. But as I write this Facebook is worth about 30% more than GE, because of its higher valuation.

There are two simple alternatives to market cap weighting, both of which assume that returns can't be forecasted. The most straightforward option is to give every firm in the index an **equal weight**. The second option is to use the **handcrafting method** which I introduced in chapter four. Handcrafted weights are allocated across, and then within, groups of assets within a portfolio. For stocks within an index this means allocating equally to industry sectors, and then equally to firms within sectors.

Here is a quick reminder of what these alternative weighting schemes assume:

Equal weighting	All shares get equal weights.
	Assumes: Correlations, risk, and risk-adjusted returns are identical. No statistical estimates are used to build the portfolio.
Handcrafted	Every industry gets an equal weight. Every relevant firm gets an equal weight within each industry.
	Assumes: Risk-adjusted returns are identical. Correlations are equal between equities in the same sector. Firms in different sectors have an equal correlation which is lower than the intra-sector figure. Risks are identical (when used with risk weighting).
	Uses historic correlations (may use estimates of historic risk when combined with risk weighting).
Market cap weighted	Weight assets by market capitalisation.
	Assumes: Market cap weights are best.
	Does not use any historic data apart from market cap weights.

How can you implement these different weighing methods? As I discussed earlier in the chapter, to buy market cap weighted portfolios you can use ETFs, or make direct investments in shares. Equal weighting can also be implemented by direct investment; whilst equally weighted ETFs are also fairly common. In contrast, funds that implement a top-down handcrafted portfolio are almost non-existent, so direct investment is the only realistic option.

Each of these alternative weighting schemes and investment routes will have their own costs and benefits.

Which weighting scheme makes sense in theory?

We now have five different options available for investing in the market:

1. Market capitalisation weighted ETFs.

2. Direct investment in a market cap portfolio.

3. Equal weighted ETF.

4. Direct investment in an equal weight portfolio.

5. Direct investment in a handcrafted portfolio.

Which is best? I'm first going to assume that expected risk-adjusted returns are identical, and see how different weighting schemes shape up in an idealised world where that is true. Later in the chapter I review the empirical evidence to see how well different weighting schemes have done in the real world.

Let's first consider equal weighting amongst groups of similar assets, such as equities in the same country and industry, like UK banks. It's reasonable to assume that these equities will have roughly the same correlation with each other, and about the same risk.

Because correlations are identical, an equally weighted portfolio will be the most diversified, which because of equal volatility will be the portfolio with the lowest risk. And because risk-adjusted returns are identical it will also have the highest return. In these circumstances equal weighting will be best.

Whilst this might be true **within** industries, it's less likely to be true **across** industries. A typical equity index will contain stocks from several different industries: utilities, technology stocks, and so on. Correlations won't be equal any more: shares from the same industry will have a higher correlation than those from different industries.

Strict equal weighting across firms will produce relatively concentrated portfolios if a few sectors are much larger than the rest. In these circumstances **handcrafting** should be better than equal weights.[125] A handcrafted portfolio that gives an identical risk weighting to each industry sector will be more diversified than one which weights every firm equally.

The advantage that equal and handcrafted weights have over any market cap alternative will depend on how concentrated the market cap portfolio is. Consider an imaginary market with 100 stocks, but where 99.99% of the index is in just one firm. That index will behave almost exactly like a portfolio with only one stock. From figure 29 earlier in the chapter, the geometric mean return for one stock is around a third less than for a large portfolio. The highly concentrated market cap index in our imaginary country will be significantly inferior to an equal weighted portfolio.

Clearly this is an unrealistic example, as in real life indices are never as skewed as that. Normally large indices in developed countries, like the S&P 500 in the US and UK FTSE 100, have less than 20% of the index in their top ten stocks.[126]

---

125. There is an unusual situation in which equal weighting and handcrafting produce exactly the same weights. This is when there are exactly the same number of stocks in each and every industry.
126. However, index weights do sometimes breach 10% in a single stock, as Vodafone did in the FTSE 100 during the late 1990s tech boom.

Smaller indices like the DAX 30 are more vulnerable to excessive concentration than those with 100 or 500 shares, like the FTSE and S&P 500. Emerging markets, and other countries with undiversified economies, will also be more concentrated. The Australian and Canada resource-heavy indices have around 50% of the index in the top ten stocks.

To evaluate different weighting schemes I'm going to use one of these relatively extreme indices: Canada. If equal weighting and handcrafting can't make the grade here, then they won't be much help in the US S&P 500. Warning: this example is quite detailed, but it will help you better understand the properties of different portfolio weighting schemes.

The Canadian TSX index has 60 constituents. At the time of writing, 12 of these firms are in the Materials sector and 14 in the Energy sector, with the rest spread across eight other sectors.[127] To construct the optimal portfolio here using my top-down **handcrafting** method, I first allocated one-tenth of my assets to each of the ten industry sectors. I then split each 10% equally amongst the stocks in a particular sector. So for example I ended up with 10% in Valeant, as it's the only firm in the health care business, whereas each of the 14 energy firms received 0.71% (one-fourteenth of 10%). Table 30 shows an extract from the portfolio.

This gives me a portfolio with the maximum diversification benefit, given my correlation assumptions (relatively high and equal correlations within industries; lower and equal correlations between industries). I did however have a 10% exposure to a single firm – Valeant – as it was unique in its sector. Of course this would be less of a problem in larger indices like the S&P 500 and FTSE 100 where there are almost always multiple firms in each sector.

---

127. This chapter was written after the standard GICS industry classification system expanded from 10 to 11 industry sectors in late 2016, but there are currently no Canadian firms in the newly created Real Estate sector.

TABLE 30: EXTRACT FROM A TSX 60 HANDCRAFTED PORTFOLIO

	Sector weight A	Stock	Stock weight in sector B	Weight A × B
Health care	10%	Valeant	100%	10%
Energy	10%	Suncor	7.1%	0.71%
Energy	10%	12 other firms	7.1% each	0.71% each
Materials	10%	Barrick gold	8.5%	0.85%
Materials	10%	11 other firms	8.5% each	0.85% each
Financials	10%	Royal Bank of Canada	10%	1%
Financials	10%	9 other firms	10% each	1% each
6 other sectors	60%	...		

Each sector gets one-tenth of the portfolio. Each firm gets an equal weight within the relevant sector.

What if I ignored sectors and equally weighted across the whole index? I'd get 1 ÷ 60 = 1.66% in each firm. So I'd be much less exposed to each individual firm. But this would mean a weight of 43.3% in the two largest sectors – energy and materials – with 26 firms between them; double their allocation in the handcrafted portfolio. This is highly concentrated, especially when you consider that these two industries are both exposed to similar economic factors. Table 31 shows an extract from the portfolio.

TABLE 31: EXTRACT FROM THE TSX 60 EQUAL WEIGHT PORTFOLIO

	Sector weight Sum (W)	Stock	Weight W
Health care	1.67%	Valeant	1.67%
Energy	21.7%	Suncor	1.67%
Energy	21.7%	12 other firms	1.67% each
Materials	20%	Barrick gold	1.67%
Materials	20%	11 other firms	1.67% each
Financials	14.7%	Royal Bank of Canada	1.67%
Financials	14.7%	9 other firms	1.67% each
6 other sectors	40%	...	

Each firm gets one-sixtieth of the portfolio (1.67%). The sector weights shown are the sum of weights for each firm within a sector.

In this particular example, the market cap weighted alternative is even more extreme (see table 32). At the time of writing, 38% is in just one sector, financials, while 20% is in energy. The largest firm has a weight of around 8%.

I'm now ready to compare the benefits of diversification against the costs. Remember there are five different options: (1) market cap weighting via ETFs, (2) market cap weighting with direct investment, (3) equal weighting via ETF, (4) equal weighting via direct investment, and (5) handcrafting via direct investment (not available in an ETF).

First of all I'm going to calculate the expected returns of each weighting scheme. These are shown in table 33. Notice that the pre-cost returns of each weighting scheme will be the same regardless of how we get the exposure: ETF or direct investment. I'm conservatively assuming correlation within industries is 0.85, and across industries is 0.75. These figures are based on my own research, and you can find them in Appendix B.

TABLE 32: EXTRACT FROM THE TSX 60 MARKET CAP WEIGHTED PORTFOLIO

	Sector weight Sum(W)	Stock	Weight W
Health care	0.9%	Valeant	0.9%
Energy	20.2%	Suncor	4.4%
Energy	20.2%	12 other firms	...
Materials	10.5%	Barrick gold	1.9%
Materials	10.5%	11 other firms	...
Financials	38.2%	Royal Bank of Canada	8.6%
Financials	38.2%	9 other firms	...
6 other sectors	30.1%	...	

Each firm is weighted by market capitalisation. The sector weights shown are the total weights of firms within each sector.

TABLE 33: WHAT IS THE EXPECTED PRE-COST PERFORMANCE OF DIFFERENT PORTFOLIO WEIGHTING SCHEMES FOR THE CANADIAN TSX 60 INDEX?

	Geometric mean	Sharpe Ratio
Market cap weighted	2.17%	0.0911
Equal weighted	2.20%	0.0932
Handcrafted	2.21%	0.0936

Market capitalisation weights correct as of early 2017. Hand crafted weights: Weight ten industries equally, then equal weight within industries. Assumes each stock has a standard deviation of 27% and arithmetic mean of 5%, correlation within industries 0.85, correlation across industries 0.75.

Notice how similar the numbers in the table are. Equal weighting is a little better than market cap, and handcrafting is slightly better than equal weighting, but the margin of improvement is tiny. Remember these results are for one of the most concentrated indices that's currently available in a developed equity market.

For a larger, more diversified, index like the S&P 500 there will be negligible difference between the different portfolio weighting options. However there are emerging market indices which are even smaller and more concentrated than the Canadian TSX 60 where equal and handcrafted weighting will show more of an improvement.

Now, what about costs? Earlier in the chapter I discussed the different cost structures of ETFs and shares. The management fee of the market cap weighted ETF for Canada is a relatively expensive 0.4% a year, and the equal weighted ETF is even more expensive at 0.5%. I assume that trading within the fund costs around 0.1% for the market cap ETF, and 0.4% for the equal weighted variation.[128]

Table 34 sums my findings once I include the effect of different costs levels; it shows the ranking of each option at different portfolio values.

TABLE 34: WHAT'S THE BEST WAY TO ALLOCATE ACROSS THE CANADIAN TSX EQUITY INDEX?

	Best option	2nd best	3rd best	4th best	Worst option
$7,500	ETF mkt cap	Direct H/C	Direct E/W	Direct mkt cap	ETF E/W
$10,000	ETF mkt cap	Direct H/C	Direct E/W	Direct mkt cap	ETF E/W
$15,000	Direct H/C	Direct E/W	Direct mkt cap	ETF mkt cap	ETF E/W
$100,000	Direct H/C	Direct E/W	Direct mkt cap	ETF mkt cap	ETF E/W
Institution	Direct H/C	Direct E/W	Direct mkt cap	ETF mkt cap	ETF E/W

E/W is equal weighting. H/C is handcrafting. Mkt Cap is market capitalisation weighting. Direct is investing directly in individual shares. ETF is purchasing an Exchange Traded Fund. Ranking done on geometric mean after costs. ETF management fees used: Equal weighted 0.5% a year, Market cap weighted 0.4% a year.

These results have some interesting implications. Firstly the equal weighted ETF is hopelessly uncompetitive. It has a slightly higher return than the market cap weighted ETF before costs, but the significantly higher management fee plus extra trading within the fund squanders that advantage.

128. When the price of a stock increases, its market cap weight will increase at the same weight. So rebalancing is only necessary when constituents move in or out of the index; normally every three months. With equal weighting or handcrafting a stock price increase would mean selling some of the share that has gone up, and buying others. It's for this reason that the costs of trading within the fund are higher for an equally weighted ETF than they are for the market cap weighted fund.

I wouldn't invest in an equal weighted ETF unless I expected it to have similar holding costs to a market cap weighted fund. The pre-cost return advantage is too slim to overcome any additional charges. Assuming that the trading costs within the fund are 0.3% higher, this implies the **management fee must be 0.3% lower for an equal weighted fund versus a market cap alternative to make it worthwhile.**[129] As the vast majority of equal weighted funds have a higher management fee, the smartest option is to steer clear of equal weighted funds.

Secondly all forms of direct investment have virtually identical costs. So you should select the option that has the highest pre-cost return; given the assumptions I'm making this will be the handcrafting method, followed closely by equal weighting and then market cap weighting.

Finally the breakeven point at which direct investment makes sense is around $15,000. Canada has an exceptionally low breakeven point due to its relatively costly ETF, and relatively modest index of just 60 stocks. Break-evens in other countries are much higher; around £750,000 for the FTSE100 and $325,000 for the S&P 500. Using handcrafted weights doesn't affect the breakeven point for direct investment very much, as it only adds a tiny amount to pre-cost returns. **Small investors can't afford to invest directly in the entire market**.

Later in this chapter I explore whether smaller investors can afford direct investment by buying a **partial selection** of the stocks in a given index.

Which weighting scheme makes sense in practice?

What I've done above is an entirely theoretical analysis which assumes that risk and risk-adjusted returns are the same for all assets, and assumes a certain level for correlations. But how have these different weighting schemes done in reality?

Ideally I should compare the actual performance of market cap and equally weighted passive index funds for the same index. However, there are no equally weighted funds that have been around long enough to give a statistically meaningful result from doing this kind of analysis. Plus there aren't any funds using handcrafting, so I can't analyse that method at all.

Instead I spent some time reading the available academic research on equal versus market cap weighting.[130] This research was done by looking at the returns of individual stocks to

---

129. This result is for large cap developed market equities. For small and mid cap firms, or emerging markets, an even bigger discount would be needed.

130. Here are some of the most relevant references: 'Bayes' Revenge? A review of Equal-Weighting As an Active Management Strategy' (Lloyd Kurtz), 'Optimal Versus Naive Diversification' (Raman Uppal et al), 'An Investor's Guide to Smart Beta Strategies' (Jason Hsu et al). It's also worth reading the Jan/Feb 2011 edition of the *Journal of Indexes*, which has several useful articles.

see how well a hypothetical equal weighted fund would have performed against a market cap weighted alternative.

The consensus is that equal weighting is better. Most researchers find volatility to be a little higher for equally weighted portfolios, but with even higher returns, leading to better Sharpe Ratios.[131]

There is less research on handcrafting but I did find one relevant paper.[132] This analysed the performance of 'sector equal weighting', which is effectively identical to handcrafted weights, versus the alternative of weighting equally across index constituents. Again these findings were much better than my theoretical results.

There's a clear conflict here between the very modest improvements I saw in my theoretical calculations above and these much more convincing empirical results. I can think of a few possible explanations.

Firstly, over recent years correlations between stocks have increased, so historical correlations in older research are likely to be lower. Bearing in mind the uncertainty around correlation estimates, I've used conservative figures that I think are realistic and achievable in the future.

Secondly, it is well known that smaller firms have historically done better than large capitalisation stocks. But a firm which is ranked 50–60 in the Canadian TSX index (average capitalisation $4 billion) can hardly be considered 'small'.

Finally, the market cap index will give higher weightings to stocks that have recently done well, whilst an equal weighted index will buy losers and sell winners. The past return of a stock sometimes gives us a clue as to how it will do in the future; chasing winners and selling lagging stocks works well for investment horizons of around six months to a year, but for shorter and longer holding periods it is better to sell your winners.[133] It might be that equal weighting is generating extra returns from buying recent losers and selling winners.

Although all this evidence tips the scales slightly further in favour of equal weighting and handcrafting, I'm still not convinced that the benefits will be large enough to compensate when costs are significantly higher. In particular I still think most equal weighted ETFs are far too expensive relative to vanilla market cap weighted tracking funds.

I repeat my advice: the smart option is to **stick to a market cap weighted ETF except in the unlikely event that you can find an equal weight ETF that is at least 0.3% cheaper in annual management fees.**

---

131. Larger stocks usually have lower risk, which could explain why equal weighted portfolios typically end up with higher risk than their market cap weighted counterparts.
132. Pradeep Velvadapu, 'The Evolution of Equal Weighting' (*Journal of Indexes*, 2011).
133. I explain how to exploit this effect in part three.

Are capped indices any good?

Quite recently, a number of new ETFs have been launched using **capped** indices: '25/50' and '10/40' are common variants. A 25/50 index like that used by MSCI Brazil ETF EWZ uses normal market cap weights, except that the weight of any single company is capped at 25% of the index. The weight of 5% of the companies in the index (e.g. the top 12 in the 58 company Brazilian index) is capped at 50%. 10/40 indices work in a similar way.

These make extreme indices less concentrated and more diversified. These are particularly useful for emerging markets where the weighting can be even more extreme than Canada, and the chance of a total loss in a single firm is higher than in the developed world. The turnover inside the fund will be lower than equal weighting although still higher than market cap weights, but the benefits will also be less than you'd get with full equal weighting.

Again I'd only consider a capped index if they had a **lower management fee** than a market cap weighted alternative. A discount of 0.1% a year in annual fees should be enough to compensate for the higher trading costs inside the fund. The Brazilian 25/5-EWZ ETF has a management fee of 0.48% which, unusually, is cheaper than the nearest market cap weighted competitor fund: DBBR with an annual fee of 0.6%. In this case the capped fund is clearly the smarter option.

Buy the whole index, or just part of it?

It doesn't matter whether you choose conventionally dull market capitalisation weights, boringly simple equal weighting, or my favorite handcrafted weights; buying every share in the index is too expensive unless you have serious amounts of money to invest. Even large investors might balk at the administrative costs of keeping track of thousands of holdings across multiple countries. Would it really be so bad to buy just a few of the shares in a market index?

Buying fewer shares has one big advantage: it will be much cheaper for small investors because you have to pay fewer sets of minimum brokerage fees. But there are two significant disadvantages. The first is **embarrassment**: not owning the entire index means your returns will deviate from the benchmark. The second problem is more serious: owning fewer shares means you will have a **less diversified** portfolio. This will increase your portfolio risk and, assuming risk-adjusted returns are identical, you'll end up with lower expected geometric returns and a poorer Sharpe Ratio.

How can you select shares from the index to minimise these problems? The answer is to use the top-down **handcrafting** method. Start by giving each industry sector in the index an equal risk weighting. Then decide how many stocks you can afford to buy in each industry. At a minimum you'll need one stock per industry sector; up to 11 shares. If you can't manage that, then you should stick with buying a single ETF for the whole country. This will give you the most **diversified** portfolio that is possible given the size of your investment.

Next you need to pick your stocks. Assuming that risk-adjusted returns are identical your choice of firm will have no effect on geometric mean returns or Sharpe Ratio. So to minimise embarrassment you should pick the firm, or firms, with the largest market cap in each sector. That will give you a portfolio with the lowest possible **tracking error** to the index (although there will still be some tracking error of course).

Let's see how this strategy works out. This time I'm going to evaluate it using the S&P 500 index. It's a large index, so I'd expect choosing only a few stocks to have a significant effect on performance. Choosing the largest stock in each sector will give me around 15% of the total market cap weight in the index. If this turns out okay in the S&P then it should be just fine in smaller indices like the Canadian TSX 60 where buying the largest stock in each sector adds up to 30% of the total market cap.

I considered full handcrafting: buying every single stock in each sector; and also buying just one, two or three stocks in each of the eleven sectors. The expected performance of each option is shown in table 35. Owning one stock per industry sector reduces returns versus full handcrafting, but not by much. Table 36 shows my findings once I include the effect of costs.

TABLE 35: WHAT IS THE EXPECTED PERFORMANCE OF DIFFERENT PORTFOLIO WEIGHTING, FOR DIRECT INVESTMENT IN THE S&P 500?

	Geometric mean	Sharpe Ratio
Full handcrafted 500 stocks	2.23%	0.0949
Handcrafted 3 stocks per industry	2.22%	0.0939
Handcrafted 2 stocks per industry	2.21%	0.0934
Handcrafted 1 stock per industry	2.18%	0.0920

Handcrafted weights: Weight 11 industries equally, then equal weight within industries over all stocks (full) or a limited selection of stocks. Assumes each stock has a standard deviation of 27% and arithmetic mean of 5%, correlation within industries 0.85, correlation across industries 0.75.

TABLE 36: WHAT'S THE OPTIMAL NUMBER OF SHARES TO BUY IN EACH SECTOR?

	Best option	**2nd best**	**3rd best**	**4th best**
$22,000	1 share	2 shares	3 shares	All
$44,000	2 shares	1 share	3 shares	All
$66,000	3 shares	2 shares	1 share	All
Institution	All	3 shares	2 shares	1 share

Ranking done on geometric mean after costs, for a given investment in the S&P 500 (rows). Assumes we equal weight shares bought within each sector.

This implies you need at least $66,000 to invest in a given country to buy three shares in each of the 11 industry sectors, and $44,000 to justify buying two shares in each sector. With less than that, it makes sense to buy just 11 shares, one in each sector.

These results can be summarised as follows: **don't buy less than $2,000 of each share when considering whether to buy more than one share per sector.** With less than $22,000 an ETF **might** make more sense, although the exact breakeven point will depend on the management fee you get charged and the invisible trading costs within the fund.

All these figures are accurate for the minimum brokerage fee of $1 per trade which I assume a US investor will pay. I'll explain how you can adapt these findings for different commission levels and for the UK in the next section.

These results will be different in other contexts – across countries and asset classes, where correlations are lower. With lower correlations, diversification would be significantly reduced by partial selection. I don't recommend selecting certain countries and ignoring others and I certainly wouldn't drop entire geographic regions or asset classes.

The smartest way to invest in a given country

If I pull together all the findings in this chapter so far, they boil down to two possible routes for investing in a given country.

First route: Below a certain threshold of total investment size, investors should stick to **buying a market cap weighted ETF.** Table 37 (US investors) and table 38 (UK investors) show the breakeven value for investing in a given country below which investors should stick to ETFs, given the total holding cost of the ETF (rows) and the minimum brokerage charge (columns). The total holding cost will be the annual management fee, plus the invisible trading cost inside the fund.

TABLE 37: WHAT'S THE MINIMUM INVESTMENT TO MAKE DIRECT SHARE BUYING WORTHWHILE FOR US INVESTORS?

	Minimum brokerage fee, $			
	$1	**$2**	**$5**	**$10**
ETF holding cost 0.1%	$15,000	$30,000	$65,000	$150,000
ETF holding cost 0.2%	$6,000	$12,000	$30,000	$60,000
ETF holding cost 0.3%	$4,000	$8,000	$20,000	$40,000
ETF holding cost 0.4%	$3,000	$6,000	$15,000	$30,000
ETF holding cost 0.5%	$2,350	$4,700	$12,000	$24,000
ETF holding cost 0.75%	$1,600	$3,200	$8,000	$16,000
ETF holding cost 1%	$1,200	$2,400	$6,000	$12,000
ETF holding cost 1.25%	$950	$1,900	$4,700	$9,500
ETF holding cost 1.5%	$800	$1,600	$4,000	$8,000
ETF holding cost 2.0%	$600	$1,200	$3,000	$6,000

Table shows breakeven point at which selective direct investment is cheaper than buying a market cap weighted ETF. Breakeven point based on geometric mean after costs. Direct investment: Assumes buying one share within each sector, equally weighted. Rebalancing costs assuming portfolio is turned over 10% a year. ETF holding cost is management fee plus trading cost within fund (calculate this using the methods in this chapter, or you can use 0.1% annually for large cap developed market funds). All other assumptions as per Appendix B.

TABLE 38: WHAT'S THE MINIMUM INVESTMENT TO MAKE DIRECT SHARE BUYING WORTHWHILE FOR UK INVESTORS?

	Minimum brokerage fee, £			
	£6	**£10**	**£15**	**£20**
ETF holding cost 0.1%	£120,000	£200,000	£300,000	£400,000
ETF holding cost 0.2%	£45,000	£80,000	£120,000	£160,000
ETF holding cost 0.3%	£27,000	£45,000	£65,000	£90,000

	Minimum brokerage fee, £			
	£6	**£10**	**£15**	**£20**
ETF holding cost 0.4%	£20,000	£32,000	£48,000	£65,000
ETF holding cost 0.5%	£15,000	£25,000	£37,000	£50,000
ETF holding cost 0.75%	£10,000	£17,000	£24,000	£34,000
ETF holding cost 1%	£7,500	£12,000	£18,000	£24,000
ETF holding cost 1.25%	£6,000	£10,000	£15,000	£20,000
ETF holding cost 1.5%	£4,700	£8,000	£12,000	£16,000
ETF holding cost 2.0%	£3,500	£6,000	£9,000	£12,000

Table shows breakeven point at which selective direct investment is cheaper than buying a market cap weighted ETF. Breakeven point based on geometric mean after costs. Direct investment: Assumes buying one share within each sector, equally weighted. Rebalancing costs assuming portfolio is turned over 10% a year. ETF holding cost is management fee plus trading cost within fund (calculate this using the methods in this chapter, or you can use 0.1% annually for large cap developed market funds). All other assumptions as per Appendix B.

TABLE 39: WHAT'S THE MINIMUM VALUE TO MAKE ADDITIONAL SHARE PURCHASES WORTHWHILE FOR US AND UK INVESTORS?

Minimum brokerage fee, $	**$1**	**$2**	**$5**	**$10**
US investors	$2,000	$4,000	$10,000	$20,000
Minimum brokerage fee, £	**£6**	**£10**	**£15**	**£20**
UK investors	£10,000	£18,000	£27,000	£35,000

Minimum investment per share when deciding whether to buy additional shares in each sector for a given minimum brokerage fee, assuming you are already invested in one share per sector.

Second route: If you have enough money it is feasible to **buy selected individual stocks** to get exposure to a given country. Use the handcrafted method: put equal risk weights into each industry sector within the relevant country and then buy the largest firm in each sector (the firm with the biggest market cap) first.[134] If you have the funds to do so, also buy the second largest, third largest, and so on.

Table 39 shows the minimum investment **per share** to justify buying additional shares in each sector for both the US and the UK. You should always have 11 shares (one in each sector, assuming every sector is represented in the relevant index), or 22 shares (two per sector), or 33, and so on.

By the way, the calculation works differently for the first share you buy in each sector, versus any subsequent shares, which is why there are two separate sets of tables. So, for example, in the US with a $1 commission, the minimum investment per share to buy additional firms in each sector is $2,000. If you can't afford to invest $2,000 × 22 = $44,000 into a given country then you can only have one share per sector.[135]

However, you might easily have less than $2,000 in each share, since even with the very cheapest ETF with an annual cost of 0.1% the breakeven from table 37 is a $15,000 investment in the entire country, or $1,364 per share. This apparent inconsistency isn't a problem since the calculations work differently for the first share in each sector, and subsequent shares.

Here is another example. Let's suppose you had $100,000 allocated to a given country, and pay a minimum brokerage fee of $5. You are considering investing in an ETF which charges 0.1% a year in management fee and which you estimate accrues 0.1% in invisible trading costs inside the fund. Looking at the 0.2% row and $5 column in table 37, the breakeven for individual share ownership is a total portfolio value of $30,000, which is comfortably exceeded.

Now look at table 39. For a $5 minimum fee you should hold at least $10,000 per share. To buy two stocks in each of the 11 sectors would need 11 × 2 × $10,000 = $220,000 in total to invest in the country. You don't have enough cash, so you should stick to buying one share per sector. Again it doesn't matter that $100,000 isn't enough to buy one share worth $10,000 in each sector, as there are two separate decisions with different criteria: the ETF versus buying shares directly decision, and the second decision to buy additional shares in each sector.

One more example, this time from the UK. Suppose you pay a minimum brokerage fee of £12 per share, and have £500,000 to invest in the UK. Although a £12 minimum isn't shown in table 38, the values in each column are just pro-rata multiples of each other. So you can multiply the values in the £6 minimum fee column by £12 ÷ £6 = 2.

---

134. I consider alternative methods for selecting stocks in part three. I discuss whether you should hang on to the same stocks, or replace them periodically, in part four.

135. Later, you'll see that if you invest in a given country with equal risk weights, you won't have equal cash weights since sectors don't all have the same volatility. So if you invest $88,000 in a given country some sectors will have less than $4,000; and others will have more than $4,000. I've accounted for this in my calculations for these tables.

Regardless of ETF holding cost you will easily have enough for direct investment, but how many shares can you buy in each sector? Multiplying the minimum per share amount of £10,000 (from table 39, £6 column) by a pro-rata factor of 2 gives you £20,000. To hold two shares per sector would need 11 × 2 × £20,000 = £440,000. You can afford to do this; but three shares per sector (£660,000) is out of your league.

You should divide the full £500,000 equally between 11 sectors,[136] about £45,500 each, and then split that in half for each pair of shares: around £27,200.

Does diversifying by buying multiple funds make sense?

I've now dealt pretty comprehensively with the question of whether buying individual shares or funds makes sense. However for many investors it's more relevant to ask **if they should diversify a portfolio of funds**. If for example you own a single global market capitalisation weighted equities fund, is it worth dividing it into a developing and emerging market fund?

The answer is complicated and depends on the additional return expected from diversifying away from market cap weights as well as any extra costs. I discussed the costs part of the problem in the previous chapter. Moving away from a single fund and replacing it with more granular funds normally increases costs, for a couple of reasons.

Firstly you are reducing your exposure to highly liquid markets like the US and increasing it in less liquid countries. So after diversifying you will probably end up with higher management fees, trading costs within the fund will be higher, and both bid-ask spreads and market impact can increase.

Secondly, and more significant for smaller investors, is the effect of minimum brokerage fees. If you're investing £500 in one UK fund it will cost you £6; that's £6 ÷ £500 = 1.2%, or 1.2% ÷ 20 = 0.06% annually once you've converted it into using the **rule of 20** I introduced in chapter five. However, buying two £250 chunks of two different funds will incur two chunks of minimum commission: £12, which works out to 0.12% a year. With other higher costs factored in it's unlikely that diversifying will bring in enough benefit to overcome that extra 0.06% a year in costs.

Clearly putting just £250 into a fund doesn't make sense, but what is the minimum viable investment?

Although there is no straightforward answer to this question it is possible to come with some general guidelines. If I make some assumptions about the typical increase in holding costs, execution costs and diversification benefits, then the only remaining factor is the

---

136. In practice even with equal risk weighting you'll probably not have equal cash amounts in each sector because sectors have different risk. I discuss the cash weightings you should use when allocating sector weights in chapter eleven.

effect of minimum brokerage charges. Table 40 shows the lowest viable investment per fund for a given minimum commission level.

TABLE 40: WHAT'S THE LOWEST VIABLE INVESTMENT PER FUND TO AVOID PAYING EXCESSIVE COSTS GIVEN THE MINIMUM BROKERAGE FEE?

Minimum fee	UK investors	US investors
Free		$300
1	£300	**$300**
2	£600	$600
5	£1,500	$1,500
6	**£1,800**	$1,800
10	£3,000	$3,000
15	£4,500	$4,500
20	£6,000	$6,000

Lowest investment per fund when deciding whether to split up an investment in a single fund into a more diversified portfolio. Each row shows the investment size given a minimum brokerage commission in the relevant currency. Columns are for investors in different countries. Values in bold are the defaults I use in this book. Assumes that diversification benefit cancels out higher holding costs. All other assumptions as per Appendix B.

So, for example, if you are considering splitting an investment of $6,000 into two purchases of $3,000 then that would be fine, as long as your minimum brokerage fee was $10 or lower. Notice that the values shown can also be found by multiplying the ratio of the minimum brokerage fees. The minimum investment per fund for a $2 minimum commission is exactly twice that for a $1 minimum commission, and so on.

I've highlighted in bold the default commission levels I'm using in this book in the table. **So for a UK investor (paying the default £6 minimum), the break-even minimum investment per fund is £1,800; whilst for a US investor (paying $1) the minimum is $300.** Throughout the book whenever you see a minimum portfolio value then that has been calculated assuming $1 and £6 minimum fees.

If your brokerage minimum is different then you should multiply the portfolio value shown by the ratio of your minimum to $1 or £6 respectively. For example if a minimum portfolio value of £10,000 is shown, and your minimum commission is £12, then the minimum portfolio value you should use is £10,000 × (£12 ÷ £6) = £20,000.[137]

Key points

Diversification is good...	It's the only way to enhance your portfolio's performance if you cannot predict risk-adjusted returns.
... but it costs money	Splitting scarce funds into small chunks brings diversification, but can also cost more thanks to the tyranny of minimum brokerage fees and higher ETF management fees.
All investors should:	Avoid buying less than $300 or £1,800 of any ETF. If your minimum brokerage commission is higher than $1 or £6 then you will need to multiply these values by the ratio of your minimum brokerage fee to the minima I'm using.
Smaller investors should:	Buy a market capitalisation weighted ETF to get exposure to a given country.
Larger investors should:	If you have sufficient money to invest in a given country (tables 37 and 38, page 171 onwards) then you can buy individual shares. Split your allocation equally between industry sectors (equal risk weightings). Then buy the firm with the largest market capitalisation in each sector.
Very large investors should:	If you have enough money to add an extra share in every sector (table 39, page 172) then you can add one, two, three or more firms. Add the second largest firm by market cap, third largest, and so on. Stick to equally weighting within each sector.

That's the end of part one. I use these results, and everything else I've covered in part one, to start constructing portfolios in part two.

---

137.   US investors lucky enough to have commission-free trading on some ETFs should still use $300 as their minimum investment per fund.

PART TWO
Creating
—— *Smart* ——
Portfolios

Part Two: Creating Smart Portfolios

"Diversification should be the corner stone of your investment program. If you have your wealth in one company, unexpected troubles may cause a serious loss; but if you own the stocks of 12 companies in different industries, the one which turns out badly will probably be offset by some other which turns out better than expected."

— Sir John Templeton, legendary UK fund manager

In part two I describe a top-down **handcrafting** procedure for creating diversified portfolios, based on the methods I developed in part one.

This part of the book is a highly detailed construction manual for building portfolios. In places it is very dense, and there are numerous tables. You should not expect to read this part in one sitting unless you are looking for a cure for insomnia, and there are some parts of it you may never need to read.

Everyone should read the first two chapters. Chapter seven introduces the top-down method. Subsequent chapters then talk about different levels of a top-down portfolio. Chapter eight starts at the highest level with asset allocation: between equities, bonds and the exotic fare of alternative assets.

I then delve into specific asset classes — these chapters are optional depending on the amounts you have to invest, as chapter eight will explain. Chapter nine explains how to allocate amongst alternative assets such as hedge funds and commodity ETFs. Then chapters ten and eleven discuss equities: chapter ten covering the weighting scheme to use across countries, and chapter eleven delving into equities within countries. Chapter twelve deals with bonds.

Finally, chapter thirteen brings everything together and shows several examples of top-down portfolios for different investors. This chapter is compulsory reading for everyone. Some readers may find it helpful to read this after reading chapter seven as it gives an overview of the process outlined in chapters eight to twelve. Alternatively you could follow through the examples in chapter thirteen at the same time as reading the earlier chapters.

Throughout part two I assume that nobody can or should try to predict risk-adjusted returns. Part three explains what changes you should make to your portfolio construction process if that statement is untrue.

CHAPTER SEVEN

A Top-Down Approach to Building Smart Portfolios

A BOTTOM-UP APPROACH TO BUILDING PORTFOLIOS INVOLVES picking specific firms that take your fancy. Your exposure to asset classes, countries and industries is just an accidental consequence of whatever companies you happen to favour at the moment.

In contrast, a **top-down** approach to portfolio allocation means you decide your portfolio weights at the highest level first: allocating cash between asset classes like bonds and equities. You then break down each asset class, so for equities you'd split up your portfolio into individual countries, industries, and then into specific firms. Your exposure to asset classes, countries and industries will be deliberately thought out.

In part two I use the top-down **handcrafting** method for portfolio construction that I introduced in chapter four. In this chapter I explain why I use a top-down approach for portfolio construction, and provide an overview of how the process works.

Chapter overview

Why is top-down smart?	I justify why a top-down portfolio is better than the alternative.
The top-down portfolio	Going into detail about the process of constructing top-down portfolios.
The road map	Explaining how the chapters in the rest of part two fit together.
Issues to consider	Some practical considerations when using the top-down method.

Why is top-down smart?

Why do I advocate using a **top-down** approach to portfolio construction? Wouldn't it be better to first select the equities or funds you think will do best, and let the asset allocation just happen naturally? If for example you think that Italian banking stocks are currently cheap, then what is so bad about having the majority of your portfolio in Italian banks?

If you agree with this point of view then you clearly haven't read part one very carefully. In part one I showed that it's almost impossible to predict risk-adjusted returns by using historical data. When risk-adjusted returns can't be forecasted, selecting stocks or funds is a complete waste of time and effort. Instead you should be focusing on buying the most diversified portfolio possible. Diversification is the only way to get better performance if you can't forecast returns. And diversifying means investing in a wide range of assets across asset classes, countries and industries; not just in Italian banks!

There are in fact a number of advantages to using a top-down approach:

Forces diversification – reduces home and asset class bias	A bottom-up portfolio made up of your favourite stock picks and ETFs might be heavily concentrated. Investors have a liking for equities or bonds in their own country (known as **home bias**), or in particular industries.* Furthermore, many investors have an unhealthy obsession with buying stocks, whilst others have a strong aversion to the idea of owning any equities at all. In contrast, top-down portfolios will be properly diversified across asset classes, countries and industries.
Isolated decisions	Trying to allocate a portfolio with a dozen or even hundreds of different assets is quite a daunting prospect. By using the top-down method you break this down into a series of simpler decisions about smaller groups of assets. Each of these problems can be resolved in isolation from the others.
Better for smaller accounts	Because of minimum brokerage fees, investors with smaller accounts can only buy a limited number of assets, as I discussed in chapter six. A top-down methodology ensures as much diversification as possible when the investor can only afford to buy a handful of funds.
Limited scope for hubris causing harm	In part one I pointed out that predicting future returns is difficult. Nevertheless I realise that many readers will still believe that they, or their favourite fund manager, does possess that rare ability to see into the future. This is something I will discuss more in part three. Using a top-down method means that diversification will still be maintained and potentially dangerous stock picking limited to a small part of the portfolio.**

* I used to like buying financial firms: insurance companies, investment management firms and banks, whose businesses I thought I understood. This was prior to 2008. After that I realised that nobody really understood the financial industry.

** For example, you may think you have particular expertise in Japanese car manufacturers. In a bottom up portfolio it would be tempting to put a large chunk of your money into Toyota, Mitsubishi or one of their corporate brethren. Your asset, country and sector allocation would be highly concentrated. Even if you were a genius stock picker you'd be exposed to a downturn in Japanese Autos. With a top-down allocation process you can mix and match active and passive approaches; collective funds and individual shares. So you'd allocate the correct portion of your portfolio towards equities, an appropriate allocation of your equities to Japan, and the right amount of your Japanese equities to auto stocks. Only then should you pick your favourite car marques. The rest of your portfolio can then remain in a set of passive indexed funds with a diversified set of allocations. If it turns out your crystal ball for Japanese car stocks is not totally accurate then the damage to your wealth will be relatively small.

The top-down portfolio

I'm now going to explain in more detail how a top-down allocation actually works, and show you how I present top-down portfolios throughout the rest of the book.

Imagine for a moment that you have access to every financial asset in the world. There are around 8,000 publicly listed stocks in the US market alone, to say nothing of the rest of the world, plus all the bonds and more esoteric instruments that are available. There are also something like 6,500 listed ETFs, plus countless US mutual funds and UK unit trusts. That is a *lot* of assets. Trying to properly optimise the portfolio weights of every global asset simultaneously would make even a supercomputer crash.

How on earth can you possibly start with the job of building a portfolio out of this vast pool? What is a smart way to deal with this problem? The first step is to form the assets you have into **groups** which contain similar securities. To make your task easier there should initially be a relatively small number of groups, with each group containing a large number of assets. The obvious way to start grouping is by **asset class**.

Portfolio 10 shows this initial stage of the top-down process. I've divided the portfolio into two components, one for each of the two asset classes I'm using in this example.

PORTFOLIO 10: A SIMPLE TOP-DOWN EXAMPLE STEP ONE: ASSET CLASSES

Portfolio	
Equities 50% **(29.4%)**	Bonds 50% **(70.6%)**

Remember from chapter four that there are two kinds of portfolio weight: **risk weightings** assume that all assets have the same volatility of returns, and **cash weightings** which translate these into real money weights that account for different levels of risk.

In portfolio 10 the risk weightings are in normal font and the recommended cash weightings[138] using my own estimates of volatility are shown in **bold**. I use this convention in the rest of the book. Where I show both kinds of weights the cash weightings will also be in brackets. Sometimes there will only be cash weightings – they will still be in bold but not bracketed. Notice that bonds, which are safer than equities, get a higher cash weight despite having an equal risk weight.[139]

I can now drill down into the second level of the portfolio. In this case I'm going to allocate to different countries. Portfolio 11 shows how I'd do this if there were just four countries in each asset class.

A nice way of thinking about top-down portfolios is to pretend they are a set of nested boxes. Like Russian dolls, but rectangular, and without the traditional costume. The largest outer box contains the entire portfolio. You open it up and find two more smaller boxes, one for each asset class. If you open up each of the asset class boxes you'll find yet more boxes for each country, and so on.

The appeal of the top-down strategy is that you can first decide the size and composition of the outer boxes without yet worrying about what's going on inside them. You can then deal with the inside of each box without reference to what's going on around it, or being concerned with the internal contents of any smaller boxes inside it.

---

138. As a reminder, I explained on page 96 how to calculate cash weightings from risk weightings, given the risk of each asset. The risks I am using here are 15.2% for equities, and 6.1% for bonds. All these values can be found in Appendix B, from page 485 onwards.

139. Here I'm maximising Sharpe Ratio by going for the most diversified portfolio with equal weighting in each asset class. This is only one possible option which won't suit every investor, as I discussed in chapter four. I explain in the next chapter how to create portfolios that maximise expected geometric returns, or others that compromise between Sharpe Ratio and geometric mean. Also if it isn't obvious why equal weighting gives the highest Sharpe Ratio you might want to revisit the relevant part of chapter four (page 103) and the section of chapter six beginning on page 142.

PORTFOLIO 11: A SIMPLE TOP-DOWN EXAMPLE STEP TWO: COUNTRIES

Portfolio							
Equities				Bonds			
50% **(29.4%)**				50% **(70.6%)**			
US	UK	Japan	Germany	US	UK	Japan	Germany
25%	25%	25%	25%	25%	25%	25%	25%
50% × 25% = 12.5%	50% × 25% = 12.5%	50% × 25% = 12.5%	50% × 25% = 12.5%	50% × 25% = 12.5%	50% × 25% = 12.5%	50% × 25% = 12.5%	50% × 25% = 12.5%
(29.4% × 25% = 7.5%)	**(29.4% × 25% = 7.5%)**	**(29.4% × 25% = 7.5%)**	**(29.4% × 25% = 7.5%)**	**(70.6% × 25% = 17.5%)**	**(70.6% × 25% = 17.5%)**	**(70.6% × 25% = 17.5%)**	**(70.6% × 25% = 17.5%)**

Bottom row shows weight to each component: asset class weight multiplied by country weight. Weights in normal font are risk weightings. Numbers in **(bold)** are cash weights.

Once you're down to the most granular component of the portfolio you can work out what the final portfolio weightings will look like. In this trivial example each component, like UK equities, will have a portfolio risk weighting equal to the asset class weight (50%), multiplied by the country weight within the asset class (25%).

The final row, below the double lines, shows the final weight in each individual country and asset combination. All the components have a weight of 50% × 25% = 12.5%. Again cash weights are shown in bold and bracketed. To get the final cash weights you just multiply the cash weights from each row.

So for UK equity the final cash weight is the asset class cash weight (29.4%), multiplied by the country weight within the asset class (25%), which gives 29.4% × 25% = 7.5%. Here I've shown the calculations for every asset but I'll normally omit them to improve readability.

Notice that I haven't put any cash weights in at the second level of the portfolio (there is nothing in bold). That's because I'm assuming all these countries have the same volatility,[140] so cash weights and risk weights will be the same. I've used this convention in the rest of the book.

---

140.   My research indicates that there aren't usually significant differences between the volatility of different developed country equity indices.

Now look at a different example: portfolio 12. First notice that this is only the equities component of the portfolio. The weights shown still add up to 100%, but that is 100% of the equity allocation, not 100% of the entire portfolio. I'll use this shortcut many times as it's not really practical to keep showing the entire portfolio in a single table.

PORTFOLIO 12: A SIMPLE TOP-DOWN EXAMPLE WITH MIXED LEVELS, EQUITIES ONLY

Portfolio			
Equities			
US 25%	Japan 25%	Europe 50%	
		UK 50%	Germany 50%
25%	25%	25%	25%

Bottom row shows weight to each component: regional weight multiplied by country weight. Risk weightings shown are equal to cash weightings.

Secondly I've added an intermediate regional level to the top-down hierarchy. The European region is subsequently broken down further into countries, whereas the US and Japan are not. This kind of mixed level portfolio layout will appear a lot.

There are no recommended cash weights shown here (nothing in bold). That's because I'm assuming all the volatilities are equal in this portfolio, so the risk weights and cash weights will be the same. If you are going to use your own estimates of volatility[141] then you will have to work out the cash weights yourself.

In part two I frequently show portfolios constructed using ETFs. Including the specific identifying **tickers** of my preferred ETFs in each portfolio gives you a straightforward way to implement my recommendations (at least whilst these particular ETFs survive).

ETFs are the best solution for most investors, however I explain in chapter eleven how larger investors can allocate to individual shares inside individual countries.[142]

Portfolio 13 shows an example of a portfolio built using ETFs. Here the tickers for both UK and US investors are shown. Sometimes though I'll show separate tables for the UK

---

141. See Appendix C, page 489, for an explanation of how to do this.
142. Also in part three I consider if there are other kinds of collective funds that are worth including in your portfolio.

and the US. This is because I can't get exactly the same portfolio structure in each country, due to differing availability of ETFs.

PORTFOLIO 13: EXAMPLE WITH ETF TICKERS

Portfolio								
Equity								
Developed equity								
North America **33%** VNRT (UK) IVV (US)		EMEA (Europe) **33%** XMEU (UK) VGK (US)				Asia Pacific **33%** IAPD (UK) IVV (US)		
US	Canada	UK	France	Germany	Other	Japan	Australia	Other
95%	**5%**	**29%**	**15%**	**14%**	**42%**	**65%**	**20%**	**15%**
31%	**2%**	**10%**	**5%**	**5%**	**14%**	**21%**	**7%**	**5%**

Bottom row shows weight to each component: regional weight multiplied by country weight. Cash weightings shown, which are equal to risk weightings. Borders show each fund used. Minimum allocation: £5,400 or $9,000.

In this particular portfolio I've used one ETF for each of the three regions. When I do this it's either because I couldn't find ETFs that gave me a more granular allocation, or because it's a portfolio designed for an investor who hasn't sufficient funds to split their cash further without incurring heavy costs.

The region of the portfolio invested in each ETF is shown with a thick black border. The country allocations inside each ETF are something we don't have any control over: they are determined by the index weightings. Think of the black borders as representing a wall within which the fund manager is in charge. You can change the size of each black bordered fund, but you have to live with the internal weights within.

The bottom row again shows the regional allocation multiplied by the allocation inside the country. Notice that this table only shows cash weightings – all the figures are in bold. I've omitted the brackets to avoid cluttering the table. Weightings within funds are always specified in cash terms.

Finally I've put a suggested minimum allocation figure below the table. The minimum applies to the part of your portfolio that is shown; in this case developed equities. If you don't have sufficient cash for the minimum allocation I've shown then it will be too expensive to use this portfolio. In this particular example, that would mean you'd have to use a single ETF for developed equities, rather than three regional funds.

All the minimum allocations I present are calculated based on a minimum investment in each ETF of $600 or £3,600, which I derived in chapter six based on my own default assumptions about costs. Remember that you can adjust these if you have a different minimum brokerage fee than the figures I use ($1 in the US, and £6 in the UK). Just multiply the minimum portfolio value by the ratio of your brokerage fee minimum to mine.

For example, if you are paying a £9 minimum brokerage fee, then you should multiply the minimum shown in the table above (£5,400) by £9 ÷ £6 = 1.5. Hence you should only invest in the portfolio shown if you have more than £5,400 × 1.5 = £8,100.

Portfolio 14 illustrates some other features that I use occasionally. This is a bond portfolio for US investors where I've used three ETFs: one for the US, one non-US, and one for emerging markets (EM). The non-US ETF also includes exposure to emerging markets, as well as to Canada. That means the EM allocation is coming from the explicit EM fund (EMAG) but also partly from the non-US fund (IAGG).

PORTFOLIO 14: EXAMPLE SHOWING EXTRA EXPOSURE ROW

Portfolio										
Bonds										
Developed 75% **(80%)**									Emerging 25% **(20%)**	
US 30% **(32.1%)** AGG (US)	Non-US 51% **(52.5%)** IAGG (US)								EM 19% **(15.2%)** EMAG (US)	
	Americas	Asia			Europe				Emerging markets 12%	
	Canada 6.5%	Japan 12.9%	Australia 3.4%	Other 2.8%	France 12.5%	UK 10.8%	Germany 10.3%	Other 28.8%		
30%	3.3%	6.5%	51% × 3.4% = 1.7%	1.4%	6.4%	5.5%	5.2%	14.7%	51% × 12% = 6.1%	19% × 100% = 19.0%
Americas: 44.5%		Asia: 13.0%			Europe: 42.5%				Emerging markets	

Risk weightings are shown with cash weights in **(bold)**. Penultimate row shows weight within bonds sub-portfolio. Final row shows regional weights within developed markets.

Overall I want to have risk weights of 25% in emerging markets, and 75% in developed markets, of which around 30% should be in the US. To put together this portfolio I started by getting the cash weights each fund manager allocates to a given country within their fund; these are readily available from fund manager websites. The key figure I needed was the cash weight to emerging markets within IAGG; which was around 8%. Once I'd accounted for the different volatility of emerging and developed markets that 8% cash weight translates to a 12% risk weight.

I then did a few simple calculations. Suppose the risk weighting for IAGG is Y, and for the pure emerging market fund EMAG it is Z. So the total risk weight for emerging markets will be (Y × 12%) + Z, and this should equal 25%. I also know that Y + Z = 70%, since I've allocated 30% to the US fund AGG. This is a problem most teenage school children can cope with but if you've forgotten your algebra you can use a spreadsheet solver, or trial and error.

You should get Y = 51.1% and Z = 18.9%, which I've rounded to 51% and 19% respectively. I now have the risk weights for all three ETFs: 30% in the US fund AGG, 51% in IAGG and 19% in the pure emerging market fund EMAG. I then translated these into cash weights using the usual method I introduced in chapter four.

I've only shown cash weightings in the first couple of rows. You only need these when you're actually building the portfolio. It's vital to know what the cash weights will be to each ETF so you can buy the right number of shares. It's not necessary to have the implied cash weights for each country or region.

To work out the implied risk weights for a given country, I multiplied the ETF allocation by the internal risk weight of that country within the relevant ETF. Take Australia for example. The relevant ETF IAGG has a 51% risk weight. Within that Australia has a risk weight of 3.4%. I derived that risk weight from the published cash allocations of IAGG, which I then corrected for different levels of volatility. The risk weight of Australia within the entire portfolio is 51% × 3.4% = 1.7%.

I can use a similar calculation to double check that the risk weight for emerging markets is correct. First I take the exposure we get from within IAGG. Remember IAGG has a 51% risk weight, of which 12% is in emerging markets (a figure I derived earlier). That gives a risk weight of 51% × 12% = 6.1%. However, I also have an allocation to emerging markets via the fund EMAG. That has a risk weight of 19% (calculated previously). The total in emerging markets is 6.1% + 19% = 25.1%; almost identical to the target of 25% (remember I did some rounding earlier, so it isn't quite spot on).

For reasons that will become apparent in a later chapter, I wanted to see what the regional breakdown was amongst developed markets. So I've added an extra row that shows this. These extra rows to show exposures are always in *italics* and in risk weighted terms. To calculate these figures we need to bear in mind that the total risk weighted exposure to developed markets is 75%. For North America I need to add the risk weight to the US (30% allocated to AGG) and Canada (3.3% as part of EMAG). The total, 33.3%, as a fraction of 75% is 44.4%. I can do similar calculations for the other two regions: Europe and Asia.

The road map

The road map in illustration 1 shows the journey we'll be taking in the rest of part two as we descend from the top of the portfolio downwards.

ILLUSTRATION 1: ROADMAP TO PART TWO

Portfolio Asset allocation (Chapter 8)					
Equities			Bonds		Genuine alternatives (Ch. 9)
Traditional equity (Ch. 10)		Equity-like alternatives (Ch. 9)	Traditional bonds (Ch. 12)	Bond-like alternatives (Ch. 9)	
Developed equity (Ch. 10)	Emerging equity (Ch. 10)		Developed (Ch. 12)	Emerging (Ch. 12)	
Regions (Ch. 10)			Regions (Ch. 12)		
Countries (Ch. 10)			Countries (Ch. 12)		
Sectors (Ch. 11)			Type (Ch. 12)		
Individual equities (Ch. 11)			Maturity and credit (Ch. 12)		

Key: Ch. is an abbreviation for Chapter

In chapter eight I discuss the allocation to **asset classes**: equities, bonds, and alternatives. Chapter nine goes into more detail about **alternative assets**, including those that are similar to equities and bonds, but also truly uncorrelated **genuine alternatives**.

Allocation within the traditional equity part of the portfolio is the subject of chapters ten and eleven. Chapter ten takes you to the point of allocating to individual countries, whilst chapter eleven is about what you do within each country. To finish off the process I talk about the allocation to bonds in chapter twelve.

Finally, there are complete examples of top-down portfolios in chapter thirteen (not shown on the map).

DIGRESSION: CORE AND SATELLITE

Core and satellite portfolios are a recent investment fad. There are several versions of this fashionable idea. In one flavour the core is a developed equity portfolio, with the satellite reflecting exotica like bonds, emerging markets and hedge funds.

In a second version the core contains long-term strategic holdings and the satellite consists of short-horizon tactical bets. Finally in another guise the core consists of low-cost index funds, whilst the satellite is stuffed full of active managers.

Of these the first is just a different method for asset allocation, which will probably result in a relatively overweight exposure to developed market equities. The second assumes an ability to forecast the performance of different fund management styles that is beyond the scope of this book (and which I'm also extremely sceptical of).

The third version, a passive core and an active satellite, is a more promising idea.

I think it's reasonable to allocate some of your portfolio to active managers, if you find some that you like, based on the criteria I describe in part three. But I think this decision should be taken after you've done your top-down allocation first. Only once you've decided how much to put in Germany equities, should you consider allocating to a German equity fund manager that shows consistent outperformance.

Do not begin with a shopping list of fund managers and a fixed idea of how much you should put into the active part of your portfolio, otherwise your asset allocation will be driven by your preferences for active managers. There will be a serious danger of getting your asset allocation wrong or constantly adjusting it as your preferences for fund managers change.

These problems will far outweigh any benefit you will get from selecting the best active managers: assuming you can manage to select the best managers in the first place.

Issues to consider

Top-down allocation is a beautifully simple idea, at least in theory. But in practice there are a few issues that arise when you try to do top-down portfolio allocation.

How to split up the portfolio and in what order

Sometimes this might seem obvious. I think it's pretty uncontroversial that the best way to split an equity allocation for a particular country is by industry. But sometimes things are trickier. So, for example, when allocating bond weightings within a single country: should you first split your pool of assets into corporate and government bonds, or by bond maturity? I grapple with these decisions in each of the relevant chapters.

Which assets should be included?

You might not be able to include all possible assets that could conceivably form part of a given section of your portfolio. So, for example, it might not be straightforward to invest in shares of certain countries with limited access to their markets, or in unlisted securities.

How should assets be weighted?

The **handcrafting** method I use advocates **equal weighting** of components within a group of similar assets, assuming you are using **risk weighting** which accounts for different levels of volatility. But sometimes you might want to constrain a particular part of your portfolio to a lower allocation than equal weights would suggest.

As I said in chapter four, there are several legitimate reasons for not sticking religiously to equal weights: when equal weights are very different from market cap weighting making them potentially embarrassing, when costs are likely to be very different, when risk is unpredictable or badly behaved, and where groups are of unequal size.

Does the portfolio need to be split further?

Because the process is top-down, at each stage you can decide if you need to continue dividing your portfolio into smaller parts. So, for example, after allocating to bonds and equities you must decide if it's worth splitting your equity allocation into individual regions, or just investing in two funds: a global equity fund and a global bond fund.

There may be several good reasons for not splitting up your portfolio. Firstly you might have a small account on which it isn't economic to buy large numbers of funds; so stopping your top-down process at a higher level makes sense. Alternatively it might be difficult or impossible to split your portfolio, due to a lack of the necessary assets to invest in. For example investing in individual bonds is difficult for many investors.

Finally owning individual shares in other countries can be a hassle, because of taxation and reporting rules, regulatory constraints, and capital controls. You might prefer to use ETFs for overseas holdings.

Often some parts of the portfolio will be more granular than others. For example within my own investments I own individual UK shares, but get my foreign equity and bond exposure exclusively through ETFs.

CHAPTER EIGHT

Asset Classes

Portfolio						
Equities			Bonds			Genuine alternatives
Traditional equity		Equity-like alternatives	Traditional bonds		Bond-like alternatives	
Developed equity	Emerging equity		Developed	Emerging		
Regions			Regions			
Countries			Countries			
Sectors			Type			
Individual equities			Maturity and credit			

IN THIS CHAPTER, WE BEGIN THE TOP-DOWN ALLOCATION OF OUR smart portfolio journey at the highest level: asset classes.

Chapter overview

Which asset classes?	Which asset classes should you include in your portfolio?
What division?	How should you divide up the world of asset classes?
What appetite for risk?	The effect of risk tolerance on asset allocation.
How to weight asset classes	Using the handcrafted method to decide portfolio weights.

How should retail investors weight their portfolio and get exposure to asset classes?	What's the smartest way for a small retail investor to get exposure to different asset classes? This section suggests specific ETFs for different portfolio sizes.

Which asset classes?

This would have been a much easier chapter to write 20 years ago. For the vast majority of investors there were only two asset classes: equities and bonds. Only sophisticated investors like US university endowments knew better; investing in a much wider set of assets and earning extra returns for their efforts.

Now even the average investor has access to a much longer menu of asset classes. A complete list of asset classes would have to include exotica such as private equity, venture capital, real estate, infrastructure, commodities, asset-backed securities, gold, alternative currencies like Bitcoin, and peer-to-peer lending. There are also hedge funds which, strictly speaking, are not asset classes in themselves, but a way of accessing trading strategies that buy and sell different underlying assets.[143]

Alternative assets are a sufficiently complicated subject that I have devoted the whole of the next chapter to them.

What division of asset classes?

Traditionally investment managers have used a three asset class[144] approach – equities, bonds[145] and alternatives – as shown[146] in portfolio 15.

---

143. I'm ignoring here derivatives like futures and options. These are a complicated way of getting exposure to certain underlying assets rather than a separate asset class, and are out of scope for this book.
144. I'm ignoring any allocation to cash. As you might recall from chapter four, most investors should have no cash except for those in the Ultra Cautious category.
145. It's worth remembering that in a crisis high yield (junk) corporate bonds, and bonds issued by emerging market governments, are more likely to behave like equities, and less like the safer bonds I have bundled them with. They'll have higher risk than other bonds and a higher correlation with equities. Nevertheless in the interests of simplicity I maintain a straightforward demarcation between equities and bonds.
146. You've probably noticed that there are no portfolio weights in these tables. I haven't forgotten them and there is no typesetting error: they will come later. At the moment I'm just showing you possible groupings.

PORTFOLIO 15: TRADITIONAL VIEW OF ASSET CLASSES: ALTERNATIVES AS A SEPARATE BUCKET

Portfolio				
Equities	Bonds	Alternatives		
		Equity-like	Bond-like	Genuine uncorrelated

This traditional approach no longer makes sense. During the financial crisis of 2008, many alternatives ended up highly exposed to the market downturn. Plenty of so-called alternatives turned out to be highly correlated with equities, and others with bonds. However there were some rare examples of genuine alternatives which provided wholly uncorrelated returns. As you can see I've divided the alternatives asset class into these different types of alternatives.

The grouping I use, which is shown in portfolio 16, better reflects the risks inherent in the various different types of alternatives.

PORTFOLIO 16: NEW VIEW OF ASSET CLASSES: MOST ALTERNATIVES INCLUDED IN RELEVANT ASSET CLASS

Portfolio				
Equity-like		Bond-like		Genuine alternatives
Traditional equity	Equity-like alternatives	Traditional bonds	Bond-like alternatives	

If you are short of capital then you should remove the alternatives that are too similar to the traditional asset classes. This will leave you with portfolio 17.

PORTFOLIO 17: ASSET CLASSES WITHOUT BOND-LIKE OR EQUITY-LIKE ALTERNATIVES

Portfolio		
Equity-like	Bond-like	Genuine alternatives
Traditional equity	Traditional bonds	

Finally, very small investors will have to eschew alternatives entirely. If you are highly sceptical about alternative assets then you should also select this option.

What appetite for risk?

Before we start thinking about asset class allocation we need to determine the type of investor, what type of portfolio they will have, and how this will translate into specific weights.

Here's a summary of what I discussed back in chapter four, starting on page 86. It might be worth rereading that section of the earlier chapter to see what investor profile fits you best.

Ultra safe	Tolerance: very low risk. No access to leverage.
	Invested in cash plus the maximum Sharpe Ratio portfolio.
	No limit on allocation to bonds: hold most diversified portfolio.
Careful	Tolerance: low risk. No access to leverage.
	Entirely invested in maximum Sharpe Ratio portfolio.
	No limit on allocation to bonds: hold most diversified portfolio.
Average	Tolerance: medium risk. No access to leverage.
	Entirely invested in compromise portfolio.
	Maximum 30% of risk weight in bonds.
Brave	Tolerance: high risk. No access to leverage.
	Entirely invested in maximum geometric mean portfolio.
	Maximum 10% of risk weight in bonds.
Borrower	Risk tolerance: medium to high. Can use leverage.
	Invested with leverage in maximum Sharpe Ratio portfolio.
	No limit on allocation to bonds: hold most diversified portfolio.

You should now know whether you will be (a) limited to 10% risk weighted in bonds, (b) limited to 30% in bonds, or (c) have no limit to your bond exposure. You will need this figure in the rest of this chapter.

You will also know the amount of cash to hold alongside risky assets: zero (most investors) or some (ultra safe investors). Also the amount of leverage you will be using to invest: zero (most investors) or some (borrowers). However I won't be using this information; this chapter is about setting the weights in your investment portfolio. You will need to add on cash or leverage to suit your risk profile.

The smart way to weight asset classes

Remember from chapter three that the optimal portfolio weights will depend on expected correlations, volatilities, and average returns.

As I discussed back in chapter three, I assume that all asset classes have the same expected risk adjusted return: the same Sharpe Ratio. They do not however have the same risk. Annualised standard deviation of returns for bonds, assuming you avoid very low-risk short maturity issues,[147] comes in around 6%. Equity asset class risk is around 15%.

Alternatives are more difficult to quantify. I assume that bond-like alternatives have bond-like volatility, and equity-like alternatives are about as risky as traditional equities.

Amongst the group of potentially genuine alternatives that I categorise in the next chapter, some[148] have equity-like volatility, whilst others have an unusual risk pattern that is a little lower on average.[149] I assume similar levels of risk for genuine alternatives as for equities. Overestimating an asset's risk is safer than underestimating it.

These different levels of risk mean that you will need to use **risk weighting**, which I introduced in chapter four (page 96).

That leaves me with correlations. The correlation between equities and bonds varies over time, but has averaged around zero. By design the correlation of genuine alternatives to both equities and bonds is similarly low, and may even be negative. This is because I've moved alternatives which are really equities or bonds in lambswool costume to be with their close cousins, leaving only the genuine diversifying assets in the alternative bucket.

Since all three pairs of correlation values (equity/bond, bond/alternatives, equity/alternatives) are close to zero, it's safe to assume they are identical. If you're using risk weighting then with identical correlations and equal risk-adjusted returns all the assumptions of equal weighting hold, and in theory you should invest in portfolio 18.

---

147. Remember I explained why you should avoid ultra safe short-term bonds back in chapter four, page 92.
148. If you're interested these include managed futures, short biased hedge funds, and precious metals.
149. I'm thinking here of tail protect and long volatility funds. These usually have low risk (and small negative returns) with occasional periods of high risk (and large positive returns), so it's difficult to measure their risk.

PORTFOLIO 18: BEST ASSET CLASS ALLOCATION FOR MAXIMUM SHARPE RATIO WITH NO CONSTRAINTS ON ALTERNATIVES (NOT RECOMMENDED)

Portfolio				
Equity-like 33% **(22%)**		Bond-like 33% **(55%)**		Genuine alternatives 33% **(22%)**
Traditional equity 50%	Equity-like alternatives 50%	Traditional bonds 50%	Bond-like alternatives 50%	
16.5% **(11%)**	16.5% **(11%)**	16.5% **(28%)**	16.5% **(28%)**	33% **(22%)**

Risk weightings shown. Cash weights in **(bold)**.

Most people would be uncomfortable with 66% of their risk in alternative assets (33% in genuine alternatives, and the rest split between equity-like and bond-like alternatives). I'd suggest 10% was a more reasonable allocation.

CONCEPT: WHY ALTERNATIVES SHOULD GET A LOWER WEIGHT

Is one-third of the portfolio in alternatives really justified, or are there grounds to think this is too high? Remember I discussed various reasons for legitimately deviating from equal weights back in chapter four (from page 110).

The use of equal risk weighting assumes that future volatility can be predicted from the past. It also assumes that the risk of returns is well behaved, in the sense that using standard deviation alone is sufficient to describe it. Unfortunately **many alternatives don't have well behaved risk**, and have a nasty habit of becoming much riskier very quickly.

I assume that expected pre-cost Sharpe Ratios for bonds, equities and alternatives are identical. However the same cannot be said of **after-cost** Sharpe Ratios. For bonds and equities I can choose ETFs with very competitive cost figures. But as you'll see in chapter nine, it's a lot more expensive to access alternatives. ETFs for alternative assets usually cost a lot more, and direct investment via hedge funds and other exotic legal entities is an equally expensive business.

Finally I have said before that although slavishly sticking to market capitalisation weights isn't necessary, it might be **embarrassing** to deviate too much from them.

The total market value of alternative assets is much smaller than that of bonds and equities.

Smaller market cap, lower post-cost returns and unpleasantly un-forecastable risk; putting these together justifies a lower weight to alternatives.

On top of this many investors are just uncomfortable with alternatives: they don't understand or like them. It's better to stick to a lower weight which you are happy with, than to go with a weight that is too high and then have to cut it later. I've chosen 10% but in my opinion any initial allocation between 0% and 25% is reasonable. I wouldn't go higher than 25%.

Fortunately it's very easy to apply constraints to top-down risk weighted portfolios. If I apply a maximum limit of 10%[150] on alternative assets I get portfolio 19. Notice I've put 5% into genuine alternatives, and then allocated 5% of the equities group into equity-like alternatives, with an identical proportion carved out of bonds.

PORTFOLIO 19: BEST ASSET CLASS ALLOCATION FOR SHARPE RATIO MAXIMUM PORTFOLIO WITH 10% IN ALTERNATIVES

Portfolio				
Equity-like 47.5% (28%)		Bond-like 47.5% (69%)		Genuine alternatives 5% (3%)
Traditional equity 95%	Equity-like alternatives 5%	Traditional bonds 95%	Bond-like alternatives 5%	
45.1% (26.4%)	2.4% (1.4%)	45.1% (65.9%)	2.4% (3.5%)	5% (2.9%)

Risk weightings shown. Cash weights in **(bold)**.

This is the **maximum Sharpe Ratio portfolio**, suitable for a **low-risk** investor. But the expected return on this would be too low for other investors. Investors who can cope with more risk should buy a **maximum geometric mean portfolio**, and cap their exposure to low-risk bonds at 10% risk weighting. Portfolio 20 is for such an investor.

---

150. It's easy to construct similar portfolios with for example only 5%, or up to 25% in alternatives.

PORTFOLIO 20: BEST ASSET CLASS ALLOCATION FOR MAXIMUM GEOMETRIC MEAN PORTFOLIO INVESTOR WITH 10% IN ALTERNATIVES

Portfolio				
Equity-like 85% **(74%)**		Bond-like 10% **(22%)**		Genuine alternatives 5% **(4%)**
Traditional equity 95%	Equity-like alternatives 5%	Traditional bonds 95%	Bond-like alternatives 5%	
80.7% **(70.2%)**	4.3% **(3.7%)**	9.5% **(20.7%)**	0.5% **(1.1%)**	5% **(4.3%)**

Risk weightings shown. Cash weightings in **(bold)**.

It's also possible to put together portfolios without any alternatives; the maximum Sharpe Ratio version would have 50% in each asset class, and the maximum geometric mean would have 90% in equities with 10% in bonds. Clearly these two portfolios represent fairly extreme views on risk. You can also construct a **compromise portfolio** which lies somewhere between the two, with risk weightings of 30% in bonds and 70% in equities.

I've summarised the cash weightings of the various different permutations in table 41.

TABLE 41: CASH WEIGHTINGS OF NINE DIFFERENT ASSET ALLOCATION PORTFOLIOS

	Bonds	Bond-like	Equities	Equity-like	Genuine alternatives
All alternatives (Max SR)	65.9%	3.5%	26.4%	1.4%	2.9%
All alternatives (Compromise)	49.1%	2.6%	42.6%	2.2%	3.4%
All alternatives (Max GM)	20.7%	1.1%	70.2%	3.7%	4.3%
True alternatives only (Max SR)	67.2%		26.9%		6.0%
True alternatives only (Compromise)	51.7%		41.4%		6.9%
True alternatives only (Max GM)	21.7%		69.6%		8.7%
No alternatives (Max SR)	71%		29%		
No alternatives (Compromise)	52%		48%		
No alternatives (Max GM)	22%		78%		

First three rows: 10% in alternatives; half of which is in genuine alternatives, the rest split between bond-like and equity-like. Second three rows: 10% in genuine alternatives only. Final three rows: no alternatives. Maximum Sharpe Ratio ('Max SR') portfolio has an even split between equities and bonds. Compromise portfolio has 30% in bonds. Maximum geometric mean portfolio ('Max GM') has 10% in bonds. All percentage limits are based on risk weightings.

How should smaller investors weight their portfolio and get exposure to asset classes?

Investors with small accounts will struggle with some of the cash weightings shown in table 41. If they have just $5,000 then it isn't really practical to put 1.1% of that, which is just $55, into a single ETF. As you might remember from chapter six, the minimum purchase for an ETF is at least $300 or £1,800, depending on your minimum brokerage commission. In this part of the chapter I analyse the different options available with a relatively small amount of money to invest.

Is there a single fund solution?

In an ideal world we could invest in a single collective fund that would give exposure to the two main asset classes. Sadly, as I'm writing this, there are no passive multi-asset ETFs available in the UK. In the US however there is currently a wide choice. Amongst the cheaper options are the iShares Core Allocation funds which come in four flavours: conservative (30% equity), moderate (40%), growth (60%), and aggressive (80%).

These weights are of course **cash weightings**. From table 41, a **maximum geometric mean** portfolio corresponds to around a 20% cash weighting in bonds, and 80% in equities, whereas a **maximum Sharpe Ratio** portfolio would have 70% in bonds (30% in equities). This would equate to the aggressive and conservative flavours of the iShares ETF. Either of the iShares moderate or growth funds would be suitable for a **compromise** portfolio.

These multi-asset funds can be useful for the very smallest investors. There is some limited freedom in selecting the proportion of bonds and equities. But you definitely cannot change the underlying weightings to individual countries within each asset classes.

Global stock and bond funds

You ought to be able to buy a single fund that invests in all global equities, and a second for bonds. This allows you to fine-tune the equity and bond exposure, and get a closer match to the target weights in table 41. With enough capital you could also add a third fund for alternatives, but I'll discuss this later.

Single global equity fund

There are numerous passive funds available to get access to global equities. In the US the cheapest global equity fund is the Vanguard Total World Stock product (VT) with an annual management charge of 0.14%. The UK also has a cheap Vanguard product, the FTSE All World Equity ETF (VWRL) which costs 0.25% a year. There is a cheaper fund from HSBC charging only 0.15% a year, but this excludes emerging markets so you should avoid it.[151]

Single bond fund

Life is more difficult in the fragmented global bond market. It's hard to find ETFs that cover **all types** of bonds, listed **all over the world**. There are ETFs that give global coverage for government bonds (like IGLO in the UK, or IGOV in the US). And there are ETFs that cover corporate bonds across the world (like CORP in the UK). Finally

---

151. My analysis indicates that losing the EM exposure will knock about 0.30% off your geometric average return; far more than the extra 0.1% of management fee.

there are ETFs that encompass all bonds in the US (AGG, BND), and complementary funds that span the non-US markets.[152]

But as I'm writing this there does not seem to be a single passive ETF for all global bonds, of all types, covering all geographic regions. One UK fund (XBAG) comes closest, but excludes high yield bonds. It is managed by DBX and has an annual management fee of 0.30%.

Due to the lack of a passive equivalent, US investors might want to consider an **active** global bond fund. One of the cheapest is the RIGS RiverFront Strategic Income fund, coming in at a net expense ratio of 0.22%. Although this has a mandate to hold both corporate and government bonds, at the time of writing it is 100% in corporate bonds.

Funds for alternatives

Alternatives are a very complex asset class which I will discuss in more detail in the next chapter.

Summary

Decide on risk appetite	Before you begin deciding your top level asset class weights, you need to work out your risk appetite. Which of the investor types on page 86 are you? Which portfolio are you going to use?
Decide on ideal allocation to alternatives	What is your preferred allocation to alternatives? Although I use a 10% risk weighted allocation in this chapter, a reasonable range would be between 0% and 25%. Stick to a level you are comfortable with.
Find cash weightings	If you're happy to use one of the standard portfolios I've put together, use table 41 to determine your cash weightings given your preferences for risk and alternatives allocation. If you're not putting 10% into alternatives you'll need to calculate the final risk weightings yourself, and then work out the cash weightings. Use the technique in chapter four, page 96. If you don't want to use my rough estimates of asset class volatility from Appendix B (page 485), you'll need to measure the risk of each asset class and work out your own cash weights. See page 489 in Appendix C.

---

152. I discuss all of these in chapter twelve.

UK investors

There is no single multi-asset ETF available in the UK. The breakeven levels shown here assume you are paying a minimum £6 brokerage fee.[153] If you are paying more then you should multiply these breakeven levels by the ratio of your minimum fee to £6. For example if you are paying £12 then you should double the values shown.

Investment from £1,800 to £30,000	Separate global bond (XBAG) and global equity (VWRL) funds. No alternatives allocation. Cash weights as per bottom three rows of table 41 (page 201).
Investment of £30,000 or more	A 10% risk weighted alternatives allocation is viable. Cash weights as per middle three rows of table 41.
Investment of £130,000 or more	Use a 10% risk weighted alternatives allocation, with separate bond-like and equity-like allocations. Cash weights as per top three rows of table 41.

US investors

The breakeven levels shown here assume you are paying a minimum $1 brokerage fee.[154] If you are paying more then you should multiply these breakeven levels by the ratio of your minimum fee to $1. For example if you are paying $2 then you should double the values shown.

	Use a multi-asset ETF like the iShares Core Allocation funds.
	Maximum Sharpe Ratio portfolio: Single multi-asset fund: ideally 70% bonds, 30% equities (cash weights). For example: iShares Core conservative product.
Investment of $300 to $1,500	Compromise portfolio: Single multi-asset fund: ideally 50% bonds, 50% equities (cash weights). For example: iShares Core moderate (40% equities) or growth (60% equities) product.
	Maximum geometric mean portfolio: Single multi-asset fund: ideally between 20% and 25% in bonds, remainder in equities (cash weights). For example: iShares Core aggressive product (80% equities).

---

153. I'm using the minimum ETF purchase size from table 40, page 175.
154. I'm using the minimum ETF purchase size from table 40, page 175.

Investment of $1,500 or more	Separate global bond (e.g. RIGS ETF) and global equity funds (e.g. VT ETF). Cash weights as per bottom three rows of table 41 (page 201).
Investment of $5,000 or more	Separate global bond (RIGS ETF) and global equity funds (VT ETF). A 10% risk weighted alternatives allocation is possible. Cash weights as per middle three rows of table 41.
Investment of $22,000 or more	A 10% risk weighted alternatives allocation is viable, with specific bond-like and equity-like allocations. Cash weights as per top three rows of table 41.

Now see chapter nine for suggestions on which genuine alternatives ETF to invest in. See chapters ten and twelve for discussion on further disaggregating equity and bond allocations.

Alternatives

Portfolio						
Equities			Bonds			Genuine alternatives
Traditional equity		Equity-like alternatives	Traditional bonds		Bond-like alternatives	
Developed equity	Emerging equity		Developed	Emerging		
Regions			Regions			
Countries			Countries			
Sectors			Type			
Individual equities			Maturity and credit			

O PINION IS CERTAINLY DIVIDED OVER ALTERNATIVE ASSETS. ARE they a genuinely wonderful source of almost unlimited extra diversification that you should unthinkingly buy? Or just a way for cynical fund managers to extract fat fees for supposedly uncorrelated performance which vanishes when things get tough? In this chapter I explore the place of alternatives in smart portfolios.

Chapter overview

Different groups of alternatives	How I classify alternative assets.

Genuine alternatives	Classifying and weighting the alternatives that really live up to their name.
Equity-like alternatives	Ditto for alternatives whose returns closely resemble equities.
Bond-like alternatives	… and for bond-like alternatives.
Alternative assets for retail investors	How retail investors should weight and get exposure to alternatives, including suggested ETFs.

Different groups of alternatives

In the previous chapter I classified alternative assets into three groups: **genuinely uncorrelated** alternatives, alternatives that are likely to be similar to **equities**, and those that behave more like **bonds**.

1. Equity-like alternatives will do badly when there is poor economic news, or when investors get scared. Certain hedge fund strategies also rely on risk remaining low, and lose money when it increases. The many "hedge funds" running supposedly uncorrelated strategies that went bankrupt in the financial crisis of 2008 are testimony to this.

2. Bond-like alternatives are sensitive to higher interest rates and spikes in inflation. Some assets fall into this category because they are positively correlated to US treasury bonds, as in times of panic they are also safe havens for scared money.

3. Genuine alternatives have relatively little to do with either of the main asset classes. Some of them even have a negative average return; but because owning them is like buying an insurance policy they are still worth throwing into your portfolio shopping basket (I'll explain what this means shortly).

I do not discuss off-the-wall alternatives like BitCoin, rare stamps, art, antiques, vintage cars, or expensive wines. I am no expert in these assets, and the research budget for this book did not run to Ferrari 250 GTOs and premier cru bottles of Bordeaux.

Genuine alternatives

Which assets to include

I divide the world of genuine alternatives into two subcategories: insurance-like alternatives and standalone alternatives.

Insurance-like assets

The first group of genuine alternatives comprises assets that are negatively correlated with bonds and stocks, and which I expect to have negative expected returns.[155] However they add diversification to the portfolio which more than compensates for any downward drag on returns. I call these **insurance-like assets**. Let me explain why.

I pay an annual premium for home insurance. Since my insurance company is profitable I don't expect to make a net positive return out of the deal. But I'm still happy to pay for the insurance and be protected from a huge loss should my house burn down. Similarly you should be happy to put up with expected negative returns for insurance-like assets. When the rest of your portfolio metaphorically burns down you'd expect them to reduce your losses.

Here are the main types of insurance-like asset:

Gold and precious metals	Gold is a classic safe haven, as are silver and platinum.* For at least 2000 years people have been buying gold at the first sign of trouble.**
Long volatility	The simplest kind of insurance-like asset involves buying a type of derivative called a **put option**, which is a bet that the market will go down.*** In the long run this costs money as stock markets tend to rise, but also because options are usually overpriced, reflecting unwarranted fears of regular market crashes. However in the event of a market meltdown the options will pay out.
Tail protect hedge funds	Tail protect funds are a more sophisticated long volatility strategy which try to reduce the size of the insurance premium by selectively buying certain options when they are relatively cheap.
Short biased equity funds	Certain hedge funds have a consistent bias to being short equities (betting the market will go down). Many claim they will make positive returns in the long run, but in reality short biased funds struggle to be consistently profitable as equity markets usually go up.

---

155. Technical note: An asset with a negatively correlated return, which is also expected to have positive expected returns, shouldn't exist. If it did then it would be possible to construct a portfolio that is profitable but which has zero expected risk.

	Certain currencies are seen as safe havens and attract *scared money* when things go badly wrong. The Swiss franc is probably the most well known example.
Insurance currencies	Countries with large overseas investments like Japan and the US also have currencies that behave like safe havens because in a global panic Japanese and US investors will liquidate foreign holdings and bring their capital home to safety. (Be careful: safe havens will change over time. Until European Monetary Union the Deutschmark was a safe haven; in the early 20th century it was the British pound.)
	Holding safe haven currencies is like buying an insurance policy because their interest rates are usually derisory or even negative; it effectively costs you money to own them.

* Non-precious metals like copper are used for industrial purposes, and behave like other commodities such as oil. These are not included here, but classified as equity-like alternatives.

** Gold also has industrial uses like non-precious metals, and is perceived as an inflation hedge, so you could argue it belongs with the equity-like alternative asset group. However in the historical data I've analysed gold has no significant positive correlation with either equities or bonds.

*** Technical note: Strictly speaking long volatility funds bet on both large rises and falls in asset prices. However, it's the downside protection that is important in this context.

Standalone alternatives

The second category of genuine alternatives are uncorrelated assets which I'd expect to have positive returns, and so are worth including in a portfolio in their own right on a **standalone** basis. In my opinion these can only be found in two specific niches of the hedge fund world:

Managed futures	These are a particular type of hedge fund. Managed futures or Commodity Trading Advisors (CTAs) seem to provide genuine diversification to both stocks and bonds§ whilst giving positive returns. This is because they benefit from both up and down markets.
Global macro hedge funds	Global macro funds, like George Soros' famous Quantum or John Paulson's eponymous firm, have a similar return profile to CTAs. They tend to buy options or similar assets to express their view with limited downside when they are wrong. Although option buying drags down returns, skilled managers can overcome this headwind.

§ I should disclose that I worked at a large CTA for many years (AHL), and most of my own active trading is done in this particular style. So yes, I'm biased. But there is plenty of independent evidence that CTAs provide genuine diversification e.g. 'Managed Futures: Portfolio Diversification Opportunities', CME Group, May 2011.

How to get exposure to genuine alternatives

Hedge funds: Long volatility, CTA's and Global macro, short biased, and tail protect

Large institutions can invest directly in hedge funds which use these kinds of strategies.[156] I will talk more about choosing the right fund manager in part three; for now all you need to know is that it's difficult to pick one fund over another. Investing in multiple funds within a particular category is a safer option if you have enough capital, or you can pay another layer of fees to a **fund of funds** which will select the managers for you.

US retail investors have the option of buying ETFs which fall into one of these categories.[157] With the exception of tail protect I managed to find ETFs for each of the strategies in this bucket, although their performance was disappointing and their fees relatively high. The UK ETF market is less well developed and didn't have anything in these categories when I checked.

Other long volatility

ETFs that increase in price when equity volatility rises are a straightforward way to buy insurance for your portfolio; they will give you similar performance to buying options. This is another category where US investors are served by several ETFs, all of which track the VIX (the volatility of the S&P 500). I only found one product in the UK which also tracks the VIX.

Insurance currencies

Despite what popular films might suggest, it's not that easy for foreigners to open a bank account in Switzerland, or Japan for that matter, although it would be straightforward for large institutional investors. Large investors could also use derivatives like futures to get currency exposure.

For retail investors in the US there are CurrencyShares ETFs that track the Swiss franc and the yen. Unfortunately no such product is available in the UK. However some brokers offer the option to hold foreign currency in a brokerage account.

Gold and precious metals

Gold is probably the most popular alternative asset and it's found in many portfolios. Fortunately you don't need to go to the trouble of buying Krugerrand coins or gold bars, and paying to store and insure them. Many gold ETFs are available in both the US and

---

156. A braver option is to replicate these funds in house. I describe how to replicate a common managed futures strategy in chapter 15 of my first book, *Systematic Trading*.

157. Some hedge funds also sell their products inside mutual funds. These also tend to be expensive and mean that you have to pick the right manager.

the UK, with quite reasonable annual management charges. Other precious metals such as platinum, palladium and silver can also be purchased through ETFs, though the fees tend to be slightly higher.

How to weight genuine alternatives

Portfolio 21 shows a suggested breakdown for genuine alternatives, for an institutional investor who can access all the different categories I mentioned above.

PORTFOLIO 21: SUGGESTED ALLOCATION FOR GENUINE ALTERNATIVES SUB-PORTFOLIO

Portfolio						
Genuine alternatives						
Standalone: Zero correlation, positive return 50%		Insurance-like: Negative correlation, negative return 50%				
Managed futures 50%	Global Macro 50%	Short biased funds 20%	Long volatility 20%	Tail protect 20%	Safe haven currencies 20%	Gold & precious metals 20%
25% **(32.4%)**	25% **(26.1%)**	10% **(10.0%)**	10% **(3.0%)**	10% **(3.0%)**	10% **(10.3%)**	10% **(15.1%)**

Final row shows weight within genuine alternatives sub-portfolio. Weights are risk weightings, cash weightings in **(bold)**.

The equal split between standalone and insurance-like alternatives is a matter of taste; I've used 50% here for simplicity. Because they are negatively correlated with other assets, a larger share for insurance-like assets will bring down the risk of the total portfolio, and so might conceivably improve Sharpe Ratios. But this will be at the expense of lower returns. Bear in mind that you will already have some exposure to safe haven currencies through owning stocks and bonds in the relevant countries.[158]

---

158. Unless you've ignored my advice from chapter one and hedged your currency exposure.

Equity-like alternatives

Which assets to include

Here is a list of assets I think should be categorised as **equity-like alternatives**. Many of these were thought to be genuinely uncorrelated alternatives until the 2008 financial crisis, when it turned out they weren't.

Private equity and venture capital	These are equity in unlisted firms. It should be no surprise that they behave very much like publicly listed equities.
Real estate	Commercial real estate is exposed to the same economic cycle as stocks (US commercial real estate prices fell around 13% in 2008, and 30% in 2009). Also rents, like equity earnings, tend to rise with inflation.
Commodities (excluding precious metals)	Like equities, commodity prices are closely linked to inflation. Many equity indices are also heavily weighted towards energy stocks. Finally the inclusion of commodity ETFs in many retail investors' portfolios from the 2000s onwards has made them behave more like other assets.*
Most hedge fund strategies	Most hedge fund strategies are correlated with equities and they tend to suffer when general de-leveraging events occur. These include equity neutral,** fixed income relative value,§ FX Carry,¶ and volatility selling.ꝺ If you want to know if a hedge fund manager is selling an equity-like strategy, ask them how they did in 2008. If they lost money they're probably running an equity-like strategy.

* Technical note: Although commodity prices are positively correlated with equity returns there is considerable debate as to whether commodities can provide positive long run returns (once storage costs or futures contango has been factored in). If not then arguably they should be insurance-like assets. However, unlike other insurance-like assets, which hedge against general market panics, they are supposed to hedge against inflation (although they haven't done a great job at this in the past). Feel free to change their classification in your own portfolio if you disagree.

** Equity neutral: A hedge fund which buys and sells different equities so it has no net exposure to the stock market. Such funds use significant leverage to boost returns which leaves them highly vulnerable to things going wrong.

§ Fixed income relative value: Buying undervalued bonds and selling overvalued bonds. This is negatively correlated to bond returns, which is great for diversifying a portfolio of bonds, but does make them more like equities. Again they use significant leverage.

¶ FX Carry: Buying currencies with high interest rates, and selling those with low rates. The differential in interest rates gives a positive return; unless the currency you are buying depreciates. These depreciations tend to occur when people are selling equities and other risky assets. Again, considerable leverage is employed by FX Carry managers.

ꝺ Volatility selling: Selling options, betting that the market will remain roughly unchanged. This is profitable in the long run but will occasionally result in very large losses, often when equity markets collapse.

How to get exposure

Private equity (PE) and venture capital (VC)

Large institutions can access PE and VC funds directly. Minimum investments often start at eight figures, so this isn't an option available to everyone. This is especially true if you are sensible and diversify your holdings amongst several managers. **Fund of funds** have lower minimum investments, but with the disadvantage of an extra layer of fees.

Individual investors can invest in suitable ETFs. However bear in mind you are usually not investing in the PE fund, but in the shares of the company that manages it. Your returns will be more correlated to the overall equity market than if you owned the underlying fund.

Real estate

Institutional investors frequently invest directly in real estate, such as undeveloped or agricultural land, or commercial and residential property. Real estate often makes up a large proportion of the portfolio of university endowments and similar funds. Are these large proportions in a single asset class sensible?[159]

With an allocation to equity-like alternatives of 3.7% (as in table 41 in the previous chapter, page 201), if you use the breakdown I show below in portfolio 22 with 25% in land, that comes out to 3.7% × 25% = 0.9% of your entire portfolio. I'm not suggesting that any holding in real estate above 1% is a bad thing, but if your exposure is already well above 10% you should probably avoid adding to it.

Similarly nearly all retail investors already have a stake in real estate in the form of their home. For many people the value of this probably dwarfs their investment portfolio. Adding further property investments might not make a lot of sense.

For private investors who do not already own property, or who wish to diversify their holdings, there are many ETFs available for this purpose. These allow you to get exposure to commercial property in different countries across the globe. You can also buy other listed property vehicles such as Real Estate Investment Trusts (REITs).

Commodities

In theory it's possible to invest directly in commodities. You can buy agricultural farmland, stuff warehouses with copper ingots, or fill a super tanker with liquid black gold. It's much

---

159. Of course, it's worth bearing in mind that the value of global real estate makes it larger than any other asset class, although only a small fraction of this is publically traded in the form of investable securities.

easier to use derivatives such as futures to speculate on the future price of commodities. But the vast majority of investors will gain access to commodities through ETFs.[160]

CONCEPT: WHAT GOES ON INSIDE COMMODITY ETFS?

You might expect that if you bought a crude oil ETF like USO, and the price of crude oil went up by nearly 40% over a year (as WTI Crude, which USO invests in, did in 2016), that you'd make 40% (less the management fee of around 0.5%). But you'd be wrong: you'll probably make less than that. In fact, investors in USO earned a mere 7% over 2016. Why?

Commodity ETFs[161] work in one of three different ways. Firstly there are **physical backed** ETFs, where the fund actually owns the physical asset. These are fairly common for gold (the GLD ETF is an example) and other metals funds, but you're unlikely to find a physically backed oil ETF that owns some actual oil sitting in a storage tank somewhere. The second type of commodity ETFs use publicly listed **derivatives**, usually futures contracts (USO is one of these). Thirdly, there are funds that do a **total return swap** with a bank: an agreement where the bank pays the fund if prices go up, and vice versa (Barclays OIL ETF is of this type).[162]

In the long run there shouldn't be any significant difference in the performance of funds that variously use these three methods.[163] Because the prices of futures are readily accessible, it's easiest to use futures prices to work out why there is a discrepancy between the price of, say, physical oil (for which the jargon is **spot**) and the returns an investor in an oil ETF might earn.

Futures traders distinguish between **contango** markets (where the futures price is above the current **spot** price), and those in **backwardation** (the futures price is below spot). If markets are in backwardation then on average an investor will earn an extra return from buying futures (via an ETF), over and above how the spot price moves. However if the market is in contango then it's more likely that investors will lose money from buying an oil ETF.[164]

---

160. Master Limited Partnerships (MLPs) are another way to get exposure to commodity assets through listed equities, albeit only in the US. The underlying assets are normally gas and oil pipelines whose value is highly correlated to the price of oil. Some ETFs which invest in MLPs are also available.
161. Warning for US investors: Some commodity ETFs issue a special tax statement (K-1) which makes life very painful if you're investing in them outside of a tax wrapper.
162. Total return swaps tend to closely follow futures as the bank will usually hedge their exposure by trading futures, although swaps are slightly more expensive to reflect the banks profit margin and there is an extra layer of risk as the fund will lose out if the bank fails.
163. Technical note: Otherwise significant arbitrage opportunities would be available.
164. Sophisticated investors should consider employing a strategy where you switch in and out of futures or ETFs depending on the level of contango. This is the carry rule described in chapter seven of my first book, *Systematic Trading*.

There are a few different factors which affect the level of contango or backwardation. If you buy oil you have to store it somewhere, and pay storage and insurance costs. This extra cost is a drag on returns. These costs are also baked in to futures prices. Futures prices also include an element reflecting the different demand for the commodity now and in the future.

When all these effects are added up we find that most markets tend to be in contango most of the time, with backwardation relatively rare. So investors will rarely see the full benefit from an increase in the underlying price of oil or other commodities, regardless of how they are getting exposure to the relevant market.

Incidentally this isn't a serious problem for metals like gold, which tends to have only very slight contango as it is relatively cheap to store, and the interest on excess cash usually just about cancels out the resulting drag on returns.

Equity-like hedge funds

Institutions have the ability to invest directly in hedge funds, which the ordinary person on the street does not. As I'll discuss in part three, it's hard to forecast future returns of individual managers, so ideally multiple funds should be purchased for each style bucket. Funds of funds are an easier way of doing this, but with higher fees.

Very large institutions with the necessary expertise could even consider in-house replication of hedge fund strategies,[165] which is a relatively cheap way of accessing hedge fund-like returns. Sophisticated investors of all sizes can also try replicating short volatility strategies like selling delta hedged straddles (if you don't understand what this means you probably shouldn't be doing it!). Extreme caution should be exercised with these strategies.

Retail investors who can't access hedge funds or replicate their strategies have to use ETFs. In the US there are multiple ETFs offering hedge fund access. However I would avoid trying to replicate a short volatility strategy using an **inverse ETF** like IVOP that bets on the VIX (the volatility index) falling.

Firstly investors will probably already own VXX in their genuine alternatives portfolio, which bets on the VIX going up! Owning both IVOP and VXX is utterly pointless as you'll just end up paying two sets of fees with nothing to show for it. IVOP is also a very nasty asset whose risk isn't well behaved or especially predictable. I also have a strong aversion to inverse ETFs. They share many evil characteristics with leveraged ETFs, which I critiqued in chapter four (page 95).

Sadly the UK currently lacks ETFs in the hedge fund space.

---

165. Again I refer you to my previous book, *Systematic Trading*, which includes plenty of advice on replicating hedge fund strategies. *Efficiently Inefficient: How Smart Money Invests and Market Prices Are Determined* by Lasse Pedersen is also a great source of specific ideas for different hedge fund strategies.

How to weight them

A weighting scheme for an investor who is willing and able to have an extensive portfolio of alternatives is shown in portfolio 22. As usual I've used the handcrafting method to do this allocation in a top-down fashion.

PORTFOLIO 22: SUGGESTED WEIGHTING FOR EQUITY-LIKE ALTERNATIVES

Portfolio										
Equities										
Equity-like alternatives										
Private equity & Venture capital 25%		Real Estate 25%		Commodities (ex precious metals) 25%			Equity-like hedge funds 25%			
Private equity 50%	Venture capital 50%	Commercial 50%	Private housing 50%	Agricultural 33%	Energies 33%	Non-precious metals 33%	Equity neutral 25%	FX Carry 25%	Fixed income relative value 25%	Short volatility 25%
12.5%	12.5%	12.5%	12.5%	8.3%	8.3%	8.3%	6.25%	6.25%	6.25%	6.25%
(8.8%)	**(8.8%)**	**(16.8%)**	**(12.0%)**	**(9.3%)**	**(5.8%)**	**(11.6%)**	**(10%)**	**(6.8%)**	**(6.8%)**	**(3.4%)**

Final row shows weight within equity-like sub-portfolio. Weights are risk weightings, cash weightings in **(bold)**.

Bond-like alternatives

The third group of alternative assets are highly correlated to the bond market.

Which assets to include

Private debt	You'd expect these close cousins of their publicly listed equivalents to be very similar to, if a little riskier than, public debt.
Peer-to-peer lending	Peer-to-peer lending is like buying an extremely risky bond. The loan is backed by the credit of a small number of random strangers you have found on the internet (yes: I'm a sceptic).
Infrastructure, real assets, and asset-backed securities	Buying these assets gives you access to a stream of future revenue. For example an infrastructure bond might be backed by the revenues from a toll road or bridge. The revenue stream is very dependable, just like a bond coupon. It may also include an implicit or explicit inflation guarantee, just like an inflation-linked bond.
Hedge funds with long bias in bonds	Some hedge funds invest in fixed income securities like corporate bonds. **Long bias** means they usually bet on the overall bond market going up; this makes them more correlated to the underlying asset class.

How to get exposure

Nowhere is the gap between large institutional and other investors more obvious than in this category of alternatives. Private debt is by its very nature an opaque and difficult market to access, whilst hedge funds require large minimum investments. There are a few ETFs which are labelled as infrastructure funds, although many of these actually invest in equities. Similarly there are funds for timber[166] and agri-business, but arguably these actually belong in the commodities part of the **equity-like** alternatives group.

Peer-to-peer lending is the exception; a truly democratic investment opportunity. But before you sign up it's worth comparing the interest rate, after fees, on peer-to-peer lending with something like the dividend yield on an ETF of high yielding corporate bonds (also known as junk). As I'm writing this, peer-to-peer rates in the UK average around 4.5% compared to over 5% for a comparable high yielding corporate bond ETF (HYLD).

Even if the rates were identical I'd rather lend to a diversified set of a thousand large companies spread across the world via the HYLD ETF than to 100 or so ordinary

---

166. It's also possible to invest directly in forestry under various unregulated schemes. I wouldn't go near these with a 20-foot tree trunk. The same applies to bamboo (an asset you might remember from the beginning of the book).

people who live in the same country. I'd want to see peer-to-peer interest rates offering a significant premium over junk bonds before I even considered them.

How to weight them

Portfolio 23 shows a suggested breakdown for bond-like alternatives. Obviously you could break private debt down further into regions and countries, as I will do for public debt (bonds) in chapter twelve.

PORTFOLIO 23: SUGGESTED WEIGHTING FOR BOND-LIKE ALTERNATIVES

Portfolio					
Bonds					
Bond-like alternatives					
Private debt 25%	Peer-to-peer lending 25%	Infrastructure, real assets, ABS 25%			Long fixed income Hedge funds 25%
		Infrastructure 33%	Real assets 33%	Asset-backed securities 33%	
25% **(30.6%)**	25% **(18.4%)**	8.3% **(6.2%)**	8.3% **(5.2%)**	8.3% **(8.7%)**	25% **(30.7%)**

Final row shows weight within bond-like alternatives sub-portfolio. Weights shown are risk weightings, cash weightings in **(bold)**.

Alternative assets for ETF investors

As I've already mentioned, there are a limited range of alternatives that investors can access when they are restricted to using ETFs. In this section I'll explain how US and UK investors should make the most of the ETFs currently available in their local market to build a diversified portfolio of alternatives.

General recommendations

In the previous chapter, in the section starting on page 204, I gave the following recommendations for alternative investment, given the total size of a portfolio, and assuming a 10% risk weighting in alternatives:

Total portfolio less than £30,000 or $5,000*	No alternatives.
Total portfolio at least £30,000 or $5,000	Invest only in genuine alternatives.
Total portfolio at least £130,000 or $22,000	Invest in genuine alternatives, equity-like and bond-like alternatives.

* As usual I'm assuming here you are paying $1 or £6 in fixed commissions. Otherwise multiply the minimum portfolio sizes shown by the ratio of your minimum commission to the values I'm using.

In this section of the chapter I show the weighting scheme given different size allocations to each type of alternatives. This will be in reverse order of size; largest investors first. This should allow you to see the logic for each element in the portfolio more clearly.

Genuine alternatives

US investors

A large US retail investor using ETFs would be able to replicate most of the exposure in portfolio 21, with the exception of tail protect, as portfolio 24 shows. Portfolios 25 and 26 show suitable portfolios for medium and small accounts.

PORTFOLIO 24: SUGGESTED WEIGHTING FOR GENUINE ALTERNATIVES SUB-PORTFOLIO (LARGE US ETF INVESTOR)

Portfolio									
Genuine alternatives									
Standalone 50%		Insurance-like 50%							
Managed futures	Global Macro	Short biased	Long volatility	Safe haven currencies 25%		Precious metals 25%			
WDTI * 50%	MCRO 50%	DYB 25%	VXX 25%	Swiss FXF 50%	Yen FXY 50%	Gold IAU 25%	Silver SLV 25%	Platinum PPLT 25%	Palladium PALL 25%
25% (28.8%)	25% (23.2%)	12.5% (11.1%)	12.5% (3.4%)	6.25% (5.7%)	6.25% (5.7%)	3.13% (4.2%)	3.13% (4.2%)	3.13% (4.2%)	3.13% (4.2%)

Final row shows weight within genuine alternatives sub-portfolio. Weights are risk weightings, suggested cash weightings shown in **(bold)**. Minimum investment in genuine alternatives: $9,000. * WDTI does not invest in managed futures hedge funds, but tries to replicate their strategy.

PORTFOLIO 25: SUGGESTED PORTFOLIO WEIGHTING FOR GENUINE ALTERNATIVES SUB-PORTFOLIO (MEDIUM US ETF INVESTOR)

Portfolio				
Genuine alternatives				
Standalone 50%		Insurance-like 50%		
Managed futures WDTI * 50%	Global Macro MCRO 50%	Short biased DYB 33.3%	Safe haven currencies 33.3%	Precious metals 33.3%
			Swiss Franc FXF 100%	Gold IAU 100%
25% (24.4%)	25% (19.7%)	16.7% (12.6%)	16.7% (24.1%)	16.7% (19.1%)

Final row shows weight within genuine alternatives sub-portfolio. Weights are risk weightings, cash weightings shown in **(bold)**. Minimum investment in genuine alternatives: $2,400. * WDTI does not invest in managed futures hedge funds, but tries to replicate their strategy.

PORTFOLIO 26: SUGGESTED PORTFOLIO WEIGHTING FOR GENUINE ALTERNATIVES SUB-PORTFOLIO (SMALL US ETF INVESTOR)

Portfolio			
Genuine alternatives			
Standalone 50%		Insurance-like 50%	
Managed futures WDTI * 50%	Global Macro MCRO 50%	Safe haven currencies 50%	Precious metals 50%
		Swiss Franc FXF 100%	Gold IAU 100%
25% **(22.2%)**	25% **(18.1%)**	25% **(33.2%)**	25% **(26.3%)**

Final row shows weight within genuine alternatives sub-portfolio. Weights are risk weightings, cash weightings shown in **(bold)**. Minimum investment in genuine alternatives: $1,700. * WDTI does not invest in managed futures hedge funds, but tries to replicate their strategy.

If you have less than $1,700 and so only enough cash for a single genuine alternatives fund you should invest entirely in gold, because it's usually the cheapest alternative ETF available and there is plenty of choice. In this situation, put your entire genuine alternatives allocation entirely in a gold ETF, e.g. IAU or similar.

UK investors

In the UK the availability of alternative ETFs is somewhat limited: for example there are no funds that meet my criteria as **standalone** genuine alternatives. We are limited to just the five funds shown in portfolio 27, all of which fall into the **insurance-like** category.

PORTFOLIO 27: SUGGESTED WEIGHTING FOR GENUINE ALTERNATIVES SUB-PORTFOLIO (LARGE UK ETF INVESTOR)

Portfolio					
Genuine alternatives					
Standalone 0%	Insurance-like 100%				
	Long volatility SPVG 50%	Precious metals 50%			
		Gold ETF SGLN 25%	Platinum ETF SPLT 25%	Silver ETF SSLN 25%	Palladium ETF SPDM 25%
0%	50% **(16.7%)**	12.5% **(20.8%)**	12.5% **(20.8%)**	12.5% **(20.8%)**	12.5% **(20.8%)**

Final row shows weight within genuine alternatives sub-portfolio. Weights are risk weightings, cash weightings shown in **(bold)**. Minimum investment in genuine alternatives: £11,000.

If you have less than £11,000 allocated to genuine alternatives then invest it entirely in a single gold ETF, e.g. SGLN or similar.

DIGRESSION: A NOTE ABOUT GOLD

You might be wondering how the modest allocations of 26% cash weighting or less in gold shown in the previous few portfolios can be reconciled with populist recommendations to put a **quarter of your entire portfolio** into the shiny metal.

Let's think about what would be a reasonable allocation to gold in the context of your entire portfolio. For a smaller retail investor it makes sense to allocate the entire genuine alternatives portfolio in gold, as it's straightforward and cheap to get exposure to it. If they've also set 10% of their entire portfolio aside for genuine alternatives, and none for equity-like and bond-like pretenders, they'd end up with a 10% risk weighted allocation in gold.

The resulting cash weighting for gold comes out at 8%. This is probably the largest amount of gold I'd countenance holding. I certainly think that the 25% weight to gold proposed by many people is far too much for an insurance-like asset that you shouldn't expect to earn a positive return on.[167]

Incidentally if you weighted your asset class allocation by global **market capitalisation** then only around 2.5% of your portfolio would be in gold.[168]

Equity-like alternatives

US investors

PORTFOLIO 28: SUGGESTED WEIGHTING FOR EQUITY-LIKE ALTERNATIVES SUB-PORTFOLIO (LARGE US ETF INVESTOR)

Portfolio						
Equities						
Equity-like alternatives						
Private equity & venture capital 25%	Real estate 25%	Commodities (ex-precious metals) 25%				Hedge funds 25%
Private equity 100% PEX	Commercial 100% GQRE	Agricultural 33% GSG	Energies 33% USO	Non-precious metals 33% JJM	Equity neutral 33% QMN	Other hedge funds 66% QAI
25% **(16.1%)**	25% **(30.7%)**	8.3% **(8.5%)**	8.3% **(5.3%)**	8.3% **(10.6%)**	8.3% **(12.2%)**	16.7% **(16.6%)**

Final row shows weight within equity-like alternatives sub-portfolio. Weights are risk weightings, cash weightings shown in **(bold)**. Minimum investment in equity-like alternatives: $6,000.

---

167. Remember from earlier in the chapter that you will not usually earn the full increase in the spot price of gold from investing in a gold ETF because of the slight contango in the futures.
168. Based on market values in early 2017.

A large US investor using ETFs would be able to implement something like portfolio 28, which is the closest possible replication of portfolio 22, page 216. I couldn't find a venture capital ETF, whilst in the real estate category there is limited geographic availability so I chose to use a single global fund. I've also replaced the FX carry and fixed income relative value with an 'other hedge funds' ETF. Portfolio 29 is suitable for smaller investors.

PORTFOLIO 29: SUGGESTED WEIGHTING FOR EQUITY-LIKE ALTERNATIVES SUB-PORTFOLIO (SMALL US ETF INVESTOR)

Portfolio			
Equity			
Equity-like alternatives			
Private equity & venture capital 25%	Real estate 25%	Commodities (ex-precious metals) 25%	Hedge funds 25%
Private equity 100% PEX	Commercial 100% GQRE	Energies 100% USO	Equity neutral 100% QMN
25% (16.1%)	25% (30.9%)	25% (15.9%)	25% (37.0%)

Final row shows weight within equity-like alternatives sub-portfolio. Weights are risk weightings, cash weightings shown in **(bold)**. Minimum investment in equity-like alternatives: $2,000.

With less than $2,000 in equity-like alternatives there's only sufficient cash for a single fund. I'd choose a global property fund like GQRE, as this the cheapest ETF in the equity-like category.

UK investors

For UK investors I've put together portfolio 30. The short volatility bucket has been removed due to a lack of funds, and there are no sub-allocations within commodities. I have however taken advantage of the wider selection of property ETFs. Portfolio 31 is for investors with more modest funds.

PORTFOLIO 30: SUGGESTED WEIGHTING FOR EQUITY-LIKE ALTERNATIVES SUB-PORTFOLIO (LARGE UK ETF INVESTOR)

Portfolio					
Equities					
Equity-like alternatives					
Private equity ETF 33.3% XLPE	Real estate 33.3%				Commodities ETF 33.3% CMFP
	US property 25% IUSP	Asia property 25% IASP	UK property 25% IUKP	Europe property 25% IPRP	
33.3% **(25.6%)**	8.3% **(12.3%)**	8.3% **(12.3%)**	8.3% **(12.3%)**	8.3% **(12.3%)**	33.3% **(25.2%)**

Final row shows weight within equity-like alternatives sub-portfolio. Weights are risk weightings, cash weightings shown in **(bold)**. Minimum investment in equity-like alternatives: £15,000.

PORTFOLIO 31: SUGGESTED PORTFOLIO WEIGHTING FOR EQUITY-LIKE ALTERNATIVES SUB-PORTFOLIO (SMALL UK ETF INVESTOR)

Portfolio		
Equities		
Equity-like alternatives		
Private equity ETF 33.3% XLPE	Global real estate 33.3% GBRE	Commodities ETF 33.3% CMFP
33.3% **(25.6%)**	33.3% **(49.1%)**	33.3% **(25.2%)**

Final row shows weight within equity-like alternatives sub-portfolio. Weights are risk weightings, cash weightings shown in **(bold)**. Minimum investment in equity-like alternatives: £7,200.

With less than £7,200 I'd select a single fund. The commodities ETF CMFP is currently the cheapest in this category.

Bond-like alternatives

US investors

US ETF investors have a much more limited set of options than in the other categories, as shown in portfolio 32. As I said earlier I would avoid peer-to-peer lending, except in the unlikely case you can earn a decent spread over high yield corporate bonds.

PORTFOLIO 32: SUGGESTED WEIGHTING FOR BOND-LIKE ALTERNATIVES (US ETF INVESTOR)

Portfolio								
Bonds								
Bond-like alternatives								
Private debt 0%	Peer-to-peer lending 0%	Infrastructure, real assets, ABS 100%						Long fixed income
		Infrastructure 50%		Real assets 50%		Asset-backed securities		Hedge funds 0%
		Developed 50% IGF	Emerging 50% EMIF	Timber 50% WOOD	Agribusiness 50% IGE	0%		
0%	0%	25% (36.9%)	25% (19.4%)	25% (19.8%)	25% (23.9%)	0%	0%	

Final row shows weight within bond-like alternatives sub-portfolio. Weights are risk weightings, cash weightings shown in **(bold)**. Minimum allocation: $1,600.

With less than $1,600 and only enough cash for a single fund in the portfolio, I'd allocate to the developed infrastructure ETF IGF as this is the cheapest option.

UK investors

Portfolio 33 reflects the paucity of suitable ETFs in the UK. Again I'd avoid peer-to-peer lending.

PORTFOLIO 33: SUGGESTED WEIGHTING IN BOND-LIKE ALTERNATIVES (UK ETF INVESTOR)

Portfolio								
Bonds								
Bond-like alternatives								
Private debt 0%	Peer-to-peer lending 0%	Infrastructure, real assets, ABS 100%						Long fixed income
		Infrastructure 50%		Real assets 50%		Asset-backed securities 0%		Hedge Funds 0%
		Developed 50% XSGI	Emerging 50% IEMI	Timber 50% WOOD	Agribusiness 50% SPAG			
0%	0%	25% **(36.9%)**	25% **(19.4%)**	25% **(19.8%)**	25% **(23.9%)**	0%		0%

Final row shows weight within bond-like alternatives sub-portfolio. Weights are risk weightings, cash weightings shown in **(bold)**. Minimum allocation £10,000.

With less than £10,000 I'd opt for the relatively cheap developed infrastructure ETF XSGI.

Summary

Retail investors: total portfolio less than £30,000 or $5,000*	Do not invest in alternatives. You could have skipped this chapter!
Total portfolio at least £30,000 or $5,000	Invest only in **genuine alternatives**. US investors should allocate to ETFs according to the advice from page 219 onwards, depending on exactly what their cash weighting to genuine alternatives is. UK investors should turn to page 221.

Total portfolio at least £130,000 or $22,000	Invest in **genuine alternatives**, **bond-like** alternatives and **equity-like** alternatives. Genuine alternatives: US investors from page 219 onwards. UK investors should turn to page 221. Equity-like alternatives: US page 223. UK page 224. Bond-like alternatives: US page 226. UK page 226.
Institutional investors	Genuine alternatives: Portfolio 21 (page 211) shows a suggested breakdown. Equity-like alternatives: portfolio 22 (page 216). Bond-like alternatives: portfolio 23 (page 218).

* As usual these account values assume you are paying £6 or $1 in minimum commissions. If not then multiply the values shown by the ratio of your minimum commission to my values. For example if you're paying £12 then you need at least (12 ÷ 2) × £130,000 = £260,000 to invest in all three kinds of alternatives.

CHAPTER TEN

Equities Across Countries

Portfolio					
Equities			Bonds		Genuine alternatives
Traditional equity		Equity-like alternatives	Traditional bonds	Bond-like alternatives	
Developed equity	Emerging equity		Developed	Emerging	
Regions			Regions		
Countries			Countries		
Sectors			Type		
Individual equities			Maturity and credit		

THE DAYS WHEN MYOPIC INVESTORS WOULD PATRIOTICALLY PUT all their money into their domestic stock market should be long gone. In this chapter I discuss how to allocate the equity part of your portfolio amongst different countries in the smartest possible way – to achieve maximum diversification.

Chapter overview

How to structure an equity portfolio	Comparing some alternative ways to group the assets in a portfolio of equities.

My framework for top-down allocation in equities	My proposed method for deciding my equity allocation to different regions and countries. Includes suggested weightings for investors using ETFs, given portfolio size.

The next chapter dives into allocating within each country's equity market.

How to structure an equity portfolio

There are least 50,000 publicly listed firms in the world. How do we classify and group them? The two main equity classifications are by **country** and **sector**. The relevant country is the location where the stock has its main listing and usually its headquarters. The sector is the industry which the firm operates in. I use the terms sector and industry interchangeably.[169]

Almost every country in the world has a stock exchange. However in most of them access for non-domestic investors is very difficult or expensive, and the liquidity of many smaller markets is pretty sluggish. So what is the set of countries which you can realistically invest in?[170]

Nearly all passive tracking funds are based on equity indices from two main index providers: MSCI and FTSE. There are currently 46 countries in the MSCI All Country World Index, of which 23 are classified as emerging. The FTSE All-World Index is a similar size.[171] For nearly all investors this universe of countries is more than enough.[172] I use the MSCI index in the rest of this book.

You can also split countries into groups. A traditional grouping is emerging and developed markets. Another is by region; a common split is America, Asia, and EMEA (Europe, Middle East, and Africa).

The widely used MSCI Global Industry Classification Standard (GICS) scheme has 11 top-level sectors,[173] and numerous sub-classifications.

---

169. Note for pedants: In the GICS® industry classification scheme sector and industry refer to different levels of granularity: sector is the top level, and industry the second level. However in this book I do not go below the top level classification. So at the risk of offending GICS geeks I sometimes use the more familiar term industry but I'm always referring to the top sector level of the GICS scheme

170. Exclusion or inclusion of any country is not a political statement but reflects their omission from, or presence within, the MSCI All Country index I've used in this chapter.

171. There are some very minor differences between the FTSE and MSCI indices; I use the MSCI indices in this book.

172. If you're more adventurous another 24 much smaller markets make up the MSCI Frontier Markets Index; with another dozen or so minnows in standalone indices. I ignore these, but there are funds that you can buy to get exposure to them.

173. Energy, Materials, Industrial, Consumer Discretionary, Consumer Staples, Health Care,

Alternative grouping methods

There are several ways to group the countries in a portfolio of equities:

Single fund: global market cap weighted	You could use a single global equity fund. These are market capitalisation weighted, so over half their exposure is in one country: the US.
US and non-US	A simple way to get round the problem of US concentration is to put a proportion of your portfolio into a US specific fund, and the rest into a non US fund, both market cap weighted. Of course the latter will still be biased towards other large countries like Japan, but it's still an improvement over a global market cap index.
By region	Countries which are in the same geographical region tend to have closely integrated economies, and so more correlated markets.
Developed and emerging	Emerging markets (EM) are usually more correlated with each other than with wealthier neighbours in the same region, especially in a crisis. It's also easier to constrain emerging markets if you first split your portfolio accordingly; I discuss this later in the chapter.
By industry	Arguably a pair of oil firms, like BP in the UK and Exxon Mobil in the US, have more in common than two UK firms like BP and Sainsbury's, a supermarket chain. Perhaps it makes more sense to allocate directly to global **industries**. However if you're using global sector ETFs then your portfolio will still be US dominated, as the relevant indices are market capitalisation weighted. This is an important problem which I examine in the next section, 'The allocation conundrum'.

The allocation conundrum

The handcrafting portfolio weighting suggests you should group the most closely related assets first. Should you (a) group firms in the same geographic area together (region or country), or (b) in the same industry? If you're buying individual firms it won't really matter, as you'll probably end up with the same final portfolio weights.

But even very large institutions are unlikely to want to hold individual shares in 40 or more countries. When you have to use ETFs to take some, or all of your exposure, then you have to make compromises.

Financials, Information Technology, Telecommunication services, Utilities and Real Estate (added in September 2016).

If you go for option (a) and allocate to market cap weighted country ETFs, this will leave you exposed to concentration in industries. Whereas going for option (b) and allocating to market cap weighted global industry ETFs means your country exposure will still be heavily biased towards the US. We can't solve both of these problems, so which is more problematic?

In reality **country concentration is more dangerous than industry concentration**. Over half of the global equity index is in one country, the US. In contrast, financials, the largest industry sector, has a weight of only 16% in the real world global market cap weighted portfolio.

In summary, it's **better to allocate to countries first, sectors second**. Top-down allocation to market cap weighted global sectors is inferior, because it will leave you exposed to large country concentration risk. Allocating to sectors within countries is the subject of the next chapter.

My framework for top-down allocation in equities

With the above analysis in mind, I'm going to show you how to weight a portfolio across countries with the top-down **handcrafting method**. I perform the top-down allocation in the following order:

1. Emerging/developed markets

2. Regional groupings

3. Countries within regions

Throughout the process I suggest ETFs to replicate the portfolios I put together. Larger investors who can decompose their portfolio within each country can also use these country weightings; then the next chapter will explain how to split up your allocation for each country.

Emerging and developed markets

The first grouping I'm going to use in my top-down weighting of the equity sub-portfolio is between developed markets (DM) and emerging markets (EM). A naive application of my handcrafting method would split the portfolio equally[174] in **risk weighted** terms between developed and emerging markets.

But there are several different scenarios when equal risk weighting wouldn't make sense. I outlined these back in chapter four: different group sizes, embarrassment, expensive assets and unpredictable unpleasant risk.

---

174. Technical note: Incidentally if I do a formal portfolio optimisation I get an answer that is very close to this: 53% for EM, 47% for developed.

As it happens, **different group sizes** aren't a problem since the MSCI All Country Index has 23 developed countries and also 23 emerging countries. Deviating from the market capitalisation weighted consensus, which can cause **embarrassment**, is more of a problem. Fifty percent in EM looks dangerously racy if I compare it to the market cap weighted MSCI All Country World Index, which has a risk weighted equivalent allocation of 14% in EM.

Emerging market funds are also a little more **expensive**, especially at the level of individual countries. They are also **riskier**. The simple risk measure I'm using in this book is particularly misleading when dealing with assets like EM equities that go through prolonged periods of relatively low volatility, followed by *risk-off* panic events.

I'm going to use a **25% risk weighted allocation to EM**. In cash terms using my preferred volatilities[175] this is **17% to EM**, leaving 83% in developed markets. Of course it's straightforward to adapt your own portfolio differently according to taste, or any regulatory constraints you have. But I'd strongly advise never going above 40% in emerging markets by risk weighting.

ETF options

If you are a very small investor then you can only afford to put a single fund into the equity part of your portfolio without incurring significant costs. Your first port of call should be a market capitalisation weighted global equity fund. These funds will have over half of their weight in the US, as portfolio 34 shows.

PORTFOLIO 34: A SINGLE GLOBAL FUND HAS MASSIVE US CONCENTRATION RISK

Portfolio						
Equity Global index ETF VWRL (UK) VT (US)						
US **53%**	Japan **8%**	UK **7%**	France **3%**	Canada **3%**	Germany **3%**	Other **23%**
53%	8%	7%	3%	3%	3%	23%

Weights shown are cash weights from MSCI World AC Index as of May 2016. Final row shows weight within equity sub-portfolio.

---

175. You can find all the standard deviations I used in this chapter for converting risk weighting to cash weighting in Appendix B, page 485. These are based on my own analysis.

If you have a little more capital then you can split out emerging markets, invest in a non-US developed markets fund, and separately in a US specific fund. This is the most efficient way to reduce concentration risk.

Suppose you wanted to limit the US to 20% risk weighting.[176] Portfolio 35 shows how this could be done.

PORTFOLIO 35: DEVELOPED AND EMERGING PORTFOLIO FOR A US ETF INVESTOR

Portfolio							
Equity							
Emerging 25% (17.5%) VWO	US 27% (22.2%) IVV	Developed 75%					
		Developed non-US 73% (60.3%) EFA					
China 24%	Other 76%		Japan 20%	UK 18%	France 9%	Canada 8%	Other 45%
6.0%	19.0%	20.2%	11.0%	9.9%	4.9%	4.4%	24.6%

Risk weightings are shown. Cash weightings for each fund in **(bold)** Final row shows risk weighting within equity sub-portfolio. Minimum investment in traditional equities: $1,750.

This option isn't available in the UK, where I couldn't find an ex-US developed markets fund. Instead portfolio 36 shows a developed and EM allocation.

---

176. This is the same allocation I use later in this chapter.

PORTFOLIO 36: DEVELOPED AND EMERGING PORTFOLIO WITH EXAMPLE ETF TICKERS FOR UK INVESTORS

Portfolio								
Equity								
Emerging 25% **(17%)** EIMI			Developed 75% **(83%)** VEVE					
China 24%	South Korea 16%	Other 60%	US 58%	Japan 9%	UK 7%	Canada 3%	Germany 3%	Other developed 20%
6%	4%	15%	43.5%	6.8%	5.3%	2.3%	2.3%	15%

Risk weightings are shown, cash weights for each fund in **(bold)**. Final row shows weight within equity sub-portfolio. Minimum investment in traditional equities: £11,000.

Investors with enough capital can disaggregate their emerging and developed market allocations further. I discuss this in the next couple of parts of this chapter.

Developed market regions

The usual regional grouping used in the investment industry is North America, EMEA (Europe, Middle East, Africa), and Asia Pacific. Personally I'm comfortable with an **equal regional allocation**: a third of my sub-portfolio in each region.

None of the potential alternatives to equal weighting make sense. The market capitalisation weight is far too skewed – nearly two-thirds in North America, a quarter in Europe and just 12% in Asia. Equal weight across countries would put far too much in Europe with its numerous countries, and hardly anything in the two-country region of North America. I also have no concerns about risk or costs that would justify deviating from equal weights.

All weights shown in this section are **risk weights**, but it's not strictly necessary to adjust for different volatility in these portfolios of fairly similar countries, so you can also use these as **cash weights**.

ETF options

Portfolio 37 shows the appropriate allocation after putting a third of the sub-portfolio into a market capitalisation weighted fund for each region, suggested ETF tickers to get the appropriate exposure, and the resulting implied weights to some key countries.

Whilst the exposure shown here is better than a single global market cap weighted fund, it's still very overweight the US, and to a lesser extent Japan and the UK. For this reason I wouldn't recommend it for US investors; the previous portfolio (35) has the same minimum investment but better diversification.

PORTFOLIO 37: DEVELOPED EQUITY BREAKDOWN BY REGION WITH SUGGESTED ETF TICKERS

Portfolio								
Equity								
Developed								
North America 33.3% VNRT (UK) IVV (US) *		EMEA (Europe) 33.3% XMEU (UK) VGK (US)				Asia Pacific 33.3% IAPD (UK)*** VPL (US)		
US 95%	Canada ** 5%	UK 29%	France 15%	Germany 14%	Other 42%	Japan 65%	Australia 20%	Other 15%
31.4%	1.7%	9.6%	5.0%	4.6%	13.9%	21.5%	6.6%	5.0%

Risk weightings are shown (suggested cash weightings are identical). Regional exposures taken use market cap indices. Final row shows weight within equity sub-portfolio. Column widths do not reflect actual weights. Minimum investment in developed market equities: £5,400 or $900 (not recommended for US Investors – use portfolio 35). * The North American IVV ETF is actually just the US. I could not find a US listed North American ETF. ** The Canadian weight with US listed ETFs is zero *** IAPD is not market cap weighted, but a fund selected on dividend yield.

With sufficient capital I can repeat my earlier magic trick and split each region into a single large country and 'ex-' pairing. In the case of the two-country North American group this is just a matter of using a US and Canadian fund. Similarly for Asia Pacific there are plenty of ex-Japan funds to which we can add a Japan only allocation. There are also UK listed 'Europe ex-UK' funds, but sadly none in the US.

Portfolios 38 and 39 have the detail with some explicit tickers. The weightings here are set to try and get as close as possible to my preferred country weights, which I'll discuss later in this chapter.

PORTFOLIO 38: DEVELOPED EQUITY BREAKDOWN BY REGION, USING 'EX-' FUNDS TO REDUCE CONCENTRATION, WITH SUGGESTED ETF TICKERS FOR US INVESTORS

Portfolio								
Equity								
Developed								
North America 33.3%		EMEA (Europe) 33.3% VGK				Asia Pacific 33.3%		
US 80% IVV	Canada 20% EWC	UK 29%	France 15%	Germany 14%	Other 42%	Japan 40% HJGP *	Asia ex-JP 60% AXJL	
							Australia 58%	Other 42%
26.7%	6.7%	9.7%	5.0%	4.7%	14.0%	13.3%	11.6%	8.4%

Risk weightings are shown (cash weightings are identical). Regional exposures taken using market cap indices. Final row shows weight within equity sub-portfolio. Minimum investment in developed market equities: $4,500. * HJGP is currency hedged, but is 0.17% a year cheaper than the cheapest non-hedged alternative.

PORTFOLIO 39: DEVELOPED EQUITY BREAKDOWN BY REGION, USING 'EX-' FUNDS TO REDUCE CONCENTRATION, WITH SUGGESTED ETF TICKERS FOR UK INVESTORS

Portfolio								
Equity								
Developed								
North America 33%		EMEA (Europe) 33%				Asia Pacific 33%		
US 80% CSPX	Canada 20% UC24	UK 20% ISF	Europe ex-UK 80% IEUX			Japan 40% HMJP	Asia ex-JP 60% CPJ1	
			France 21%	Germany 20%	Other 59%		Australia 58%	Other 42%
26.7%	6.7%	6.7%	5.6%	5.3%	15.7%	13.3%	11.6%	8.4%

Risk weightings are shown (cash weightings are identical). Regional exposures taken use market cap indices. Final row shows weight within equity sub-portfolio. Minimum investment in developed market equities: £27,000.

Larger investors will be able to break this allocation down further to specific countries, and I discuss this later in the chapter.

Emerging market regions

How should we divide up the emerging market (EM) countries? There are three geographical regions that are commonly used by index providers: Latin America, Asia[177] and EMEA (Europe, Middle East, Africa).[178]

Again we need to check if a move away from equal weighting is justified. Both risk and ETF costs are similar across EM regions, so no problem there. But by market capitalisation weighting, Asia is over represented in the EM regions mainly due to the behemoth that

---

177. There is some debate about whether South Korea belongs in the EM or developed group, so be aware there might be double counting if you mix and match funds using different index providers.
178. Sometimes Brazil, Russia, India and China are grouped together as the BRIC countries. I won't be using that conveniently named grouping here. Nor will I be using MINT (Mexico, Indonesia, Nigeria and Turkey), CIVETS (Colombia, Indonesia, Vietnam, Egypt, Turkey and South Africa), or any other arbitrary group of countries chosen partly on the basis that they make a neat acronym.

is the Chinese market, although South Korea and Taiwan also have large weights. EMEA and the Americas represent just 16% and 13% respectively of the EM cap weighted index.

Because there is such a large difference between equal and market cap weighting, I'm going to compromise: my recommended weighting gives 40% to Asia – slightly higher than a strict equal weighting of 33%. The other two regions are left with 30% each.

In theory portfolio 40 would be suitable for an investor with at least £6,000 or $1,000 to invest in emerging market equities. There are no serious concentration issues so I do not advise bothering with a China/ex-China split or similar; especially given coverage is patchy for funds of this type.

PORTFOLIO 40: EMERGING MARKET EQUITY BREAKDOWN BY REGION WITH SUGGESTED ETF TICKERS

Portfolio								
Equity								
Emerging								
Americas 30% ALAT (UK) ILF (US)		EMEA 30% XMEA (UK) GUR (US)			Asia 40% EMAS (UK) GMF (US)			
Brazil 50%	Other 50%	South Africa 44%	Russia 25%	Other 31%	China 34%	South Korea 23%	Taiwan 18%	Other 25%
15.0%	15.0%	13.2%	7.5%	9.3%	13.6%	9.2%	7.2%	10.0%

Risk weightings are shown (suggested cash weightings are identical). Regional exposures taken use market cap indices. Final row shows country weight within emerging equity sub-portfolio. Minimum investment in emerging market equities: $1,000 or £6,000.

Again, larger investors can break this allocation down further to specific countries, and I discuss this in the next section.

Within regions, down to countries

In this part of the chapter I explain how to allocate to individual countries within geographic regions.

All weights shown are risk weights, but it's probably unnecessary to adjust for different volatility in these portfolios of fairly similar countries, so you can also use the weights given as cash weights.

Developed markets: North America

This is the most trivial breakdown into two countries, and I did it in portfolios 38 and 39 (page 237), with suggested weights of 80% in the US and 20% in Canada.

Developed markets: Europe

Portfolio 41 shows my ideal allocation within developed Europe. The good news is that US investors are spoilt for choice and have an ETF for every country shown.

PORTFOLIO 41: IDEAL DEVELOPED EQUITY BREAKDOWN FOR EUROPE, WITH US ETF TICKERS

Portfolio													
Equity													
Developed													
Europe													
Anglophile 20%		Northern Europe 40%								Latin Europe 40%			
UK 80% QGBR	Ireland 20% EIRL	Germanic 50%			Benelux 20%		Nordic 30%			France 35% EWQ	Italy 20% EWI	Iberian 35%		Israel 10% EIS
		Germany 40% VGK	Austria 20% EWO	Switzerland 40% EWL	Netherlands 50% EWN	Belgium 50% EWK	Sweden 33% EWD	Finland 33% EFNL	Norway 33% NORW			Spain 80% QESP	Portugal 20% PGAL	
16%	4%	8%	4%	8%	4%	4%	4%	4%	4%	14%	8%	11%	3%	4%

Risk weightings are shown (suggested cash weightings are identical). Final row shows country weight within developed European equity sub-portfolio. Minimum investment in developed European equities: $11,000.

But there are fewer ETFs in the UK, as Portfolio 42 shows.[179]

PORTFOLIO 42: DEVELOPED EQUITY BREAKDOWN FOR EUROPE WITH UK ETF TICKERS

Portfolio							
Equity							
Developed							
Europe							
Anglophile 20%	Northern Europe 40%				Latin Europe 40%		
UK 100% ISF	Germanic 50%		Benelux 20%	Nordic 30% CN1	France 35% ISFR	Italy 30% CI1	Iberian 35%
	Germany 50% DAXX	Switzerland 50% CSWCHF	Netherlands 100% CH1				Spain 100% CS1
20%	10%	10%	8%	12%	14%	12%	14%

Risk weightings are shown (suggested cash weightings are identical). Final row shows country weight within developed European equity sub-portfolio. Minimum investment in developed European equities: £23,000.

---

179. For instance, I couldn't find an Irish ETF with a UK listing. This is deeply ironic, given that many UK listed ETFs are Irish domiciled legal entities.

Developed markets: Asia

Portfolio 43 shows my recommended allocation for both UK and US investors.

PORTFOLIO 43: DEVELOPED EQUITY BREAKDOWN FOR ASIA PACIFIC WITH SUGGESTED ETF TICKERS

Portfolio				
Equity				
Developed				
Asia Pacific				
Japan 40% HMJP (UK) JPP (US)	Antipodean 30%		Asian mainland 30%	
	Australia 70% LAUS (UK) DBAU (US)	New Zealand 30% ENZL (US)	Hong Kong 50% HSI (UK) EWH (US)	Singapore 50% XBAS (UK) EWS (US)
40%	21% *	9% *	15%	15%

Risk weightings are shown (suggested cash weightings are identical). Final row shows country weight within equity sub-portfolio. Column widths do not reflect actual weights. Minimum investment in developed Asia Pacific equities: $3,400 or £12,000. * There is no New Zealand ETF listed in the UK. For a UK investor the weights would be 30% in Australia, 0% in New Zealand.

Emerging markets: Asia

My suggested breakdown for emerging Asia for both UK and US investors is shown in portfolio 44.

PORTFOLIO 44: EMERGING MARKETS EQUITY BREAKDOWN FOR ASIA WITH SUGGESTED ETF TICKERS

Portfolio							
Equity							
Emerging							
Asia							
China 30%	India 20%	Asian Tigers 30%		South East Asia 20%			
CSIL (UK) CHNA (US)	CI2G (UK) INDA (US)	Taiwan 50% HTWN (UK) EWT (US)	South Korea 50% HKOR (UK) HKOR (US)	Malaysia 25% XCX3 (UK) EWM (US)	Indonesia 25% XCX5 (UK) IDX (US)	Thailand 25% THAG (UK) THD (US)	Philippines 25% XPHG (UK) EPHE (US)
30%	20%	15%	15%	5%	5%	5%	5%

Risk weightings are shown (suggested cash weightings are identical). Final row shows country weight within EM Asia Pacific equity sub-portfolio. Minimum investment in emerging Asian Equity: £36,000 or $6,000.

Emerging markets: Latin America

I've put together a suggested US ETF allocation for Latin America in portfolio 45.

PORTFOLIO 45: EMERGING MARKETS EQUITY BREAKDOWN FOR LATIN AMERICA WITH SUGGESTED ETF TICKERS FOR US INVESTORS

Portfolio				
Equity				
Emerging Markets				
Latin America				
Brazil 35% DBBR	Mexico 35% DBMX	Smaller Latin America 30%		
		Chile 33% ECH	Colombia 33% ICOL	Peru 33% EPU
35%	*35%*	*10%*	*10%*	*10%*

Risk weightings are shown (suggested cash weightings are identical). Final row shows country weight within EM Latin American equity sub-portfolio. Weights and funds shown are for US investors. Minimum investment in emerging Latin American equities: $3,000.

For UK investors I recommend sticking with the single regional fund ALAT, since there are no ETFs available for the smaller countries.

Emerging markets: Europe, Middle East, Africa (EMEA)

The final emerging region is EMEA. A theoretically ideal breakdown is show in portfolio 46. However, it isn't possible to make this allocation using ETFs; there just aren't enough of them available.

PORTFOLIO 46: EMERGING MARKET EQUITY BREAKDOWN FOR EMEA (INSTITUTIONAL INVESTORS)

Portfolio									
Equity									
Emerging									
Europe, Middle East, Africa									
Europe 50%						Middle East 25%			Africa 25%
Russia 33%	Central & Eastern Europe 33%			South East Europe 33%		Qatar 33%	UAE 33%	Egypt 33%	South Africa 100%
	Poland 33%	Hungary 33%	Czech Republic 33%	Greece 50%	Turkey 50%				
17%	6%	6%	6%	8%	8%	8%	8%	8%	25%

Risk weightings are shown (suggested cash weightings are identical). Final row shows country weight within EM EMEA equity sub-portfolio.

Portfolio 47 shows the best job you could do with ETFs that are currently available in the US.[180]

PORTFOLIO 47: EM EQUITY BREAKDOWN FOR EMEA WITH US ETF TICKERS

Portfolio				
Equity				
Emerging				
Europe, Middle East, Africa				
Europe 50%			Middle East 25%	Africa 25%
Russia 33% RBL	Central & Eastern Europe 33%	South East Europe 33%	GULF	South Africa 100%
	Poland 100% PLND	Turkey 100% TUR		EZA
17%	17%	17%	25%	25%

Risk weightings are shown (suggested cash weightings are identical). Final row shows country weight within EM EMEA equity sub-portfolio. Minimum investment: $1,800.

In the UK there's a different set of available countries, hence portfolio 48.

---

180. There is also an All Emerging Europe ETF in the US, but this would be massively overweight Russia, to a degree that outweighs the benefit from getting exposure to additional countries.

PORTFOLIO 48: EM EQUITY BREAKDOWN FOR EMEA WITH UK ETF TICKERS

Portfolio				
Equity				
Emerging				
Europe, Middle East, Africa				
Europe 50%			Middle East 25%	Africa 25%
Russia 33% CRU1	CEE 33% CE9G	SE Europe 33%	SGCC	XMAF
		Turkey 100% UB36		
17%	17%	17%	25%	25%

Risk weightings are shown (cash weightings are identical). Final row shows country weight within EM EMEA equity sub-portfolio. Minimum investment: £11,000.

Summary

Large institutional investors

I recommend putting 75% into developed markets, and 25% into emerging markets (EM). If you have a low tolerance for embarrassment the market cap weight is 14% EM; the maximum EM weight I'd advocate would be 40% in EM. These are all risk weightings. My suggested cash weightings are 82.5% and 17.5% respectively.

All other weights given below are risk weightings, but you can safely use them as cash weightings if you assume that all countries have the same volatility.

Developed markets: Allocate one-third of your sub-portfolio in each region: North America, EMEA and Asia Pacific. Allocate 80% of your North American region to US equities, 20% to Canada. Use the weightings in portfolios 41 (for EMEA), and 43 (Asia Pacific).

Emerging markets: Put 40% of your sub-portfolio in Asia, 30% in Latin America, and 30% in EMEA. Use portfolios 44 (Asia), 45 (Latin America), and 46 (Europe) for each emerging market region.

Now read chapter eleven to work out the best way to get exposure to each individual country.

UK retail traders using ETFs

£515,000 upwards allocated to equities*	Risk weightings: 75% developed markets, 25% emerging markets. Cash weightings: 82.5% developed markets, 17.5% emerging markets. Developed markets: Allocate one-third of your sub-portfolio in each of the developed market regions: North America, EMEA and Asia Pacific. Allocate 80% of your North American region to US equities, 20% to Canada. Allocate EMEA using portfolio 42 and Asia Pacific using portfolio 43. Emerging markets: Put 40% of your sub-portfolio in Asia, 30% in Latin America, and 30% in EMEA. Use portfolios 44 (Asia) and 48 (EMEA) for each emerging market region. For Latin America use the single fund ALAT. Now read chapter eleven to work out the best way to get exposure to each individual country.
£82,000 to £515,000	Risk weightings: 75% developed markets, 25% emerging markets. Cash weightings: 82.5% developed markets, 17.5% emerging markets. Developed markets: Allocate one-third into each of North America, EMEA and Asia Pacific. Allocate 80% of your North American allocation to US equities, 20% to Canada. Use the weightings in portfolios 42 (for EMEA), and 43 (Asia Pacific). Emerging markets: Use portfolio 40. Now read chapter eleven.
£36,000 to £82,000	Risk weightings: 75% developed markets, 25% emerging markets. Cash weightings: 82.5% developed markets, 17.5% emerging markets. Developed markets: Use portfolio 39. Emerging markets: Use portfolio 40.
£33,000 to £36,000	Risk weightings: 75% Developed markets, 25% Emerging markets. Cash weightings: 82.5% Developed markets, 17.5% emerging markets. Developed markets: Use portfolio 39. Emerging markets: Single fund: EIMI.
£11,000 to £33,000	Risk weightings: 75% developed markets, 25% emerging markets. Cash weightings: 82.5% developed markets, 17.5% emerging markets. Developed markets: Use portfolio 37. Emerging markets: Single fund: EIMI.

£1,800 to £11,000	Single fund: VWRL.

* These minimum portfolio sizes assume you are paying £6 minimum brokerage commission. As usual if you are paying more you need to multiply them by the ratio of your commission to mine. For example if you're paying £18 minimum you need to multiply these values by £18 ÷ £6 = 3.

US retail traders using ETFs

$86,000 upwards allocated to equities**	Risk weightings: 75% developed markets, 25% emerging markets.
	Cash weightings: 82.5% developed markets, 17.5% emerging markets.
	Developed markets: Allocate one-third of your sub-portfolio to each region: North America, EMEA and Asia Pacific. Allocate 80% of your North American region to US equities, 20% to Canada. Allocate EMEA using portfolio 41 and Asia Pacific using portfolio 43.
	Emerging markets: Put 40% of your sub-portfolio in Asia, 30% in Latin America, and 30% in EMEA. Use portfolios 44 (Asia), 45 (Latin America), and 47 (EMEA) for each emerging market region.
	Now read chapter eleven to work out the best way to get exposure to each individual country.
$28,000 to $86,000	Risk weightings: 75% developed markets, 25% emerging markets.
	Cash weightings: 82.5% developed markets, 17.5% emerging markets.
	Developed markets: Allocate one-third of your sub-portfolio in each region: North America, EMEA and Asia Pacific. Allocate 80% of your North American region to US equities, 20% to Canada. Allocate EMEA using portfolio 41 and Asia Pacific using portfolio 43.
	Emerging markets: Use portfolio 40.
	Now read chapter eleven.
$5,700 to $28,000	Risk weightings: 75% developed markets, 25% emerging markets.
	Cash weightings: 82.5% developed markets, 17.5% emerging markets.
	Developed markets: Use portfolio 38.
	Emerging markets: Use portfolio 40.
$1,750 to $5,700	Risk weightings: 75% developed markets, 25% emerging markets.
	Cash weightings: Use portfolio 35.
$300 to $1,750	Single fund: VT (US).

** These minimum portfolio sizes assume you are paying $1 minimum brokerage commission. If you're paying more you need to multiply them by the ratio of your commission to mine. For example if you're paying $5 minimum you need to multiply these values by $5 ÷ $1 = 5.

CHAPTER ELEVEN

Equities Within Countries

Portfolio							
Equities			Bonds			Genuine alternatives	
Traditional equity		Equity-like alternatives	Traditional bonds		Bond-like alternatives		
Developed equity	Emerging equity		Developed	Emerging			
Regions			Regions				
Countries			Countries				
Sectors			Type				
Individual equities			Maturity and credit				

WHAT IS MORE EXCITING – READING A FINANCIAL WEBSITE AND seeing news about a firm you own a small part of, or following the daily movement of abstract market indices?

Personally I prefer the former, and I'm sure many other investors agree. Buying individual equities is a lot more fun than purchasing index funds. There is also the satisfaction of knowing, for example, that you own a piece of the energy company that's providing your electricity (it might even make paying the bill less galling). However, we need to be smart and not get drawn into the excitement of equity investing. Buying shares in individual firms doesn't make sense for everyone, and it needs to be done correctly if you're to maintain a properly diversified portfolio.

This chapter is about investing in equities within countries: into industry sectors, and then specific firms within each sector.

Chapter overview

Allocating to sectors within a country	How to break down exposure to the sector level.
Allocating to individual equities within sectors	Buying equities within each industry sector.
Ethical investment	Doing the right thing.

Allocating to sectors within a country

Which sectors should we include?

There are a couple of well known industry classification schemes, but I'll be using the Global Industry Classification System (GICS®) developed by MSCI and S&P. The GICS is a four-tier system. At the top level are 11 sectors: energy, materials, industrials, consumer discretionary, consumer staples, health care, financials, information technology (often abbreviated to IT, or just plain tech), telecommunications, utilities and real estate (which was added in 2016).

Below the top level there are a veritable cornucopia of classifications: industry groups, industries and sub-industries. But for simplicity I'll be sticking to the highest layer within the scheme; the 11 sectors.

How to weight each sector

A key tenet of handcrafting is: **thou shalt use equal risk weightings** (unless there is a good reason not to). To use equal risk weightings you need to make the usual assumption about identical risk-adjusted pre-cost returns, but you must also assume that correlations between different assets are very similar.

But are industry correlations really similar enough to be treated as close to identical? The truthful answer is: not really. Using data from US sectors[181] I got an estimated correlation for the IT and utilities sectors of just 0.19. After all, you cannot get more different firms than a sexy tech stock like Apple and a boring, highly regulated, utility business like a power plant operator.

In contrast, consumer staples and health care come out 0.91 correlated. *Staples* are things people **have** to buy, like food (without which you die) and tobacco (which will probably kill you, but is awfully addictive). Health care isn't usually a discretionary purchase either.

---

181. The results are based on annual US sector returns from 1990 to 2016.

Both industries are regarded as defensive plays in an economic downturn. Even in a recession consumers still need pasta, cigarettes and headache pills.

I considered trying to herd similar sectors into several sub-groups, and perform a top-down allocation starting with these sub-groups,[182] but: (a) this would probably have given me something pretty close to equal weighting across sectors, (b) it would be difficult to come up with a single grouping that everyone would agree was reasonable,[183] and (c) it seemed like unnecessary complexity which would probably yield little benefit.

My conclusion: it's acceptable to pretend intra-industry correlations are similar.

Now for the second part of the key tenet of handcrafting: thou shalt use equal risk weightings **unless there is a good reason not to**. Remember that the good reasons not to use equal weighting are: (1) groups of assets that are of radically different size, (2) embarrassment when underperforming with weights which are radically different from the market capitalisation portfolio, (3) significantly different cost levels, and (4) assets with unusual or unpredictable risks.

Let's address (1) **different group sizes** first. It's true that some countries do have an uneven spread of firms across sectors. But if you allocate to individual stocks, and follow the top-down process I outline later in this chapter, you'll end up with a portfolio that has sectors with equal numbers of stocks by design.

To calibrate (2) possible **embarrassment** you should look at the weights you'd get with a vanilla market cap weighted country index tracker. As I'm writing this a US ETF covering the S&P 500 or similar index would have around 20% in glamorous technology, 16% in financials, but just 3% in unfashionable utilities stocks.

These are cash weightings; the risk weightings would be even more extreme because tech has around two-thirds more volatility than utilities. This is some way from an equal risk weighting which would be 9.1% in each of the 11 sectors.[184] However correlations

---

182. To see how correlations affected sector allocations in the US I also performed a formal portfolio optimisation on the returns of the original ten sectors, since sufficient data history wasn't available for the newest sector, Real Estate. The results were pretty interesting. Large risk weighted allocations went to Utilities (23%), IT (21%) and Materials (14%). Losing out were Consumer Staples (7.8%), Consumer Discretionary (3.4%), Financials (1.6%), and Industrials (which got a zero allocation). The other three sectors got close to equal weighting; between 9% and 10%. Although these results are intellectually interesting I wouldn't want to use these weights in any real portfolio. Over 20% in one sector and nothing in another is too extreme for my taste. I'd also need to repeat the exercise for every country we could potentially allocate to – a lot of work, even if I could find sufficient data. Technical note: I used a bootstrapped method to find the best risk weightings, assuming identical Sharpe Ratios. There is more information on this method in Appendix C, page 496.

183. For example, should you group defensive stocks like health care, consumer staples and utilities together, or lump consumer staples with consumer discretionary? Where do financials fit in? IT and telecoms seem to make obvious bedfellows, but telecommunications firms are large and highly regulated companies with consistent cash flow; which makes them more like utilities.

184. Actually the market cap industry weights in the US are relatively diversified compared to other countries. Many markets are dominated by firms in a particular industry, with many emerging markets

between sectors in the same country are relatively high, so there shouldn't be too much tracking error if you use equal risk weights instead of market cap weights.

The latter two problems, (3) **cost levels** and (4) **unpredictable risk**, do not seriously affect sector weights within countries.

Weighing up all these factors, **I am going to stick to using equal risk weightings across equity sectors** within a given country.

Which cash weightings to use

This still leaves us with the problem of finding cash weightings. As I said in chapter two, you have several options. Firstly you can ignore the problem, assume all sectors have the same volatility of returns, and set cash shares which are equal to risk weightings.

Secondly you can use the suggested values for volatility I recommend in Appendix B, in the section starting on page 485. This will give you the cash weights shown in portfolio 49.

PORTFOLIO 49: SECTOR ALLOCATION WITHIN COUNTRIES – CASH WEIGHTINGS IMPLIED BY EQUAL RISK WEIGHTING

Portfolio										
Equities										
Traditional equities										
Developed or emerging										
Region										
Country										
Consumer discretionary	Consumer staples	Energy	Financials	Real estate	Health care	Industrials	IT	Materials	Telecom	Utilities
9.1%	9.1%	9.1%	9.1%	9.1%	9.1%	9.1%	9.1%	9.1%	9.1%	9.1%
(8.2%)	**(13.5%)**	**(11.1%)**	**(7.5%)**	**(8.2%)**	**(8.6%)**	**(10%)**	**(5.6%)**	**(10%)**	**(8.2%)**	**(9%)**

Risk weightings shown. Cash weights in **(bold)**. Minimum allocation to a given country when using sector ETFs: $5,500 or £32,000.

---

suffering from a concentration of resource related stocks in the materials and energy sectors.

Finally you can find some sector data and calculate the actual standard deviations yourself, using the technique in Appendix C (page 489).

What is the benefit of sector allocation?

A single market cap weighted fund will inherit the sector exposure of a particular country. This could mean a portfolio which is far too exposed to just one or two sectors and thus relatively undiversified. What benefit should you expect if you allocate to sectors separately?

You've seen this kind of comparison already, in chapter six. According to my earlier calculations the theoretical benefit of a top-down allocation to sectors was around 0.04% in annual returns in Canada: a country with relatively extreme sector concentration. In a more diversified country like the US the benefit will be a little lower, but there are also some emerging markets with really dire sector concentration problems where you'd see a large improvement.

On average though there is only a small improvement from allocating directly to sectors, and it will be worth having only if you can get exposure to individual sectors relatively cheaply.

Getting exposure to each sector

There are two main methods to create a portfolio of sectors for a given country. You could use market cap weighted sector ETFs, assuming they are available in the country you are allocating to. The alternative is to buy individual shares.

The US seems to be the only country where there is a full suite of sector ETFs available, with several managers offering them. Right now the Select Sector Spider ETFs are the best value, with an expense ratio of 0.14%. This sounds cheap but compares poorly to the 0.07% charged by the cheapest single country fund, IVV. This extra 7 basis points[185] of management fee expense is too high relative to the maximum 4 basis points of benefit I calculated above.

There are also sector ETFs that span Europe, although not within individual countries. In Europe the cheapest sector funds I can find come in at around 0.30% management fee, pretty similar to a Europe-wide market cap weighted fund. However should you have enough capital to split your European equity portfolio into a dozen or so funds it's better to diversify amongst European **countries**, than across a similar number of European **sectors**.[186]

In conclusion, sector ETFs are either too expensive (US), do not provide enough diversification (Europe), or are entirely absent (everywhere else). This implies the only

---

185. Remember a basis point is 0.01%.
186. I explained why in 'The allocation conundrum' section on page 231.

viable options are: (a) forgetting about allocating to individual sectors, and putting your cash into a single market cap weighted country ETF, or (b) buying individual stocks using a handcrafted top-down sector allocation.

There are a number of reasons why holding individual stocks won't always make sense, and this is especially true for foreign equities. It's difficult and costly to keep track of holdings in many different countries, some emerging markets might have rules against foreign ownership, and understanding different tax regimes, disclosures and bilateral agreements is a further headache. In contrast buying a London-listed Chinese equity ETF is no different to buying any other London-listed share.[187]

These problems don't apply to buying equities in your own country. So, for example, in my own personal portfolio I don't own a single overseas listed share, but I have purchased a number of individual UK shares.

However you can only buy single equities if you have sufficient capital. Allocating to all the individual shares in each sector would mean buying dozens or hundreds of shares in a given country, even if you limited yourself to large capitalisation stocks. This is prohibitively expensive for most retail investors, because of the tyranny of high fixed trading costs,[188] and managing vast numbers of holdings could be a headache even for relatively large institutions.

Fortunately you don't need to buy more than a few firms in each sector to be well diversified. I discuss precisely how many you need in the next part of this chapter, when I delve into weighting for individual equities within a sector.

In conclusion:

Avoid sector ETFs	Unless you can find them with management fees no more than 0.04% basis points higher than the relevant whole country ETF, otherwise there will be no net benefit. Even then I'd suggest a minimum investment of $300 or £1,800* in each sector, so you'd need about $5,500 or £32,000 to put into each country where you use sector ETFs.**
Smaller investors	The best option will usually be to allocate to an entire country using a single market cap weighted ETF.
Larger investors	Where you have sufficient capital you should consider allocating to individual equities within a top-down handcrafted allocation, after splitting your portfolio into sectors. I talk about this option in more detail later in the chapter.

---

187. This is an over simplification. Most UK listed ETFs are actually domiciled in Ireland or Luxembourg. But it's still an awful lot easier than directly owning a basket of Chinese shares.
188. I discussed this problem in chapter six, page 154.

* All values in this chapter are based on my usual assumption of minimum trading commissions of £6 and $1. If you are paying more you need to multiply the suggested values by the ratio of your commission levels to the values I am using. ** This isn't exactly 11 times $300 or £1,800 (my suggested minimum for each fund) because in cash weighting terms the smallest sector has 5.6% of the portfolio (see portfolio 54, page 271).

These methods can also be mixed. You can buy individual shares in countries where it's easiest, like your own domestic market, and then allocate to the rest of the world using country ETFs.

Small and mid cap ETFs

Equal weighting implies you should have the same weight in a large firm as in a small one. But smaller firms with lower market capitalisation (**small caps**) have historically had better performance. In this part of the book I'm assuming all risk-adjusted returns are equal; but small caps definitely have higher risk, and so I'd still expect to see a higher geometric return if you up-weight small cap stocks in your portfolio.

However, if you're buying market cap weighted sector ETFs small caps will be under represented; indeed most country and sector ETFs have no small cap stocks at all. It may be worth adding some extra funds for mid cap and small cap stocks if they're available in a given country.

Are mid cap and small ETFs worth buying, given they are likely to cost more to hold? I estimate that ETFs for mid cap and small cap stocks cost around 0.05% and 0.30% respectively in invisible trading costs compared to large caps, to which you would need to add on any premium in management fee costs. But if I assume that geometric Sharpe Ratios are equal then you should also receive an extra 0.25% (mid cap) or 0.65% (small cap) in geometric returns in compensation for their higher volatility. That gives a net benefit of 0.2% (mid cap) and 0.35% (small cap).

This all means you should avoid investing in mid cap or small cap stock ETFs which charge a significantly higher management fee than any large cap funds you are using. If you can find a small cap fund with an annual fee of less than 0.35% extra, or a mid cap fund with a management fee premium below 0.2%, then they are worth buying.

The cheapest mid cap ETF in the US I could find was SCHM, which has a management fee of just 0.06% – this is worth buying. The relevant small cap fund, SCHA, has the same low annual fee and is also a good investment. In contrast, passive UK mid and small ETFs are thin on the ground; the cheapest mid cap fund, the Lyxor FTSE 250 ETF, charges 0.35%, which is too high, and I couldn't find a small cap fund which costs less than 0.5% a year.

How much of your portfolio should be in small and mid cap stocks? An equally weighted portfolio of all the stocks in the UK would have around 16% of it's cash weighting in large cap, 40% in mid cap and 44% in small cap stocks.[189] These allocations would make most people nervous. In contrast, the relevant market cap weights would be 82% large cap, 15% mid, and around 3% in small cap. Deviating too much from these would be potentially embarrassing. I'd personally advocate a maximum weight of about 20% in each of the mid and small cap groups, leaving 60% in large cap, as in portfolio 50.

PORTFOLIO 50: LARGE CAP FUND PLUS MID/SMALL CAP FUNDS

Portfolio		
Equities		
Developed or emerging		
Region		
Country		
Large cap 60% **(66.5%)**	Mid cap 20% **(18.5%)**	Small cap 20% **(15%)**
60%	20%	20%

Risk weightings shown. Cash weights in **(bold)**. Minimum investment in a given country: $2,000 or £12,000.

What if you have access to sector ETFs, and they are cheap enough? Since mid cap and small cap funds aren't normally sector specific you should construct a portfolio with a risk weighting of 60% split equally between 11 funds covering the large cap sectors, 20% in a single mid cap fund, and 20% in a single fund for small caps. The result is shown in portfolio 51.

---

189. There are 100 shares in the large cap FTSE 100, 250 in the mid cap FTSE 250 and about 280 in the small cap FTSE Small Cap index. There are another 1,000 or so microcaps which are listed on the exchange but are too small to qualify for membership even in the small cap index. The proportions in the US are similar.

PORTFOLIO 51: LARGE CAP SECTOR ALLOCATION WITHIN COUNTRIES PLUS A MID/SMALL CAP ALLOCATION

Portfolio												
Equities												
Developed or emerging												
Region												
Country												
Large cap 60% (66.5%)											Mid cap 20% (18.5%)	Small cap 20% (15%)
Cons. Discr.	Cons. Staples	Energy	Financials	Real Estate	Health care	Industrials	IT	Materials	Telecom	Utilities		
5.4% (5.5%)	5.4% (9%)	5.4% (7.4%)	5.4% (5%)	5.4% (5.5%)	5.4% (5.7%)	5.4% (6.6%)	5.4% (3.7%)	5.4% (6.6%)	5.4% (5.5%)	5.4% (6%)	20% (18.5%)	20% (15%)

Key: 'Cons.' = Consumer. 'Discr.' = Discretionary. Risk weightings shown. Cash weights in **(bold)**. Minimum investment in a given country: $8,100 or £50,000 (assuming sector ETFs used to get exposure).

You should also use the allocations in portfolio 51 if you're planning to invest in large cap sectors using individual equities; I discuss this possibility in the next section.

Allocating to individual equities within sectors

This section applies if you wish to use individual equities to achieve exposure to a given sector for a particular country.

When is it worth investing directly?

Costs are the crucial factor when deciding whether to allocate to a market cap ETF for the entire country, or to buy individual stocks in each sector.[190] Small positions in lots of

---

190. As I said earlier in the chapter, sector ETFs usually aren't available or come a poor third in this race: don't buy them unless their cost premium is 0.04% or less.

different stocks will cost more to hold and trade, which means they'll only make sense if the country ETF is relatively expensive.

I already covered this problem back in chapter six. Table 37 and 38 (page 171 onwards, and in the reference section at the end of the book) show the breakeven point at which direct investment in one share per sector becomes viable, depending on your minimum brokerage charge and the holding cost for a single countrywide ETF (remember the holding cost is the annual fund management fee, plus the invisible cost of trading within the fund which is around 0.1% for a developed market).

So, for example, with a super cheap holding cost of 0.2% and my default assumption of a $1 or £6 minimum brokerage commission, the break-even for direct investment is $6,000 or £45,000. This is the minimum you'd need to buy one share in each sector. However you wouldn't actually put the same amount into every stock because different sectors have smaller or larger cash weights (portfolio 49, page 254). That means, for example, you'd only put 6.5% × $6,000 = $490 into the share you choose to represent the tech sector.

Which equities should be included?

In principal if you're a large enough investor then you would want to buy up shares in every public company in the relevant country. In the US alone that's about 20,000 firms! So in practice you will probably want to restrict yourself to a subset of these.

You should only buy shares listed on a reputable exchange. Less reputable shares, traded in venues like the US over-the-counter pink sheets, may not have especially stringent corporate governance rules. Stocks on certain other markets might be off limits for other regulatory or tax reasons; for example to put foreign shares into a UK ISA they need to be listed on a recognised exchange. This excludes markets like the US over-the-counter bulletin board.

Listed collective investment vehicles like ETFs[191] should also be excluded; an ETF tracking Chinese equities on the London Stock Exchange does not belong in the UK part of your portfolio! Large multinationals often have multiple listings in different countries. Secondary listings are usually excluded from major indices.

You will probably want to avoid highly illiquid stocks, or those with a tiny market capitalisation (which are usually the same firms). Limiting yourself to an index like the Russell 3000 or FTSE All-Share will ensure you avoid the very smallest stocks.

Personally I'd advise direct investment only in large cap stocks[192] such as the FTSE 100 or S&P 500. This is safer for retail investors, and means that large institutional investors can avoid the large market impact costs they'd get from trading smaller firms.

---

191. Also things like investment trusts, listed mutual funds, limited partnerships and royalty trusts.
192. Sophisticated investors who feel they can find better value in mid and small cap stocks will probably want to ignore this advice. I explain how they should do this in part three.

You can combine direct large cap equities with small and mid cap allocations using ETFs, if they're available and not too expensive, using the weightings in portfolio 51.

How many stocks to buy

Let's say you want to get exposure to the US consumer discretionary sector, and you're sensibly limiting yourself to the large cap S&P 500 index. As I'm writing this that would mean buying shares in 86 different firms. Is this really necessary? How much benefit would you get from owning the entire sector, rather than just a few firms?

Remember that equities in the same country and sector are very similar, and will have relatively high correlations. Back in chapter six (figure 29, page 146) I pointed out that diversification amongst highly correlated assets adds very little extra performance. The calculations I did earlier show that including just one stock per sector loses just a few basis points of theoretical performance every year (again from chapter six, table 35, page 169).

So a single stock per sector in each country is enough assuming you have sufficient money to afford it, given your brokerage fee and the cost of buying a countrywide ETF (consult tables 37 and 38 on page 171, also repeated in the reference section at the end of the book). But with even more capital it makes sense to split sector allocation into two, three or more stocks. Table 39 on page 172 shows the investment required to allocate to more than one stock in each sector, depending on the minimum brokerage charge.

With my standard minimum brokerage fee of $1 or £6, the minimums for extra investment in another stock per sector are $2,000 or £12,000. These are the average investments you need to make **in each stock**; so to buy two stocks in each of 11 sectors, or 22 stocks in total, would need a total allocation to the entire country of 2 × $2,000 × 11 = $44,000 or 2 × £12,000 × 11 = £264,000.

In practice you would not actually put $4,000 or £24,000 into every sector because looking back at portfolio 49 (page 254), different sectors have smaller or larger cash weights. So for example you'd only put 6.5% × £264,000 = £17,160 into the tech sector. Split equally between two shares that's £8,580 each.

You should buy either one stock in every sector, or two, or three, etc: 11, 22 or 33, and so on in total (assuming the full 11 sectors are represented in the relevant stock index). **Do not buy extra stocks in some sectors and not in others**. If you do this you will either have an unbalanced portfolio with uneven allocations to each sector, or if you maintain the correct sector allocations you will have positions that are too small to meet my recommended minimum size.

Institutional investors can afford even more diversification; at least five or ten stocks in each sector.[193] Such investors do not have an issue with high minimum fixed costs on

---

193. Large institutions could also break down their sector allocations further using the GICS® classification system.

small purchases. But there is a risk of potential embarrassment. They don't want to be telling clients they had exposure to just one energy firm in the US… and it turned out to be the next Enron.[194]

How to choose which stocks to buy and how to weight them

In theory, if you can't predict risk-adjusted performance, then randomly throwing a dart at a list of stocks in a given sector and country is as good as any other method. Larger retail investors would need more than one dart. Institutional investors will need a whole quiver full.

Okay, I'm not really expecting you to pick stocks using a dartboard. But what is a sensible method for choosing stocks if you assume that stock selection will have no effect on your returns? Because it doesn't really matter which stock you pick, you can instead focus on minimising your **embarrassment**. Remember my definition of embarrassment is the deviation of your portfolio from the market capitalisation weighted consensus.

To minimise embarrassment you should **buy the stock with the largest market capitalisation in a given sector**. If you have sufficient capital you should buy the second largest, third largest, and so on. Depending on how many stocks you buy you will end up with something that is a reasonably close match to a market cap weighted sector index. For institutions, limiting themselves to the largest stocks will also keep market impact costs as low as possible.

Give each of the stocks you buy within a given sector an equal risk weighting. To go from risk weightings to cash weightings you can either[195] measure the volatility of each stock using the method shown in Appendix C on page 489, or assume they are equal and just use risk weightings directly. Equities in the same sector should be fairly similar so assuming equal risk is perfectly okay: it's what I do with my own portfolio.

Portfolio 52 has an example for the US. I've used the sector cash weights I derived earlier in the chapter, and chosen the current largest firm in each sector.

---

194. If your memory is short (or you're very young), Enron was a giant US energy firm that went bankrupt in 2001 after massive accounting irregularities and fraud were discovered, resulting in the share price plummeting from $90 in mid-2000 to less than $1 just over a year later.
195. I don't include indicative volatilities for individual stocks in this book – or it would be several thousand pages longer!

PORTFOLIO 52: EXAMPLE OF DIRECT INVESTMENT IN THE US, ONE STOCK PER SECTOR, CHOOSING LARGEST MARKET CAP STOCK

Portfolio										
Equities										
Traditional equities										
Developed										
North America										
US										
Consumer discretionary	Consumer staples	Energy	Financials	Real estate	Health care	Industrials	IT	Materials	Telecom	Utilities
Amazon	Proctor & Gamble	Exxon	Berkshire Hathaway	Simon Property	Johnson & Johnson	General Electric	Apple	Dow Chemical	AT&T	NextEra
9.1% **(8.2%)**	9.1% **(13.5%)**	9.1% **(11.1%)**	9.1% **(7.5%)**	9.1% **(8.2%)**	9.1% **(8.6%)**	9.1% **(10%)**	9.1% **(5.6%)**	9.1% **(10%)**	9.1% **(8.2%)**	9.1% **(9%)**

Risk weightings shown. Cash weights in **(bold)**.

Ethical investment

People are increasingly concerned that the firms they invest in should be socially and environmentally responsible.

Proponents of ethical investing argue that *good* firms should outperform the wider market. A counter claim is made by others who promote *sin portfolios* which deliberately buy arms dealers, tobacco firms and the like. Unfortunately there isn't clear evidence either way, and perhaps never will be. The application of ethical screens has a degree of subjectivity which makes it hard to apply a rigorous test. Screens do not usually exclude enough stocks to give a statistically significant difference in performance.

If you assume that you can't predict risk-adjusted returns then the only effect of applying an ethical screen will be a reduction in diversification. An ethically screened portfolio will have slightly lower geometric returns, and a lower Sharpe Ratio, than an unscreened version (although to be fair the same is true of a *sin* portfolio!). I think it is reasonable to be aware that ethical investing might lower your returns slightly, but to still be in favour of it. After all plenty of people buy organic or free range food even though it is a little more expensive.

Ethical collective funds

Most people will invest ethically through an ethical fund set up specifically for that purpose. These funds are usually actively managed. I will cover active funds in more detail in part three.

A few passive funds do exist such as the UK listed Legal & General Ethical Global Equity fund which tracks the FTSE4Good index. Inevitably these charge more than non-ethical alternatives. However they are usually still market cap weighted funds, so there should be no hidden cost differential in the form of invisible trading costs within the fund; unless the fund manager keeps changing their mind on how ethical each firm is.

Direct investment in shares

For direct investors the effect of ethical investment will depend on how aggressive your ethical screening is. A screen which excludes 10% or even 90% of the stocks in each sector is going to make almost no difference. After all you wouldn't be buying every single stock in the sector even without a screen.

A screen which excluded most or all of an entire sector would be more problematic. For example very committed ethical investors might think that every single listed firm in the energy industry for their country is terribly bad, due to their reliance fossil fuels.

Table 42 shows the effect on your portfolio of excluding one or more sectors. Because there are diminishing returns to diversification, performance is mostly unchanged until you have eliminated six out of 11 sectors, and then it falls off dramatically.

TABLE 42: WHAT HAPPENS TO RETURNS WHEN SECTORS ARE REMOVED ENTIRELY FROM A PORTFOLIO?

	Geometric mean	Sharpe Ratio
11 sectors	2.59%	0.117
10 sectors	2.58%	0.117
9 sectors	2.57%	0.117
8 sectors	2.56%	0.116
6 sectors	2.53%	0.113

	Geometric mean	Sharpe Ratio
5 sectors	2.50%	0.112
2 sectors	2.27%	0.097
1 sector	1.88%	0.075

Table shows the effect of eliminating industry sectors from a country portfolio. Uses average correlation between sectors of 0.75, assuming arithmetic mean of returns is 5% and standard deviation for a sector is 25%.

I think ethical investors should be pleased with these results. Even the most ardent screen is unlikely to remove more than one or two sectors from consideration in your portfolio.

Summary

This chapter summary is more complicated than usual, because of the permutations that are available depending on ETF availability. Remember, an affordable sector ETF (if you can find one) should have a management fee that is no more than 0.04% higher than a market cap country ETF. Affordable mid cap funds would have a management fee no more than 0.2% above a large cap fund, and 0.35% is the relevant figure for small cap funds.

	Sector ETFs cheap and available		Sector ETFs expensive or unavailable	
	Mid / small cap ETFs cheap & available	**Mid / small cap ETFs expensive or unavailable**	**Mid / small cap ETFs cheap & available**	**Mid / small cap ETFs expensive or unavailable**
(A) Less than $2,000 / £12,000	Market cap weighted country ETF (You could substitute this for an equal weighed country ETF. See chapter six.)			
(B) More than $2,000 / £12,000	Market cap country ETF		Portfolio 50 (Large, mid and small cap ETF)	Market cap country ETF
(C) More than $5,500 / £32,000	Market cap country ETF	Portfolio 54 (sector ETFs)		

	Sector ETFs cheap and available		Sector ETFs expensive or unavailable	
	Mid / small cap ETFs cheap & available	Mid / small cap ETFs expensive or unavailable	Mid / small cap ETFs cheap & available	Mid / small cap ETFs expensive or unavailable
(D) More than $8,100 / £50,000	Portfolio 51 (sector ETFs, plus mid and small cap ETF)	Portfolio 49 (sector ETFs) or row E in next table if sufficient capital	Portfolio 50 (Large, mid, small cap ETF) or row E in next table if sufficient capital	Market cap country ETF or row E in next table if sufficient capital

In rows A, B, C and D, multiply the values in the left-hand column by the ratio of your minimum brokerage fee and the ones I use: $1 and £6.

Larger investors can consider direct investment:

	Mid / small cap ETFs cheap and available	Mid / small cap ETFs expensive or unavailable
(E) More than $6,000 / £45,000	*If sector ETFs cheap and available:* Portfolio 51 (sector ETFs, plus mid and small cap ETF) i.e. row D in previous table *If sector ETFs expensive or unavailable:* Sector weights from portfolio 49 (direct investment, buy largest stock in each sector)	Sector weights from portfolio 49 (direct investment, buy largest stock in each sector)
(F) More than $9,040 / £67,770	Sector weights from portfolio 51 (direct investment, buy largest stock in each sector, plus mid and small cap ETF)	Sector weights from portfolio 49 (direct investment, buy largest two stocks in each sector)
(G) More than $28,000 / £155,000		
(H) More than $42,170 / £233,400	Sector weights from portfolio 51 (direct investment, buy largest two stocks in each sector, plus mid and small cap ETF)	
I) More than $50,000 / £265,000		Sector weights from portfolio 49 (direct investment, buy largest three stocks in each sector)
J) More than $75,300 / £399,000	Sector weights from portfolio 51 (direct investment, buy largest three stocks in each sector, plus mid and small cap ETF)	

Notes:

- The exact break-even for direct investment (row E) depends on your minimum brokerage cost and the holding cost of a market cap weighted ETF. See tables 37 and 38 on page 171. For the subsequent rows, refer to the following:
- Row F: Equal to the minimum for the previous row E, plus an additional 50.6% to invest in small and mid cap funds.
- Row G: Equal to the minimum for row E, plus the minimum investment required for additional shares in each country; I assume $22,000 or £110,000 but see tables 37 and 38 on page 171.
- Row H: Equal to the minimum for the row G, plus an additional 50.6%.
- Row I: Equal to the minimum for row G, plus the minimum investment required for additional shares in each country; I assume $22,000 or £110,000 but see tables 37 and 38 on page 171.
- Row J: Equal to the minimum for the previous row H, plus an additional 50.6%.

Notice that investing in mid and small cap funds, when they are available, is preferable to adding another share in each sector. Hopefully you can see how the table can be extended to larger portfolio values.

CHAPTER TWELVE

Bonds

Portfolio						
Equities			Bonds			Genuine alternatives
Traditional equity		Equity-like alternatives	Traditional bonds		Bond-like alternatives	
Developed equity	Emerging equity		Developed	Emerging		
Regions			Regions			
Countries			Countries			
Sectors			Type			
Individual equities			Maturity and credit			

I SPENT MY FORMATIVE YEARS IN THE FINANCE INDUSTRY TRADING in the bond market, and the last few years of my career managing a portfolio of bond derivatives. I love bonds. But most people don't. The bond market is the dull and boring cousin of the stock market. Bond analysts are rarely quoted in newspapers. The evening news on TV doesn't conclude by telling you the movements in bond indices. There are currently over 7,000 books about the stock market listed on Amazon.com, but less than 700 about bonds.

This is all somewhat unfair. After all, the bond market is actually larger than the stock market.[196] Yes it is true that in the long run bonds will earn you a lower return than stocks, but everyone should have some exposure to bonds in their portfolio. Remember:

---

196. As of the end of 2016 roughly 30% of publically listed assets are equities and 60% bonds, with the rest in various kinds of alternatives.

including a small proportion of bonds in your portfolio has no effect on your expected geometric mean return but will improve your Sharpe Ratio, as figure 18 (chapter four, page 82) illustrated. Ignoring bonds is not smart, so it's worth understanding them.

Chapter overview

The world of bonds	Naming and explaining the wide variety of different types of bonds.
How to get exposure to bonds	Different ways to organise the bonds in a portfolio.
How to weight bonds	My suggested framework for top-down weighting of bond funds, depending on the size of your account.

The world of bonds

Equities are a relatively straightforward asset. But when you want to buy bonds there are a bewildering variety of categories available.

A bond is essentially a tradeable **loan**. The two most important features of bonds in this context are: (1) **how long** the money is being borrowed for, the bond's **maturity**, and (2) **who** is borrowing the money, the bond's **issuer**.

Longer maturity bonds have a higher yield because people need to be compensated for lending further out into the future. Longer maturity bonds are also riskier because the effect of interest rate changes is magnified.

I assume that all bonds have the same risk-adjusted return, as I've done for other assets so far in part two. This means the higher risk and return of longer bonds should cancel each other out.

The maturity profile of the Barclays Global Aggregate Bond Index is shown in portfolio 53. The cash weights are copied from the bond index weighting. I then used my own estimates of volatility to work out the risk weightings.

PORTFOLIO 53: GLOBAL BOND INDICES HAVE A GOOD SPREAD OF MATURITIES

Portfolio						
Bonds Global Bond Index ETF XBAG (UK)						
1–3 years	3–5 years	5–7 years	7–10 years	10–15 years	15–25 years	25+ years
5.1% **(22%)**	8.0% **(18%)**	7.7% **(12%)**	14.3% **(14%)**	9.8% **(7%)**	23.0% **(12%)**	32.6% **(14%)**

Cash weights in **(bold)** from Barclays Global Aggregate Bond Index as of January 2017. Risk weightings are derived from cash weights using my own estimates of bond volatility.

A common method of summarising the maturity profile of a bond portfolio is by its **duration**.[197] Back in chapter four (page 92) I said that if you're a Sharpe Ratio maximising investor then you should avoid putting too many low volatility assets into your portfolio, as it will reduce your expected returns significantly without improving Sharpe Ratio. For this reason, it's important to keep the duration of your bond allocation from getting too low. A duration below 4 would be a cause for concern.

When assessing different bonds it's also vital to have a good idea of how **creditworthy** the borrower is. The safest issuers are governments issuing bonds in their own local currency. Other public sector entities like cities, municipalities[198] (munis), and government lending **agencies** come next in the pecking order.

Private firms issuing **corporate** bonds come next. Within the corporate bond world there is another hierarchy of credit ratings. At the top are **investment grade** bonds issued by blue chip firms. The bluest of blue chips can have better credit ratings than many governments.[199]

---

197. The duration of a bond is its sensitivity to interest rate changes. If a bond has a duration of 10, and interest rates rise by 1%, then it's price will fall by 10% since higher interest rates mean lower bond prices. Longer maturity bonds have a higher duration. A ten-year bond has a duration of about 8. The duration of portfolio 58 is around 6.9. Bond fund managers normally state their fund's current duration on their websites. Technical note for fellow bond geeks: obviously I am ignoring convexity here to make the explanation simpler.

198. Municipal bonds have highly favourable tax status in the US, especially if held to maturity. I discuss the effects of tax on investments in part four.

199. For example, as I'm writing this the five year credit default swap (a measure of bond riskiness) for the giant consumer staples manufacturer Procter & Gamble is 0.24%. Only a few governments have lower levels which imply they are safer than P&G; including Switzerland, Germany and Sweden, but not the US or the UK. Technical note of caution: Credit spreads on most countries are thinly traded

At the bottom of the credit totem pole are the euphemistically named **high yield** bonds, for which the impolite name is **junk** bonds. Across the global bond market around 90% is in investment grade corporate and government bonds; the remainder is in high yield junk (because of disagreements over ratings it's hard to be precise). These are cash weights: in risk weighed terms the proportion of high yield will be greater. Note that the Barclays Global Bond Index, and the ETFs that track it, are entirely in investment grade.

It's also important which **country** the issuer is domiciled in. A government in a stable developed country will be much safer than an emerging market. Also emerging market borrowers frequently issue their bonds in a stable foreign currency, like dollars or Euros, for which there is more demand from international investors. This is great in theory, but also means that in a crisis they'll struggle to find foreign reserves to meet their obligations.

About 40% of the market capitalisation weighted global bond index is in the US, as portfolio 54 shows. This is not as extreme as the situation in global equities (with over half in the US), but it's still far from ideal.

PORTFOLIO 54: A SINGLE GLOBAL BOND FUND HAS SIGNIFICANT US OVERWEIGHTING

Portfolio						
Bonds Global Bond index ETF XBAG (UK)						
US	Japan	UK	France	Germany	Other developed	Emerging markets
37.7% **(39%)**	18.3% **(19%)**	6.8% **(7%)**	5.8% **(6%)**	4.8% **(5%)**	13.5% **(14%)**	12.9% **(10%)**

Cash weights in **(bold)** from Barclays Global Aggregate Bond Index as of July 2016; risk weightings implied using my own calculations.

There are a few other important categories of bonds. Most bonds are **nominal**; you get the same coupons and final payment regardless of what happens to inflation. But some governments, and a few select corporates, issue **inflation linked** bonds whose value is linked to inflation indices.

---

and are not especially meaningful given the unlikely probability of a default amongst developed country governments.

Some bonds are secured by certain underlying assets. **Mortgage backed** securities became famous – for all the wrong reasons – when they were at the epicentre of the 2007–8 global financial crisis. There are asset-backed securities for other kinds of consumer debt, like credit card receivables and car loans. There have even been bonds backed by the back catalogue of music legend David Bowie. **Covered bonds** are a variation on the asset-backed theme. **Convertible bonds** are in effect backed by the equity of the firm: when certain conditions are met they will be converted into shares.

Short-term **money market** and **floating rate** securities are sometimes lumped in with bonds. In reality they are much closer to cash than to bonds, so I don't consider them in this chapter. Remember that your allocation to cash should be determined solely by your risk profile, as I discussed in chapter four (page 86 onwards).

How to get exposure to bonds

It's relatively difficult to buy and sell bonds. The bond market is highly fragmented compared to the equity market. Bonds are thinly traded over numerous trading venues, many of which are inaccessible to private investors and smaller institutions. Minimum order sizes are large. Owning bonds is complicated: portfolios need to be regularly rebalanced to hit maturity targets as their components age and mature.

For these reasons I don't recommend direct investment in the bond market, except for very large institutions that can hire significant numbers of specialist portfolio managers and traders.

Medium sized institutions are better off using **derivatives** to get exposure: futures, interest rate swaps, and credit derivatives (if you don't understand all of these terms this paragraph isn't for you!). These may be prohibited for regulatory reasons and also require some specialist management, although with fewer people than you need for trading a global portfolio of individual bonds. When I was working at AHL, a hedge fund, I managed a team responsible for a multi billion dollar portfolio of fixed income derivatives. The group which executed the orders was relatively small: the equivalent of just three full-time traders.

In this chapter I stick exclusively to investment via passive index tracking ETFs. This is the right solution for the vast majority of investors. ETFs trade on ordinary markets and liquidity in bond ETFs is usually much better than the underlying bonds, plus the fund manager will rebalance the portfolio for you.

How to weight bonds – in theory

With so many different possible dimensions it's difficult to know where to start with a top-down allocation process in the bond market. After analysing all the correlations across the bond market I came up with the following **theoretically** ideal order for allocation:

1. Emerging and developed markets

2. Regions

3. Countries

4. Bond type (standard nominal, inflation linked, foreign currency)

5. Bond maturity

6. Credit rating (government quality, municipal, government agency, investment grade corporate, high yield corporate)

7. Backing (none, asset-backed, covered bond, convertible)

But the weighting scheme above is highly theoretical. In reality it will be impossible to replicate, since funds don't exist for many of the conceivable parts of this portfolio. For example you can't buy a fund containing just Chinese long maturity covered nominal corporate high yield bonds; at least not when I last checked.

The availability of bond ETFs is also radically different in the US and the UK. Unlike in equities, the UK has a much wider offering. Although there are hundreds of bond ETFs listed in the US, nearly all of them focus on the US bond market. So opportunities for international diversification are radically curtailed, although you can allocate to every tiny niche of the highly variegated US bond market.

For this reason I present two quite different top-down weighting schemes in this chapter: one for the US, and one for the UK. As I did for equities and alternatives I'll show portfolios for varying sizes of bond allocations.

Weighting bonds for US investors

Single and double fund options

Before beginning the top-down allocation process let's look at the options for very small investors who can only invest in one or two ETFs.

A very small investor can only stick a single fund in their bond sub-portfolio. But in the US there doesn't seem to be a suitable passive fund. You can instead opt for the active RIGS RiverFront Strategic Income fund which has a global mandate for all bonds; although as I'm writing this it's invested 100% in corporate bonds. The net expense ratio is currently 0.22%.

As with equities, an investor who can buy two ETFs should invest in a non-US fund and a separate US fund. This is the most efficient way to reduce concentration risk. Suppose you wanted to limit the US to a 23% weighting – the weight I use later in this chapter. Portfolio 55 shows how this is done using ETFs listed in the US.

PORTFOLIO 55: USING A NON-US FUND TO GET BETTER DIVERSIFICATION WITHIN BONDS FOR SMALL US-BASED ETF INVESTORS

Portfolio						
Bonds						
US 23% **(25%)** AGG	Non-US 77% **(75%)** IAGG					
	Japan 12.9%	France 12.5%	UK 10.8%	Germany 10.3%	Other developed 41.6%	Emerging markets 12%
30%	9.0%	8.7%	7.5%	7.2%	29.1%	8.4%

Risk weightings are shown with cash weightings for each fund in **(bold)**. Final row shows risk weight within bond sub-portfolio. Minimum investment in traditional bonds: $1,250.

This portfolio currently costs 0.10%[200] in annual management fees, which is cheaper than the RIGS fund.

Emerging and developed markets

The first step in a top-down allocation for bonds is to carve up your money between emerging market (EM) and developed market (DM) bonds. The most diversified, maximum Sharpe Ratio option would be a 50:50 split in **risk weightings**.

However as with equities there are several good reasons for not sinking half of your portfolio into emerging market bonds. Firstly there is the embarrassment of departing from market capitalisation weights (EM bonds make up only around 10% of the market cap weighted aggregate global bond index in cash weighted terms). Emerging market bond funds also have higher ETF management fees.

EM bonds are not just more volatile on average; but also in a crisis they get even riskier and in an unpredictable way. They also become more correlated with equities; this implies that to get maximum diversification in your portfolio you should own less of them.

The right weight to EM will depend on your preferences, although I'd advise never going beyond a 40% risk weighting for EM bonds. Exactly as I did for equities I'm going to

---

200. Remember to find the average cost of a portfolio you need to find the weighted average of the costs of each component, where the averaging weights are the cash weightings.

suggest that you opt for a 25% risk weight in emerging markets. This works out to a 20.5% cash weighting assuming volatility of 6% for developed and 8% for emerging market bonds.[201]

Portfolio 56 shows a suitable portfolio for an investor who wants a 25% emerging market exposure. Notice that IAGG already includes some emerging markets; hence the explicit weight given to the emerging markets ETF EMAG is less than you might expect.

PORTFOLIO 56: DEVELOPED AND EMERGING PORTFOLIO WITH US ETF TICKERS

Portfolio								
Bonds								
Developed 75%							Emerging 25%	
US 23% (24.5%) AGG	Non US ETF 59% (61.2%) IAGG						EM ETF 18% (14.4%) EMAG	
	Japan 12.9%	France 12.5%	UK 10.8%	Germany 10.3%	Other developed 41.6%	Emerging markets 12%	Mexico 10%	Other 90%
23%	7.7%	7.7%	7.1%	6.5%	39.8%	5.9%	1.8%	16.2%
Developed: 75%							Emerging: 25%	

Risk weightings are shown, cash weightings for funds in **(bold)**. Penultimate row shows weight within bonds sub-portfolio. Bottom row checks risk weightings for developed and emerging markets. Minimum investment in bonds: $2,100.

Developed and emerging market regions

In the equities chapter I used three regional groupings: Americas, EMEA (Europe, Middle East, Africa), and Asia Pacific. I also suggested an equal allocation to each. Because bond issuance is highly concentrated in a few countries[202] this does not make as much sense.

---

201. These and other assumptions about bond volatility can be found in Appendix B, page 485.
202. There are 24 countries represented in the Barclays Global Aggregate Index for bonds of which 14 are developed markets, compared to the 46 in the MSCI All world equity index, including 23 developed. Of the 14 developed bond markets, two are in the America region, five in Asia, and seven in Europe.

An equal weight across countries would put 14% in the Americas, 36% in Asia, and 50% in Europe. The market cap weights would be 41% Americas, 23% Asia and 36% Europe. But there is much greater scope for diversification within the US and European bond markets; and for UK investors at least also within the UK bond market.

So for US investors I'd suggest **35% in the Americas, 25% in Asia, and 40% Europe**. Unfortunately these weights are purely theoretical because of the poor availability of relevant collective funds.

There aren't specific US listed ETFs for Asia and Europe. Portfolio 57 is a copy of portfolio 56, but this time I've added an effective breakdown of regional exposure within developed markets.

PORTFOLIO 57: EXTENDED COPY OF PORTFOLIO 56 WITH REGIONAL EXPOSURES ADDED

Portfolio									
Bonds									
Developed 75%								Emerging 25%	
US 23% AGG (US)	Non US ETF 59% IAGG (US)								EM ETF EMAG (US)
	Americas	Asia			Europe			Emerging markets 12%	18%
	Canada 6.5%	Japan 12.9%	Australia 3.4%	Other 2.8%	France 12.5%	UK 10.8%	Germany 10.3%	Other 28.8%	
23%	3.8%	7.6%	2%	1.7%	7.4%	6.4%	6.1%	17%	5.9%	18.0%
Americas: 35.7%		Asia: 15.1%			Europe: 49.2%				Emerging markets

Risk weightings are shown. Penultimate row shows risk weight within bonds sub-portfolio. Final row shows regional weights within developing markets.

Notice that compared to my preferred weights this is rather overweight Europe, with a lower weight to Asia. Although there aren't regional bond ETFs in the US, all is not lost because there are specific ETFs for both Japan[203] and Australia. In portfolio 58 I've included an allocation to these ETFs to bump up the Asian exposure.

PORTFOLIO 58: DEVELOPED AND EMERGING BOND ALLOCATION FOR A US ETF INVESTOR TARGETING SPECIFIC REGIONAL EXPOSURES

Portfolio									
Bonds									
Developed and emerging									
US 23% (24.1%) AGG	Non US 48% (50.4%) IAGG						Japan 5% (5.2%) JGBL	Australia 5% (5.2%) AUNZ	Emerging markets 19% (14.9%) EMAG
	Americas	Europe			Asia				
					Emerging markets 12%				
	Canada 6.5%	France 12.5%	UK 10.8%	Other 39.1%	Japan 12.9%	Australia 3.4%	Other 2.8%		
23%	3.1%	6%	5.2%	18.8%	6.2%	1.6%	1.3%	5.8%	5% 5% 19%
Americas: 34.7%	*Europe: 39.8%*			*Asia: 25.4% (Japan: 11.2%, Australia: 6.6%)*					
Developed: 75%								*Emerging: 25%*	

Risk weightings are shown, cash weightings for funds in **(bold)**. Final row shows emerging and developed risk weightings. Penultimate row shows regional risk weights within developing markets. Row above that shows risk weight within bonds sub-portfolio. Minimum investment in bonds: $6,000.

Some explanation is probably necessary. As before, the emerging market exposure is coming from a portion of IAGG, and an investment in EMAG. The regional exposures shown are only for developed markets. The Americas weighting is coming from AGG and the Canadian part of IAGG. Europe is entirely derived from the relevant countries in IAGG. The Asian exposure comes from what is left of IAGG, plus the weight that is in JGBL and AUNZ.

---

203. Actually the fund shown here for Japan, JGBL, is an Exchange Traded Note (ETN), not an ETF, as I couldn't find a proper ETF for Japan. Exchange Traded Notes have counterparty risk as they aren't secured by the underlying assets and so are riskier than ETFs.

Emerging market regions

Within emerging markets I'd stick to a simple equal weight of one-third in each region: Asia, EMEA and Latin America. By market cap Asia is larger, but there is more scope for diversification in the EMEA region. However this is purely theoretical: there is no comprehensive set of ETFs for different emerging market regions.

Bond types and credit rating (within emerging and developed markets)

An alternative way to categorise bonds within the emerging and developed markets groups is by bond **type** and **credit rating**.[204] The main **types** of bond are **normal** (issued in a domestic currency, and without inflation linking), **inflation linked**, and those that are issued in a safe **foreign** currency like Euros or dollars.[205] In risk-weighted terms these make up around 65%, 2%, and 33% respectively of the total market.[206]

I'd suggest putting **90% in normal bonds and 10% in inflation linked** in developed markets; there aren't enough foreign issued bonds amongst developed markets to justify their inclusion. The negative returns that we currently expect on inflation linked bonds make them more like the **insurance-like** genuine alternative assets I discussed in chapter nine: not likely to yield a positive return, but insuring against a scary event; in this case, hyperinflation. Thus a lower weight is justified. Within emerging markets I'd allocate **50% to normal bonds, 40% to foreign currency issued bonds, and 10% to inflation linked bonds**.

The three key **credit** categories are **Investment Grade Government**,[207] **Investment Grade Corporate**, and **High Yield**. These make up roughly 50%, 40%, and 10% respectively of total market capitalisation. I recommend putting about **40% of your portfolio into government bonds, 30% into corporate bonds, and 30% into high yield bonds**. This is something of a compromise between equal weighting and market cap, and reflects our preference of avoiding very low-risk bonds which are over represented in the government bond category.

These are all **risk weightings**; your **cash weightings** will reflect the higher risk of corporate bonds, particularly high yield. Portfolio 59 shows how to allocate your portfolio if you

---

204. You will notice that I haven't bothered with a breakdown by maturity. There are several reasons for this. Firstly, bonds which are identical in all respects apart from maturity are likely to be highly correlated, so there is little benefit in allocating to separate maturity groups. Secondly, it's difficult to find maturity specific ETFs in many areas of the bond universe. Finally, most ETFs are already well diversified with respect to maturity, as portfolio 53 illustrates. Remember you should avoid funds with too many short maturity bonds, where you can, because of the problems I highlighted in chapter four (page 92). I will however use a maturity breakdown within the US ETF market later in this chapter.
205. Although they are issued in a safer currency, foreign issued bonds may actually be riskier, since issuing governments can't just print money to pay them off.
206. Figures derived from cash weights of the global market capitalisation weighted index.
207. This includes municipal securities and those issued by government agencies, including mortgage backed securities.

had access to ETFs in every subcategory. Sadly in reality you can't create a portfolio exactly like this, as there just aren't the right funds available.

PORTFOLIO 59: HYPOTHETICAL BREAKDOWN OF BOND PORTFOLIO BY TYPE AND CREDIT

Portfolio										
Portfolio										
Bonds										
Developed 75%				Emerging 25%						
Normal 90%			Inflation linked 10%	Normal 50%			Foreign 40%			Inflation linked 10%
Govt. 40%	Corp. 30%	High yield 30%	Govt. 100%	Govt. 40%	Corp. 30%	High yield 30%	Govt. 40%	Corp. 30%	High yield 30%	Govt. 100%
27% **(32.1%)**	20.3% **(22.1%)**	20.3% **(16.6%)**	7.5% **(8.9%)**	5% **(4.5%)**	3.8% **(3.1%)**	3.8% **(2.5%)**	4% **(3.6%)**	3% **(2.5%)**	3% **(2.0%)**	2.5% **(2.2%)**

Risk weightings are shown, cash weightings in **(bold)**. Final row shows weight within bonds sub-portfolio. Key: Govt.: Government bonds. Corp.: Investment grade corporate bonds. High yield: Sub investment grade corporate bonds.

It's rare for corporates to issue inflation linked bonds, hence the lack of corporate or high yield bonds in that category.

US ETF investors with sufficient capital can use portfolio 60. This is a refinement of portfolio 58. Remember the specific funds for Japan and Australia are there to beef up the Asian developed regional weighting. Unlike the previous portfolio there are no emerging markets (EM) hidden inside the non-US funds.

I've replaced the IAGG non-US exposure with specific funds for non-US developed market bonds of various types and credit ratings. I've also broken down the emerging markets into type and creditworthiness. Notable absences are funds to invest in EM inflation, or separately in foreign denominated corporate EM debt.

PORTFOLIO 60: DEVELOPED AND EMERGING BOND ALLOCATION WITH BREAKDOWN BY TYPE AND CREDIT FOR US ETF INVESTOR

US AGG 22%	Australia AUNZ 5%	Japan JGBL 5%	Developed non-US 43%				Emerging 25%				
			Normal 90%			Inflation 10% GTIP	Normal 55%			Foreign 45% EMB	
			Govt. 40% IGOV	Corp. 30% VCLT	High yield 30% IHY	Govt. 100%	Govt. 40% VWOB	Corp. 30% EMLC	High yield 30% EMHY	Govt. 84%	Corp. 16%
22% (24.7%)	5% (5.6%)	5% (5.6%)	15.5% (17.4%)	11.6% (12.0%)	11.6% (9.8%)	4.3% (4.8%)	5.5% (4.6%)	4.1% (3.1%)	4.1% (2.8%)	9.5% (9.5%)	1.8%
Americas: 34.7%			Europe: 39.8%		Asia: 25.4%		Emerging markets				

Penultimate row shows risk weighting within bonds sub-portfolio; cash weights in **(bold)**. Notice the cash weight for EMLC is shown below two risk weights. Final row shows risk weighted regional breakdown within Developed Markets. Minimum allocation to bonds: $11,500.

Countries within regions

In the theoretical order I presented earlier, the next step after dividing up your bond portfolio into regions was to allocate to countries. US investors have already done this to an extent, with direct allocations to the US, Japanese and Australian bond markets. Sadly there aren't enough individual country ETFs listed in the US for further geographical division within the bond market.

Bond types and credit rating (within regions and countries)

The next stage is to break down bonds within each country or region into different types and credit ratings. As usual you don't have the option of doing this in every country. US investors have a huge variety of options to break down their US bond exposure, but can't do anything elsewhere.

Portfolio 61 shows how you can break down your US bond exposure. Notice that for reasons of space I haven't shown the rest of the world; this will be the same as portfolio 60.

PORTFOLIO 61: BREAKDOWN OF US EXPOSURE FOR A US ETF INVESTOR

Portfolio													
Bond													
US 22%													Non US 78%
Normal 90%											Inflation 10% SCHP		See portfolio 60
No specific maturity 50%							Medium maturity 25%		Long-term maturity 25%		All 60% SCHP *	15 years+ 40% LTPZ	
Government 40%		Investment Grade Corporate 30%			High yield Corporate 30%		Govt 50% SCHR	IG Corp 50% VCIT	Govt 50% TLO	IG Corp 50% LWC			
High yield Muni 50% HYD	MBS 50% VMBS **	MBS 40% CMBS **	Convert. 30% ICVT	Covered bond 30% COBO	Cross-over 50% QLTB	Junk 50% QLTC							
2% **2.3%**	2% **2.6%**	1.2% **1.5%**	0.9% **1.1%**	0.9% **1.1%**	1.5% **1.6%**	1.5% **1.4%**	2.5% **3.3%**	2.5% **3.0%**	2.5% **2.2%**	2.5% **1.6%**	1.3% **1.7%**	0.9% **1.2%**	78% **75.3%**

All figures are risk weighting; cash weightings in **(bold)**. Final row shows risk weighting within bonds sub-portfolio. Minimum allocation to all bonds: $30,000 (including the non-US component). Key: Muni: Municipal. MBS: Mortgage Backed Security. Conver.: Convertible bonds. Cross-over: A corporate bond with a yield between investment grade and high yield. Junk: True high yield corporate bonds. IG Corp: Investment grade corporate bonds. Govt: Government bonds. * Around 12% of SCHP is in 15 year plus maturity inflation linked bonds. ** 6% of VMBS is in non agency securities, 38% of CMBS is in agency securities.

Weighting bonds for UK investors

Single fund

A very small investor can only choose a single fund for their bond sub-portfolio. As I mentioned in chapter eight, the cheapest UK option would be the XBAG ETF, although this excludes high yield bonds. This has a management fee of 0.30%.

Looking at portfolio 54 from earlier in the chapter, it's clear this global fund is overweight the US and Japan; but the spread of maturities is relatively diversified (see portfolio 53). UK ETF investors don't currently have the option of breaking down their bond exposure into geographic regions.

Developed market regions

For UK investors I'd create a separate geographic region just for the UK, and use ideal risk weightings of **33% in the Americas, 21% in Asia, 25% in the UK, and 21% in the rest of Europe**. Unfortunately there is a dearth of suitable bond ETFs for UK investors, which makes reproducing these ideal regional weights impossible. UK investors are better off grouping bonds by bond **type** and **credit rating** in their top-down allocation.

Bond type and credit rating

Portfolio 62 is the starting point for a UK investor who wants to begin breaking down their bond exposure into multiple funds. I use the same weights for type and credit allocations that I introduced for US investors earlier in the chapter.

It isn't possible for a relatively small investor to allocate to inflation linked bonds; or to foreign or corporate bonds in emerging markets. This portfolio will have an excessive exposure to the US and other large countries. However in the absence of decent regional ETFs for bonds it's the best option for this portfolio size.

PORTFOLIO 62: DEVELOPED AND EMERGING BOND ALLOCATION WITH BREAKDOWN BY TYPE AND CREDIT FOR UK ETF INVESTOR

Portfolio			
Bonds			
Developed 75%			Emerging 25%
Normal 100%			Normal 100%
Government 40% SAAA	Corporate 30% CRPS *	High yield 30% IGHY	Government 100% SEML
30.0% **(34%)**	22.5% **(26%)**	22.5% **(19%)**	25% **(21%)**

Risk weightings are shown, cash weightings in **(bold)**. Final row shows weight within bonds sub-portfolio. Column widths do not reflect actual weights. Minimum allocation to bonds: £10,000. * CRPS ETF includes a modest amount of emerging market exposure.

With more money you can include developed inflation linked bonds, plus most of the emerging market universe, as portfolio 63 shows.

PORTFOLIO 63: DEVELOPED AND EMERGING BOND ALLOCATION WITH BREAKDOWN BY
TYPE AND CREDIT FOR UK ETF INVESTOR – WITH DEVELOPED INFLATION AND EMERGING
BREAKDOWN

Portfolio						
Bonds						
Developed 75%				Emerging 25%		
Normal 90%			Inflation 10%	Normal 55%	Foreign 45%	
Government 40% SAAA	Corporate 30% CRPS *	High yield 30% IGHY	Government 100% SGIL	Government 100% SEML	Govt. 40% LEMB	Corporate 60% EMCP
27.0% **(31.2%)**	20.3% **(21.6%)**	20.3% **(17.5%)**	7.5% **(8.7%)**	13.8% **(11.9%)**	4.5% **(3.9%)**	6.8% **(5.2%)**

Risk weightings are shown; Cash weightings in **(bold)**. Final row shows weight within
bonds sub-portfolio. Minimum allocation to bonds: £46,000. * CRPS ETF includes a
modest amount of emerging market exposure.

If you're a UK investor with sufficient capital then you can allocate to portfolio 64. This
has a rather large minimum size of £86,000 to ensure a reasonable allocation to emerging
market inflation linked bonds. Of course this portfolio will still be rather overweight the
US, which forms a significant proportion of each of the developed market ETFs. I fix this
problem in due course.

PORTFOLIO 64: DEVELOPED AND EMERGING BOND ALLOCATION WITH BREAKDOWN BY TYPE AND CREDIT FOR UK ETF INVESTOR – WITH EMERGING MARKET INFLATION

Portfolio								
Bonds								
Developed 75%				Emerging 25%				
Normal 90%			Inflation 10%	Normal 50%	Foreign 40%		Inflation 10%	
Government 40% SAAA	Corporate 30% CRPS *	High yield 30% IGHY	Government 100% SGIL	Government 100% SEML	Govt. 40% LEMB	Corporate 60% EMCP	Government 100% EMIN	
27.0% **(31.1%)**	20.3% **(21.5%)**	20.3% **(17.5%)**	7.5% **(8.7%)**	12.5% **(10.8%)**	4.0% **(3.4%)**	6.0% **(4.6%)**	2.5% **(2.1%)**	

Risk weightings are shown; cash weightings in **(bold)**. Final row shows weight within bonds sub-portfolio. Minimum allocation to bonds: £86,000. * CRPS ETF includes a modest amount of emerging market exposure.

Type, credit, and regional allocation

Portfolio 65 further breaks down the allocation for a UK bond investor into different regions where this is possible. For reasons of space I've not shown the breakdown for emerging markets; this would be the same as shown in portfolio 64.

PORTFOLIO 65: DEVELOPED AND EMERGING BOND ALLOCATION WITH EXTRA BREAKDOWN FOR UK, EUROPEAN AND US BONDS – FOR UK ETF INVESTOR

Portfolio												
Bonds												
Developed 75%												Emerging 25%
Americas 33%				Europe 30%				UK 27%			Asia 10%	See portfolio 64
US 100%				Normal 90%			Inflation 10%	Normal 90%		Inflation 10%	Australia 100%	
Normal 90%			Inflation 10%	Govt. 40%	Corp. 30%	High yld. 30%	MTIX	Govt. 50%	Corp. 50%	GILI	XCS2	
Govt. 40% USTY	Corp. 30% UC84	High yld. 30% SHYU	UTIP	VETY	IBCX	SHYG		GILS	COUK			
8.9%	6.7%	6.7%	2.5%	8.1%	6.1%	6.1%	2.3%	9.1%	9.1%	2.0%	7.5%	25%
(11%)	**(7.6%)**	**(6.2%)**	**(2.7%)**	**(8.9%)**	**(6.2%)**	**(5.0%)**	**(2.5%)**	**(10%)**	**(9.2%)**	**(2.2%)**	**(8.2%)**	**(20.5%)**

Risk weightings are shown; Cash weightings in **(bold)**. Final row shows weight within entire bonds portfolio. Column widths do not reflect actual weights. Minimum allocation to all bonds: £86,000.

If you have £900,000 to put into bonds then you can split your developed Europe government bond exposure out further. Rather than having a single ETF, VETY, you can instead use the funds shown in portfolio 66.

PORTFOLIO 66: DEVELOPED EUROPE GOVERNMENT BOND PORTFOLIO (AS PART OF PORTFOLIO 65) WITH UK ETF TICKERS

Bonds						
Developed 75%						
Europe 30%						
Nominal 90%						
Government 40%						
Northern Europe 50%				Southern Europe 50%		
Germanic 50%		Benelux 20%	Nordic 30%	France 39%	Italy 22%	Iberian 39%
Germany 90% SDEU	Austria 10% SAUT	Netherlands 100% SNLD	Finland 100% SFIN	SFRB	SITB	Spain 100% SESP
1.8% **(2.0%)**	0.2% **(0.2%)**	0.8% **(0.9%)**	1.2% **(1.3%)**	1.6% **(1.7%)**	0.9% **(1.0%)**	1.6% **(1.7%)**

Risk weightings within entire bond portfolio are shown in penultimate row; cash weightings in **(bold)**. Replaces VETY ETF to get more granular allocation. Minimum allocation to bonds: £900,000 (as part of portfolio 65).

Summary

Institutional investors investing directly in bonds	Put 75% in developed and 25% in emerging markets (EM); cash weightings of **79.5%** and **20.5%** respectively.
	Otherwise the allocation you use will depend on whether you group by region, country, type and credit; and in which order.
	If using a regional weighting for developed markets:
	US-based: 35% Americas, 25% Asia, and 40% Europe.
	UK-based: 33% Americas, 21% Asia, 25% UK, and 21% rest of Europe.
	These are risk weightings that can also be used as cash weightings.
	If using a regional weighting for emerging markets:
	One-third in each of Asia, Latin America, and EMEA.
	If you can and wish to allocate directly to countries then use the regional weightings from the equities chapter. For developing markets: portfolios 41 and 43, plus for North America: 80% US, 20% Canada. For emerging markets: portfolios 44, 45 and 46.
	If allocating to bond type and credit use portfolio 59.
	To get exposure: Consider using the ETFs listed throughout the chapter, derivatives like bond futures, swaps or credit derivatives; or investment in baskets of individual bonds in each category.

US investors using ETFs

More than $30,000*	Portfolio 60 with US exposure broken down in portfolio 61.
$11,500 to $30,000	Portfolio 60.
$6,000 to $11,500	Portfolio 58.
$2,100 to $6,000	Portfolio 56.
$1,250 to $2,100	Portfolio 55.
$300 to $1,250	Currently the best single fund option is the actively managed (but relatively cheap) RIGS RiverFront Strategic Income fund.

* As usual I'm assuming a minimum commission of $1 here. If your commission is higher then you need to multiply these values appropriately. For example, if you're paying $5 then the minimum for this portfolio would be $28,000 × ($5 ÷ $1) = $140,000

UK investors using ETFs

At least £900,000* **allocated to bonds**	Portfolio 65 with developed Europe government bond exposure from portfolio 66.
£86,000 to £900,000	Portfolio 64 with developed market exposure from portfolio 65.
£46,000 to £86,000	Portfolio 63.
£10,000 to £46,000	Portfolio 62.
£1,800 to £10,000	Invest in the cheapest diversified global bond ETF you can find; currently this is XBAG.

* Here I assume you are paying a £6 minimum commission. If you are paying £12 then the minimum for this portfolio will be (£12 ÷ £6) × £900,000 = £1.8 million.

CHAPTER THIRTEEN

Putting It All Together

Portfolio						
Equities			Bonds			Genuine alternatives
Traditional equity		Equity-like alternatives	Traditional bonds		Bond-like alternatives	
Developed equity	Emerging equity		Developed	Emerging		
Regions			Regions			
Countries			Countries			
Sectors			Type			
Individual equities			Maturity and credit			

DECIDING ON PORTFOLIO WEIGHTINGS CAN BE OVERWHELMING and complex. The beauty of the top-down method is that you can separate out this problem into many smaller decisions: how much to hold in equities or bonds, what the breakdown should be across different countries, and so on. However, after reading the last few chapters you are probably drowning in detail and struggling to see the big picture: what a fully completed smart portfolio actually looks like.

In this chapter I show a few examples of how to go about building a complete portfolio, from start to finish. Hopefully these will illustrate how straightforward it is to follow the top-down method. This should help you to follow the process yourself, and create a portfolio that suits you best. However, if you already have a portfolio which will require serious changes before it resembles the examples in this chapter, then I will cover the best way of going about this in part four.

Chapter overview

Example 1: Sarah	US-based institutional investor (risk tolerance: brave)
Example 2: David	UK investor with £500,000 (risk tolerance: average)
Example 3: Paul	US investor with $40,000 (risk tolerance: ultra safe)
Example 4: Patricia	UK investor with £50,000 (risk tolerance: brave)

These are just arbitrary names. No resemblance is intended to anyone living or dead.

This is the concluding chapter of part two. After reading this you should be able to construct a portfolio to suit your own requirements.

Example 1: Sarah – US institutional investor

My first example is for a university endowment based in the US with $1 billion, which is overseen by an investment committee but also employs a full time Chief Investment Officer, Sarah, who has recently been recruited from a similar role at a hedge fund manager.

The investment committee are comfortable holding individual equity positions, but for bonds they are going to use ETFs. They don't believe in active management except in the alternatives asset class where they believe that Sarah can find the best hedge funds.

Determine risk tolerance

The first stage in any portfolio allocation is to determine risk tolerance (see the summary section on page 507). Because the committee is running a university endowment with a theoretically infinite investment horizon, it decides it is a **brave** investor. A brave investor will invest in the **maximum geometric mean portfolio**, and limit bond allocation to a 10% risk weight.

Asset allocation

Sarah decides to adapt portfolio 20 (chapter eight, page 200) for her asset allocation. Because she feels confident about her ability to choose good hedge funds, she decides to increase the alternatives allocation to a higher level than I normally recommend: 20% rather than 10%.

PORTFOLIO 67: ASSET CLASS ALLOCATION (EXAMPLE ONE)

Portfolio **$1,000 million**				
Equity-like 80% **(73.6%)**		Bond-like 10% **(17.2%)**		Genuine alternatives 10% **(9.1%)**
Traditional equity 90%	Equity-like alternatives 10%	Traditional bonds 90%	Bond-like alternatives 10%	
72% **(66.2%)** **$662 million**	8% **(7.4%)** **$74 million**	9.0% **(15.6%)** **$156 million**	1.0% **(1.7%)** **$17 million**	10% **(9.1%)** **$91 million**

Risk weightings shown. Cash weightings in **(bold)**. Dollar amounts in bold.

Alternatives

Genuine alternatives

Sarah knows about hedge funds. She will have done the type of analysis I will cover in part three to evaluate their active management skills, along with even more complex techniques. However she is comfortable using ETFs to access precious metals, and she will hold safe haven currencies like the Japanese yen and Swiss franc in bank accounts. Portfolio 68 is a copy of portfolio 21 (page 211), with selected ETFs from portfolio 24 (page 220).

PORTFOLIO 68: GENUINE ALTERNATIVES (EXAMPLE ONE)

Portfolio **$1,000 million**										
Genuine alternatives **$91 million**										
Standalone 50%					Insurance-like 50%					
Managed futures 50%	Global Macro 50%	Short biased 20%	Tail protect 20%	Long volatility 20%	Safe haven currencies 20%		Precious metals 20%			
					Swiss franc 50%	Yen 50%	Gold IAU 25%	Silver SLV 25%	Platinum PPLT 25%	Palladium PALL 25%
4 x Hedge funds	4 x Hedge funds	Hedge fund	2 x Hedge funds	Hedge fund	Bank account	Bank account	ETF: IAU	ETF: SLV	ETF: PPLT	ETF: PALL
25% (28.8%) $29m	25% (23.2%) $23m	10% (8.9%) $8.8m	10% (13.6%) $13m	10% (2.7%) $2.7m	5% (4.6%) $4.6m	5% (4.6%) $4.6m	2.5% (3.4%) $3.4m	2.5% (3.4%) $3.4m	2.5% (3.4%) $3.4m	2.5% (3.4%) $3.4m

Final row shows weight within genuine alternatives sub-portfolio. Weights are risk weightings, cash weightings shown in **(bold)** cash amounts shown in $m (millions).

Notice that in some hedge fund categories I have included multiple funds. It makes sense to diversify amongst different managers if you can still meet their minimum investment requirements.

Equity-like alternatives

Portfolio 69 is a copy of portfolio 22 (page 216) with selected ETF tickers from portfolio 28 (page 223).

PORTFOLIO 69: EQUITY-LIKE ALTERNATIVES (EXAMPLE ONE)

Portfolio **$1,000 million**										
Equities **$736 million**										
Equity-like alternatives **$74 million**										
Private equity & venture capital 25%		Real estate 25%		Commodities (ex. precious metals) 25%			Hedge funds 25%			
Private equity 50%	Venture capital 50%	Commercial 50%	Private housing 50%	Agricultural 33%	Energies 33%	Non-precious metals 33%	Equity neutral 25%	FX Carry 25%	Fixed income relative value 25%	Short volatility 25%
Private equity fund	VC fund	Private real estate partnership	Student housing	ETF: GSG	ETF: USO	ETF: JJM	Hedge fund	Hedge fund	Hedge fund	Hedge fund
12.5% **(7.6%)** **$5.7m**	12.5% **(7.6%)** **$5.7m**	12.5% **(14.6%)** **$11m**	12.5% **(12.1%)** **$9m**	8.3% **(8.1%)** **$6m**	8.3% **(5%)** **$4m**	8.3% **(10%)** **$7m**	6.25% **(8.7%)** **$6m**	6.25% **(8.7%)** **$6m**	6.25% **(8.7%)** **$6m**	6.25% **(8.7%)** **$6m**

Final row shows weight within equity-like sub-portfolio. Weights are risk weightings, cash weightings in **(bold)** cash allocations in bold $m (millions).

Sarah is able to access private equity and venture capital funds directly. She also has an investment in a real estate partnership, and the endowment fund had already co-invested in some student housing in partnership with the university.

Finally she has selected four fund managers for each of the equity-like sub categories of hedge funds. Sarah is comfortable using passive ETFs to get her commodity exposure.

Bond-like alternatives

Portfolio 70 is a copy of portfolio 23 (page 218) with selected ETFs from portfolio 32 (page 226).

PORTFOLIO 70: BOND-LIKE ALTERNATIVES (EXAMPLE ONE)

Portfolio **$1,000 million**						
Bonds **$172 million**						
Bond-like alternatives **$17 million**						
Private debt 33%	Peer-to-peer lending 0%	Infrastructure, real assets, ABS 33%				Long fixed income Hedge Funds 33%
		Infrastructure 50%		Real assets 50%	Asset-backed securities 0%	
		Developed 50%	Emerging 50%			
Private debt fund		ETF: IFG	ETF: EMIF	Direct investment in farmland		Hedge fund
33% (33.6%) $5.7m	0%	8.3% (11.2%) $1.9m	8.3% (5.9%) $1m	16.7% (12.0%) $2m	0%	33% (37.6%) $6.4m

Final row shows weight within bond-like alternatives sub-portfolio. Weights shown are risk weightings, cash weightings in **(bold)**.

The final alternatives sub category is for bond-like assets. Again there is a mixture of actively managed funds and ETFs, and the endowment fund owns a farm on the outskirts of the university campus. Sarah does not believe the returns of peer-to-peer lending compensate for the risk and has excluded them. She is also excluding asset-backed securities, since these also appear in her traditional bond portfolio.

Equities

The advice from chapter eight is to put 75% into developed markets and 25% into emerging markets, with suggested cash weightings of 83% and 17% respectively. For institutional investors I suggested allocating one-third of their developed markets exposure to three regions: North America, EMEA and Asia Pacific; with 80% of North America in the US. However the university investment committee is concerned that this would leave them an insufficiently patriotic allocation to the US (about 22%).

So they take the decision to put 40% of the regional exposure into North America, with 90% of that in the US, bringing the US risk weighting up to just under 30%. This higher weighting is a reasonable thing to do, as long as the university is consistent and sticks to it. It's much smarter to make decisions like these in a conscious way using the top-down methodology, rather than in an arbitrary or haphazard way.

For the other developed regions Sarah is happy to use portfolios 41 and 43 for EMEA and Asia Pacific respectively. She also follows my advice to put 40% of emerging market equities into Asia, 30% in Latin America, and 30% in EMEA; using portfolios 44 (Asia), 45 (Latin America), and 46 (Europe) for each emerging market region.

Tables 43 and 44 show how Sarah calculated the allocation to each country's equity market using this information.

TABLE 43: ALLOCATION TO EACH COUNTRY WITHIN EQUITIES – DEVELOPED EQUITIES (EXAMPLE ONE)

	Emerging or developed A	Emerging or developed (cash) B	Region C	Within region D	Risk weight E = A×C×D	Cash weight F = B×C×D	Cash allocation G = F × $662m
US	75%	83%	40%	90%	27%	30%	$198m
Canada	75%	83%	40%	10%	3.0%	3.3%	$22m
UK	75%	83%	30%	16%	3.6%	4%	$26m
Ireland	75%	83%	30%	4%	0.9%	1%	$6.6m
Germany	75%	83%	30%	8%	1.8%	2%	$13m
Austria	75%	83%	30%	4%	0.9%	1%	$6.6m
Switzerland	75%	83%	30%	8%	1.8%	2%	$13m
Netherlands	75%	83%	30%	4%	0.9%	1%	$6.6m
Belgium	75%	83%	30%	4%	0.9%	1%	$6.6m
Sweden	75%	83%	30%	4%	0.9%	1%	$6.6m
Finland	75%	83%	30%	4%	0.9%	1%	$6.6m
Norway	75%	83%	30%	4%	0.9%	1%	$6.6m
France	75%	83%	30%	14%	3.2%	3.5%	$23m

	Emerging or developed A	Emerging or developed (cash) B	Region C	Within region D	Risk weight E = A×C×D	Cash weight F = B×C×D	Cash allocation G = F × $662m
Italy	75%	83%	30%	8%	1.8%	2%	$13m
Spain	75%	83%	30%	11%	2.5%	2.7%	$18m
Portugal	75%	83%	30%	3%	0.7%	0.8%	$5m
Israel	75%	83%	30%	4%	0.9%	1%	$6.6m
Japan	75%	83%	30%	40%	9%	10%	$66m
Australia	75%	83%	30%	21%	4.7%	5.2%	$35m
New Zealand	75%	83%	30%	9%	2%	2.2%	$15m
Hong Kong	75%	83%	30%	15%	3.4%	3.7%	$25m
Singapore	75%	83%	30%	15%	3.4%	3.7%	$25m

Table shows the calculation of country weights for a large institutional investor allocating $662 million to equities. All weights shown are risk weights unless specified otherwise. Values shown are as a proportion of entire equity portfolio. Note I am not using my preferred weights here: there is a 40% allocation to North America, and 90% within that region to the US.

TABLE 44: ALLOCATION TO EACH COUNTRY WITHIN EQUITIES – EMERGING EQUITIES (EXAMPLE ONE)

	Emerging or developed A	Emerging or developed (cash) B	Region C	Within region D	Risk weight E = A×C×D	Cash weight F = B×C×D	Cash allocation G = F × $662m
China	25%	17%	40%	30%	3%	2%	$14m
India	25%	17%	40%	20%	2%	1.4%	$9m
Taiwan	25%	17%	40%	15%	1.5%	1%	$6.8m
South Korea	25%	17%	40%	15%	1.5%	1%	$6.8m

	Emerging or developed A	Emerging or developed (cash) B	Region C	Within region D	Risk weight E = A×C×D	Cash weight F = B×C×D	Cash allocation G = F × $662m
Malaysia	25%	17%	40%	5%	0.5%	0.3%	$2.3m
Indonesia	25%	17%	40%	5%	0.5%	0.3%	$2.3m
Thailand	25%	17%	40%	5%	0.5%	0.3%	$2.3m
Philippines	25%	17%	40%	5%	0.5%	0.3%	$2.3m
Brazil	25%	17%	30%	35%	2.6%	1.8%	$12m
Mexico	25%	17%	30%	35%	2.6%	1.8%	$12m
Chile	25%	17%	30%	10%	0.8%	0.5%	$3.4m
Colombia	25%	17%	30%	10%	0.8%	0.5%	$3.4m
Peru	25%	17%	30%	10%	0.8%	0.5%	$3.4m
Russia	25%	17%	30%	17%	1.3%	0.9%	$5.7m
Poland	25%	17%	30%	6%	0.5%	0.3%	$2m
Hungary	25%	17%	30%	6%	0.5%	0.3%	$2m
Czech Republic	25%	17%	30%	6%	0.5%	0.3%	$2m
Greece	25%	17%	30%	8%	0.6%	0.4%	$2.7m
Turkey	25%	17%	30%	8%	0.6%	0.4%	$2.7m
Qatar	25%	17%	30%	8%	0.6%	0.4%	$2.7m
UAE	25%	17%	30%	8%	0.6%	0.4%	$2.7m
Egypt	25%	17%	30%	8%	0.6%	0.4%	$2.7m
South Africa	25%	17%	30%	25%	1.9%	1.3%	$8.4m

Table shows the calculation of country weights for a large institutional investor allocating $662 million to equities. All weights shown are risk weights unless specified otherwise. Values shown are as a proportion of entire equity portfolio (emerging and developed).

The next step is to determine sector weightings within each country. I've copied portfolio 49 (page 254), and worked out the dollar allocations for UK equities as an example.

PORTFOLIO 71: SECTOR ALLOCATION WITHIN COUNTRIES – UK (EXAMPLE ONE)

Portfolio **$1,000 million**										
Equities										
Developed										
Region: Europe										
Country: UK **$26 million**										
Consumer discretionary	Consumer staples	Energy	Financials	Real estate	Health care	Industrials	IT	Materials	Telecom	Utilities
9.1%	9.1%	9.1%	9.1%	9.1%	9.1%	9.1%	9.1%	9.1%	9.1%	9.1%
(8.2%)	(13.5%)	(11.1%)	(7.5%)	(8.2%)	(8.6%)	(10%)	(5.6%)	(10%)	(8.2%)	(9%)
$2.1m	$3.5m	$2.9m	$2m	$2.1m	$2.2m	$2.6m	$1.5m	$2.6m	$2.1m	$2.3m

Risk weightings shown. Cash weights in **(bold)**. Actual cash in **bold**.

Notice that even the smallest country in table 44 has a couple of million dollars of allocation. From chapter six (table 37 on page 171), this is more than enough to justify direct investment. In theory the institution could economically buy dozens of stocks in each country.

However, Sarah has a small team of just two analysts to help her manage the portfolio: she doesn't want the hassle of owning tens of thousands of individual stocks. Sarah also doesn't want to end up holding dozens of tiny illiquid firms just to make up the numbers in small emerging markets, and incurring huge market impact costs.

So she decides to enforce some rules: a minimum position size of $100,000, a maximum of five stocks in each industry sector, and a minimum market cap of $100 million. This will exclude small cap stocks, but Sarah is more concerned about market impact and owning too many stocks than any potential for lost return.

For example, looking at portfolio 71, Sarah needs to work out if she can hold the maximum of five stocks in each of the 11 UK sectors. If she bought five stocks in the UK technology sector in equal cash and risk weightings, then each would have a position of one-fifth, or 20%, of $1.5 million: $300,000. This comfortably exceeds the minimum of

$100,000 specified above. Because tech is the sector with the smallest cash weight there won't be any problems with the minimum elsewhere.

Sarah then checks that there are five stocks with a market cap of at least $100 million in each of these sectors. In the UK as of early 2017 the telecoms sector has the fewest stocks available in the FTSE 350 index of large and mid cap stocks, but there are still exactly five telecommunications stocks in the index; each of which has a market cap of at least $500 million.

In other large developed countries like the US she will also own the maximum number of stocks: 55, five for each of the 11 sectors. But in a small emerging market with an allocation of just $2 million Sarah will probably hold just one or two in each sector. For some smaller emerging markets there may be no stocks that are liquid enough in certain sectors.

Bonds

Sarah isn't an expert on bonds and doesn't want the hassle of employing specialist dealers – she is happy to use ETFs to get her bond exposure. From chapter ten the suggested portfolio is number 61, with non-US exposure from portfolio 60. These are copied below with the size of each investment included.

PORTFOLIO 72: BOND ALLOCATION (EXAMPLE ONE)

US 22%	Australia 5%	Japan 5%	Developed non-US 43%				Emerging 25%				
			Normal 90%			Inflation 10%	Normal 55%			Foreign 45%	
			Govt. 40%	Corp. 30%	High yield 30%	Govt. 100%	Govt. 40%	Corp. 30%	High yield 30%	Govt. 84%	Corp. 16%
See portfolio 73	ETF: AUNZ	ETF: JGBL	ETF: IGOV	ETF: VCLT	ETF: IHY	ETF: GTIP	ETF: VWOB	ETF: EMLC	Fund manager	ETF: EMB	
22% (24.7%) $39m	5% (5.6%) $8.7m	5% (5.6%) $8.7m	15.5% (17.4%) $27m	11.6% (12%) $19m	11.6% (9.8%) $15m	4.3% (4.8%) $7.5m	5.5% (4.6%) $7.2m	4.1% (3.1%) $4.8m	4.1% (2.8%) $4.4m	9.5% (9.5%) $15m	1.8%

Portfolio $1,000m — Bonds $172m — Traditional bonds $156m

All values are risk weights; cash weights in **(bold)**, cash allocation in **bold** in $1m (millions). Notice the total cash weight for EMB is shown below the two separate risk weights for each of its components (government and corporate).

PORTFOLIO 73: US BOND ALLOCATION (EXAMPLE ONE)

Portfolio **$1,000m**													
Bonds **$172m**													
Traditional bonds **$156m**													
US **$39m** 22%													Non-US 78% See portfolio 68
Normal 90%											Inflation 10% SCHP		
No specific maturity 50%							Medium maturity 25%		Long term maturity 25%		All 60%	15 years+ 40%	
Government 40%		Investment Grade Corporate 30%			High yield Corporate 30%		Govt. 50%	IG Corp 50%	Govt. 50%	IG Corp 50%			
High yield Muni 50%	MBS 50%	MBS 40%	Conv. 30%	Covered bond 30%	Cross-over 50%	Junk 50%							
ETF: HYD	ETF: VMBS	ETF: CMBS	ETF: ICVT	ETF: COBO	ETF: QLTB	ETF: QLTC	ETF: SCHR	ETF: VCIT	ETF: TLO	ETF: LWC	ETF: SCHP	ETF: LTPZ	
2%	2%	1.2%	0.9%	0.9%	1.5%	1.5%	2.5%	2.5%	2.5%	2.5%	1.3%	0.9%	
(2.3%)	(2.6%)	(1.5%)	(1.1%)	(1.1%)	(1.6%)	(1.4%)	(3.3%)	(3.0%)	(2.2%)	(1.6%)	(1.7%)	(1.2%)	
$3.6m	$4.1m	$2.3m	$1.7m	$1.7m	$2.5m	$2.2m	$5.1m	$4.7m	$2.4m	$2.5m	$2.7m	$1.9m	

All figures are risk weighting; cash weightings in **(bold)**, cash allocation in **bold** $1m (millions). Final row shows risk weighting within bonds sub-portfolio. Key: Muni = Municipal. MBS = Mortgage Backed Security. Conver. = Convertible bonds. Cross-over = A corporate bond with a yield between investment grade and high yield. Junk = True high yield corporate bonds. IG Corp= Investment grade corporate bonds. Govt. = Government bonds.

Example 2: David – UK investor with £500,000

Risk tolerance

This portfolio is for David, a UK-based investor with £500,000 in his self directed pension plan. David is in his late 50s and considering early retirement, so he is worried about taking on too much risk. He decides that his risk tolerance is **average**, and a **compromise portfolio** would suit him best. David is paying the same £6 minimum commission as I am, so he can use the same default minimum portfolio values I've used throughout part two.

Asset allocation

David is happy with a 10% weight in alternatives and reading the guidance in chapter eight he realises he has enough money for allocating to all three categories of alternatives (genuine, equity-like, and bond-like). David puts together portfolio 74 using table 41 (chapter eight, page 201) to get the appropriate cash weights.

PORTFOLIO 74: ASSET CLASS ALLOCATION (EXAMPLE TWO)

Portfolio **£500,000**				
Equity-like 65% **(44.8%)**		Bond-like 30% **(51.7%)**		Genuine alternatives 5% **(3.4%)**
Traditional equity 95%	Equity-like alternatives 5%	Traditional bonds 95%	Bond-like alternatives 5%	
61.8% **(42.6%)** £212,800	3.3% **(2.2%)** £11,200	28.5% **(49.1%)** £245,600	1.5% **(2.6%)** £13,000	5% **(3.4%)** £17,000

Risk weightings shown. Cash weightings in **(bold)**. GBP amounts in **bold**.

Alternatives

Following the advice in chapter nine, David constructs portfolios 75, 76, and 77 (these are copies of portfolio 27 (page 222), portfolio 31 (page 225) and portfolio 33 (page 227), with the specific amounts added). He feels happier knowing that some of his money is in assets that sound robust, like gold, property and timber. Although David also owns his own home he is happy to put a few thousand pounds into real estate ETFs.

PORTFOLIO 75: GENUINE ALTERNATIVES (EXAMPLE TWO)

Portfolio **£500,000**					
Genuine alternatives **£17,000**					
Standalone 0%	Insurance-like 100%				
	Long volatility SPVG 50%	Precious metals 50%			
		Gold ETF SGLN 25%	Platinum ETF SPLT 25%	Silver ETF SSLN 25%	Palladium ETF SPDM 25%
0%	50% (16.7%) £2,850	12.5% (20.8%) £3,550	12.5% (20.8%) £3,550	12.5% (20.8%) £3,550	12.5% (20.8%) £3,550

Final row shows weight within genuine alternatives sub-portfolio. Weights are risk weightings, cash weightings shown in **(bold)**. GBP amounts in **bold**.

PORTFOLIO 76: EQUITY-LIKE ALTERNATIVES (EXAMPLE TWO)

Portfolio **£500,000**		
Equities **£224,000**		
Equity-like alternatives **£11,200**		
Private equity ETF 33.3% XLPE	Global real estate 33.3% GBRE	Commodities ETF 33.3% CMFP
33.3% **(25.6%)** **£2,900**	33.3% **(49.1%)** **£5,500**	33.3% **(25.2%)** **£2,800**

Final row shows weight within equity-like alternatives sub-portfolio. Weights are risk weightings, cash weightings shown in **(bold)**. GBP amounts in **bold**.

PORTFOLIO 77: BOND-LIKE ALTERNATIVES (EXAMPLE TWO)

Portfolio **£100,000**							
Bonds **£258,600**							
Bond-like alternatives **£13,000**							
Private debt 0%	Peer-to-peer lending 0%	Infrastructure, real assets, ABS 100%					Long fixed income hedge funds 0%
		Infrastructure 50%		Real assets 50%		Asset-backed securities 0%	
		Developed 50% XSGI	Emerging 50% IEMI	Timber 50% WOOD	Agribusiness 50% SPAG		
0%	0%	25% **(36.9%)** **£4,800**	25% **(19.4%)** **£2,520**	25% **(19.8%)** **£2,570**	25% **(23.9%)** **£3,110**	0%	0%

Final row shows weight within bond-like alternatives sub-portfolio. Weights are risk weightings, cash weightings shown in **(bold)**.

Equities

David has £212,800 to put into traditional equities. He follows my advice in chapter eight to put 75% risk weighted into developed markets, and 25% into emerging markets. Subsequently he allocates one-third of his developed markets portfolio to individual countries in each of the three regions: North America (60% US, 40% Canada), EMEA (portfolio 42) and Asia Pacific (portfolio 43).

David puts his emerging markets allocation into three regions using the weights I suggest: 40% in Asia, 30% in Latin America, and 30% in EMEA. He finds that he doesn't have enough money to buy individual countries in any emerging markets region (although he's close to the minimum in EMEA, portfolio 48).

The final allocations and calculations are shown in table 45.

TABLE 45: ALLOCATION TO EACH COUNTRY WITHIN EQUITIES (EXAMPLE TWO)

	Emerging or developed A	Emerging or developed (cash) B	Region C	Within region D	Risk weight E = A×C×D	Cash weight F = B×C×D	Cash allocation G = F × £212,800	ETF
US	75%	83%	33.3%	80%	20%	22.1%	£47,210	CSPX
Canada	75%	83%	33.3%	20%	5%	5.5%	£11,700	UC24
UK	75%	83%	33.3%	20%	5%	5.5%	£11,700	ISF
Germany	75%	83%	33.3%	10%	2.5%	2.8%	£5,960	DAXX
Switzerland	75%	83%	33.3%	10%	2.5%	2.8%	£5,960	CSWCHF
Netherlands	75%	83%	33.3%	8%	2%	2.2%	£4,700	CH1
Nordic	75%	83%	33.3%	12%	3%	3.3%	£7,020	CN1
France	75%	83%	33.3%	14%	3.5%	3.9%	£8,300	ISFR
Italy	75%	83%	33.3%	12%	3%	3.3%	£7,020	CI1
Spain	75%	83%	33.3%	14%	3.5%	3.9%	£8,300	CS1
Japan	75%	83%	33.3%	40%	10%	11.1%	£23,620	HMJP
Australia	75%	83%	33.3%	30%	7.5%	8.3%	£17,660	LAUS
Hong Kong	75%	83%	33.3%	15%	3.8%	4.2%	£8,900	HSI

	Emerging or developed A	Emerging or developed (cash) B	Region C	Within region D	Risk weight E = A×C×D	Cash weight F = B×C×D	Cash allocation G = F × £212,800	ETF
Singapore	75%	83%	33.3%	15%	3.8%	4.2%	£8,900	XBAS
EM EMEA	25%	17%	30%		7.5%	5.1%	£10,850	XMEA
EM Asia	25%	17%	40%		10%	6.8%	£14,470	GMF
EM Latam	25%	17%	30%		7.5%	5.1%	£10,850	ALAT

Table shows the calculation of country weights for a UK investor allocating £212,800 to equities. All weights shown are risk weights unless specified otherwise. Values shown are as a proportion of entire equity portfolio.

David would ideally like to buy individual stocks in the UK equity market but after looking at table 38 in chapter six (page 171) he can see that it doesn't make sense. Given the low holding costs of UK tracking ETF ISF (expense ratio 0.07% plus invisible trading costs within the fund of 0.10%) he would need to allocate at least £60,000 to UK equities[208] before being able to buy one stock in each sector. He will have to wait until he has saved more money.

Traditional bonds

Finally let's examine David's bond portfolio. Portfolios 78 and 79 are appropriate for his bond allocation of just under £250,000. They are copies of portfolios 64 and 65 from chapter twelve.

---

208. The precise holding cost of 0.17% isn't show in table 38; I found this value by interpolation.

PORTFOLIO 78: BOND ALLOCATION (EXAMPLE TWO)

Portfolio **£500,000**				
Bonds **£258,600**				
Traditional bonds **£245,600**				
Developed 75% See portfolio 84	Emerging 25%			
	Normal 50%	Foreign 40%		Inflation 10%
	Government 100% SEML	Govt. 40% LEMB	Corporate 60% EMCP	Government 100% EMIN
75% **(79.1%)** **£204,550**	12.5% **(10.8%)** **£27,930**	4.0% **(3.4%)** **£8,790**	6.0% **(4.6%)** **£11,900**	2.5% **(2.1%)** **£5,430**

Risk weightings are shown; cash weightings in **(bold)**; GBP allocation in **bold**. Final row shows weight within bonds sub-portfolio.

PORTFOLIO 79: DEVELOPED BOND ALLOCATION (EXAMPLE TWO)

Portfolio **£500,000**											
Bonds **£258,600**											
Traditional bonds **£245,600**											
Developed 75%											Emerging 25%
Americas 33%				Europe 30%				UK 27%			Asia 10%	See portfolio 67
US 100%				Normal 90%			Inflation 10%	Normal 90%		Inflation 10%	Australia 100%	
Normal 90%			Inflation 10%	Govt. 40%	Corp. 30%	High yld. 30%	MTIX	Govt. 50%	Corp. 50%	GILI	XCS2	
Govt. 40% USTY	Corp. 30% UC84	High yld. 30% SHYU	UTIP	VETY	IBCX	SHYG		GILS	COUK			
8.9%	6.7%	6.7%	2.5%	8.1%	6.1%	6.1%	2.3%	9.1%	9.1%	2.0%	7.5%	25%
(11%)	(7.6%)	(6.2%)	(2.7%)	(8.9%)	(6.2%)	(5.0%)	(2.5%)	(10%)	(9.2%)	(2.2%)	(8.2%)	(20.5%)
£28.5k	£19.7k	£16k	£7k	£23k	£16k	£12.9k	£6.5k	£25.9k	£23.8k	£5.7k	£21.2k	£53,010

Risk weightings are shown; Cash weightings in **(bold)**. GBP allocation in **bold**. Final row shows weight within entire bonds portfolio. Amounts are shown in £1000 amounts (1k = 1000).

Example 3: Paul – US investor with $40,000

Risk tolerance

Paul is a US investor with $40,000 to invest. He has just retired and will be using the income to supplement a very modest defined benefit employer pension. Paul is a very cautious individual who after reading the relevant part of chapter four (page 77 onwards) decides he fits into the **ultra-safe** category, as even a low-risk maximum Sharpe Ratio portfolio is too racy for him.

Rather than risk his entire nest egg to the whims of the market Paul decides to put $10,000 into a savings account, and invests the remaining $30,000 into the **maximum Sharpe Ratio** portfolio.

Paul is paying $1.30 in minimum commission rather than the $1 minimum I've assumed. This means he needs to invest at least $400 in each ETF, rather than the default value of $300.

Asset allocation

Paul likes the idea of holding some gold, so he is happy with a 10% risk allocation to alternatives. At this level of investment it isn't possible to split up alternatives into sub categories of equity-like and bond-like. Portfolio 80 shows the resulting asset allocation for a low-risk portfolio.

PORTFOLIO 80: ASSET ALLOCATION (EXAMPLE THREE)

Assets **$40,000**			
Portfolio **$30,000**			Cash
Equity-like 45% **(26.9%)**	Bond-like 45% **(67.2%)**	Genuine alternatives 10% **(6%)**	**$10,000**
Traditional equity 100%	Traditional bonds 100%		
45% **(26.9%)** **$8,070**	45% **(67.2%)** **$20,160**	10% **(6%)** **$1,800**	

Risk weightings shown, cash weights in **(bold)**, actual amounts in **bold**. Weights are a proportion of the invested portfolio of $30,000, not the entire $40,000.

Alternatives

With only $1,800 Paul can only buy a single fund; the cheapest gold ETF he can find is IAU.

Equities

Paul is very nervous about emerging markets, so rather than my recommended allocation of 25% he decides to allocate just 10% of his equity portfolio, with the remaining 90% in developed markets. For developed markets he buys the regional funds in portfolio 38. The result is portfolio 81.

PORTFOLIO 81: EQUITIES (EXAMPLE THREE)

Portfolio **$30,000**									
Equity **$8,070**									
Developed 90% **(93%)**									Emerging 10% **(7%)** VWO
North America 33%		EMEA (Europe) 33% VGK				Asia Pacific 33%			
US 60% IVV	Canada 40% EWC	UK 29%	France 15%	Germany 14%	Other 42%	Japan 40% JPP	Asia ex-JP 60% EPP		
							Australia 58%	Other 42%	
18%	12%	9%	4%	4%	12%	12%	10%	8%	10%
(18.4%) **$1,490**	**(12.3%)** **$1,000**	**(30.7%)** **$2,480**				**(12.3%)** **$1,000**	**(18.4%)** **$1,490**		**(7%)** **$807**

Risk weightings are shown, cash weightings in **(bold)** and actual amounts in **bold**. The emerging market allocation is lower than I normally recommend; 10% rather than 25%.

Bonds

Finally we come to Paul's favourite asset class: safe and secure bonds. Portfolio 82 is a copy of portfolio 60, in chapter twelve. The US exposure is broken down further in portfolio 83. This is based on portfolio 61, but I've taken out a few sub categories so that there is at least $400 invested in each ETF.

PORTFOLIO 82: BOND ALLOCATION (EXAMPLE THREE)

US 68%	Australia AUNZ 16%	Japan JGBL 16%	Govt 40% IGOV	Corp 30% VCLT	High yield 30%	Inflation Govt 100%	Govt 40%	Corp 30%	High yield 30%	Foreign Govt 84% / Corp 16%
	Portfolio **$30,000**									
	Bonds **$20,160**									
	Traditional bonds **$20,160**									
Developed 75%							Emerging 25%			
Country by country 43%			Rest of the world 57%							
US 68%	Australia AUNZ 16%	Japan JGBL 16%	Normal 90%			Inflation 10%	Normal 55%			Foreign 45%
			Govt 40% IGOV	Corp 30% VCLT	High yield 30%	Govt 100%	Govt 40%	Corp 30%	High yield 30%	Govt 84% / Corp 16%
See portfolio 83	ETF: AUNZ	ETF: JGBL	ETF: IGOV	ETF: VCLT	ETF: IHY	ETF: GTIP	ETF: VWOB	ETF: EMLC	ETF: EMHY	ETF: EMB
22% **(24.7%)** **$4,980**	5% **(5.6%)** **$1,130**	5% **(5.6%)** **$1,129**	15.5% **(17.4%)** **$3,510**	11.6% **(12.0%)** **$2,420**	11.6% **(9.8%)** **$1,980**	4.3% **(4.8%)** **$970**	5.5% **(4.6%)** **$930**	4.1% **(3.1%)** **$625**	4.1% **(2.8%)** **$564**	9.5% 1.8% **(9.5%)** **$1,920**

Final shows risk weighting within bonds sub-portfolio; cash weights in **(bold)**, cash amounts in **bold**.

PORTFOLIO 83: US BOND EXPOSURE (EXAMPLE THREE)

Portfolio **$30,000**									
Bonds **$20,160**									
Traditional bonds **$20,160**									
US **$4,980** 22%									Non US 78%
Normal 90%								Inflation 10%	See portfolio 82
Government 40%			Investment grade corporate 30%			High yield corporate 30%			
Muni 25%	MBS 25%	Other Govt. 50%	MBS 25%	Covered bond 25%	Other corporate 50% LWC	Cross-over 50%	Junk 50%		
ETF: HYD	ETF: VMBS	ETF: TLO	ETF: CMBS	ETF: COBO	ETF: LWC	ETF: QLTB	ETF: QLTC	ETF: SCHP	
2% (2.5%) $500	2% (2.8%) $560	4% (3.8%) $760	1.5% (2%) $410	1.5% (2%) $400	3% (2.1%) $420	3% (3.4%) $690	3% (3%) $610	2.2% (3.2%) $630	

Figures in plain font are risk weighting; cash weightings in **(bold)**, cash allocation in **bold**. Final row shows risk weighting within bonds sub-portfolio. Key: Muni = Municipal. MBS = Mortgage Backed Security. Cross-over = A corporate bond with a yield between investment grade and high yield. Junk = True high yield corporate bonds. Govt. = Government bonds.

Example 4: Patricia – UK investor with £50,000

We return to the UK for my final example. Patricia is a young and well paid banker who has been working and saving for a couple of years, and has already put away £50,000 for her retirement which she expects will be around 30 years away. With such a long investment horizon and a relatively high salary she is very comfortable with risk, and will be taking on the brave option of a **maximum geometric mean** portfolio.

Patricia is financially switched on, and is using the same ultra-cheap broker as I am. So she can use the same default minimum portfolio values as shown throughout part two. She goes with the default options for the size of her investments in chapters eight through twelve and ends up with portfolio 84.

PORTFOLIO 84: STARTING ALLOCATION (EXAMPLE FOUR)

Portfolio £50,000												
Equities 80%							Bonds 10%					Genuine alternatives 10%
Developed 75%						Emerging 25%	Developed 75%			Emerging 25%		Insurance-like 100%
North America 33%		Europe 33%		Asia 33%			Normal 100%			Normal 100%		Precious metals 100%
US 60%	Canada 40%	UK 20%	Other 80%	Japan 40%	Other 60%		Govt. 60%	Corp. 40%	High yield 40%	Govt. 100%		Gold 100%
ETF: CSPX	ETF: UC24	ETF: ISF	ETF: IEUX	ETF: HMJP	ETF: CJP1	ETF: AEUM	ETF: SAAA	ETF: CRPS	ETF: IGHY	ETF: SEML		ETF: SGLN
12%	8%	4%	16%	8%	12%	20%	3%	2.3%	2.3%	2.5%		10%
(11.5%)	(7.6%)	(3.8%)	(15.3%)	(7.6%)	(11.5%)	(12.5%)	(7.2%)	(5%)	(4%)	(4.5%)		(9.6%)
£5,750	£3,800	£1,900	£7,650	£3,800	£5,750	£6,250	£3,600	£2,500	£2,000	£2,250		£4,800

Risk weightings shown. Cash weightings in **(bold)**. Actual cash amounts in **bold**.

I return to Patricia's case study in parts three and four of the book.

Summary

Risk appetite	Decide on your risk appetite, and the appropriate portfolio: maximum Sharpe Ratio, compromise, or maximum geometric mean.
	Careful investors: Determine cash holding to reduce risk to comfortable levels.
	Borrowing investors: Determine amount of leverage required.

Asset allocation	Follow the advice in chapter eight to set up the appropriate asset allocation for your portfolio type.
Alternatives	Chapter nine will help you decide on the best allocation for alternatives.
Equities	Read chapters ten and eleven to determine your equities allocation.
Bonds	Use chapter twelve to decide on your bond allocation.

PART THREE
Predicting
Returns

Part Three: Predicting Returns

"I think that the first thing is you should have a strategic asset allocation mix that assumes that you don't know what the future is going to hold."

—Ray Dalio, founder of giant quantitative hedge fund Bridgewater

After reading parts one and two you should have met Ray's requirements, and know how to build a smart portfolio of assets which assumes nothing about the future; or to be precise assumes that risk-adjusted returns can't be forecasted. But what if you do know what the future holds, or think you do? What should you do about it?

There are two chapters in this part of the book. The first part of chapter fourteen explains how to use **simple systematic models** to predict risk-adjusted returns and adjust your portfolio accordingly. But perhaps you believe you possess real skill in forecasting asset prices or stock picking, which no simple model can replicate. The second half of chapter fourteen shows you how to exploit this skill in the safest possible way.

The next chapter is about investing in **funds**. The first half of chapter fifteen is about **smart beta**: a recent innovation in passive fund management which goes beyond the traditional world of market capitalisation weighted index tracking. In the second half of the chapter I explore the world of **active fund management**. I ask whether real skill exists amongst active managers, and show you how to work out if their performance is just a fluke.

CHAPTER FOURTEEN

Predicting Returns and Selecting Assets

$\mathcal{S}$O FAR I'VE INSISTED THAT NOBODY CAN PREDICT FUTURE returns, or to be pedantic future risk-adjusted returns. I'm now going to backtrack slightly from that extreme ideological position.

During my career working in hedge funds I've created many trading models that have had some success in predicting the future. In this chapter I show you how to use similar models to make adjustments to your handcrafted portfolio weights from part two.

I'm less convinced that there are large numbers of people who can forecast future returns using some kind of special skill that can't be replicated with simple models. However many people will still want to try. So in the second half of the chapter I explain how to adjust your portfolio to account for any predictions you've made yourself. Allowing limited changes to your portfolio as a result of intuitive forecasts will constrain the damage done if you aren't as skilled as you think.

Chapter overview

Why predicting risk-adjusted returns is so difficult	A reminder of why I assumed you couldn't predict risk-adjusted returns in the first two parts of this book, and why forecasting models offer some hope.
How can we use forecasting models to construct portfolios	The nuts and bolts of what you should do with your carefully handcrafted portfolio when you unleash some forecasting models.
Introducing my forecasting models	I use two models in this chapter: a **momentum** model, and a **dividend yield** model.

Using forecasting models in a top-down portfolio	A detailed guide to using my preferred forecasting models to adjust your portfolio weights.
Adjusting portfolio weights when you don't have a model	How you can use your own forecasts without needing a formal forecasting model.
Stock selection when you don't have a model	Some advice for would-be discretionary stock pickers.

Why predicting risk-adjusted returns is so difficult

I spent seven years working for a multi-billion dollar quantitative hedge fund, AHL. For the last three years of my time there, I managed a portfolio of trading strategies that were heavily exposed to interest rate changes.[209] When I started that job in September 2010 the key Fed funds interest rate was 0.25%[210] and it cost the US government 2.5% to borrow for ten years. This was the lowest rate since the Second World War. Every week there were predictions that the US Fed would be raising interest rates within the next few months, and that we would lose a ton of money because our strategies had a predilection for buying bonds.

That all happened almost exactly six years before I started to write this book. Since then the Fed funds target rate has barely moved; it was increased to a mere 0.5% in December 2015, and has recently increased to 0.75%. As I write this sentence in February 2017 it still costs the US government just 2.5% to borrow for 10 years: exactly the same as in September 2010. Owning an ETF tracking US 10 year bonds would have earned you over 20% since 2010. Investors in that ETF have made a positive return in every calendar year except 2013, where they lost around 6%.

All the people who predicted bonds would lose a ton of money have ended up with several tons of egg on their face. Anyone who had followed their advice and cut bonds entirely out of their portfolio would have felt pretty **embarrassed**.[211]

There are a couple of lessons I think we can learn from this story. Firstly – as I have said before – prediction is hard. No matter how low (or high) things can go, they can always go even lower or much higher. Many people thought it was impossible for interest rates

---

209. This included bonds and bond futures, interest rate futures, and other fancy derivatives like interest rate swaps and credit default swaps.

210. Strictly speaking the Fed sets a target range for interest rates not a single level. The target was 0–0.25% from December 2008, 0.25%–0.5% from December 2015, and 0.5%–0.75% after December 2016.

211. Of course equities have also done very well in this period with a total return of around 100%, though obviously with much higher volatility.

to be negative: over the last few years this has happened in several countries. **Market extremes only become turning points in retrospect.** Even if you can accurately see what's coming, it's extremely difficult to predict **when** something will happen. Interest rates probably will go considerably higher at some point, but a forecast that is at least six years too early is almost worthless.[212]

The second point is that it's not enough to predict the future, **you have to predict it better than anyone else can.** Remember market prices already account for the market's best collective prediction of the future. Bond yields were consistently pricing in Fed interest rate increases since 2010. Even if interest rates had increased, investors in bonds would still have made money unless rates had risen faster and higher than the market expected them to.

Does this mean that prediction is impossible? Not completely. I do think that it is smart to use **systematic models** to forecast future risk-adjusted returns. Unlike human gut feeling, these models have been tested on a wide variety of financial instruments and have consistently performed well in the past.

For example, take the models we created at AHL, the hedge fund I was working for. These accurately predicted the positive returns that could be earned from owning bonds between 2010 and 2016. Our models didn't run scared at the widely forecast prospect of higher interest rates. Because the market assumed rates would rise, there were higher returns available to those who were still happy to buy bonds: this meant that bonds were great value. One set of models took advantage of this. But when interest rates did temporarily rise in 2013 another group of models automatically reduced the position they had in bonds to limit future losses.

CONCEPT: SYSTEMATICALLY REDUCING THE UNCERTAINTY OF THE PAST

Systematic models can't predict the future perfectly, but they can reduce the **uncertainty of the past** problem that I talked about at length in part one. Remember that uncertainty of the past means you can't be sure exactly what the underlying parameters of the **statistical model** were in historical data.

The resulting uncertainty is so large that it makes historical estimates of Sharpe Ratios effectively useless for determining the best portfolio weights; although volatility and correlation aren't so badly affected.

Consider figure 32. You have seen this kind of plot before, back in chapter three (figure 13, page 67). The figure shows the distribution of Sharpe Ratio estimates

---

212. If you'd like another example I accurately predicted the dramatic fall in 2008 of global house prices... in 2004.

for US equities. However this time I've added a model to filter different periods of history to use for my estimates.

FIGURE 32: DISTRIBUTION OF SHARPE RATIO ESTIMATES IS QUITE DIFFERENT FOR HIGH VERSUS LOW MOMENTUM

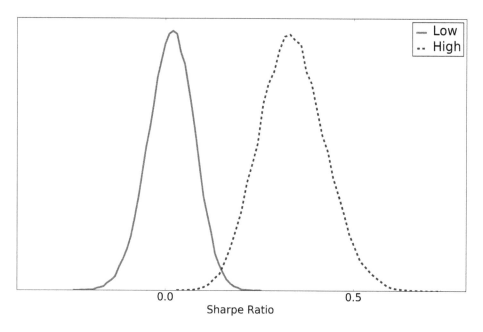

I've used the **momentum** model here. I explain this properly later in the chapter, but for now all you need to know is that it's a very simple and entirely systematic model which is based on the returns of an asset in the last 12 months.

The distribution on the left shows the range of Sharpe Ratio estimates drawn from history when momentum is low; periods when equities have recently underperformed relative to their historic average. On the right I've shown the distribution when relative momentum is high and equities have done very well in the last year.[213]

---

213. Technical details: Sharpe Ratio estimates were bootstrapped from series of monthly returns, conditioned on the value of momentum in the previous month. High momentum is a 12 month Sharpe Ratio above 2.00, low momentum is a 12 month Sharpe Ratio below -0.57. These values are based on the +1 and -1 standard deviation points on the distribution of past momentum. This plot is drawn from a dataset of monthly US equity returns which is different to the longer history of annual data I used in chapter 3; hence the unconditional distribution of Sharpe Ratio estimates will not be quite the same. The plot for bonds is equally striking. If I run the analysis on relative performance of equities versus bonds, conditioned on relative momentum, I get similar results.

Notice that there is still considerable uncertainty about the correct Sharpe Ratio in both historical periods; the **uncertainty of the past** hasn't gone away.[214] But the true Sharpe Ratio in high momentum periods was almost certainly higher than that in low momentum periods because the distributions barely overlap.

This doesn't mean that equities will definitely have higher returns if momentum is high: although you have more information about the parameters of the statistical model, a statistical model still produces random returns. But it does mean that some adjustments to your portfolio weights to reflect the output of the momentum model should improve your returns; at least if history repeats itself and the model continues to work as well in the future as it has done before.

I can understand why many people are wary of trusting their money to mysterious computer models. But my own experience is that these smart and simple models do a much better job of predicting the future than the vast majority of human investors, experts and market pundits. Better still, anyone can use them, regardless of skill or experience. I introduce specific models later in the chapter, which are very similar in spirit to those I managed at AHL.

Implementing these models requires some effort: perhaps one day a year on a portfolio with several dozen assets. However, they can boost your returns by around one-fifth; a 5% expected return might become 6%. On a portfolio of $100,000 that is $1,000; not bad for a day's work. Those with significantly smaller portfolios will not make this kind of additional return, and might want to skip this chapter.

Introducing risk factors

How can very simple models predict future returns, something I've consistently said is virtually impossible, even for highly intelligent human beings? It's because the extra returns that these simple models provide don't come for free – there is a downside. These models expose you to additional **risk**.

This isn't the simple **standard deviation of returns** that I've been using to measure risk so far. To understand these new risks we need to take a temporary detour, in which I introduce the concept of **risk factors**.

Why should investing in equities or bonds earn more than merely placing your money in a *risk free*[215] investment, such as a bank account or a very short-term loan to a stable government? Simple: for an investment to earn more than the risk free rate, it must be

---

214. In fact there will be slightly more uncertainty because I'm dividing the data up into smaller pieces, and with less data parameter uncertainty is higher.
215. Remember from chapter one that risk free assets don't really exist: even cash isn't risk free, because of inflation.

risky. Investments with no risk cannot earn more than the risk free rate. By definition this is the highest return available without taking on any risk. Any risky investment that earned less than the risk free rate would (in theory) receive no takers.

Any extra return above the risk free rate must properly compensate investors for the additional risk. There are many different kinds of risk which investors worry about. Professors of finance call these **risk factors**.

The most famous risk factor is **beta**: the additional compensation for exposure to the overall equity market. You can earn it by investing in a passive market capitalisation weighted index tracker such as an ETF that tracks the S&P 500 US equity index.

In this chapter I introduce two simple forecasting models which I'd expect to improve your returns as they will expose you to different risk factors: specifically the **momentum** and the **dividend yield** risk factors.

How can we use smart forecasting models to construct portfolios?

You have two ways to use the information you get from forecasting models. Firstly you can use it to **adjust** your portfolio weights. Secondly you can use it to **select** certain assets, and drop others.

Adjusting handcrafted weights when returns are forecasted

The basic **handcrafting** method assumes all assets in a group have the same expected **Sharpe Ratio (SR)** and gives them equal risk weighting. If you think some assets will do better, they should have a higher portfolio weight. But by how much should you change your weights?

I remember having this discussion with Bill,[216] a fellow investor. Bill suspected a market crash was coming within the next 12 months, and he had liquidated most of his portfolio, which was now 95% in cash and 5% in equities (down from around 80% before). That was a massive change in position which suggested a huge amount of confidence in his prediction (which incidentally turned out to be wrong).

Going from 80% in equities to 5% is definitely far too extreme, but what would be a reasonable adjustment to your weights given some expectations about risk-adjusted returns?

We have to think once again about **uncertainty**. Remember from chapter two, there is huge uncertainty in historic estimates for Sharpe Ratios. In chapter three I pointed out this means we can never be sure exactly what the right portfolio weights should have been in the past, never mind the future.

---

216. Not his real name.

Now have another look at figure 32, on page 324. Using forecasting models can reduce the uncertainty of Sharpe Ratio estimates, but never to the point where they are known precisely. I've calibrated the models I'm using to reflect this residual uncertainty.[217] When a model thinks the Sharpe Ratio is likely to be higher the portfolio weight is increased – but only modestly, to reflect the fact the model forecast still has considerable uncertainty.

Using return forecasts to select assets

Selection is the hard core version of adjusted portfolio weighting. Under this method, if the forecasting model doesn't like certain assets they aren't just modestly down-weighted: instead they're kicked out of the portfolio entirely.

Generally selective weighting works best when the resulting loss in diversification will be small. This will be the case when:

1. The choice of assets is large.

2. The components of a portfolio are quite similar and highly correlated.

I don't recommend using forecasting models to select substantial elements of your portfolio. Imagine if you dropped one or two asset classes and only kept a subset. There are only two or three asset classes to begin with! Removing one entirely would make the portfolio highly concentrated. There would be a large drop in diversification, and if the model is wrong about its prediction of expected risk-adjusted returns you would end up seriously underperforming, and feel very embarrassed.

However things are different when you are at the level of individual stocks within a sector: for example when trying to decide whether to hold every financial institution in Italy, or just buy a selection. From chapter six we know that choosing just a few shares in a sector barely affects diversification, and once we account for costs it is the best strategy for all but the very largest investors. If you can use forecasting models to select some shares that will perform better than average, then that will be the icing on the cake.

Introducing two smart forecasting models

I use two smart forecasting models in this book.[218] The first is a **momentum** model, which you've briefly seen already. Things that have recently gone up in price seem to continue doing so. The converse is true if prices have recently fallen. So you should buy recent *winners*, and sell *losers*.

---

217. Technical note: I measured the uncertainty in the ex-post conditional Sharpe Ratio against the model forecast. I explain in more detail in Appendix C, page 498, how you can calibrate your own forecasting models.
218. This is a cursory look at what is a very complex subject. If you're interested and can cope with the technical details I'd highly recommend Anti Illmanen's book *Expected Returns*, *Efficiently Inefficient: How Smart Money Invests and Market Prices Are Determined* by Lasse Pedersen, and *Systematic Trading* by me.

The second model is based on **yield**.[219] Stocks with high dividend yields, or bonds with higher yield to maturity, seem to do better than others. This is a specific case of the more general **value** risk factor, which forecasts that *cheap* stocks such as those with higher yields tend to beat *expensive* shares like lower yielders.[220]

These models often complement each other. Assets that have gone up in price recently tend to have lower yields, and vice versa. But an asset which has gone up in price and still has a high yield is doubly attractive.

The momentum model

The first forecasting model uses **momentum:** assets that are going up in price tend to continue doing better. So if equities outperformed bonds last year, that will probably continue into the future. You may also hear this described as **trend following**. Here is how you should implement this model (don't worry if you don't follow the explanation as I give a specific example later in the chapter):

Starting portfolio weights	The method assumes you begin with some portfolio weights that you've found through handcrafting.
	You can either adjust cash weightings or risk weightings. It doesn't matter as long as you're consistent across assets.
Get the returns from the last 12 months	You need the percentage returns over the last year for each asset (fund or direct equity investment). Ideally you should use the total return (including equity dividends and bond coupons),* or if unavailable just the change in price; but again you must be consistent across assets. If you use an index or another ETF make sure it is in the same currency as the ETF that you actually intend to buy.
Work out trailing Sharpe Ratios	You need to convert the annual returns into trailing Sharpe Ratios by dividing by the historic standard deviation of the returns of each asset: either estimated using the technique in Appendix C (page 489) or the fixed values I suggest in Appendix B (page 485).
Get portfolio weight adjustment factors	You now have a trailing Sharpe Ratio (SR) for each asset. Find the portfolio weight adjustment factors by looking up the SR in the first column of table 46 to adjust your portfolio weights.
	Either round or use interpolation if the SR difference is not shown.

---

219. Equity dividend yield: dividends divided by share price. Bond yield to maturity: the annualised value of future bond coupons and the final repayment. ETF yields may be different from the yield of the underlying assets and I discuss this later.

220. Unlike the forecasting records of most market experts these models have a long and successful history, and are supported by large numbers of academic research papers. If you're interested then 'Value and Momentum Everywhere' by Cliff Asness and co-authors (*Journal of Finance*, 2013) is a relatively recent and pretty comprehensive study.

Adjust portfolio weights	Use the adjustment factors from table 46 to adjust your portfolio weights: multiply each weight by the adjustment factor. Note: these weights aren't guaranteed to add up to 100%.
Normalise the weights	See the discussion below.

* Technical note: If assets have higher yields then using total return will introduce a bias towards those assets which may already be overweight in the yield forecasting model. Using total return will also introduce more of a long bias in the absolute momentum model and will mean average risk is closer to the long-term average.

TABLE 46: HOW MUCH TO ADJUST HANDCRAFTED WEIGHTS GIVEN TRAILING RETURNS

Trailing SR	Adjustment factor
−1.0 or less	0.60
−0.80	0.66
−0.60	0.77
−0.40	0.85
−0.20	0.94
0	1.00
0.20	1.11
0.40	1.19
0.60	1.30
0.80	1.37
1.0 or more	1.48

The table shows the adjustment factor to use for handcrafted weights (second column) given trailing Sharpe Ratio (SR) (first column). I explain how these figures are calculated in Appendix C, page 498.

There is one final stage required which is a **normalisation** of weights. This is required because the adjusted portfolio weights could easily add up to more than 100% (if most assets have been going up in price) or less than 100% (if most have been falling). But first you need to decide whether you want to use an **absolute** or a **relative** momentum model.

In a relative momentum model you determine the relative attractiveness of different assets. **With a relative model you are always fully invested**, with no investable cash left over.[221] If equities are going up faster than bonds, then naturally you'd invest more than average in equities, and less in bonds. But if both equities and bonds are falling, but equities are falling more slowly, then you'd still be fully invested in both assets – it's just that you'd have more in equities; the asset which isn't doing quite as badly.

The normalisation procedure for relative momentum is straightforward: You **take the adjusted portfolio weights, and then normalise them so they add up to 100%**. So for example suppose you ended up with weights of 65% in equities and 85% in bonds after adjusting the weights. This adds up to 150%. To get the weights back to a total of 100% you divide by 150% ÷ 100% = 1.5, giving you weights of 65% ÷ 1.5 = 43.3% for equities, and 85% ÷ 1.5 = 56.7% in bonds.

In contrast an **absolute momentum model** does not like holding assets that are falling in price, regardless of whether they are doing well on a relative basis. If both equities and bonds are falling, but equities are falling more slowly, then you'd be investing less than average in equities although still more than in bonds.

With an absolute momentum relative model you **will not be fully invested if there are any assets in the portfolio that are falling in price**. This also means that the risk of your portfolio will be lower on average if you're using absolute momentum, because there will be many times when you aren't fully invested. As with so many decisions in this book the choice of relative or absolute momentum will depend on your preferences for return and risk.

The normalisation for absolute momentum is a little more complex. **If the adjusted portfolio weights add up to 100% or less you should do no normalisation**. This means we'll hold cash if some assets are falling in price. **If the adjusted weights add up to more than 100% you normalise them so they add up to exactly 100%**,[222] using the same method as for relative momentum.

I explore the advantages and disadvantages of the relative and absolute momentum alternatives later in the chapter.

---

221. Unless of course you are deliberately holding some back because you are an ultra-safe investor of the type I discussed back in chapter four.
222. Technical note: A leveraged investor would not need to do this. However, if you're interested in varying leverage when using forecasting models, then you ought to read my first book *Systematic Trading*.

CONCEPT: CURRENCIES AND RETURNS

If your portfolio is properly diversified you'll often be buying funds or shares denominated in a foreign currency (especially if you've taken my advice back in chapter one to avoid currency hedged products).

For foreign currency assets there is a subtle difference between measuring trailing returns using (a) the cash returns of the assets in your portfolio, (b) the price of a currency hedged ETF in your domestic currency, or (c) the foreign currency price of an unhedged equity, ETF or index. The first two methods (a and b) will measure returns in your domestic currency, whilst the latter will be denominated in the currency of the index.

So, for example, a UK investor measuring the performance of the S&P 500 in December 2016 will have seen a large annual increase in the value of their US stocks measured in GBP and in the price of a currency hedged ETF like IGUS; but only a modest rise in the S&P 500 index and the dollar price of an unhedged ETF such as VUSA. This is because of the massive depreciation in the pound after the June 2016 Brexit vote.

The good news is that it doesn't matter whether you measure trailing returns using a foreign or domestic currency value. My research suggests that there is no interaction of currency rates and stock or bond prices which would make one measurement technique systematically better than the other.

However as usual you must be consistent and stick to a specific method. If you've followed my advice to spurn currency hedged ETFs then using the foreign currency price of the ETF is simplest.

One final point: you should avoid using the momentum model if your total portfolio[223] is less than £10,000 or $2,000 as the trading costs will be too high. I explain why in part four, starting on page 407. Also, the modest gains in performance for small amounts of capital won't justify the extra time spent getting the data and calculating the right positions.

The yield model

Traditionally, conservative investors liked to buy high dividend paying stocks. And decades of research by finance professors have consistently shown that stocks that pay higher dividends outperform others. It turns out that this works pretty well in bonds as

---

223. As usual these values assume you are paying a minimum brokerage commission of £6 or $1; if you are paying more then you'll need to multiply them by the ratio of your minimum brokerage fee and mine.

well, and across different asset classes. I put these ideas together to create a forecasting model that uses **yields** to try and predict Sharpe Ratios.[224]

Here is how to use the yield model. Again there will be examples later in the chapter.

Starting portfolio weights	The method assumes you begin with some portfolio weights that you've found through **handcrafting**.
	You can either adjust cash weightings or risk weightings. It doesn't matter as long as you're consistent across assets.
Get the yield for each asset	Ideally you need the dividend yield (equities or equity funds) or yield to maturity (bond funds).
	With ETFs you should ideally use the underlying yield of the assets within it, but you can also use the ETF's own dividend yield (as long as you are consistent). If you own the accumulating version of an ETF, then instead find the distributing version to measure the dividend yield.
	Watch out for ETFs that deduct their management fee from the dividend. If necessary add this back to make sure you have the correct yield.*
Work out Sharpe Ratios	You need to convert the yields into Sharpe Ratios by dividing by the standard deviation of the returns of each asset class.
	You can use my preferred approximate volatilities from Appendix B (page 485), or you can estimate these yourself using the formula in Appendix C (page 489).
Get the return difference versus the average	Work out the **median** Sharpe Ratio, and each asset's relative difference to the median. The median is more stable than the mean, and will protect you against particularly large or small yields.
Get portfolio weight adjustments	You now have a difference between each asset's Sharpe Ratio (SR) and the average. Find the portfolio weight adjustments by looking up this difference in the first column of table 47 to adjust your portfolio weights.
	Either round or use interpolation if the SR difference is not shown.
Adjust and normalise portfolio weights	Use the adjustment weights from table 47 to adjust your portfolio weights: multiply the weights by the adjustment factors, then normalise them to add up to 100%.

* Alternatively a nice variation on the basic yield model for ETFs is to consistently use dividend yields that **always** have the management fee deducted (and if you wish to calculate them, any other relevant holding costs). This will penalise more expensive funds.

224. Technical note: I chose yields because they are simple to calculate and comparable across asset classes. However you could also use other metrics within asset classes. For example, within equities you could use earnings yield (the inverse of the price-to-earnings ratio), and for all assets you could use carry (the yield, less an appropriate short term interest rate like LIBOR or the Fed funds rate).

TABLE 47: HOW MUCH TO ADJUST HANDCRAFTED WEIGHTS GIVEN THE DIFFERENCE IN YIELD SHARPE RATIOS

SR yield difference	Adjustment factor
−0.10 or less	0.60
−0.08	0.66
−0.06	0.77
−0.04	0.85
−0.02	0.94
0	1.00
0.02	1.11
0.04	1.19
0.06	1.30
0.08	1.37
0.10	1.48

The table shows the adjustment factor to use for handcrafted weights (second column) given current difference in yield Sharpe Ratio (SR) versus the average (first column). I explain how these figures are calculated in Appendix C, page 498.

Notice that the yield model is **always a relative model**: we use relative Sharpe Ratios when calculating portfolio weight adjustments, and we always normalise weights to add up to 100%.

An absolute yield model wouldn't make much sense. With trailing returns there is a clear neutral point where we don't need to do any adjustment: when an asset has a zero trailing return. This allows us to use an absolute model if we wish. But there is no neutral yield,[225] so it's meaningless to use an absolute forecasting model for yields.

One final point: you should avoid using the yield model if your total portfolio[226] is less than £7,500 or $1,500, as the trading costs will be too high. I explain why in part four, on page 407.

---

225. Technical note: Although we could introduce a neutral rate by subtracting the risk free interest rate. The yield model would then be closer in spirit to a carry model. But I prefer this simpler implementation.
226. As usual these values assume you are paying a minimum brokerage commission of £6 or $1; if you

Creating your own forecasting models

Maybe you don't like my momentum and yield models, and you want to use your own favourite forecasting model, or create a new model from scratch. If so, there's advice on how to do so in Appendix C, on page 498.

Using forecasting models in a top-down handcrafted portfolio

I'll now explain how to use these forecasting models in practice for different parts of your handcrafted smart portfolio.

This is quite a long and detailed section. I start by explaining how to use forecasting models at the top level of your portfolio: asset allocation. I then discuss how you should combine the forecasts of the two models together, and the method for adjusting weights at multiple levels of a portfolio. Next I outline how you use the models in the rest of your portfolio: for equity country weights, equity sectors, individual equities, and bonds.

Finally I show an example of how to adjust portfolio weights across a complete portfolio.

Using models to weight asset classes

Using the momentum model for asset class weights

How do we use trailing returns in different asset classes to adjust portfolio weights?

Starting portfolio weights	Use handcrafting to find portfolio weights: this assumes Sharpe Ratios are all identical.
	I'm going to use a simple example here of a portfolio with 50% in bonds, and 50% in equities. But you can use the momentum model with more complex portfolios that contain alternative assets.

are paying more then you'll need to multiply them by the ratio of your minimum brokerage and mine.

Get the returns from the last 12 months	You need the percentage returns over the last year for each asset class. You can get these by looking at either: (a) the average return of the funds you plan to use to get exposure to each asset class, (b) the single ETFs I've suggested for each asset class in chapter eight (for equities VWRL (UK), VT (US); for bonds XBAG (UK), RIGS (US)), or (c) benchmarks like the MSCI All Country World Index (equity) and the Barclays Capital Global Aggregate Bond Index. It doesn't matter which method you use, as long as you are consistent.
	You should use the total return (including equity dividends and bond coupons), or if unavailable just the change in price, but again you must be consistent across asset classes. If you use an index or another ETF make sure it is in the same currency as the ETF that you actually hold.
	For example, as I write this chapter the db x-trackers Global Aggregate Bond ETF has returned 18.5% in the last year; whilst the iShares MSCI World equity ETF has gone up 8.2%.
Work out Sharpe Ratios	You need to convert the returns into Sharpe Ratios by dividing by the historic standard deviation of the returns of each asset class. Use my preferred approximate volatilities in Appendix B (e.g. 15% for global equities and 6% for bonds), or estimate the figures yourself.
	For example this currently gives me figures of 18.5% ÷ 6.0% = 3.1 for bonds and 8.2% ÷ 15% = 0.55 for equities.
Get portfolio weight adjustments	You now have a trailing Sharpe Ratio (SR) for each asset class. Find the portfolio weight adjustments by looking these up in the first column of table 46 to adjust your portfolio weights.
	Either round or use interpolation if the SR difference is not shown.
	A trailing Sharpe Ratio difference of 3.1 for bonds corresponds to a multiplier of 1.48, and the SR for equities of 0.55 equates to a multiplier of 1.27 (interpolated from the table).
Adjust portfolio weights	Use the adjustment weights from table 45 to adjust your portfolio weights. For the simple example:
	1.48 x 50% = 74% bonds
	1.27 x 50% = 63.5% equities
Normalise the weights	Either:
	For **relative momentum** always normalise the weights to add up to exactly 100%.
	For **absolute momentum** you only need to normalise the weights if they add up to more than 100%. Otherwise leave them alone.
	In this simple example the weights add up to more than 100%, so normalisation is definitely required. The adjusted weights add up to 137.5%; so the normalised weights are 74% ÷ 1.375 = 53.8% for bonds; and 63.5% ÷ 1.375 = 46.2% for equities.

Figure 33 shows the effect of applying this model to a simple 50:50 risk weighted portfolio of stocks and bonds.

FIGURE 33: EFFECT OF APPLYING VARYING WEIGHTS TO US BOND AND EQUITY PORTFOLIO

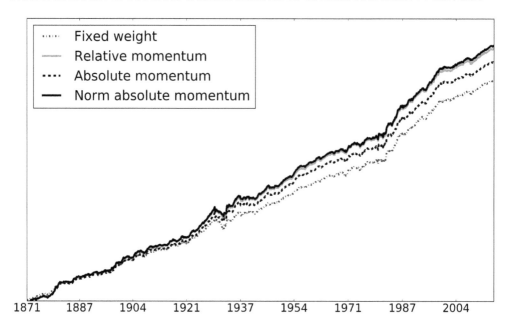

US data: S&P 500 and US 10 year bonds. Y axis is a log scale of cumulated total returns. Fixed risk weightings 50% in each asset. Relative and absolute momentum use trailing returns to adjust portfolio weights. Norm absolute momentum: the returns from absolute momentum, normalised to have the same volatility as the returns from relative momentum. Costs of monthly rebalancing are not included.

The results[227] are also summarised in table 48.

---

227. This plot has a couple of important caveats. Firstly, I've used US stock and bond returns as there is more historic data available. The effect of these models is quite weak, so it's important to use as much history as possible. However, the results are similar for global indices over a more recent period (which in any case have a large weight to the US). More significantly the results also ignore costs. Because I'm changing portfolio weights every month these could be quite high. I look at costs in part four when I consider rebalancing in more detail.

TABLE 48: PERFORMANCE OF US BOND AND EQUITY PORTFOLIO WITH DIFFERENT FORECASTING MODELS

	Geometric mean	Volatility	Geometric Sharpe Ratio
Fixed weight	6.67%	6.17%	1.081
Relative momentum	7.68%	6.70%	1.146
Absolute momentum	7.25%	6.28%	1.154
Normalised absolute momentum	7.75%	6.70%	1.156

Fixed weight is 50:50 risk weightings. Normalised absolute momentum is absolute momentum, adjusted to have the same volatility as relative momentum.

Using fixed weights – with no forecasting model – is the worst option. Both relative and absolute momentum are better on a geometric return and Sharpe Ratio basis. Relative versus absolute momentum is not a clear-cut contest. As you'd expect, absolute momentum has lower risk because it spends much of its time out of the market, not fully invested. In fact in an average month 7% of the portfolio is in cash.

Although going to absolute momentum improves the Sharpe Ratio, it's not a large improvement, and it harms the geometric mean.

If you're lucky enough to be able to leverage your portfolio then you can use this leverage to multiply all your positions by the ratio of the risk of relative momentum (6.7%) and absolute momentum (6.28%); or 1.07. This will give you the risk **normalised** version of absolute momentum. This has the same risk as relative momentum, so you can earn the extra performance and get some additional geometric mean (though strictly speaking you will have to pay interest costs when you leverage). Unfortunately this normalised absolute momentum model is unavailable to the average investor who can't borrow.

Using relative yield

The second forecasting model I'm going to use for asset allocation is the **relative yield** model. However, using such a model with different asset classes isn't straightforward.

In figure 34 I've plotted the risk normalised yield on US equities and bonds. To calculate this I've taken the dividend yield (for equities) and yield to maturity (for bonds), and divided both by the approximate volatility I'm using for each asset class. So this figure shows the Sharpe Ratio of the yield for each asset.

FIGURE 34: HISTORY OF RISK NORMALISED YIELDS ON US ASSETS

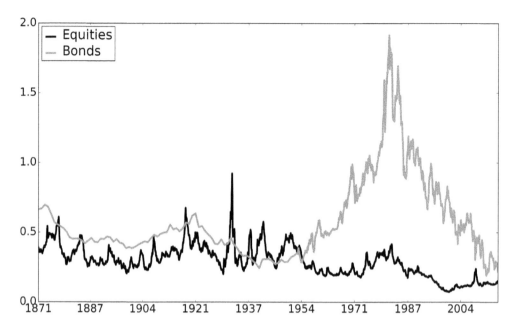

Prior to the great crash of 1929 bonds consistently yielded more than equities in risk-adjusted terms. Then there was a 30-year period where they traded places every few years. For the last 60 years the normalised yield has always been higher for bonds over equities; sometimes many times higher. Should we have been overweight bonds for 60 years?

There are other ways to try to predict equity and bond returns: the Fed model[228] and the CAPE[229] model to name just two. However, they all suffer from the same shortcomings. Firstly it's not always obvious what the correct or equilibrium relative yield should be: the point at which you wouldn't apply any adjustment to your portfolio weights, except perhaps with hindsight. Secondly they are subject to **regime changes**; periods when the equilibrium changes as it appears to do in 1929 and 1955. These changes are not predictable in advance and it can take years for the new equilibrium to become clear.

Yet another problem is that the yield for many alternative assets is not a straightforward thing to measure or compare. I'd leave alternatives out of any yield forecasting model. Finally the forecasts in these models rarely change direction, spending many years favouring one asset or another, making it impossible to decide whether their performance is statistically different from pure randomness.

---

228. Probably invented by Ed Yardeni. This compares the equity earnings yield to the government bond yield and does not do any volatility normalisation.

229. Cyclically Adjusted Price earnings Ratio, invented by Robert Shiller. It looks only at price-to-earnings ratios adjusted for inflation and does not use government bond yields at all.

CONCEPT: THE DIFFERENT PROPERTIES OF MOMENTUM AND DIVIDEND YIELD MODELS

There are good reasons why momentum and dividend yield models do better in some situations than others.

As a general rule, when assets are very similar, value type models like dividend yield tend to do better. There are a couple of plausible explanations for this effect.

Firstly it makes more sense to compare ratios like yields for very similar assets. Two US banks should be pretty similar. But a US bank and a grocery store are quite different. The former will have a lot of debt on its balance sheet; the latter probably has plenty of cash. This problem is even worse across asset classes where we're comparing very different things. As we've already seen, the risk-adjusted yields on different asset classes can be wildly different for long periods of time.

Secondly it's unusual for very similar assets to see their prices drift apart for long – they tend to **mean revert**. Value models like the yield model buy assets that have become cheaper, and sell those that have gone up in price. So they benefit from this mean reversion effect.

Conversely if assets are very different then value models won't do as well, and momentum models are likely to be more successful. Dissimilar assets can easily spend long periods experiencing quite different price movements which can be exploited by the momentum model.

In this section the models are looking at very different assets, drawn from completely separate asset classes. So it's no surprise that momentum does well and dividend yield does badly. Later in the chapter as we proceed deeper into the top-down portfolio allocation process, the assets will get more similar. Momentum will become less attractive, and the performance of dividend yield will improve.

Despite my misgivings I tested this model, using the same US data I used for experimenting with the momentum model. The results were so bad I did not feel it was worth wasting paper by plotting them. The risk of the portfolio rose from 6.2% to 6.4% a year, and the geometric mean fell from 6.7% to 6.0%. Obviously the Sharpe Ratio is also much worse. The yield model is not a great success at predicting risk-adjusted returns for different asset classes.

Recommendations

My recommendation for asset allocation is to use a **relative momentum model**. I would not use an absolute momentum model, as the reduction in geometric mean with only modest improvement in Sharpe Ratio is a deal breaker for me. I would also avoid the yield model: it doesn't make sense, it doesn't work, and it adds unnecessary complexity.

I'm writing this book at a time when interest rates are still relatively low, but have started to rise from their recent historic lows, and are expected to get much higher (early 2017). Many readers will have digested the suggested weightings to bonds in chapter eight, and will be looking at the bond market, and then getting nervous. At some point interest rates will have to go up. Holding cash weightings of up to 70% in bonds seems kind of insane. Wouldn't the yield model sensibly reduce the bond allocation in this situation?

Unfortunately using the dividend yield model as described above will not alleviate that stress, since at the time of writing it would still be overweighting bonds (see figure 34, page 338). Although there are some negative yielding bonds the overall asset class still has a higher risk-adjusted yield than equities. Yields would have to fall much further before this was no longer the case; and then they would only have to rise modestly before the model began overweighting bonds again.

In contrast the momentum model will reduce your exposure to bonds once bond returns have begun to fall consistently, providing some protection. Later in this chapter I discuss how to use the dividend yield model **within** your bond holdings. That will allow you to tactically reduce your exposure to parts of the bond market with low or even negative yields.

Using both models

To reiterate, I don't recommend using the yield model for asset allocation, just the momentum model. However later in the chapter I use both models together when I show you how to adjust portfolio weights within asset classes. You might also want to combine my momentum model with some invented forecasting model of your own. So, for the sake of completeness, here is an example of how you would combine the forecasts from two models together.

Get starting portfolio weights	Assume you have a simple portfolio with a risk weighted 50% in bonds, and 50% in equities.
Get portfolio weight adjustments for momentum	From the earlier example I had adjustments of: equities 1.27, bonds 1.48.
Get portfolio weight adjustments for yields	From my own calculations I get adjustments of: equities 0.60, bonds 1.48.

Get the geometric mean of the adjustment factors	Multiply the adjustment factors from each model together for each asset. Then take the square root (if you're using 3 models take the cube root; and so on) Equities $\sqrt{(1.27 \times 0.60)} = \sqrt{0.762} = 0.87$ Bonds $\sqrt{(1.48 \times 1.48)} = \sqrt{2.19} = 1.48$
Adjust portfolio weights	Adjust your portfolio weights, by multiplying them by the adjustment factors. For the example you would end up with: 0.87 x 50% = 43.5% equities 1.48 x 50% = 74% bonds
Normalise the portfolio weights	I'd use combined models in a **relative** way. This means always normalising adjusted portfolio weights so they add up to 100%. After normalising the weights in the example to sum to 100% you'd have 37% in equities and 63% in bonds.

This can be extended to combine as many forecasting models as you like.

Forecasting models with multiple levels

You should now be pretty confident about using forecasting models in simple portfolios with a single group of assets. But most portfolios will be a little more interesting, and have multiple levels. You need to apply the same method to each part of the portfolio in turn. Here is a simple example.

PORTFOLIO 85: SIMPLE EXAMPLE TO DEMONSTRATE MODELS WITH MULTIPLE LEVELS

Portfolio			
Equity 50%		Bonds 50%	
UK equities 40%	US equities 60%	UK bonds 30%	US bonds 70%
20%	30%	15%	35%

Risk weightings shown. Example only: don't invest in this!

Portfolio 85 is the starting point for the example. We're going to run three sets of forecasting models on this. The first will be relative momentum only in equities and bonds. Then we'll use momentum and yields within equities (as I recommend later in the chapter). Finally we'll use the same two models within bonds.

The models are all run separately. This means, for example, when finding the yield multipliers within equities you should compare the Sharpe Ratio of yields for US equities against UK equities. You wouldn't take any other assets in the portfolio into account.

As a starting point, table 49 shows some illustrative Sharpe Ratios for this simple example.

TABLE 49: SIMPLE PORTFOLIO TO DEMONSTRATE MODELS WITH MULTIPLE LEVELS – SOME ILLUSTRATIVE SHARPE RATIOS

	Momentum SR	Yield SR
US equities	1.2	0.2
UK equities	0.9	0.24
US bonds	0.5	0.3
UK bonds	−0.3	0.36

These figures are arbitrary.

How do we work out the combined Sharpe Ratio of each asset class? We could use a benchmark index, but in this case we're going to use **aggregate** Sharpe Ratios.[230] For example, to work out the aggregate trailing Sharpe Ratio (SR) for equities we need to take a weighted average of the trailing SR for US equities (1.2) and UK equities (0.9); using the risk weightings of 60% and 40% respectively[231] from portfolio 85. This gives an aggregate SR of (1.2 × 0.6) + (0.9 × 0.4) = 1.08. We can then perform a similar calculation for bonds. Table 50 shows the aggregated Sharpe Ratios.

---

230. There is more detail on aggregation in Appendix C, page 489.
231. Strictly speaking these should be the risk weightings after you've already applied the forecasting model multipliers within this group; however it won't make much difference if you just use the starting risk weightings created using the top-down handcrafting method.

TABLE 50: SIMPLE PORTFOLIO TO DEMONSTRATE MODELS WITH MULTIPLE LEVELS –
AGGREGATED AND MEDIAN SHARPE RATIOS

	Aggregate: momentum SR
Equities	1.08
Bonds	0.26

Aggregated Sharpe Ratios (weighted mean, weighted by risk weightings) across asset classes.

Within each group I then looked up the correct multipliers in tables 47 and 48. For example, for UK bonds momentum the SR is –0.3. From table 46 this corresponds to a multiplier of 0.9. Table 51 shows the multipliers for each of these models, and the final combined multiplier (which is the geometric mean of the other multipliers).

TABLE 51: SIMPLE PORTFOLIO TO DEMONSTRATE MODELS WITH MULTIPLE LEVELS – COMBINING
MULTIPLIERS

	Momentum	Yield	Combined
Equities	1.48		1.48
Bonds	1.13		1.13
US equities	1.48	0.94	1.18
UK equities	1.42	1.11	1.26
US bonds	1.25	0.9	1.06
UK bonds	0.9	1.15	1.02

Combined multiplier is the geometric mean of the multipliers for each model. We only use momentum for asset classes.

I can now apply the multipliers, and portfolio 86 shows how it's done.

PORTFOLIO 86: SIMPLE PORTFOLIO TO DEMONSTRATE MODELS WITH MULTIPLE LEVELS –
APPLYING MULTIPLIERS

Portfolio			
Equity 50% × 1.48 = 74% Normalised: 56.7%		Bonds 50% × 1.13 = 56.5% Normalised: 43.3%	
UK equities 40% × 1.26 = 50.4% Normalised: 41.6%	US equities 60% × 1.18 = 70.8% Normalised: 58.4%	UK bonds 30% × 1.02 = 30.6% Normalised: 29.1%	US bonds 70% × 1.06 = 74.2% Normalised: 70.8%
56.7% × 41.6% = 23.6%	56.7% × 58.4% = 33.1%	43.3% × 29.1% = 12.6%	43.3% × 70.8% = 30.7%

Risk weightings shown. Example only: don't invest in this!

I've applied all the relevant multipliers and then normalised the weights within each group so they add up to 100%. Remember there are three groups: asset classes (equities and bonds), within bonds, and within equities; the normalisation to 100% happens in each of these, not across them.

Finally we just need to follow the normal top-down procedure and multiply the normalised weights from each level to get the final risk weightings. We could then apply the method from chapter four to get cash weightings. Alternatively we could do this entire procedure starting with cash weightings.

This might seem rather time consuming, but with a spreadsheet it just takes a few minutes even for a large portfolio with dozens of assets. Sample spreadsheets are available on the website for this book (www.systematicmoney.org/smart).

Adjusting equity country weights

You can also adjust the portfolio weights you have for funds exposed to equities in different countries; again using the 12 month momentum and dividend yield models.

I tested both forecasting models with 22 developed equity markets, and the results are shown in figure 35. Dividend yield (Sharpe Ratio 1.41) manages to beat fixed allocations (Sharpe 1.37), although it still doesn't do quite as well as relative momentum (Sharpe 1.54). I didn't include absolute momentum in this test for the reasons I mentioned earlier in the chapter.

FIGURE 35: USING FORECASTING MODELS TO ADJUST THE PORTFOLIO WEIGHTS OF EQUITY COUNTRIES

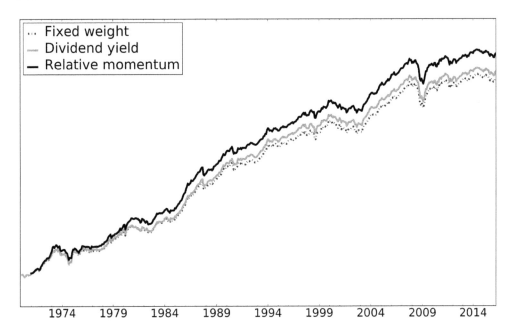

Fixed weights are the handcrafted weights from chapter ten. Dividend yield adjusts those weights using dividend yields. Relative momentum adjusts weights using relative momentum.

I recommend using both models, and combining them. Equities from different parts of the world are sufficiently similar that a dividend yield model makes more sense than it does in asset classes.

Instead of having a single group of assets (equities, bonds and possible alternatives), you now have the two types of country (emerging and developed), three regions within each country type, and then the individual countries in your equity portfolio. So you could have up to nine sets of forecasting models: one to decide the weights of emerging versus developed markets, two to decide the regional weights within developed and emerging markets, and then a model for each of the six regions (three within developed, and three within emerging markets).

The models should all be run separately; this means, for example, when finding the yield multipliers within developed European equities you are only comparing the yield Sharpe Ratios of countries in developed Europe.

As with asset classes, you have several different methods you can use to find trailing returns and yields for each asset. You can either use the historic returns and dividends from the relevant ETF, or get figures for benchmark indices. Just make sure that you use a consistent method within each group, and don't mix up different currency denominations, or confuse total return including dividends with price return.

You can also find the relevant aggregate returns or yields by taking a weighted average of the returns or yields for the individual assets that make up that aggregate asset, using within group risk weightings. So for developed European equities you'd take a weighted average of returns or yields for the individual countries within developed Europe: UK, Germany, France, and so on.

Finally, to combine the multipliers from the momentum and yield models you need to find their geometric mean, as I discussed on page 340.

This is only a brief overview, but you can find an example of how to use these methods in an actual equity portfolio later in the chapter.

Weighting equity sectors within a country with a model of returns

How can you use forecasting models to change the weight to equity sectors within a country, like US tech stocks versus US utility stocks, and so on?

I'd recommend using both dividend yield and absolute momentum models to adjust sector weights, then using the geometric mean of their relevant multiplying factors as I discussed earlier in the chapter (page 340). Both momentum and yield are widely used in the financial industry for allocating capital across equity sectors, and there is considerable evidence showing they have performed well in the past.

If you're using sector ETFs then it's straightforward to get the trailing 12 month return and dividend yield figures you need to use the model.

If you are exposed to one or more sectors through individual shares then things are a little more complicated. For momentum you need to calculate the average trailing return for your sub-portfolio of shares for a given sector, weighted by the current portfolio cash weights of each share.

Similarly you need to calculate the average dividend yield across the sector. If you already own the stocks it will be the total dividend received divided by the current value of all the stocks owned in that sector.

Alternatively you can get the sector trailing return and yield from the relevant sector ETF or an index. Regardless of how you get your yields, make sure you are consistent with the method you use.

Weighting and selecting individual stocks with a model of returns

How can you use models to change the weights of stocks within each sector, for example how much Apple, Microsoft or Facebook within the US tech sector? Should you use models to select certain stocks, and not others?

Personally **I don't recommend using forecasting models for both weighting and selection**. This means you're using the same models twice and putting too much confidence in them, as well as requiring a lot of extra work. If you want to use a model to select your equities, then just hold them in fixed weights. Whereas if you want to use a model for weighting then you should stick to the method I proposed for selection back in chapter eleven: picking the largest firms in each sector.

What is likely to be more effective, weighting or selection? As I mentioned earlier in this chapter selection works best when (a) there are plenty of assets to choose from, and (b) they are fairly similar. Groups of equities in the same country and sector fulfil both of these criteria. They are highly correlated and there are usually plenty of firms to choose from. The only caveat is that selecting by model will increase the chances of embarrassment compared to choosing the largest firms by market cap, as I recommended in chapter 11.

Which type of model should you use for selection? I've already pointed out that value based models like dividend yield tend to work better when assets are very similar. It makes more sense to compare accounting ratios on businesses if they're operating in the same industry and country.

In contrast the momentum model doesn't work quite as well when assets are very similar. Also if you're using momentum for asset classes, countries and sectors then you've already got a significant exposure to the momentum risk factor.[232]

Recommendations

I would propose **using dividend yield to select one or more equities in each sector**, and then **hold those in equal weights**.[233] So if you are buying one stock then for each sector choose the stock with the highest dividend yield; and if you have enough capital then add the firm with the second highest yield, and so on.

For example, suppose you wanted to use the dividend yield model to select equities in the French utilities sector, and you had enough capital to buy five firms. First you'd start with a list of all French utility firms that met your minimum criteria, like index membership or minimum market capitalisation. You'd then **rank** them by dividend yield. Finally you would buy the five firms with the highest dividend yields.

---

232. Technical note: If you disaggregate the performance of individual stock momentum most of the value is coming from the asset class, country and sector level.

233. If you follow this process with the minimum amount of capital you'll end up with one share in each sector, each the highest yielding. This kind of portfolio construction is by no means original. I first came across it on the Motley Fool's UK website fool.co.uk where the idea was proposed by Stephen Bland, who named this approach the 'High Yield Portfolio' (HYP). An important difference between this and my approach is that Stephen advocates putting everything you have got into this HYP strategy, which leaves you exposed to a single country (the UK) and asset class (equities). I personally think it's extremely important to enforce geographic and asset class diversification before considering stock selection.

DIGRESSION: DIVIDEND INVESTING – SOME TRAPS FOR THE UNWARY

Buying the highest yielding stock in a given industry is superficially appealing, but can be quite dangerous. It may result in you holding some fairly nasty and toxic companies whose dividend yield is only impressive because the price has recently plummeted on the back of bad news, and the dividend is unsustainably high. There are a number of ways to avoid this.

Firstly I would avoid firms with **very high dividend yields**. There is strong evidence that these have lower risk-adjusted returns.

Next you can use **forecasted dividends:** the future dividends expected by equity market analysts. Unlike historic dividends these will account for any dividend cuts that have been announced, or are widely expected. They are no panacea however; not all stocks are covered by brokers, analysts are sometimes slow to update their forecasts, and equity analysts don't have a great track record at predicting anything.

The third technique is to set a minimum level of **dividend cover**. The dividend cover ratio is the earnings per share divided by the dividend per share. Higher numbers are better. Alternatively you can divide the earnings yield (which is the inverse of the price-to-earnings ratio) by the dividend yield. At a minimum dividend cover should be 1, indicating dividends are fully covered by earnings, and preferably higher.[234]

You can easily set minimum and maximum thresholds for other accounting ratios. Here is the full list of criteria I use in my own portfolio:

- Dividend yield: less than 10%

- Price-to-earnings ratio: less than 12

- Next year's forecast earnings divided by current earnings: greater than 1

- Price-to-book value: less than 1.5

- Forecast dividend cover (forecast earnings per share divided by forecast dividends per share): greater than 1.2

- Gearing (debt divided by shareholders equity):[235] less than 0.5

---

234. So, for example, if a firm has a dividend of $0.05 per share and earnings of $0.075 per share then the cover ratio is 1.5. If the share price was $1 then the dividend yield would be 5% and the PE ratio 13.33, giving an earnings yield of 7.5%, so again the cover comes out at 1.5. Regardless of how you calculate it the ratio is well above the minimum of 1.

235. I do not use this ratio for banks and other industries that are naturally highly leveraged.

There is nothing magic about these numbers and I don't claim they are the best possible values. I'm including them only to illustrate the kind of filter you might want to use.

If you're confident then you can also use other valuation factors like price-to-book ratios. Appendix C, page 500, explains how you can extend the dividend yield selection model to using multiple factors, or design a stock ranking and selection system based on any criteria you like.

It's also sensible to add and remove firms from a portfolio as their ranking changes. I discuss how to do this in the most cost-efficient way in part four.

Direct investment in small cap stocks

In chapter eleven I recommended avoiding direct investment in small and mid cap stocks. But these stocks generally offer better risk-adjusted returns. This is because they're exposed to the size **risk factor**. Value risk factors like dividend yield also seem to work better on small and mid cap stocks where the market isn't as efficient.

You could benefit from the size risk factor by ignoring my earlier advice and including small and mid cap stocks in the pool you use to fish out the highest yielding equities. However there is a serious risk that you will end up with only small cap stocks in your portfolio if it just happens that they are the highest yielding firms. I don't know about you, but that would leave me lying awake at night worrying.

There is a smart way to avoid this scenario, but only if you have enough money to hold multiple shares in each sector. In chapter eleven I recommended a risk weighted allocation of 60% in large cap, 20% in mid cap, and 20% in small cap stocks; using ETFs to get the mid cap and small cap exposure. However if you have a large enough account there is an alternative which involves direct investment in small and mid caps.

Suppose you can hold five shares per sector. The first three you should choose are the highest yielding large cap stocks from that industry (3 out of 5 is 60%). You then include the single highest yielding mid cap (1 out of 5 is 20%), and highest yield small cap firm (1 out of 5 is 20%).

That will limit your exposure to risky mid cap and small cap stocks to safe levels. Similarly with ten stocks you'd have six large cap, two mid cap, and two small cap.

TABLE 52: HOW TO SQUEEZE SMALL AND MID CAP STOCKS INTO YOUR SECTOR SUB-PORTFOLIO

	Large cap			Mid cap			Small cap		
	Number	**Risk weight**	**Cash weight**	**Number**	**Risk weight**	**Cash weight**	**Number**	**Risk weight**	**Cash weight**
<3 stocks	All	Equal	Equal	Consider ETF			Consider ETF		
3 stocks	2	33.3%	35.2%	1	33.3%	29.7%	Consider ETF		
4 stocks	3	25%	26.0%	1	25%	22.0%	Consider ETF		
5 stocks	3	20%	22.2%	1	20%	18.6%	1	20%	15%
10 stocks	6	10%	11.1%	2	10%	9.3%	2	10%	7.5%
15 stocks	9	6.7%	7.4%	3	6.7%	6.2%	3	6.7%	5%
20 stocks	12	5%	5.5%	4	5%	4.7%	4	5%	3.7%

Table shows the number of stocks held in a given sector, risk weight per stock within your sector sub-portfolio, cash weight per stock within your sub-portfolio: for different cap levels (sets of columns), and sub-portfolio sizes (rows). For five or more shares the total risk allocation to large cap stocks is 60%, mid cap 20% and small cap 20%. For fewer shares we have at least 66% in large cap stocks.

The appropriate portfolios for different numbers of stocks in each sector are shown in table 52. If your portfolio size doesn't fit neatly into this table you should overweight your large stocks. So, for example, with seven stocks you'd have one mid cap and one small cap, and five large caps.

With three or four stocks you don't have sufficient capital for a small cap stock, so you should stick to large and mid cap.

These stocks should all be held with equal risk weightings within each market cap group; this does mean you'll have a lower cash weight for riskier small and mid cap stocks.

If you can afford to invest directly, but only have enough capital for one or two stocks in each sector, then you are better off sticking to portfolio 51 (page 259), putting your mid cap and small cap allocation into ETFs if any are available and sufficiently cheap. Your large cap exposure would be divided into sectors, and you'd select stocks for each sector using a dividend yield ranking. If mid and small cap ETFs weren't available or too expensive then stick to direct investment only in large cap stocks (portfolio 49, page 254).

Adjusting bond portfolio weights

It's also possible to use momentum and yield forecasting models with the bond ETFs in your portfolio. The 12-month momentum model can be used without any modification; just make sure you are consistently using either total return or price return.

Ideally you should use the **yield to maturity** measure as a substitute for dividend yield. Most bond fund managers publish and regularly update this figure on their websites. If it's unavailable then the dividend yield of the ETF you're investing in is a reasonable substitute, assuming it is a distributing share class. Just don't mix and match the two measures across different funds within the same group as they aren't quite the same thing.

As I've touched on before, you might be a little nervous about investing in "safe" bonds. As I'm writing this at the start of 2017, investors are terrified by two thoughts: widespread negative yields, and the prospect of central banks sharply increasing interest rates.

Using these two simple models can help alleviate your concern. The yield model will ensure you are underweight in bonds which have very low or negative yields; whilst the momentum model will reduce relative exposure in countries where interest rates have started to rise, causing bond prices to begin falling. If you also use the relative momentum model for asset classes then you'll also be protected against a general rise in global interest rates.

Using forecasting models: an example

To finish this section here is a complete example of how to apply forecasting models in a real portfolio. We met Patricia back in chapter eleven, where she put together portfolio 84. Remember Patricia is a young investment banker. As I know from my own career, young investment bankers spend most of their early working lives creating PowerPoint presentations full of dull tables and graphs (then once they've finished their apprenticeship they graduate to actually giving the boring presentations).

So it's fair to say that Patricia will be very comfortable with spreadsheets and financial modelling, and she is a natural candidate for using my two forecasting models. Let's see how she went about adjusting her portfolio allocations.

First of all Patricia puts her initial portfolio into table 53. This will make all the calculations easier.

TABLE 53: STARTING ALLOCATION

	Asset class A	Emerging or developed B	Region or credit C	Within region D	Risk weight E = A×B×C×D	Volatility	Cash weight
US equities	80%	75%	33.3%	80%	16%	15%	15.3%
Canada equities	80%	75%	33.3%	20%	4%	15%	3.8%
UK equities	80%	75%	33.3%	20%	4%	15%	3.8%
Europe ex-UK eq.	80%	75%	33.3%	80%	16%	15%	15.3%
Japan equities	80%	75%	33.3%	40%	8%	15%	7.6%
Asia ex-JP eq.	80%	75%	33.3%	60%	12%	15%	11.5%
EM equities	80%	25%			20%	23%	12.5%
Dev. govt. bonds	10%	75%	40%		3%	6%	7.2%
Dev. corp. bonds	10%	75%	30%		2.3%	6.5%	5%
Dev. HY bonds	10%	75%	30%		2.3%	8%	4%
EM bonds	10%	25%			2.5%	8%	4.5%
Gold	10%				10%	15%	9.6%

Table shows the portfolio weights I calculated earlier assuming all risk-adjusted returns are equal. All weights shown are risk weights unless specified otherwise. Values shown are as a proportion of entire portfolio.

Forecasting model adjustments

Now the hard work begins. First Patricia needs to collect the 12 month return and current yield for each ETF. She then works out the Sharpe Ratio of the trailing return and yield. The results are shown in table 54.

TABLE 54: DATA FOR FORECASTING MODELS

	Trailing return A	Current yield B	Volatility C	Sharpe Ratio, trailing return A ÷ C	Sharpe Ratio, yield B ÷ C
US equities	7.5%	1.6%	15%	0.37	0.11
Canada equities	33.5%	1.7%	15%	2.23	0.11
UK equities	15.0%	4.4%	15%	1.00	0.29
Europe ex-UK eq.	−4.0%	2.4%	15%	−0.27	0.16
Japan equities	24.1%	1.6%	15%	1.61	0.11
Asia ex-JP eq.	20.0%	2.6%	15%	1.33	0.17
EM equities	10.8%	1.6%	23%	0.47	0.07
Dev. govt. bonds	26.7%	0.8%	6%	4.45	0.14
Dev. corp. bonds	32.7%	2.4%	6.5%	5.03	0.37
Dev. HY bonds	34.3%	4.6%	8%	4.29	0.58
EM bonds	36.1%	4.6%	8%	4.51	0.58
Gold	18.4%	N/A	15%	1.23	N/A

All volatility figures from Appendix B

Patricia has a little more calculating to do, because she also needs to know the Sharpe Ratios (SR) for each region, each area (emerging or developed markets), and each asset class. These values are needed so that she can apply the forecasting model in each part of the portfolio, and at every level. To do this Patricia is going to work out the weighted average using the relevant risk weightings.

So, for example, to find the European equity Sharpe Ratio for yield, she takes the UK SR (0.29) and the Europe ex-UK SR (0.16), and then uses the starting risk weights[236] for European equities of 20% (UK) and 80% (Europe), which gives her an average SR of 0.19.[237] She then repeats this for North American (SR of yield 0.11), and Asian developed

---

236. Strictly speaking she should find the average using the risk weights after applying forecasting model multipliers within the North American group, but this is simpler and makes almost no difference to the final result.
237. $(0.2 \times 0.29) + (0.8 \times 0.16) = 0.19$

equities (SR of yield 0.15). To find the developed market Sharpe Ratio she takes the average of each region[238], which gives her 0.15.

Finally for the entire asset class of equities she takes the SR for emerging markets (0.07) and for developed markets (0.15); and then using the respective weights of 25% and 75% she gets a weighted average of 0.13. Patricia uses a similar technique to find the SR for developed equities, and for all bonds.

Patricia has also included the alternatives asset class in her forecasting model for asset class returns. Although gold produces no dividend, it does have a trailing return.

Patricia also needs to find the median SR for dividend yields in each group so she can calculate the multipliers. So, for example, the median yield SR for developed equities is the median of the SR for Europe (0.19), North America (0.11) and Asia (0.15), which is 0.15.

The aggregated and median numbers are in table 55.

TABLE 55: AGGREGATED AND MEDIAN DATA FOR FORECASTING MODELS

	Sharpe Ratio, trailing return	Sharpe Ratio, yield	Median Sharpe Ratio, yield
North American equities	1.11	0.11	0.11
European equities	-0.01	0.19	0.23
Asian equities	1.44	0.15	0.14
Developed market equities	0.85	0.15	0.15
Emerging market equities	0.47	0.07	N/A
Equities	0.65	0.13	0.11
Developed bonds	4.57	0.33	0.37
Emerging bonds	4.51	0.58	N/A
Bonds	3.58	0.40	0.46
Alternatives	1.23	N/A	N/A

Table shows the aggregated Sharpe Ratios for each region, area, and asset class (first two columns), and the median Sharpe Ratios for each group (second two columns).

238. Average of 0.11, 0.19 and 0.15 is 0.15. This is just a simple average because each region has the same weight within Developed markets: one-third.

These are calculated using risk weightings across each group. N/A indicates there is only one asset in the group and a median is not required, or that a particular model is not being used.

Next Patricia has to find the relevant multipliers. First, using table 46 she works out the multipliers for the momentum model. So, for example, amongst asset classes the relevant SR are 0.65 for equities, 3.58 for bonds, and 1.23 for alternatives. These correspond to multipliers of 0.78 for equities, and 1.48 for bonds and alternatives.

Table 56 shows the multipliers for each asset. For each asset there are different multipliers for different levels of the portfolio. So, for example, all the equities have 0.78 as their asset class multiplier, because that is the relevant multiplier at the asset class level for equities.

TABLE 56: MULTIPLIERS FROM MOMENTUM MODEL

	Asset class	Emerging or developed	Region or credit	Within region
US equities	0.78	1.39	1.48	1.18
Canada equities	0.78	1.39	1.48	1.48
UK equities	0.78	1.39	1.0	1.48
Europe ex-UK eq.	0.78	1.39	1.0	0.9
Japan equities	0.78	1.39	1.48	1.48
Asia ex-JP eq.	0.78	1.39	1.48	1.48
EM equities	0.78	1.24		
Dev. govt. bonds	1.48	1.48	1.48	
Dev. corp. bonds	1.48	1.48	1.48	
Dev. HY bonds	1.48	1.48	1.48	
EM bonds	1.48	1.48		
Gold	1.48			

Table shows the multipliers to be applied to each asset, based on the momentum forecasting model for each group.

Then Patricia turns to table 47 for the yield model and follows the same procedure; the results are shown in table 57. Notice that she is following my advice and not using the yield forecasting model for asset classes.

TABLE 57: MULTIPLIERS FROM YIELD FORECASTING MODEL

	Asset class	Emerging or developed	Region or credit	Within region
	A	B	C	D
US equities	N/A	1.19	0.85	1
Canada equities	N/A	1.19	0.85	1
UK equities	N/A	1.19	1.19	1.3
Europe ex-UK eq.	N/A	1.19	1.19	0.77
Japan equities	N/A	1.19	1	0.90
Asia ex-JP eq.	N/A	1.19	1	1.15
EM equities	N/A	0.85		
Dev. govt. bonds	N/A	0.6	0.6	
Dev. corp. bonds	N/A	0.6	1	
Dev. HY bonds	N/A	0.6	1.48	
EM bonds	N/A	1.48		
Gold	N/A	N/A	N/A	N/A

Table shows the multipliers to be applied to each asset, based on the yield forecasting model for each group.

Now Patricia can combine the multipliers from each model using the technique on page 340; the result is in table 58. So, for example, to get the combined figure for European equities she takes the momentum multiplier of 1.0, and the yield multiplier of 1.19. Multiplying and taking the square root gives a combined value of 1.09. Notice that the multipliers at the asset class level are just those from the momentum model.

TABLE 58: COMBINED MULTIPLIERS FROM BOTH MODELS

	Asset class	Emerging or developed	Region or credit	Within region
	A	**B**	**C**	**D**
US equities	0.78	1.29	1.12	1.09
Canada equities	0.78	1.29	1.12	1.22
UK equities	0.78	1.29	1.09	1.39
Europe ex-UK eq.	0.78	1.29	1.09	0.85
Japan equities	0.78	1.29	1.22	1.15
Asia ex-JP eq.	0.78	1.29	1.22	1.30
EM equities	0.78	1.03		
Dev. govt. bonds	1.48	0.94	0.94	
Dev. corp. bonds	1.48	0.94	1.22	
Dev. HY bonds	1.48	0.94	1.48	
EM bonds	1.48	1.48	1.00	
Gold	1.48			

Table shows the multipliers to be applied to each asset, based on the yield and momentum forecasting model for each group.

Final portfolio weights

Patricia's work is nearly done. She just has to multiply each of the group risk weights from table 53 by the figures in table 58, and then multiply the new weights out to get the new risk weight. For example, the original asset class weights were 80% in equities, 10% in bonds, and 10% in alternatives. The multipliers from the momentum model were 0.78, 1.48 and 1.48 respectively (remember we don't use the yield model for asset classes). This gives weights of 62.4%, 14.8% and 14.8% for each asset class. After normalising the weights to add up to 100% Patricia ends up with asset class weights of 67.8% in equities, 16.1% in bonds, and 16.1% in alternative assets.

Finally she has to apply the usual procedure to get the cash weights. Table 59 shows the final risk and cash weights.

TABLE 59: FINAL ALLOCATION USING FORECASTING MODEL

	Asset class A	Emerging or developed B	Region or credit C	Within region D	Risk weight E = A×B×C×D	Volatility	Cash weight
US equities	67.8%	78.9%	32.7%	78.1%	13.7%	15%	12.1%
Canada equities	67.8%	78.9%	32.7%	21.9%	3.8%	15%	3.4%
UK equities	67.8%	78.9%	31.8%	29.4%	5%	15%	4.4%
Europe ex-UK eq.	67.8%	78.9%	31.8%	70.6%	12.0%	15%	10.7%
Japan equities	67.8%	78.9%	35.5%	37.1%	7.1%	15%	6.3%
Asia ex-JP eq.	67.8%	78.9%	35.5%	62.9%	11.9%	15%	10.6%
EM equities	67.8%	21.1%			14.3%	23%	8.3%
Dev. govt. bonds	16.1%	65.6%	31.8%		3.4%	6%	7.5%
Dev. corp. bonds	16.1%	65.6%	30.8%		3.3%	6.5%	6.7%
Dev. HY bonds	16.1%	65.6%	37.4%		4.0%	8%	6.6%
EM bonds	16.1%	34.4%			5.5%	8%	9.2%
Gold	16.1%				16.1%	15%	14.3%

Table shows the calculation of risk and cash weights after applying forecasting model multipliers. All weights shown are risk weights unless specified otherwise. Values shown are as a proportion of entire portfolio.

Patricia buys the ETFs she needs, and then goes to have a well deserved rest. But she will be back (again): in part four I will use Patricia's portfolio to show you how to perform regular **portfolio maintenance**. At that point I'll also address the costs of doing this kind of adjustment, and how often you should do it.

Adjusting portfolio weights when you don't have a model

There are three ways of predicting future risk-adjusted returns: simple extrapolation of historical estimates (which doesn't work due to **uncertainty of the past**), simple forecasting models (which I've already discussed in this chapter), and **prophesy** (some other combination of gut feel, more complex analysis, or poring over chicken entrails).

It's my recommendation that you don't try prophesising at home. In my experience few people can do a better job of predicting risk-adjusted returns than a simple model.

However, I have the same view about prophesy as I do about my teenage daughter having boyfriends; I'm not keen on the idea, but if I am being realistic it is going to happen anyway – so it's better it happens in a safe and controlled way with strict rules. Similarly if you do think you can predict future risk-adjusted returns, despite my determined efforts to dissuade you, then I strongly suggest you do so using the techniques that follow in the rest of this chapter.

There are two methods you can use. One uses explicit **Sharpe Ratios**, the other a **scoring system**.

Forecast Sharpe Ratios	First of all you need to determine the expected Sharpe Ratio of each asset over some time horizon; I suggest one year. Either:
	1. You are the sort of person who can think in Sharpe Ratio units, in which case you can just do it directly.
	2. Or forecast the future return and then divide by the standard deviation that you're using (either rule of thumb from Appendix B on page 485, or estimated using the techniques in Appendix C, page 489).
	For example, suppose you think that stocks will return 5% and bonds −4% next year. Using my preferred volatilities of 15% for global equities and 6% for bonds this translates to Sharpe Ratios of 5% ÷ 15% = 0.33 for equities and −4% ÷ 6% = −0.66 for bonds.
Get the return difference versus the average	Work out the **median** Sharpe Ratio, and each asset's relative difference to the average.
	The median of 0.33 and −0.66 is −0.17.
	Bond SR versus the average is −0.66 − (−0.17) = −0.5
	Equity SR versus the average is 0.33 − (−0.17) = +0.5
Get portfolio weight adjustment factors	You now have a difference in Sharpe Ratio (SR) to the average for each asset. Find the portfolio weight adjustment factors by looking up this difference in the first column of table 60 to adjust your portfolio weights using the multipliers in the third colum*
	Either round or use interpolation if the SR difference is not shown.
	In the example, a forecasted Sharpe Ratio difference of 0.5 for equities corresponds to a multiplication factor of 1.35; −0.5 means the bond factor is 0.65.

	Multiply the initial handcrafted portfolio weights by the adjustment factors. You can either adjust cash weightings or risk weightings. These should always be normalised to add up to 100% (remember I'm not keen on absolute predictive models).
Adjust portfolio weights	Assuming a simple portfolio with a risk weighted 50% in bonds, and 50% in equities, and using the factors we've already worked out:
	1.35 x 50% = 67.5% equities
	0.65 x 50% = 32.5% equities
	These weights already add up to 100% so don't need normalising.

---

* If you're interested in how I constructed this table see Appendix C, page 498. This is worth consulting if you want to build your own forecasting models.

TABLE 60: HOW MUCH SHOULD WE ADJUST HANDCRAFTED WEIGHTS BY IF WE HAVE A PREDICTION FOR ASSET SHARPE RATIOS WHICH IS NOT BASED ON A MODEL?

SR difference to average	Relative score	Adjustment factor
−0.50	−20	0.65
−0.40	−16	0.75
−0.30	−12	0.83
−0.25	−10	0.85
−0.20	−8	0.88
−0.15	−6	0.92
−0.10	−4	0.95
−0.05	−2	0.98
0	0	1.00
0.05	+2	1.03
0.10	+4	1.06
0.15	+6	1.09

SR difference to average	Relative score	Adjustment factor
0.20	+8	1.13
0.25	+10	1.15
0.30	+12	1.17
0.40	+16	1.25
0.50	+20	1.35

The table shows the adjustment factor (third column) to use for handcrafted weights given Sharpe Ratio (SR) of asset (first column), or score (second column), versus portfolio average.

If you don't want to forecast returns or Sharpe Ratios then using a **scoring system** might be easier. This is particularly useful if you're using a very subjective or qualitative method to do your predicting, like chicken entrails.

Decide on your scores	Assign a **score** to each asset; higher scores mean higher returns. Use a range for scores between −20 and +20. A score of −20 means you are terribly bearish, +20 fantastically bullish, and 0 means you are neutral. An example forecast is: +10 for bonds and −15 for equities.
Get the score difference versus the average	Work out the **median** score, and each asset's relative difference to the average. For the example, the average of 10 and −15 is −2.5 Bond score versus the average is 10 − (−2.5) = 12.5 Equity score versus the average is -15 − (−2.5) = −12.5

Get portfolio weight adjustment factors	You now have a difference in scores relative to the average. Find the portfolio weight adjustments by looking up this relative score in the second column of table 60, getting the adjustment factors from the third column.
	Either round or use interpolation if the score you have chosen is not shown.
	A forecasted score of −12 (−12.5 rounded down), corresponds to a multiplying factor of 0.83 (equities) and a score of +12 gives a factor of 1.17 (bonds)
Adjust portfolio weights	Multiply your initial handcrafted portfolio weights by the relevant adjustment factors.
	For the example assuming a simple portfolio with a risk weighted 50% in bonds, 50% in equities, you would end up with:
	1.13 x 50% = 56.5% bonds
	0.83 x 50% = 41.5% equities
	After normalising the weights to sum to 100% you'd have 42.3% in equities and 57.7% in bonds.

These methods can be applied in any part of the portfolio. See the earlier parts of the chapter to see how to combine multipliers found in different groups and levels of a handcrafted portfolio.

Stock selection when you don't have a model

Can you do better than throwing darts to pick stocks, or as finance journalists love to do getting a chimpanzee, glamorous model, or small child to do it?

If you're in the lucky position of being able to buy individual stocks to get your sector exposure, then you may want to ignore my advice to use a forecasting model, and choose them yourself. I'm personally sceptical about the likelihood that this will be successful.

Nevertheless, discretionary stock picking will probably be a better use of your time than trying to predict the direction of asset classes: more people do better at picking stocks than forecasting the general level of equity prices and interest rates, although the returns of many successful stock pickers can mostly be attributed to exposure to risk factors like size and value.

If you follow the advice in part two you'll also be choosing stocks within a handcrafted portfolio with enforced diversification. Unless you are a very large investor you'll be limited to stock picking within just a small part of your overall portfolio. This reduces the damage you can do if your stock picking ability isn't as good as you think, or if you are a stock picking genius who just happens to be unlucky.

In Appendix C on page 502 I explain a method for putting together a qualitative systematic method for stock picking.

Summary

Simple forecasting models work	There is considerable research showing that simple models have done a pretty good job in improving the predictability of risk-adjusted returns.
But they aren't perfect	You should use forecasting models to **adjust** your portfolio weights, but never go to extremes where you almost completely remove assets from your portfolio. Forecasting models reduce the uncertainty of the past: they don't remove it entirely.
For asset allocation...	I recommend using **relative momentum**.
For choosing portfolio weights amongst equity countries, and across sectors within a country	I recommend using a combination of **relative momentum** and **dividend yields**.
For stock picking within sectors	I recommend **selecting** one or more stocks using the **dividend yield model**. Larger investors can partition off part of their portfolio of stocks for small and mid capitalisation firms.
For choosing portfolio weights amongst bond funds...	I recommend using a combination of **relative momentum** and **dividend yields**.
Do it yourself	You can also substitute my forecasting model for your own discretionary methods, predicting Sharpe Ratios directly or using a scoring system. Also you can pick stocks using your own methods.

CHAPTER FIFTEEN

Are Active Fund Managers Really Geniuses? And is Smart Beta Really Smart?

ALTHOUGH SIMPLE, THE FORECASTING MODELS IN THE PREVIOUS chapter require some effort to use. Wouldn't it be easier to leave portfolio weighting and stock selection to the really smart *experts*: active fund managers? Active fund managers charge a lot for this expert skill – are they worth it?

In the last couple of decades a cheaper alternative to active management has appeared: **smart beta**. These are passive funds which don't use market capitalisation weighting. They are cheaper than active funds, but more expensive than their plain market cap brethren. Is this smartness worth paying extra for?

Over the last few years another innovation – **robo advisors** – has arrived on the scene. Managers like Fidelity and Nutmeg invest in a portfolio of cheap passive ETFs with the added bonus of reweighting the assets on your behalf, but as usual there is a price to pay: yet more fees. Should you trust one of these *robots* with your money?

Chapter overview

Active fund managers	Is it worth investing in active fund managers? Which manager should you pick?
Smart beta	Smart beta funds use different weighting, and give you exposure to stocks that are expected to perform better. They are cheaper than active funds, but costlier than market cap weighted funds. Are they worth it?

Robo advisors	A recent innovation in the world of finance are algorithms that choose your portfolio weights for you. Should you try them out?

Active fund managers

Active management costs money. In the bargain basement world of passive indices you can get exposure to the S&P 500 for 0.05% a year in management fees, with invisible costs from trading inside the fund adding another few basis points in annual costs. But an active fund can easily cost 1% a year more to manage, plus even higher invisible costs. In exchange you're supposed to get better performance, achieved through the skill and expertise of the highly qualified investment professionals employed by the fund.

In this section I explain how you can check if this is really true, and determine whether active funds have a place in a smart portfolio.

How do we compare investment funds?

In chapter two I pointed out that it's difficult to forecast future returns. This means it's difficult to forecast what benefits different portfolios will bring in the future. Whereas in chapter five I pointed out that costs are relatively easy to predict. This leaves you with a difficult decision. Is it better to go for funds that are more expensive but which you expect to have higher returns, or for cheaper funds that might not perform as well?

To make things more tractable let's look at a specific example. I assume for now that you're trying to decide between two active fund managers who are both trying to beat the S&P 500, for which you have track records consisting of ten years of monthly returns. One manager incurs 2% a year in costs, the other 1% a year.

When you analyse their returns you find that the pricier manager seems to be worth it. On average they make 8% versus 6% annually after costs. This implies a pre-cost return that is 3% better than the cheaper manager.[239] However this doesn't tell the whole story. You can be sure that the expensive manager will continue to cost more. But how confident can you be that the expensive manager will continue to do better in the future?

This is actually a variation of the investment game I discussed in chapter two. The returns of each manager are like cards being dealt from two different decks. The track records are the cards that have been dealt so far. You want to predict what the **relative** returns will

---

239. The expensive manager has post-cost returns of 8%, adding back in costs of 2% means they must be making 10% a year before costs. The cheaper manager is making 6% after costs plus 1% in costs, equals 7% a year before costs. The difference in pre-cost returns is 3%.

be given what you've seen of each deck already. The returns of two similar managers will probably be related; they will have some **correlation**.

In figure 6 (page 45) I used some statistical wizardry to show the likelihood of the average return in a deck of cards taking a particular value, given the cards that we've already seen. Figure 36 shows a similar picture. This time I've plotted the likely distribution of the **difference** in pre-cost returns between the *better* expensive and *worse* cheap manager, assuming the ten-year track records are representative of future returns, and using a correlation of 0.85 (which is pretty typical for managers with similar fund styles).

FIGURE 36: GIVEN A TEN-YEAR TRACK RECORD HOW CONFIDENT CAN WE BE ABOUT LIKELY MANAGER RETURNS

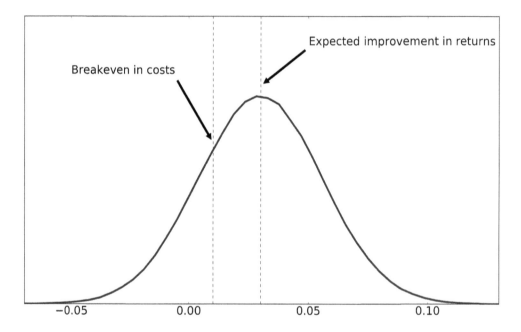

The expected difference in pre-cost returns is 3% a year, marked with the right hand vertical dotted line. But this means that over a ten-year period there is a 50% chance that the expensive manager will have less than 3% of outperformance.

The vertical dotted line on the left is set at 1% a year of outperformance. This is the **breakeven** pre-cost return where the expensive manager would become uncompetitive after costs (remember their costs are 1% higher). Over a ten-year period there is a 22% chance that the return difference between the expensive and the cheaper manager will be 1% or less.

So there's only a 78% chance that the more expensive manager will actually come out ahead after costs in any given ten-year period. You can only be 78% confident that the more expensive manager is the best option.

Personally a 78% chance isn't good enough for me. 78% is a purely theoretical number which I've calculated assuming that the statistical model I built using past returns is a good guide to the future. But in real life markets are constantly changing, and so are the approaches used by individual fund managers. It is unrealistic to assume the profile of returns will be the same if (a) a fund changes it's manager, (b) your favourite manager switches to a different firm, or (c) a manager tries their hand in a different market.[240]

For this type of comparison I'd want to see at least a 90% chance that the higher cost manager was better. This is less than the 95% most academic statisticians and economists usually want as evidence of statistical significance, but it's still a relatively high bar to jump over. In this example, for us to be 90% sure they were better the expensive manager would need to have an annual return over ten years that was 4.3% better before costs. As they only have a 3% advantage they aren't good enough.

Over the next few pages I show you how to use this concept to compare different fund options.

Active or passive

There is one perennial debate within the finance industry that will never go away: should we invest in cheap passive tracker funds, or stump up extra fees for active managers? Active managers don't just have higher management fees, they also have larger invisible costs such as trading costs inside their funds. Is all this extra cost worth it? Over the last 50 years there has been a voluminous output of academic research showing that active managers fail to outperform passive indices after costs and risk have been accounted for.[241] But maybe your favourite fund manager is different?

To find out you should first find an alternative option: a passive fund which closely matches the mandate of the active fund manager you are considering. Do not compare the fund manager against their active peers, even though managers prefer to do this, as it flatters them when active managers underperform as a group, as they normally do. Do not compare them against an index: this is unfair on the manager as you can't actually invest in an index.

Make sure you are using returns with all costs deducted; both visible and invisible. Many active funds charge opaque initial and holding costs which may not be reflected

---

240. Like UK superstar manager Anthony Bolton, who saw poor performance in the Chinese equity fund he launched in 2010, after decades focusing on the UK and Europe.

241. For example, 'Reflections on the Efficient Market Hypothesis: 30 Years later' by Burton Malkiel, *The Financial Review*, 2005. Over 44 years (1970–2004) out of 139 funds, 65 underperformed by 1% or more a year, only four outperformed by 2% a year.

in their published performance figures. I've included a discussion of active fund costs in Appendix B, page 481. Don't forget to divide initial costs by 20 to convert them into annual costs. You need to measure total returns, including dividends. Both active and passive funds also need to be in the same currency.

Measure the historic standard deviation of returns for both funds to make sure they are similar, or the riskier fund will have an advantage. Normalise the returns of both funds so they have a standard deviation of 22%, which is the typical risk of a single country equity fund.[242]

Measure the average annual outperformance of the active fund (if it doesn't outperform then your decision is easy: stick with the passive fund). Finally measure the correlation. Ideally you'd use monthly returns to get these values. There are methods in Appendix C for calculating these figures (page 489 for standard deviations, page 493 for correlations).

Table 61 shows the difference in arithmetic returns required to be 90% sure that one fund is better than another, depending on the length of the track record and the correlation between the active and passive fund. I've put this together using the technique I developed in the previous section.

TABLE 61: HOW MUCH IMPROVEMENT IN AVERAGE POST-COST RETURN DO WE NEED TO BE 90% SURE THAT AN ACTIVE FUND IS PROBABLY BETTER THAN A PASSIVE ALTERNATIVE (%)?

Correlation	1 year	2 yrs	3 yrs	5 yrs	7 yrs	10 yrs	20 yrs	50 yrs
0.25	32.0	23.0	18.4	13.7	11.6	10.0	6.9	4.3
0.50	25.0	18.0	14.9	11.2	9.8	8.0	5.6	3.6
0.75	18.0	13.0	10.6	8.2	7.3	5.6	4.1	2.6
0.80	16.0	12.0	9.2	7.4	6.2	5.0	3.6	2.3
0.85	14.0	9.9	8.2	6.4	5.4	4.3	3.0	2.0
0.90	12.0	8.2	6.6	4.9	4.4	3.6	2.5	1.6
0.95	8.2	5.5	4.7	3.6	3.0	2.5	1.8	1.1

Table shows improvement in average arithmetic mean return needed to be 90% sure that one fund is better than another given a given correlation (rows) and track record (columns). I assume that both funds have a standard deviation of returns of 22% a year;

242. For example, if fund A has a standard deviation of 20% and fund B 24%. To normalise the returns so they have the same risk: multiply the returns of fund A by 22% ÷ 20% = 1.1 and multiply the returns of fund B by 22% ÷ 24% = 0.917.

appropriate for funds that invest in the equities of a single country. First three columns, in italics, should be used with caution. If correlations are not estimated then use the 0.85 row.

This might seem like a lot of effort. If you're short of time then it's okay to (1) use the cheapest ETF that tracks the appropriate index, (2) assume an 85% correlation, and (3) pretend that the active fund and the passive fund both have the correct volatility. This just leaves you just to measure the difference in average annual returns. The table uses normal arithmetic means rather than geometric means, which means you can easily get the relevant figures from publically available information.

Just be careful: if you're comparing the returns of two bond funds then the volatility is unlikely to be correct on either fund, as I've constructed the table to reflect the risk of a typical equity fund. As a rule of thumb, if you tmultiply the return difference of two bond funds by 2.5[243] then it will give you a comparable figure that can be looked up in the table. For example if one bond fund outperforms another by 1% a year then that is equivalent to a 2.5% outperformance for an equity fund.

Looking at the table, a longer track record means you can be more certain about historic returns, and the difference needed is smaller. More highly correlated funds also have a smaller required improvement. A manager who is closely following and regularly beating the index only needs a small uplift in returns to justify their extra cost. Someone who is idiosyncratic and doing something quite different will need longer to prove themselves, or show a larger degree of outperformance.

Within the table I've included numbers for track records of less than five years in length for completeness. But I wouldn't personally trust the track record of any manager who hasn't been around for at least five years. These figures are shown in italics to reflect my cautiousness.

Let's take a real example. Fundsmith is an active global equity fund run by a high-profile UK fund manager, Terry Smith. I'll assume that Fundsmith has an 85% correlation with IGWD,[244] a passive tracking fund covering the global equity market. Fundsmith has outperformed the ETF over the last five years with average returns of 12.4% versus just 10.7% for the ETF. This annual outperformance of 1.6% sounds impressive but wouldn't actually meet the threshold of 6.4% improvement over the benchmark that is required with that correlation over five years. You should stick to the passive fund. The fund manager would need to maintain that outperformance for many more years before his improvement became significant.

---

243. Assuming of course that you've taken my earlier advice and have stayed away from bond funds containing low maturity (or low duration) bonds.

244. The real correlation is actually a little lower, so this flatters the active manager. As Fundsmith is priced in GBP it would also be fairer to use a GBP hedged ETF, rather than one priced in USD; again by using an unhedged ETF I am flattering the active manager (since GBP has fallen against USD).

In contrast, Warren Buffet has outperformed the S&P 500 by an average of 12% per year over almost 50 years (and counting). Regardless of his correlation with the index, it's safe to say that his past returns are extremely unlikely to be luck and he'd easily meet the 90% certainty threshold.

There is another statistical issue we have to consider when making this decision, known formally as the **multiple testing problem**. If you test the performance of a large number of managers then by the laws of chance some of them will pass the 90% criteria, even if none of them actually have any skill. There are thousands of active funds available, with dozens of funds in most categories, so the chances of a few lucky funds managing to pass the test without having any real merit are high.

Table 62 shows the magnitude of this problem. I created this by randomly generating some return data for a set of imaginary active managers, none of whom can actually beat the passive fund on average, but which are charging 1% more in fees and turnover. You can see that with only a few years' data, about 10% of the managers' pass the thresholds I show above (it's slightly less than 10% because of the drag of costs). As we get more data the chances of a 'lucky monkey' passing the 90% test are reduced, but some always make it through.

TABLE 62: HOW MANY MANAGERS WILL SLIP THROUGH THE NET JUST BY LUCK (%)?

Correlation	1 year	2 yrs	3 yrs	5 yrs	7 yrs	10 yrs	20 yrs	50 yrs
0.25	9.5	9.1	8.9	8.5	8.4	8.1	7.2	5.7
0.50	9.4	9.2	8.3	8.2	8.0	7.2	6.5	4.6
0.75	9.3	8.9	7.7	7.5	7.0	6.7	5.5	4.0
0.80	9.2	8.4	8.1	8.0	6.8	5.7	5.0	3.5
0.85	9.1	8.4	6.9	6.8	6.3	6.1	4.4	2.8
0.90	8.7	7.2	6.8	6.3	5.9	5.2	3.8	2.4
0.95	7.5	6.3	6.0	5.1	4.4	3.4	2.0	0.8

Table shows the percentage of poor managers who I'd expect to pass the threshold in table 61, for a given correlation (rows) and track record (columns). All managers are expected to underperform a passive tracker by 1% a year on average (due to extra costs).

All the methods I use above assume that past performance is indicative of the future. But since managers often move to different funds, or change their approach, even a long track record might be useless. Should I find a manager that passed the 90% certainty test I'd still be reluctant to allocate away from a passive option. Even if managers with persistent skill exist, it's not clear if their skill can be distinguished from luck, except after several decades when their career has probably nearly ended. The very best managers also tend to operate in niches of the market where their edge will be eliminated if they attract too much additional capital. Many will go and work for hedge funds where even higher fees will eat up most, if not all, of their outperformance.

Despite all I have said I appreciate that some people are wedded to the idea that (a) brilliant active fund managers exist, (b) can be distinguished from the herd, and (c) are worth paying for. Just make sure you pick a manager that passes the tests in this section.

Which manager? How many managers?

Suppose you've decided that it is worth choosing an active manager for a particular component in your portfolio. Whom should you pick?

To a large extent you can use exactly the same method as I showed you for the active and passive decision above. Your preferred option will be the cheaper fund. Make sure you account for all relevant costs: visible and invisible; initial and holding costs (see appendix B, page 481). If the cheaper fund outperforms after costs then your decision is easy: pick the cheaper fund. If not, then you should check to see if the outperformance of the more expensive manager passes the 90% significance test in table 61.

Sufficiently large institutional investors should allocate to multiple managers for a particular mandate; assuming they can find more than one manager with returns that pass the 90% threshold. You should then take the same approach I advocate for portfolios of underlying assets: invest in an equally weighted basket of a number of active managers.

You can also use the 90% test when considering whether to replace an existing active manager who is lagging behind with a rising star that you are considering. This is quite a stern test to pass, so it will significantly reduce the turnover of managers in your portfolio. This is undoubtedly a good thing as there is considerable evidence that people are as lousy at changing their active managers as they are at predicting the prices of underlying assets.[245]

---

245. 'The Selection and Termination of Investment Management Firms by Plan Sponsors', Amit Goyal and Sunil Warhal, *Journal of Finance*, 2008. They looked at 3,700 pension fund managers. They found that sponsors transferred money to new managers who showed positive returns in the three years prior to hiring, and fired existing managers are they had underperformed. If they'd stuck with their managers their excess returns would have been larger.

A final warning about active managers

You might find this a surprising admission coming from a self-proclaimed expert in quantitative finance, but when choosing active fund managers I wouldn't rely that heavily on statistical analysis of a fund manager's track record.

Track records aren't completely useless, because I would never trust managers whose returns are wildly different from their benchmark: relatively uncorrelated, unrealistically high, or appallingly low. However I am more interested in **how** a manager makes investment decisions and manages risk, rather than focusing purely on the track record that results from that decision making. Except for very long periods of time track records are mostly down to luck, as the tables in this part of the chapter make clear.

This kind of detailed due diligence requires deep understanding of the manager's investment strategy, and is certainly well beyond the scope of this book. Most retail investors are unlikely to have the skills or the opportunity to do this properly, and my general recommendation is that they steer clear of active managers altogether. This is a popular view: the active fund industry is slowly shrinking as investors realise they have been paying too much for too little skill.

Smart beta

Smart beta funds are passively managed funds that do something other than boring market capitalisation investing. They get their name because plain **beta** is the shorthand term used in finance for investing in market cap portfolios.

You've already seen a form of smart beta portfolio construction in this book: **equal weighting**. But there are other far more exotic smart beta weighting methods available, which I discuss in a moment.

The more interesting flavours of smart beta also use **risk factors** to try and improve their returns; either by up-weighting certain assets, or selecting only a subset of the available assets. These are similar in spirit to the simple forecasting models I discussed in the previous chapter.

In this part of the chapter I explain different weighting schemes, and the use of risk factors to alter weights and select assets.

Smart beta weighting

You've already met three different methods for portfolio weighting in this book: equal weighting, market capitalisation weighting, and handcrafting. But there are yet more sophisticated methods. These are mostly variations on the technique of **full optimisation** which uses historic risk, returns, and correlations to find the best portfolio. Because of the various flaws I exposed in chapter three, full optimisation is now discredited and rarely seen on the smart beta menu.

Here is a fairly comprehensive list of portfolio weighting schemes that will cover pretty much anything you'll see in a list of ETFs:

Fully optimised	Weights optimised for maximum expected risk-adjusted returns.
	Assumes: Nothing. Risk, return and correlation can all be different. Uses historic correlations, risk and returns.
	Pleasingly there do not seem to be any ETFs offering fully optimised weights.
Equal weighting	All assets get equal weights.
	Assumes: Correlations, risk, and risk-adjusted returns are identical.
	No statistical estimates are used to build the portfolio.
	This is the most common smart beta ETF weighting, with numerous funds available including RSP, an S&P 500 fund with an expense ratio of 0.4%.
Volatility parity	All assets get weighted inversely to their risk. Volatility parity is effectively a combination of equal weighting combined with the **risk weighting** technique I introduced in chapter four.
	Assumes: Correlations and risk-adjusted returns are identical.
	Uses historic risk.
	Volatility parity is not a common ETF strategy and I couldn't find any relevant funds when I wrote this chapter.
Risk parity	All assets get weighted inversely based on their contribution to portfolio risk.
	Assumes: Risk-adjusted returns are identical.
	Uses historic risk and correlations. These funds tend to cover multiple asset classes; one example would be Canadian listed HRA (annual fee 0.85%).
Maximum diversification	Weights optimised for maximum portfolio diversification.
	Assumes: Risk-adjusted returns are identical.
	Uses historic correlations and risk.
	The Canadian fund MUS is an example of a maximum diversification ETF (annual fee 0.6%).

Minimum variance	Weights optimised for minimum portfolio risk.
	Assumes: Risk-adjusted returns are identical.
	Uses historic correlations and risk.
	An example would be the USMV ETF (MSCI USA, minimum volatility index) with an annual fee of 0.15%.
Handcrafted	Assets are grouped and then equally weighted within, and across, groups.
	Assumes: Correlations are equal between assets in the same group. If assets are in different groups, they have an equal correlation which is lower than the intra-group figure.
	Uses historic correlations. When used with risk weighting uses historic risks.
	ETFs using this strategy are rare; the closest match I could find was the fund EQL which itself invests in ten sector ETFs with equal cash weightings (net annual fee 0.3%).
Market cap weighted	Weight assets by market capitalisation.
	Assumes: Market cap weights are best.* Don't use historic data. Virtually all passive ETFs use market cap weighting.

* Technical note: To be precise this is best if the assumptions of the Capital Asset Pricing Model are true, which implies that all investors should own the market portfolio.

Do the fancier optimisation techniques add value compared to handcrafting, simple equal weighting or the standard option of a cheap market cap weighted ETF?

Volatility weighting makes the most sense across asset classes, where volatility can be quite different. However for similar assets such as equities within the same country I am less convinced that this is necessary;[246] I think equal weighting gets close enough.[247] Volatility weighting also requires higher portfolio turnover than equal weighting since you need to respond to changes in risk as well as asset value.[248]

Risk parity, maximum diversification and **minimum variance**[249] use historic correlations as well as risk to find the portfolio which is likely to perform the best, again assuming

---

246. I'm not the only one. There is a strong body of evidence that equally weighting is better than more sophisticated methods for similar assets, e.g. Raman Uppal et al: 'Optimal Versus Naive Diversification: How Inefficient is the 1/N Portfolio Strategy', *Review of Financial Studies*, 2007.

247. Technical note: Equities with low volatility have historically outperformed those with high volatility, at least on a risk-adjusted basis. Volatility weighting will allow you to benefit from this.

248. Of course this is also a problem with using my method of risk weighting if you change your estimate of standard deviation over time. I explore this issue more in part four.

249. If all assets have the same expected risk then the minimum variance and maximum diversification

equal risk-adjusted returns for all assets. These methods are overkill if your portfolio is composed of assets with similar correlations, when equal weighting would be more appropriate. With assets like equities from the same country and industry there is less of a need to take correlations into account.

I am concerned that portfolios formed using risk parity, maximum diversification and minimum variance are at risk of the dangers of optimisation which I discussed in chapter three. As well as relatively high management fees they will also have higher trading costs, as portfolios need to be adjusted as correlation estimates change.

The minimum variance portfolio has another problem: by reducing risk to a minimum it will also reduce return. This makes it much less attractive to an investor who wants the maximum geometric mean portfolio as defined in chapter four.

However, suppose you're investing in something like the Canadian equity market, where both equal weighing and market cap weighting will give you a portfolio with high sector concentration.[250] It's preferable to deal with this by buying sector based ETFs, or by allocating to individual stocks using a top-down approach, as I discussed in chapter eleven.

But if this isn't possible or too expensive, because of a small account size and a lack of competitively priced sector ETFs, then a maximum diversification or minimum variance ETF for the entire country might make sense. However, I'd only buy such a fund if the management fee was 0.5% less than a market cap weighted fund; a little higher than the 0.3% discount I would want for equal weighting, reflecting the higher trading costs because of changes in volatility and correlation.

To summarise, I'm fairly sceptical of more complicated smart beta weighting approaches, and as they normally cost significantly more than both market cap and equal weighted I wouldn't recommend them.

Smart factor weighting and selection

In the previous chapter I introduced **risk factors**. A higher exposure to risk factors like value and momentum should improve your returns.

A **factor weighted** smart beta portfolio has a higher exposure to your chosen risk factor(s) than the market capitalisation index. If for example a fund manager wants a higher exposure to a value factor like dividend yield then they can adjust their portfolio appropriately. This could be done either by (1) **up weighting** higher dividend payers, or by (2) investing **selectively** only in equities that met some minimum dividend yield requirement, or a combination of the two methods.

Alternatively for certain value factors you can use **economic weighting**. A portfolio that was economically weighted by dividends would weight firms according to the value of

---

portfolios will be the same.
250. See tables 31 and 32 back on page 163 and page 164.

their dividends. If two firms had the same $10 billion market capitalisation, but one had twice the dividend yield of the other (say 4% versus 2%), then it would end up with twice the weight in an economically weighted smart beta portfolio (because its annual dividends would be $400 million versus $200 million).

Is factor weighting worth paying for?

Factor-based smart beta funds are nearly always more expensive than their vanilla market capitalisation weighted counterparts. Firstly they usually have higher management fees. For example, in the US Vanguard currently sells an S&P 500 ETF (VOOV) with exposure to the value risk factor. This has an expense ratio of 0.15% compared to a mere 0.05% for the cheapest market cap version (IVV); 0.1% higher. Secondly they will have higher invisible trading costs inside the fund.

You already know that equal weighted funds have higher invisible trading costs, as fund managers have to buy and sell to maintain equal weights as prices change; but factor-based smart beta funds trade even more, since they also need to take account of changes in valuation.

That is the downside, but what additional returns can you expected from a smart beta ETF that uses factors?

Unfortunately factor based smart beta passive funds haven't been around long enough to get statistically significant evidence of outperformance over market cap weighted benchmark funds. This is problematic because different risk factors come in and out of fashion[251] so their performance can only be properly judged over several full market cycles. However there has been considerable academic research on the returns of risk factors for individual equities.

Rather than regurgitate it all I'll summarise the results of one paper[252] which is relatively recent and covers all the main developed equity markets. My summary is in table 63.

---

251. For example, value type strategies did very badly during the tech boom of the late 1990s. Firms that actually had old fashioned profits were discarded in favour of dot-coms for which making money was a distant prospect at best. Value stocks only outperformed once the tech bubble had popped.
252. Eugene Fama and Ken French 'Size, Value, and Momentum in International Stock Returns', *Journal of Financial Economics*, 2012. The results I show here are derived from table 2. I've converted the monthly arithmetic means into annualised geometric means. Although the returns in the paper are excess not absolute returns it's relative performance that matters.

TABLE 63: ANNUAL GEOMETRIC MEAN OF EXCESS RETURNS FOR GLOBAL EQUITIES OF DIFFERENT SIZES AND EXPOSURE TO PRICE:BOOK (PB) AND MOMENTUM RISK FACTORS

Size	High PB	Average PB	Low PB	Low momentum	Average momentum	High momentum
Small cap	−1.27%	8.10%	13.15%	−0.07%	8.66%	17.07%
Mid cap	2.53%	5.13%	7.30%	0.71%	5.51%	8.38%
Large cap	2.26%	4.87%	4.67%	−0.91%	3.56%	5.60%

Low PB: 20% of firms with lowest price:book ratio (*cheap*). High PB: 20% of firms with highest price:book ratio (*expensive*). Average PB: firms with median price:book ratios. Low momentum: 20% of firms with lowest relative momentum, measured using trailing 12 month returns. High momentum: 20% of firms with highest momentum. Average momentum: firms with median relative momentum. Small firms: Bottom 75% of firms ordered by market cap. Large cap: Top 3% of firms ordered by market cap. Remaining firms are mid cap.

The first finding of note is that buying cheap stocks using price:book (PB) doesn't work very well amongst large firms. Smart beta ETFs are limited to selectively buying the cheapest stocks. They can only earn the extra return from owning the cheapest stocks rather than the average stock with a median PB ratio; but the average stock actually earned more (4.87%) than the cheapest stocks (4.67%). Due to higher volatility, cheaper large cap stocks also had a lower Sharpe Ratio (not shown in the table).

Yes, there is a big gap between the cheapest (low PB, mean return 4.67%) and the most expensive large cap stocks (high PB, mean return of just 2.26%), but this difference can only be earned by hedge funds who can buy the cheaper stocks whilst short selling the expensive stocks, and then use leverage to boost returns.

Value only starts working once we look beyond the very largest, most efficiently priced, firms. On average within mid cap firms the cheapest have higher geometric means (7.3% versus 5.13% for the average stock) and Sharpe Ratios. For small cap firms the cheapest stocks do significantly better than average.

Momentum – buying stocks that have gone up the most in the last 12 months – is a clear winner for all firm sizes. Large cap investors can earn over 2% a year in additional returns, before costs, by picking stocks with positive momentum rather than just holding the average stock. Mid cap and small cap investors will do even better.

Other evidence in the paper and elsewhere also suggests that a combination of risk factors does better than a single factor, something which several ETFs offer, albeit for an even higher management fee.

I'm a firm believer in both value investing and momentum, but given the available evidence I don't think there is always enough extra return in risk factor investing to pay for significantly higher costs.

How much extra management fee can you justify paying for a smart beta product? First let's look at the benefits of different kinds of smart beta versus market cap weighting, which are shown in table 64. You might recognise the modest 0.03% benefit of equal weighting which I calculated in chapter six. The other numbers are derived from table 63 or drawn from my own research. All these figures reflect the uncertainty of each benefit, as we're going to compare them to certain costs.

TABLE 64: EXTRA GEOMETRIC RETURN FROM DIFFERENT SMART BETA PRODUCTS, VERSUS MARKET CAP WEIGHTED

Size	Equal weight	Single value factor	Multiple value factors	Single momentum factor	Value plus momentum
Small cap	0.03%	5.13%	7.10%	8.44%	9.45%
Mid cap	0.03%	2.23%	3.07%	2.90%	3.56%
Large cap	0.03%	−0.17%	0.05%	2.07%	2.50%

Maximum difference in annual management fee versus a market cap weighted ETF to make investment in a smart beta product worthwhile.

If I deduct the extra invisible trading cost of smart beta (Appendix B, table 95, page 485) from the relative benefits of factor investing in table 64 I can work out the maximum viable management fee premium that should be paid for a given product. This is shown in table 65.

TABLE 65: MAXIMUM ANNUAL EXTRA MANAGEMENT FEE YOU SHOULD PAY FOR A SMART BETA FACTOR FUND

Size	Equal weight	Single value factor	Multiple value factors	Single momentum factor	Value plus momentum
Small cap	−0.82%	4.0%	6.0%	7.0%	8.0%
Mid cap	−0.58%	1.4%	2.2%	1.7%	2.3%
Large cap	−0.27%	−0.68%	−0.46%	1.2%	1.7%

Maximum difference in annual management fee versus a market cap weighted ETF to make investment in a Smart Beta product worthwhile. A negative value indicates the smart beta fee would have to be cheaper than the market cap alternative.

Let's return to the smart beta S&P 500 Value ETF (VOOV) I mentioned earlier, and use the table to see if it's worth buying. This is a large cap multi-factor value fund. From table 65, the annual management fee would need to be 0.46% **cheaper** than a market cap fund to be worthwhile. This is because the modest 0.05% benefit shown in table 64 is more than wiped out by 0.51% of additional trading costs. But VOOV is actually 0.1% more expensive than the alternative market cap fund!

We can conclude that value is unlikely to work well enough in the large cap S&P 500 to justify paying a higher management fee. However, large cap momentum funds, and funds which cover smaller firms with any risk factor, are worth paying more for. Generally, however, most smart beta funds are likely to be far too expensive to bother purchasing, relative to boring but cheap market cap weighted alternatives.

Robo advisors

A recent trend in the investment world has been the emergence of **robo advisors**. A robo advisor will invest your money for you, usually in ETFs, with portfolio weights decided by some kind of fancy algorithm, although many like Vanguard (US) and Nutmeg (UK) also have some human input, using real people to forecast future returns of different assets. Robo advisors save you a lot of effort and at first glance it looks like they implement similar methods to those I've discussed in this book, since their algorithms are usually variations on the portfolio optimisation methods I discussed in chapter three.

However, there are several reasons why I am not keen on robo advisors. First of all they aren't cheap. You have to pay the robot a hefty annual fee to look after your portfolio. In the UK, for example, the market leader Nutmeg charges between 0.25% and 0.45% for their fixed allocation product, and between 0.35% and 0.75% a year for their fully managed service. The US is cheaper but even Vanguard charge 0.3% a year. Currently only Charles Schwabs offer a robo advice service that does not charge a management fee.

You also have to pay another set of trading costs inside the robo fund when the robot or it's human master decides to switch between ETFs; although for smaller investors these costs are likely to be cheaper than doing the rebalancing yourself. On top of this you have to pay the normal costs you'd incur if you were DIY investing: the management fee of the underlying funds, plus the invisible trading cost inside the underlying ETFs.

Secondly, some of these robots do some pretty stupid things. When I took a cursory look at a single provider's fund I unearthed immediate problems.

What were the issues? The two riskiest funds included no bonds, and were 100% invested in equities. The safest fund was invested in cash and bonds; with zero allocation to equities. Both of these allocations are flawed: if you drag your memory back to chapter four you might remember that (a) when using the correct measure of expected geometric mean all investors should have some bonds in their portfolio; and (b) even ultra cautious investors should own some equities.

This suggests there are some serious flaws in the optimisation process being used by this particular advisor. This is unlikely to be an isolated problem. Who knows what gremlins lurk within other fund managers' algorithms?

Thirdly, I am not convinced these robots are robotic enough. Vanguard for example offers a hybrid of human and robot advice. Will this give the best, or the worst, of both worlds? Nutmeg employ fund managers who continuously tune their fully managed portfolios:

> "...instead of relying on rigid computer models, we carry out our own rigorous analysis of the relevant data" (from nutmeg.com, December 2016)

In other words, they try and predict risk-adjusted returns. Which I don't believe that humans can do especially well.[253]

It's almost impossible to know if this human input has added value, although it will definitely add extra trading costs. The time period is too short to evaluate the performance of any changes that humans are making to their portfolio weights: most of these funds have been going just a few years – much shorter than the periods I showed were needed to analyse the performance of active managers earlier in this chapter.

It's also hard to accurately perform a proper comparison as robo advisors use the same marketing tricks as their actively managed brethren; for example comparing themselves to expensive financial advisors rather than a fair benchmark such as a fixed and balanced portfolio of the underlying ETFs.

Finally, robo advising is relatively inflexible. You can't usually decide to own individual shares, have different allocations, invest in alternatives or do anything except choose a portfolio according to your risk tolerance.[254]

Robo advisors definitely work out cheaper than the traditional combination of an expensive financial advisor who invests in costly actively managed funds. But for those prepared to do a little more work themselves they are far too expensive.[255] If you're lazy then you should only consider a manager that offers zero additional management fee (currently just Charles Schwab). But you will probably still be paying more in rebalancing costs, and you'll definitely be giving up considerable flexibility and autonomy.

---

253. As of January 2017 Nutmeg offers a fixed allocation service with no rebalancing which is a little cheaper.

254. Some robo advisors may offer flexibility in some of these areas. For example OpenInvest, a new entrant to the robo industry, allow investors to avoid firms that have dubious ethical or sustainability credentials. But no robo advisor can ever offer the same number of options as DIY investment.

255. One claimed advantage of US robo investors is that they trade to harvest tax losses. I discuss how you can take advantage of tax losses yourself in part four.

Summary

Be sceptical about active fund management	It's unlikely that active managers will produce statistically significant performance that will justify their higher costs. In a large pool of potential fund managers some will have apparently good results just by luck.
Avoid fancy portfolio weighting	Forget minimum variance, maximum diversification, and the rest.
Forget about smart beta	Except for a limited set of funds it's unlikely that the benefits will exceed the higher costs involved.
Robo advisors	Avoid these costly gimmicks unless you are very lazy, or so well paid that the time you save outweighs the extra management fee, higher turnover costs, and lack of flexibility.

PART FOUR

Smart

— *Rebalancing* —

Part Four: Smart Rebalancing

"Our favorite holding period is forever."

—Warren Buffett, legendary investor

In a perfect world you wouldn't need to do anything once your portfolio was set up. But we don't live in a perfect world. Left unchecked your portfolio will drift away from its initial allocation as assets change in price, dividends come in and cash is added or removed. Annoyingly firms sometimes get taken over, or even more annoyingly go bust. You may even want to change your portfolio weights occasionally.

However it's important that you do the absolute minimum amount of trading, even if you end up doing slightly more than the esteemed Mr Buffett. It's vital that every single buy and sell is fully justified: they all cost money and you need to be confident that you'll benefit from each and every trade that you do.

Chapter sixteen explains the **theory** and **principles** you need to understand to do rebalancing properly. Like many decisions in this book it's about making a smart choice that involves weighing up the known costs of trading against the uncertain benefits of adjusting your portfolio weights.

In chapter seventeen I show how to use these principles when running smart portfolios of the type I showed how to construct in part two. This involves a process of regular **portfolio maintenance**; just like the annual service on a car. It's all about small changes to keep things ticking over; not big adjustments that will incur large trading costs.

Many investors reading this book will already have their own portfolios. After reading parts one, two and three you may no longer like the look of what you have got in your brokerage account. But it would be prohibitively expensive to sell everything and start again from scratch. You need to do some careful **portfolio repair**. This more extreme form of rebalancing is discussed in chapter eighteen.

CHAPTER SIXTEEN

The Theory of Rebalancing

SO YOU'VE PUT TOGETHER YOUR SMART PORTFOLIO? THINK YOU can relax? Wrong: you now need to think about possible **rebalancing**, which may involve further buying and selling. Like many financial decisions this involves calculating the trade-off between benefits and costs. Most people underestimate the costs, and overestimate the benefits, of trading. After reading this chapter you will know better.

Chapter overview

Why do you need to rebalance?	I explain why rebalancing is required, and I define two kinds of rebalancing – partial **reweighting** and total **substitution** of one asset for another.
Is it worth reweighting and by how much?	Working out whether it's worth trading to get your portfolio weights closer to their optimum values.
When to substitute and when not to	Calculating the trade-off between the benefits of substituting a new fund or equity for another.
Tax considerations	Tweaking your rebalancing to minimise your tax bill.

The next two chapters explain how to use the principles here for regular portfolio **maintenance**, and more serious portfolio **repair**.

Why do you need to rebalance?

Broadly speaking, you need to rebalance for two reasons. Firstly when your **Target Weights** (the portfolio cash weights you'd like to have) are unchanged, but the cash weights implied by the value of the underlying assets – your **Current Weights** – no longer properly reflect them. I call this **portfolio drift**. Secondly, you would rebalance if you *changed* your Target Weights. This is an **allocation change**.

In this first part of the chapter I introduce problems that need solving, but I don't offer up any solutions – yet. These come afterwards, in the rest of the chapter.

I'm going to use an ultra simple portfolio consisting of three actual firms to illustrate what's going on in this part of the chapter – please do not think this is a viable set of investments, as it violates almost every principle in parts one and two of the book! You can see it in table 66.

TABLE 66: A SIMPLE PORTFOLIO TO ILLUSTRATE REBALANCING EFFECTS. DO NOT INVEST IN THIS!

	Target risk weight	Std dev	Target cash weight A	Account value B	Allocation value C = A × B	FX rate D	Share price E	Number of shares (C × D) ÷ E
Barclays	25%	20%	24.1%	£10,000	£2,409	1.0	£2.00	1,204
Tesco	25%	15%	32.1%	£10,000	£3,212	1.0	£5.00	642
JP Morgan	50%	22%	43.8%	£10,000	£4,379	1.5	$30.00	218

The table shows how we go from target risk weights, to target cash weights, and then finally to calculating the number of shares required. All figures are arbitrary values for the purpose of the example.

I started by constructing a very simple top-down equity portfolio; split between two banks (JP Morgan and Barclays), and UK supermarket Tesco. I then calculated the cash weights implied by the standard deviation of equity returns for each firm, as usual using the method in chapter four, page 96. These are the **Target Weights** which I hope to achieve when I start buying.

Next I decided on a nominal account value of £10,000, and then worked out what value of each stock I'd need to own, in pounds. Using the share price, I calculated the number of shares to actually purchase. For JP Morgan I also need the exchange rate since the shares are valued in dollars.

For reasons that will become apparent shortly, I can also do this calculation in reverse, as in table 67. Given a particular account value, the number of shares owned, the price of each share, and the FX rate, it's straightforward to calculate the cash weighting implied by what I own (my **Current Weights**). Then using the standard deviation of each share I can find the implied risk weights.[256]

TABLE 67: WORKING BACKWARDS FROM VALUES TO WEIGHTINGS

	Number of shares F	Share price E	FX rate D	Allocation value C = (F × E) ÷ D	Account value B	Current Weight G = C ÷ B	Std dev	Implied risk weight
Barclays	1,204	£2.00	1.0	£2,408	£10,000	24.1%	20%	25.0%
Tescos	642	£5.00	1.0	£3,210	£10,000	32.1%	15%	25.0%
JP Morgan	218	$30	1.5	£4,360	£10,000	43.6%	22%	49.8%

The table shows the cash weighting (Current Weight) and risk weightings implied by a given number of shares, the share price, FX rate, and account value. Note that £22 (0.2%) of the portfolio is in cash.

Portfolio drift

Portfolio drift happens when the **Target Weights** remain the same, but the **Current Weights** have moved away. This can happen for a number of reasons: (1) changes in prices, (2) dividends and other cash transfers, and (3) bankruptcies and takeovers.

Changes in prices

UK Supermarket Tesco had an accounting scandal a few years ago. If that happens again, their share price could easily halve; to have one accounting scandal is a misfortune, to have two looks like carelessness. If the share price does halve[257] and I repeat the calculations in table 67 then I would get the result in table 68.

---

256. Notice that the implied cash and risk weights are already slightly different from the target weights in the previous table. This is because I can't buy fractional numbers of shares, so 0.2% of the portfolio is unallocated and held in cash.

257. To make the maths clearer I'm assuming that the standard deviation estimate wouldn't be affected, although this is very unrealistic: normally a plummeting share price would result in volatility increasing.

TABLE 68: WHAT HAPPENS TO CURRENT WEIGHTS WHEN PRICES CHANGE?

	Number of shares F	Share price E	FX rate D	Allocation value C = (F × E) ÷ D	Account value B	Current Weight G = C ÷ B	Std dev	Implied risk weight
Barclays	1,204	£2.00	1.0	£2,408	**£8,395**	**28.7%**	20%	**28.5%**
Tesco	642	**£2.50**	1.0	**£1,605**	**£8,395**	**19.1%**	15%	**14.3%**
JP Morgan	218	$30	1.5	£4,360	**£8,395**	**51.9%**	22%	**56.9%**

The table shows the cash weightings (Current Weight) and risk weightings implied by a given number of shares, the share price, FX rate, and account value, after Tesco's price halves. All figures in **bold** have changed. Note that £22 of the portfolio is in cash.

As you'd expect, the relative Current Weight of Tesco has fallen; and the Current Weight of the other firms has increased. Although the other firms haven't seen a price reduction they now have a higher proportion of the new lower total account value. Also notice that it's mostly relative price changes that matter. If the price of everything in the portfolio had halved the implied Current Weights would be unchanged.[258]

To bring things back into line I'd need to sell Barclays and JP Morgan; and buy Tesco. Table 69 shows the newly **rebalanced** portfolio. The Current Weights are now in line with the original Target Weights. To achieve this I had to sell and then re-buy around £1,100 of the portfolio; or about 26% of its value.

TABLE 69: THE REBALANCED PORTFOLIO

	Number of shares F	Share price E	FX Rate D	Allocation value C = (F × E) ÷ D	Account value B	Current Weight G = C ÷ B	Std dev	Implied risk weight
Barclays	1,010	£2.00	1.0	£2,020	£8,395	24.1%	20%	25.0%
Tesco	1,078	£2.50	1.0	£2,695	£8,395	32.1%	15%	25.0%
JP Morgan	184	$30	1.5	£3,680	£8,395	43.8%	22%	50.0%

The table shows the cash weighting (Current Weight) and risk weightings implied by a given number of shares, the share price, FX rate, and account value, after Tesco's price halves and the portfolio has been rebalanced.

---

258. This isn't quite true because the small amount of cash in the portfolio would become relatively more valuable, but that is a very small effect.

A similar exercise would be necessary if the exchange rate moved; even if share prices remained unchanged. This cannot be avoided unless all your holdings are denominated in a single currency. This is an impractical solution if you've followed my advice to diversify geographically whilst avoiding funds which are currency hedged.

Finally, notice that a market capitalisation weighted portfolio wouldn't need rebalancing in this example. Market cap weights adjust automatically as prices change. This is why traditional passive tracking funds have much lower rebalancing costs than funds which use equal weighting.

Dividends and other cash transfers

Most stocks and distributing funds pay dividends. If you do nothing this will gradually increase the proportion of cash in your portfolio. Reinvesting dividends when they are received in the same company or fund will maintain the correct portfolio weight. Many brokers offer a service which does this automatically.

If, for example, you are receiving an average yield of 4%, then that is 4% of your portfolio you'll need to reinvest annually. Unless you invest solely in accumulating funds then dividends are an inevitable fact of life; indeed, if you're using the relative yield model I introduced in part three then you'll probably be receiving higher dividends than average.

Cash balances can change for another reason. Investors might deposit additional funds. These need to be invested to maintain the correct portfolio weights. Alternatively you might need to withdraw money; if there is insufficient cash in the account this would require selling securities to realise the necessary funds.

Investors don't always have control over the timing and size of withdrawals. However, it's generally bad practice to add funds one year, only to withdraw them the year after. This creates unnecessary transaction costs, and may also generate additional taxes. Single company pension funds normally move from generally depositing funds (when a company is new and has no benefits to pay) to usually withdrawing (as workers retire and pensions need to be paid) .

Other institutional investors like endowment funds should also try and smooth their withdrawal of funds by budgeting over a multi-year horizon. Finally, retail investors should be cautioned against investing money they could conceivably need in the next five years.

Bankruptcy and takeovers

What happens if Tesco really screws up and goes bankrupt? Or what if JP Morgan decides to buy Barclays?

When a bankruptcy occurs the share price will probably go to zero; you won't have any extra money and you will own one less firm. After a cash takeover you'll also end up with one less holding, but with the consolation prize of some spare cash.

In both cases you should consider whether you need to replace the share with a substitute. A more difficult case is a takeover in exchange for shares. If the acquiring company is a firm you'd have substituted into your portfolio anyway then no further trading is required. If not then in theory you should sell shares in the acquirer so you can buy something more suited to your portfolio. I'll explain how to make these decisions later in the chapter.

Bankruptcies are fortunately rare amongst publicly listed companies. Takeovers are slightly more common, but are still unlikely to affect more than a few of your holdings in any given year. In either case there is little you can do about these events. At least takeovers are normally at a premium to the current share price; so rebalancing after a takeover is a nice problem to have.

Takeovers don't affect collective funds[259] like ETFs. It's theoretically possible that ETFs could go bankrupt, but unlikely if you stay away from the leveraged versions. However, ETFs do sometimes get de-listed if they no longer have sufficient assets to make them worth managing. This is effectively a cash takeover since you're forced to sell out of the ETF whether you want to or not.

If possible you should avoid ETFs which don't manage very much money: anything less than $500 million in the US or £100 million in the less developed UK market. These are more likely to be de-listed than larger funds.

Allocation change

An allocation change happens when your **Target Weights** have changed. This can happen if asset volatility changes. It will also happen if your preferred risk weights change, which could be caused by changes in correlations, risk-adjusted returns or stock selection criteria. Target Weights will also change if new funds become available, or stocks move in or out of an index.

Changes to volatility

Implied risk weightings can change even if implied cash weightings don't. How is this bizarre thing possible? Have a look at table 70. This is a copy of table 67, but now the standard deviation of returns in US bank JP Morgan has doubled (without anything happening to the price – which isn't very realistic). It's now at an implied risk weight of 80%, versus the 50% we were targeting before.

---

259. Sometimes an actively managed fund is taken over by new management who drastically change its style or increase its management fee; to the point where you'd want to deallocate from it.

TABLE 70: RISK WEIGHTINGS WILL CHANGE IF VOLATILITY MOVES

	Number of shares F	Share price E	FX rate D	Allocation value C = (F × E) ÷ D	Account value B	Implied cash weight G= C ÷ B	Std dev	Implied risk weight
Barclays	1,204	£2.00	1.0	£2,408	£10,000	24.1%	20%	**10.1%**
Tesco	642	£5.00	1.0	£3,210	£10,000	32.1%	15%	**10.1%**
JP Morgan	218	$30	1.5	£4,360	£10,000	43.6%	**44%**	**79.8%**

The table shows the cash weightings, risk weightings implied by a given number of shares, the share price, FX rate, and account value, after the volatility of JP Morgan has doubled. Figures in **bold** have changed.

To correct for this I'd need to reduce the Target Weight on JP Morgan, and sell enough shares so that the implied risk weight was correct again.

Notice that as with prices it's only *relative* volatility that matters here. If all the assets in your portfolio become twice as volatile, then your implied risk weightings will be unchanged.

Many readers will be bemused by this. They are planning to use the rule of thumb volatility estimates I provide in Appendix B, page 485. These won't ever change (unless I write a second edition of this book, and probably not even then).

But for those who are going to use their own volatility estimates this is potentially a problem. These estimates will change all the time. Theoretically you should rebalance the portfolio every time this happens; I explain what you should actually do later in the chapter.

Changes to risk weights: correlations

So far I've discussed situations where something in the outside world is conspiring to ruin your portfolio and make you trade to bring things back into line. However there are also situations where nothing is forcing you to rebalance, but where you still want to change your Target Weights.

In my preferred top-down handcrafted method for constructing portfolio weights, the only thing that determines risk weights are **correlations**, which affect how you group various assets. Small changes in correlation will have no effect on grouping, but in theory at least large changes mean you should consider changing the grouping, and thus the Target Weights.

You definitely shouldn't change your handcrafted portfolio groupings every day: only if you think there has been a permanent and significant change in correlations. For example Italian and German government bonds became highly correlated after the Euro currency came into being (although they returned to being very much uncorrelated when the Eurozone sovereign debt crisis occurred just over a decade later).

These events are rare enough that ignoring them won't significantly affect your portfolio.[260] So **I'd recommend never changing your handcrafted weights**.

Changes to risk weights: expected risk-adjusted returns

You may be considering using the two models I presented in part three for adjusting your risk weights according to **momentum** and **dividend yield**. I've already shown that these improve the performance of the portfolios they're used for. But on the downside using these models will mean that your target risk weights will always be changing, leading to continuous rebalancing. I introduce a technique for dealing with this later in the chapter.

Changes to risk weights: selection of a subset of assets

Suppose you're picking the highest yielding stock from each sector in the Eurostoxx index. As I'm writing this the Finnish firm Fortum is top of the yield charts in the utilities sector, with a yield of 7.8%.

But at some point it's likely that Fortum will be outclassed yield wise, either because its price has gone up too much (a nice problem to have), or because it's dividend is cut (a less pleasant experience). Another firm will surpass it, which means in theory you should swap Fortum for it's rightful successor.

Indeed if the universe of assets is large enough this could happen frequently, as the differences in yield that will cause the rankings to change can be quite small. It's quite plausible that one firm could be yielding 4.9% and the next 4.8%, in which case a mere 0.2% change in relative price would cause them to swap their relative rankings. Such a tiny change in relative price could happen every few seconds!

Changes to risk weights: change to index membership

If you built your portfolio by selecting your stocks from a particular index, but one of them drops out, should you sell it and replace it with a new entrant? Passive trackers have to slavishly sell stocks that fall out of an index like the FTSE 100 and buy their replacements.[261] This is why even passive market capitalisation weighted funds have to

---

260. However, if you were using another method for finding portfolio weights, like the techniques I outline in Appendix C starting on page 496, then in theory it's probably better to update your correlation estimates, and trade accordingly. I discuss how to reduce the costs of doing this later in the chapter.
261. Index providers use buffering rules to reduce trading costs. For example, a security will usually be included in the FTSE 100 at the quarterly review if it has risen to 90th ranking, and will be removed if

pay some trading costs, even though their weights usually adjust automatically as prices move.[262]

But there is no reason why stocks will underperform just because they are no longer members of an index.[263] So personally I'd avoid changing your selection of stocks based on index criteria, unless you are running an institutional fund with a constrained mandate and have no choice.

Changes to risk weights: new, and better, funds appearing

The constant innovation in the ETFs market is usually a good thing for investors, but it can also cause some decision making headaches.

Imagine you have allocated to the entire Asian emerging bond market using a single ETF, because that was all that was available. This ETF is market cap weighted, and heavily skewed towards a single country, China. Now suppose that separate ETFs become available for each individual country. Ideally you'd sell your regional ETF, and buy the ETFs for each country: China, Thailand and so on. This would add diversification, and hence improve expected risk-adjusted returns.

Alternatively what if a new Asian emerging market bond ETF was launched which was identical in terms of coverage, but was much cheaper with a lower management fee. Again if you didn't have to worry about trading costs you'd definitely want to switch to the new fund.

With nearly 250 new ETFs launched in the US alone in 2016, chasing the best new funds could lead to some serious over trading.

Conclusion

From the above discussion there are clearly two types of rebalancing: (1) weights moving out of line requiring a modest **reweighting**, and (2) a more serious situation where you'd ideally want to **substitute** one or more assets in your portfolio – selling out of the entire position and buying something else. In the next part of the chapter I discuss how you can reduce the costs of portfolio **reweighting**, and the subsequent section is about the question of **substitutions** – selling entirely out of one asset, and replacing it with another.

---

it has fallen below 111th. This reduces turnover compared to the simpler method of taking the largest 100 firms regardless of whether they are currently in the index. (Actually it's slightly more complicated than that, because with these rules it's possible that the index can end up with more or less than 100 members. Additional clauses prevent this from happening.)

262. Reinvesting dividends and dealing with takeovers also create some turnover.

263. There of course will be short-term effects as passive funds sell a particular stock but these can't be avoided unless you can correctly guess the index changes and front run them. Even if you can manage this, you'll end up with a larger tracking error to the index. Also, since being dropped from an index usually follows a share price decline there will be momentum effects, but I deal with these later in the chapter.

Is it worth reweighting and by how much?

Deciding whether it is worth reweighting is yet another problem of the trade-off between relatively unpredictable benefits versus the known costs of extra trading.

First the benefit: any delay in reweighting means portfolios will remain unbalanced for longer. Remember from chapter four, figure 24 (page 113) that having slightly different portfolio weights doesn't make much difference. However if weights get seriously out of line because you're not rebalancing at all then the cumulative effect will be significant.

Now let's consider the costs. I use costs a lot in the next few chapters so here are some indicative values for costs given trade sizes, using my usual assumptions from Appendix B for large cap stocks. Tables 71 and 72 show the all-in trading costs for UK and US investors; including commissions, bid-ask spread cost, and UK stamp duty. Notice that because of stamp duty there are different UK rates for direct stock purchases (0.5% stamp duty) and for ETF trades and direct stock sales (zero stamp duty).[264]

TABLE 71: COST PER TRADE FOR US EQUITY INVESTORS IN LARGE CAP SHARES OR ETFS

	Direct or ETF Buy or sell
$150	$1.08
$350	$1.18
$500	$1.25
$1,000	$1.50
$2,000	$2
$5,000	$3.50
$10,000	$5
$100,000	$60

Total cost per year for trade of a given value (rows), including commissions and bid-ask spread cost; but with zero market impact. Cost assumptions as per Appendix B, page 480.

---

264. If you are paying a higher minimum commission then you should add the difference between your minimum and the values I am using ($1 in the US, £6 in the UK). For example, if you're paying a $5 minimum then a $150 trade would cost the figure from table 70, $1.08, plus $5 – $1 = $4; $1.08 + $4 = $5.08.

TABLE 72: COST PER TRADE FOR UK EQUITY INVESTORS IN LARGE CAP SHARES OR ETFS

	Direct buy	Direct sell	ETFs buy or sell
£250	£7.38	£6.13	£6.13
£500	£8.75	£6.25	£6.25
£1,000	£11.50	£6.50	£6.50
£2,000	£17.00	£7.00	£7.00
£5,000	£33.50	£8.50	£8.50
£10,000	£62	£11	£11
£100,000	£580	£79	£79

Total cost per year for trade of a given value (rows) and type (columns), including commissions, stamp duty on purchases and bid-ask spread cost; but with zero market impact. Cost assumptions as per Appendix B, page 480.

How much potential trading do all the effects I described earlier in the chapter actually cause? It's difficult to quantify some of them, but others are more straightforward. In particular it's relatively easy to calculate the likely cost of price movements, dividends, using forecasting models to choose weights, and updating estimates of volatility or correlation.

To illustrate this I ran an experiment on a simple three asset model containing US and UK equities, and US bonds; where I check prices and trade every month. Figure 37 shows the results. The y-axis shows the annual portfolio **turnover**. A turnover figure of 2 indicates that you'd buy, and then sell, the entire value of your portfolio every year on average.

FIGURE 37: TURNOVER WITH THREE ASSETS AND DIFFERENT LEVELS OF PORTFOLIO REWEIGHTING

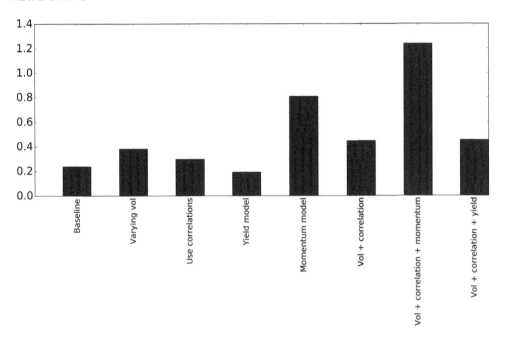

Each bar shows a different degree of portfolio reweighting. From left to right these are:

Baseline	Trading done because of changes in prices, and quarterly dividends being received. **You cannot reduce your trading below this level.** Constant standard deviations are from Appendix B, and risk weights are fixed using the handcrafting method.
Varying vol	As baseline, but standard deviations are estimated and allowed to vary over time.*
Use correlations	As baseline, but risk weights are estimated with an optimisation model that uses varying correlations.**
Yield model	As baseline, but risk weights are modified with a model which uses **dividend yields** to predict risk-adjusted returns.
Momentum model	As baseline, but risk weights are modified with a model which predicts risk-adjusted returns based on the trailing returns of the last 12 months.
Vol + correlation	Combination of 'Varying vol' and 'Use correlations'.

Vol + correlation + momentum	'Vol+correlation' and 'Momentum model'.
Vol + correlation + yield	'Vol+correlation' and 'Yield model'.***

* Technical note: I use an exponentially weighted estimate of standard deviation with a half life of 12 months, using monthly returns. A longer half life would reduce turnover; a shorter one would do the opposite. ** Technical note: I recalculate portfolio weights annually using correlations of monthly returns from the last five years. A longer window would reduce turnover, a shorter one would increase it. Correlations are more stable than volatility, hence the longer estimation period. *** In case you're wondering, using both the momentum and the yield model at the same time gives you turnover roughly the same as the momentum model.

Monthly trading to keep up with changing prices and dividends generates turnover of around 20% a year. Adjusting weights for volatility and correlations increases this further. Using a momentum model to adjust portfolio weights causes even more trading.[265]

Now consider figure 38. This shows the cost of trading a simple three asset portfolio with £5,000 in the UK, a relatively small account in a relatively expensive place to trade.[266] The figures show the same set of situations that I used when I estimated turnover for three assets earlier in figure 37. The costs shown are extremely high – at least 3.5% a year, going up to nearly 4.5% a year. These cost levels are very similar as they are mainly being driven by fixed commissions and we trade every asset in every single month, regardless of what scenario we are in. These costs would wipe out most, if not all, of this portfolio's likely performance.

265. Using a yield model **should** also ramp up turnover. The only reason it doesn't with these three assets is that relative yields remain divergent for long periods of time so the model hardly does any trading (cast your mind back to figure 34, page 338). If I check the results for a portfolio of developed 22 equity countries where the yield model makes more sense, I find that using dividend yields to adjust portfolio weights also pushes up turnover (from about 40% to 130% a year) although not as much as momentum (which has turnover of around 160% a year).
266. All the examples in the next few pages will be in the UK. This doesn't reflect patriotic bias on my part, but merely the relatively high cost of trading which makes the examples more interesting. So American readers should feel good about this, rather than ignored.

FIGURE 38: ANNUAL % COSTS OF TRADING THREE ASSET PORTFOLIO WITH £5,000

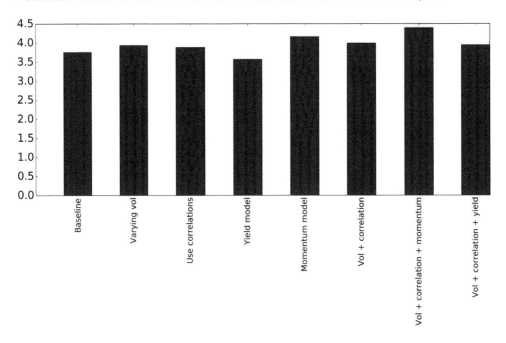

Obviously frequent reweighting costs more. This is for two reasons. Firstly many of the trades that are done will have to be reversed in the near future. If you traded because a price has gone up today then it may well go down again tomorrow, requiring yet more buying and selling.

Secondly, minimum fees make small trades highly uneconomic. For example, suppose that over the course of a year you want to buy and sell a £1,000 position in UK large cap equities. If you do this gradually with four trades of £500 each the total cost[267] will be £30. But with two trades of £1,000 it works out[268] at just £18. Trading less frequently is cheaper but it will mean having the wrong portfolio weights for longer.

Clearly the huge costs I've calculated in this section will massively outweigh any potential benefits from frequent reweighting. Although this is an extreme example, even larger investors in the relatively cheap US will still end up paying a significant proportion of their potential returns away in commissions and other costs. Naively rebalancing your portfolio on every twist and turn of the market will badly hurt performance.

---

267. From table 71 two buys of £500 are £17.50, two sales of £500 are £12.50; total £30.
268. From table 71 a £1,000 buy costs £11.50 and a £1,000 sale £6.50; total £18.

Minimising reweighting costs with a No-Trade-Zone

The obvious tactic for dealing with reweighting costs is to rebalance less frequently. But this is a blunt tool. There would be many times when you'd be doing tiny trades during a regular rebalancing, and other occasions when you'd have to wait too long to reweight after a significant market move.

A better solution to this problem is to create a **No-Trade-Zone** around your Target Weights. This will allow you to reap the benefits of reweighting with minimal cost; by only reweighting when you have to, rather than at fixed intervals. With a No-Trade-Zone you ignore small reweighting trades; if your Current Weights are only slightly out of line you don't bother adjusting them.

But when your portfolio weights are outside of the zone you trade as necessary to bring them back in line. This makes rebalancing less expensive as you only rebalance when it's absolutely necessary and likely to provide the largest benefit.[269]

For example, suppose that the current Target Weight for BP shares in your portfolio is 1.5% (all figures in this section are **cash weights**).[270] If you have set your **No-Trade-Zone** to 2.0% then you would be happy with any weight between 0.5% and 2.5%. If your Current Weight was 0.75% then no trade would be needed, as illustration 2 shows.

ILLUSTRATION 2: NO TRADE IS NEEDED HERE

---

269. I return to the question of how often you should check if your Current Weights are outside the zone later in the chapter.

270. Technical note: It's also possible, and theoretically better, to use a No-Trade-Zone with risk weights; comparing implied risk weights to optimal risk weights. However, this is much more complicated and the benefits from using risk weights are tiny.

401

But now see illustration 3: if your Target Weight subsequently changes to 2% then your No-Trade-Zone would also move to between 1% and 3%. You should now buy, investing another 0.25% of your portfolio into BP to bring its Current Weight up from 0.75% to 1.0%, the border of the No-Trade-Zone.

ILLUSTRATION 3: CURRENT WEIGHT IS TOO LOW – WE NEED TO BUY

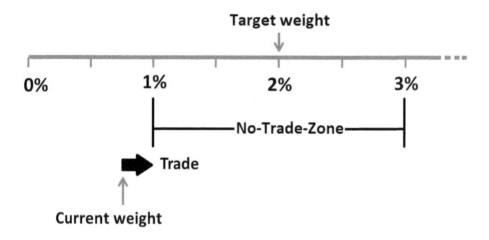

You're probably wondering why you wouldn't keep buying to take your BP holding from 0.75% all the way up to the new Target Weight of 2%. This doesn't reduce turnover as much as the method I've presented here; you do fewer trades as you spend longer inside the zone, but then the trades you do are all relatively large – at least half the size of the width of the zone. The effect of these larger trades swamps the benefit of doing fewer of them, and you end up with higher turnover if you trade to the centre of the zone rather than the edge. This is particularly problematic if you are an institutional trader who has to worry about market impact.

Introducing a Minimum-Trade-Size

A No-Trade-Zone reduces turnover dramatically by preventing you from buying, and then selling shortly afterwards, if Target Weights change slightly. But it doesn't help with the problem of minimum fees on small trades. Buying just 0.25% of your portfolio in extra BP shares as you did in illustration 3 above is fine if the portfolio is massive, and your main concern is minimising market impact. But for an investor with a £5,000 portfolio that would mean doing a tiny trade with a value of just £12.50 and paying prohibitively high costs.

The solution is to combine the No-Trade-Zone with a **Minimum-Trade-Size**. You should specify this in cash terms (i.e. £100) and then convert it into a percentage of your account value. After calculating any required trade you should then check that it's larger than the Minimum-Trade-Size.

Suppose, for example, that the minimum for a UK investor was £250. With a £50,000 portfolio this corresponds to 0.5%. Using the figures from illustration 3, with a Current Weight of 0.75% and a No-Trade-Zone of 1% to 3% the required trade of 0.25% would be too small. See illustration 4.

ILLUSTRATION 4: THE TRADE REQUIRED (0.25%) IS SMALLER THAN THE NO-TRADE-ZONE (0.5%) – WE DO NOTHING

No trading would be possible unless the target weight moved to 2.25%, at which point the No-Trade-Zone would be 1.25% to 3.25%. Only then would it worth buying any more BP shares.

At this point the required trade shown in illustration 5 takes us from the Current Weight of 0.75% up to the edge of the No-Trade-Zone at 1.25%; this is a buy of 0.5% which meets the Minimum-Trade-Size.

ILLUSTRATION 5: THE REQUIRED TRADE OF 0.5% NOW MEETS THE MINIMUM TRADE REQUIREMENT

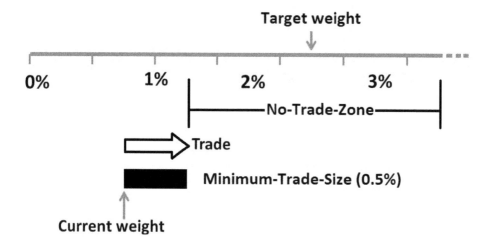

How wide a No-Trade-Zone? What Minimum-Trade-Size?

What No-Trade-Zone and Minimum-Trade-Size should you use? The optimum size of these two values depends on two factors: (a) the number of assets in your portfolio, and (b) the level of costs that you are paying.

If you own just two assets, each with a 50% weight, then a No-Trade-Zone that is 10% wide works out to a fifth of the weight of each asset. But if you have 100 assets with 1% each then a No-Trade-Zone that is 10% wide equates to ten times your average weight: you'll never do any rebalancing.

Higher costs mean a wider No-Trade-Zone is necessary. In chapter three I explained that costs can be divided into variable percentage costs (like minimum brokerage commissions) and fixed percentage costs (like bid-ask spread execution costs). Variable percentage costs are the same for all investors. However, fixed percentage costs are lower for larger investors. Smaller retail investors should set their No-Trade-Zone wider than large institutions.

A higher minimum brokerage fee also means a higher Minimum-Trade-Size: if you have to pay $20 in commission on every trade you'd need a Minimum-Trade-Size that is 20 times larger than someone who is paying just $1.[271]

We can conclude that (a) the correct Minimum-Trade-Size is invariant to portfolio size, but should be related to minimum brokerage fees, and (b) the optimum levels of No-Trade-Zone will be different depending on the number of assets owned, and the value of your portfolio.

If you've followed the advice in this book then there should be a direct relationship between the value of your portfolio and the number of assets it contains: larger investors can afford to buy more assets and gain more diversification. So when setting the No-Trade-Zone we can simplify things by focusing just on the number of assets in the portfolio.

After running experiments with different portfolios I calculated that the best No-Trade-Zone width to use is **one half of the average portfolio weight**, which is also equal to 100% divided by the number of assets you own.[272] For example, if you have ten assets in your portfolio then the average portfolio weight will be 10%. One half of this is 5%. So if you had one asset with a Target Weight of 12% then you wouldn't trade as long as the Current Weight was between 9.5% and 14.5%.

I calculated an optimal minimum trade size of £250 in the UK, and $150 in the cheaper US market.[273]

What effect does applying these two techniques have on the simple three asset £5,000 UK portfolio I analysed earlier? First let's look at the baseline scenario where rebalancing occurs due to change in price, and dividends. Without using any cost reduction, costs are nearly 4% a year. Using my recommend No-Trade-Zone of half the average cash weight substantially cuts costs, to just 0.043% a year. Adding a £250 Minimum-Trade-Size reduces annual costs even further to a mere 0.025%. That is *less than a hundredth* of the original cost of 4%!

---

271. Actually it wouldn't be exactly 20 times larger because both investors will also be paying other costs like bid-ask spread cost, and stamp duty in the UK. However, it's more conservative, and easier, to apply a pro-rata adjustment to Minimum-Trade-Size based on relative minimum brokerage fees.

272. Technical note: If you're familiar with the theory behind No-Trade-Zones you will understand that I'm simplifying this problem a great deal. (See 'Optimal trading under proportional transaction costs' by Richard Martin, *Risk* magazine, 2014. I should probably point out that Richard is an ex-colleague of mine from AHL.) Nevertheless, this is an appropriately conservative value to use across most scenarios.

273. This assumes that your brokerage fee minimums are £6 and $1 respectively. If not, you need to multiply this figure by the ratio of your brokerage fee to the numbers I'm using. For example, if you're a US investor paying $5 minimum brokerage your Minimum-Trade-Size will be $150 × ($5 ÷ $1) = $750. By the way, the UK value isn't exactly six times the US value because both investors will also be paying other costs like bid-ask spread cost as well as the minimum brokerage commission. However, it's more conservative, and easier, to apply a pro-rata adjustment to Minimum-Trade-Size based on relative minimum brokerage fees.

It's worth remembering that I'm using an account value of £5,000 here. Because it's a UK account, and a relatively small one at that, the costs are initially quite high and are dramatically reduced by using the No-Trade-Zone and Minimum-Trade-Size. However there are still significant improvements in costs for larger UK investors, and for US investors of all sizes.

Further reductions in the width of the No-Trade-Zone beyond this leads to extremely modest further reductions in costs; as would introducing a Minimum-Trade-Size larger than £250. Slowing down trading further by using a wider zone or larger minimum will result in portfolio weights being out of line for much longer. This does potentially serious harm to your gross returns that will far outweigh the tiny improvements in costs.

Investors with larger accounts should use a higher Minimum-Trade-Size as it would be pretty silly for a hundred million dollar fund to place an order for $150 worth of shares. I'd recommend using the lower of £250 (or $150), and 0.1% of your portfolio value. This implies that investors with more than £250,000 or $150,000 will use higher minimum values. If, for example, you had a million dollar portfolio[274] you'd use a Minimum-Trade-Size of 0.1% of $1 million, or $1,000.

So far my analysis has only accounted for rebalancing caused by price changes and dividends. Does the recommended no trade zone and minimum trade size also reduce costs if you are changing volatility, correlations, or expected risk-adjusted returns because of a forecasting model?

You bet it does. See figure 39. This is a rerun of figure 38 (page 400), only this time I've applied a no trade zone and minimum trade size.

It's clear that in most cases the costs in figure 39 are many orders of magnitude lower than the annual costs of 3.5% upwards which you'd pay in figure 38, in which I didn't use any techniques for reducing costs. However, using the momentum model to periodically adjust portfolio weights is still relatively expensive, either alone or in combination with varying volatility and correlations.

Earlier in chapter fourteen I estimated that the additional return from using the momentum model was around 1% a year. But the certain extra costs of using momentum for the UK investor with £5,000 in figure 39 are around 0.6%, which wipes out most of this benefit. As there is considerable uncertainty about any estimate of geometric return I would recommend that any UK investor with just £5,000 avoids using the momentum model.

---

274. However, all investors should keep their minimum trade size below the level where they would start to pay market impact costs. If a fund manager with a billion dollar portfolio is reading this then a minimum trade size of 0.1%, which is $1 million for a billion dollars, may be too large. For large cap stocks in developed markets they should use a minimum of $50,000, with lower minima elsewhere.

FIGURE 39: ANNUAL % COSTS OF TRADING THREE ASSET PORTFOLIO WITH £5,000, USING NO TRADE ZONE AND MINIMUM TRADE SIZE

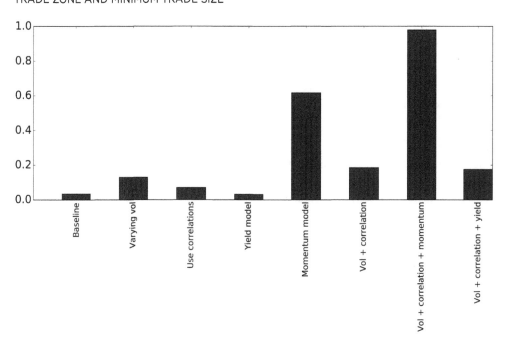

Generally it is not sensible for the very smallest investors in any country to use the momentum model. Even with the No-Trade-Zone and Minimum-Trade-Size I've recommended, you'd pay trading costs which would wipe out any additional returns; and these are returns which are uncertain, unlike the costs. Further increasing the width of the No-Trade-Zone or the Minimum-Trade-Size would certainly reduce the costs of using momentum, but this would be at the expense of bringing down returns. The accuracy of momentum forecasts decays quickly with time, so introducing additional delay into the rebalancing process would seriously damage the benefits of the momentum model.

I'd recommend avoiding the momentum model unless you have a portfolio of **at least £10,000 or $2,000**.[275] At this point the benefits of using the model comfortably exceed the extra costs, as long as you're using my suggested levels for the No-Trade-Zone width and Minimum-Trade-Size.

The yield model is a little slower and cheaper, although remember that figure 39 underestimates the real likely cost of using the yield model, because in this specific example bonds and stocks spend long periods of time looking relatively cheap or expensive.

---

275. As usual all of these figures assume you are paying £6 and $1 minimum brokerage commission. If your minimum commission is higher you need to multiply them by the ratio of your commission and the levels I use.

I reckon that the yield model is also too expensive for the very smallest investors. I wouldn't use it unless your portfolio is at least **£7,500 or $1,500**.

How often?

We can now return to the question of **how often** reweighting should occur: how frequently you should check your Current Weights to see if they are out of line with the Target Weights, then using the No-Trade-Zone and Minimum-Trade-Size to check if a trade is justified. One advantage of using these techniques is that more frequent reweighting will not increase your costs.

Generally the longer you wait for a reweighting the larger your trades will be, leading to slightly higher costs for institutional investors who have to worry about market impact. If you have the resources to do it then large institutional portfolios should be rebalanced daily. Of course this doesn't mean they will trade every day since most of the time portfolio weights will be inside the No-Trade-Zone. Monthly or quarterly rebalancing is also acceptable.

However, retail investors can rebalance less frequently; as they are more likely to be constrained by Minimum-Trade-Sizes they will do relatively few trades in any case. Annual rebalances are perfectly adequate.

When to substitute and when not to

The previous section dealt entirely with **reweighting**: any situation when you want to continue owning all the assets in your portfolio but with different cash weights. However there are also scenarios where you want to completely dispose of an existing asset, and **substitute** it with a new purchase. To recap, these are: (1) Changes to model derived selections of stocks within sectors (i.e. highest dividend yields), (2) takeovers where you are paid in stock, and (3) new and better (cheaper, or more diversifying) ETFs appearing on the market.

Changes to model selection of stocks

Back in chapter fourteen I proposed getting exposure to a particular sector within each country by choosing the highest yielding stock (page 346); or, if you have the funds, the two highest yielding stocks (or three, or four...).[276]

So what happens when you've bought a firm that subsequently drops to second place (or third, or fourth...) in the yield rankings within its sector, either because the dividend has been cut (bad news) or the price has gone up (better news). Should you buy the share that now outranks it and cut the old stock out of your portfolio?

---

276. This also applies if you're using another method for ranking stocks, as I discuss in Appendix C, page 500.

Again this is another example of a trade-off between a known cost and an uncertain benefit. To evaluate this decision you first need to calculate the cost of doing the substitution. For example, if the relevant stock forms 5% of your portfolio, then on a $100,000 portfolio you'd do two trades of $5,000 (a sell, and a buy). Referring to table 71 earlier in the chapter, this would cost $7.

What benefit do you expect to get from switching to a higher yielding stock? To start with you should calculate the expected improvement in yield. For example, going from 4.5% to 4.7% is a 0.2% pickup. On a $5,000 position that translates to $10 a year in additional dividends.

Next you need to work out the value of receiving the extra $10 dividend every year, for the period of time you expect to be holding the new stock.

CONCEPT: DISCOUNTING AND UNCERTAINTY

Back in chapter five I said you should divide by 20 to translate any initial costs of purchasing stocks or funds into an annual rate. You can also do the reverse calculation: multiply an annual cost by 20 to find its present value.

But you know costs with a high degree of accuracy; the same can't be said of future benefits. To work out the value of future dividends you need to factor in uncertainty.

For dividend yields my research suggests dividing by a factor of 5 will reflect the uncertainty involved. So, for example, I'd be pretty confident that an increase in dividends from 4% to 5%, which is a 1% improvement, would improve expected future returns by 1% ÷ 5 = 0.2% a year. This has a present value of 0.2% × 20 = 4%.

This relatively high discount for uncertainty isn't because future dividend payments are extremely uncertain – they're actually more predictable than future stock returns. Instead it reflects how much confidence you can have in using the dividend yield model to forecast total stock returns.

Going back to the example, a $10 a year expected improvement in dividends adjusted for uncertainty equates to one-fifth of that: $2 a year. Then multiplying by 20 to convert it to an initial value, equals $40. This comfortably exceeds the up front cost of $7 that we calculated earlier, so the substitution is easily worth doing.[277]

---

277. If you're using your own methods to pick stocks you'll have to adapt this technique. See Appendix C, page 502.

What happens if we work backwards to find the smallest yield improvement that would justify trading? In this case it's less than 0.05%.[278] That kind of yield improvement could be a result of a stock yielding 5% moving in price by just 1%. If you have several candidate stocks with very similar yields you could end up wanting to replace your stocks every few hours!

For this reason I'd recommend checking yields and doing substitutions relatively infrequently: every six months or annually, regardless of how often you check to see if a portfolio reweighting is required.[279]

Stock takeovers

Suppose you own shares in US retailer Costco. Imagine that Costco then gets taken over by Walmart, and you're paid with Walmart stock. Have you lost any portfolio diversification? No, the acquiring firm is in the same sector (consumer staples) and country (US) as the existing company. Of course if you're using dividend yields to select your equities then you should refer back to the previous section to see if the Walmart shares you now hold should be replaced with a higher yielding substitute.

However, what if Costco gets bought out by eBay, the online auction site, having decided it needs a physical presence? As the new stock is in a different sector you now have an unbalanced portfolio. If you only previously had one stock in each US sector then your portfolio now has zero exposure in the consumer staples, and twice the exposure in technology.[280]

In theory you should now sell the eBay shares you have picked up in the takeover, and replace them with a new firm in the original consumer staples sector. The new firm should be selected using the same method that you used to select the original share.[281]

It's straightforward to calculate how much it will cost to sell the shares you've acquired through a takeover, and buy something more suitable. But the benefits of recovering the correct sector diversification are harder to quantify, since they depend on the return correlations of the old and new firm with the rest of your portfolio. I calculate that the likely improvement in annual geometric return is around 0.05%[282] per proportion of the portfolio that is reallocated from the overweight back to the newly underweight sector.

---

278. Divide the cost of $7 by 20 (to get an annual cost) then multiply by 5 (to reflect uncertainty), which gives us $1.75; the minimum annual yield pickup. $1.75 divided by $5,000 equates to 0.04%.

279. Also to make sure the comparison is fair you should only compare stocks which are all priced *cum-dividend* or all priced *ex-dividend*.

280. Similarly, if Costco gets bought by UK retailer Tesco your sector exposure will be unchanged, but you will now be slightly overweight the UK and underweight the US.

281. If you're following my advice this would either be the largest firm remaining in the sector, or the firm with the highest dividend yield.

282. Assuming inter sector correlations of 0.8 and intra sector correlations of 0.9; with equal weights across the portfolio. These relatively high correlation values account for the uncertainty involved in estimating diversification benefits. The exact improvement will depend on the precise weights in the

So, for example, suppose you had a $1,000 stake in Costco, which gets bought by eBay. You decide that the best replacement firm in the consumer staples sector would be health junkie nirvana Whole Foods. Selling $1,000 worth of eBay and buying Whole Foods will cost $1.50 for the buy and the same for the sell; $3 in total (from table 71, page 396).

The annual improvement in return will be 0.05% × $1,000 = $0.50, and if I multiply this by 20 to get an equivalent up front benefit I get $0.50 × 20 = $10. This is much higher than the initial cost of $3: you should not delay in dumping eBay and purchasing Whole Foods.

Better, more diversifying, funds

A nice problem to have is the appearance of new and better ETFs. In this section I concentrate on funds which are better because they bring more diversification to the portfolio. For now I'll assume both the current and new fund have the same level of costs. I consider funds with different cost levels in the next section of this chapter.

New fund replaces part of old fund allocation

If you've read part two recently you may remember that I was unable to find ETFs for every country's equity market. For example, there are currently no ETFs tracking Portugal available in the UK – although they do exist in the US. Exposure to sunny Iberia is only possible for UK investors via a Spanish equity ETF.

Now suppose that a new UK listed Portuguese ETF was launched. Should you sell some of your Spanish ETF holding to buy the newly available Portuguese ETF? From portfolio 41 (page 240) using my handcrafted weights, 20% of the Iberian peninsula allocation should be in Portugal, with the remainder still in Spain.

This isn't a total substitution: it's a **reweighting**. So you can use the No-Trade-Zone method from earlier in the chapter. If Spain currently has a 5% cash weight in your portfolio, then the new Target Weights would be 80% × 5% = 4% in Spain and 80% × 5% = 1% in Portugal.

If, for example, you had a No-Trade-Zone that was 1% wide then the respective zones would be 3.5% - 4.5% in Spain, and 0.5% - 1.5% in Portugal. This implies you should buy 0.5% of Portugal, funded by selling 0.5% of Spain, resulting in new cash weights of 0.5% in Portugal and 4.5% in Spain that are on the edge of their respective zones. Subsequently over the next few years you'd probably trade more, and gradually get closer to the right weights.

---

portfolio, and the change in correlation patterns between the old and the new asset(s). However, 0.05% is a conservative value which is reasonable to use in most circumstances. This assumes we are maximising geometric returns. Technically speaking, investors who are maximising Sharpe Ratio would see a slightly higher benefit, but it's better to be conservative.

New fund or funds entirely replaces old fund

Now suppose instead that you're replacing one ETF entirely with one or more new funds which brings more diversification to the portfolio. For a complete substitution you need to work out how much improvement in diversification you are likely to get adjusted for uncertainty, measure this using the expected increase in annual geometric mean of returns, and then apply the **rule of 20** to see if it covers your initial costs.

This is complicated because it depends on which type of fund is being replaced. If, for example, you're replacing an ETF that covers the financial sector in France with an equal weighted basket of French banks and asset managers, then there will be minimal improvement in geometric returns. In contrast you'll get a big improvement in expected returns if you replace a single global market capitalisation weighted equity ETF with a diversified portfolio of country ETFs.

Table 73 requires some explanation. Each row shows a particular type of diversifying substitution trade that you can do in the left-hand column. The middle column shows a conservative estimate for the annual benefit for each portion of your portfolio that is being rebalanced.[283]

The right-hand column shows the up front value of this benefit after multiplying by 20. This is also the breakeven level – if initial costs are higher than this value then it isn't worth doing the substituting trades.

TABLE 73: BREAKEVEN COSTS WHEN SUBSTITUTING FOR MORE DIVERSIFIED ASSETS

	Annual benefit	Breakeven cost
1) Global bond only portfolio to MC bonds & MC equities	0.77%	15.4%
2) Global stock only portfolio to MC bonds & MC equities	Depends	N/A
3) Single stock to global MC equity portfolio	2.9%	58%
4) Single sector to global MC equity portfolio	2.4%	48%
5) Single country to global MC equity or bond portfolio	1.7%	34%
6) MC global equities to HC weighted DEV/EM	0.24%	4.8%
7) MC global bonds to HC weighted DEV/EM	0.12%	2.4%

---

283. These are approximations, the exact benefits will vary slightly depending on what the precise handcrafted weights and correlations are in the relevant portfolios. Technical note: I've done this by using correlations estimated at the 75% confidence interval.

	Annual benefit	Breakeven cost
8) MC DEV or EM equities to HC weighted regions	0.05%	1.0%
9) MC DEV or EM bonds to HC weighted regions	0.03%	0.6%
10) MC region equities to HC weighted countries	0.06%	1.2%
11) MC region bonds to HC weighted countries	0.02%	0.4%
12) MC equity country to HC sectors (ETF or stocks)	0.03%	0.60%
13) MC equity sector ETF to HC individual equities	0.02%	0.4%
14) MC DEV / EM bonds to HC EM/DEV bond types/credits	0.02%	0.4%
15) Regional MC Bonds to HC regional bond types/credits	0.02%	0.4%
16) Country MC Bonds to HC country types/credits	0.02%	0.4%

Table shows the annual benefit, and maximum initial cost (annual benefit multiplied by twenty) for which a particular type of incremental diversification makes sense. All figures assume you are maximising geometric mean. MC: Market capitalisation weights. HC: Handcrafted weights.

The different rows refer to the following:

Global bond only portfolio to MC bonds & MC equities	Selling: A portfolio of bonds. Buying: A portfolio containing an ETF with market cap weighted global equity exposure, and a second ETF with global bond exposure.*
Global stock only portfolio to MC bonds & MC equities	Selling: A portfolio containing only stocks. Buying: A portfolio containing an ETF with market cap weighted global equity exposure, and a second ETF with global bond exposure. A 10% risk weighted allocation to bonds won't affect the geometric mean; beyond that the geometric mean will be reduced.
Single stock to global MC equity portfolio	Selling: A portfolio consisting of a single stock in one country. Buying: A market cap weighted global stock ETF.

Single sector to global MC equity portfolio	Selling: A portfolio consisting of shares in only one sector and one country, e.g. US tech stocks. Buying: A market cap weighted global stock ETF.
Single country to global MC equity or bond portfolio	Selling: A portfolio exposed to stocks (or bonds) in only one country, e.g. US stocks (or bonds). Buying: A market cap weighted global stock (or bond) ETF.
MC global bonds/ equities to HC weighted DEV/ EM	Selling: A market cap weighted exposure to global stocks (or bonds). Buying: A global emerging market and a global developed market equity (or bond) fund using my suggested handcrafted weights of 25% risk weighting in emerging markets.
MC DEV or EM bonds/equities to HC weighted regions	Selling: A market cap weighted global emerging market or developed market equity (or bond) fund. Buying: Regional ETFs covering the emerging or developed market, using my suggested handcrafted weights.
MC region bonds/equities to HC weighted countries	Selling: A market cap weighted regional ETF covering part of the emerging or developed market equity (or bond) market. Buying: A set of country ETFs covering the same region, using my suggested handcrafted weights. You will see similar benefits with equal weights.
MC equity country to HC sectors (ETF or stocks)	Selling: A market cap weighted fund covering the equities in a single country. Buying: A set of sector ETFs covering the same country or at least one individual stock per sector.**
MC equity sector ETF to EW individual equities	Selling: A market cap weighted fund covering the equities in a single country and sector (e.g. UK health care stocks). Buying: At least ten individual equities covering the same sector, with equal weights.
MC DEV/EM bonds to HC EM/ DEV bond types/ credits	Selling: A market cap weighted global emerging market or developed market bond fund. Buying: Multiple funds covering the emerging or developed bond market, but with different bond types and credit ratings.
Regional MC Bonds to HC regional bond types/credits	Selling: A market cap weighted bond fund covering a particular developed or emerging market region. Buying: Multiple funds covering the relevant emerging or developed region, but with different bond types and credit ratings.

Country MC Bonds to HC country types/ credits	Selling: A market cap weighted bond fund covering a particular country.
	Buying: Multiple funds covering the country, but with different bond types and credit ratings.

* This improvement assumes you put half your portfolio by risk weighting in equities (maximum Sharpe Ratio portfolio). For the maximum geometric mean and compromise portfolios, the improvement will be even larger. Including alternatives would add even more diversification, but to be conservative I've ignored that here. ** In the table the benefit shown for this switch is 0.03% a year. In chapter six (page 164) I showed that for the Canadian TSX 60 it was around 0.04%. However, remember the Canada index is relatively extreme in terms of sector diversification, so the benefits of getting away from market cap weighting are a little higher than average.

Notice that some of these rows apply to entire portfolios, whereas others will only be applicable to part of a portfolio. The benefits shown apply only to the proportion of your portfolio that you are considering substituting.

Let's look at an example. Suppose you have a $1,000 allocation to a single regional ETF for Australia and New Zealand, which you plan to replace with two ETFs, one for each country. To keep things simple let's assume the two new funds are equally weighted. Looking at table 71 (page 396), selling the regional ETF position of $1,000 will cost $1.50, and rebuying two ETFs of $500 each will cost $1.25 per trade; altogether the total cost is $4.

The relevant row in table 73 is row 10: 'MC region equities to HC weighted countries'. The improvement in return is 0.06%, which multiplied by 20 is 1.2% worth of benefit, and $1,000 × 1.2% = $12. This is quite a bit higher than the total cost of $4 so this switch is worth doing.

You can add up benefits from different rows if you're doing multiple degrees of diversification simultaneously. Suppose, for example, you own a global equity ETF with market cap weightings, and you plan to buy country ETFs with handcrafted weights.

As table 74 shows, this takes you through three different levels of diversification. First you go from a global equity ETF to owning a developed and emerging market ETF with handcrafted weights. Then you split each of those into regional exposures. Finally the regional holdings are put into individual countries. In practice you wouldn't do these separately, but as a single trade: selling the global equity ETF, and then buying the individual country ETFs.

Adding all this up the total benefit comes to 0.35%, this accumulates to a benefit of 7% over the life of the trade (using the rule of 20), so the trades are worth doing if their total cost is less than 7%.

TABLE 74: EXAMPLE OF BREAKEVEN COSTS FOR MULTIPLE DIVERSIFICATIONS

	Annual benefit	Breakeven cost
MC global equities to HC weighted DEV/EM (row 6)	0.24%	4.8%
MC DEV or EM equities to HC weighted regions (row 8)	0.05%	1%
MC region equities to HC weighted countries (row 10)	0.06%	1.2%
Total	0.35%	7%

Row numbers shown refer to table 73.

Cheaper assets

Sometimes new funds appear which don't bring better diversification to your portfolio, but which have lower annual management fees; whilst annoyingly funds which improve diversification sometimes cost more.

How should you calculate the benefits of switching between funds if the old and new funds have different costs? To work out the future cost benefits of switching between funds with different costs you simply multiply the cost differential between funds by 20. Of course if the new fund is more expensive then the value of switching will be negative.

You should then include the up front benefit from diversification as calculated above; and then compare the total benefit to the initial trading costs.

Up front diversification benefit = 20 × annual diversification benefit

Total benefit = (up front div. benefit) + 20 × (cost old fund − cost new fund)

Substitute the fund if: Total benefit > initial trading cost

Let's return to the example I used a moment ago: a $1,000 allocation to a single ETF for Australia and New Zealand, which we plan to replace with two ETFs for different countries. The switching cost was $4 (0.4% of $1,000), and the diversification benefit had a present value of $12 (1.2% of $1,000).

Now suppose that the old fund has a management fee of 0.1%, but the new funds have annual fees of 0.1% (Australia) and 0.3% (New Zealand). Because you're buying these in equal weights the weighted average management fee will be 0.2%. There is no reason to believe that the other types of costs associated with these particular funds will be different so you can disregard invisible costs like trading costs within the fund.

Using the rule of 20 the extra annual cost has an equivalent initial value of 0.1% × 20 = 2%, which in cash terms is 2% × \$1,000 = \$20. So now the benefit of switching is negative (since the additional cost of \$20 outweighs the \$12 diversification benefit).

Let's check this using the formula above:

Total benefit = diversification benefit + 20 × (cost old fund – cost new fund)

Total benefit = 1.2% + 20 × (0.1% – 0.2%) = 1.2% – 2% = –0.8%

The higher management fee means this switch is no longer worth doing, even before you consider the initial trading costs you'd have to pay.

Tax considerations

Not every investor has to worry about tax. Many institutions hold their funds inside tax exempt trusts. Retail investors can stash their money in tax protected wrappers like 401Ks and IRAs in the US, or ISAs and SIPPs in the UK.

But those who exceed annual or lifetime contribution limits will be subject to tax on some or all of their investments. If this applies to you then this section of the chapter will help you legally minimise the amount of tax you're paying.[284]

Tax law is complicated, different for every country, and always changing. The few pages I've written here cannot possibly be an exhaustive guide to the subject. However there are some general characteristics of tax systems which I assume you can exploit:

1. When it comes to rebalancing, it's capital gains tax that is relevant. Sell something at a profit, and you have to cough up some of your gain to the US IRS or UK HMRC.

2. If you make a loss you can probably offset this against your profits.

3. Normally there is an annual tax free exemption on net profits.

4. Often tax will be lower on investments that have been held for longer.

5. Taxes are also due on dividends. There may be an annual tax free allowance before you start incurring this.

6. There are tax sheltered accounts which do not incur capital gains or dividend tax liabilities. But there are annual limits on how much can be contributed to these.

7. Some special types of assets are tax free.

---

284. This might seem like a morally dubious position but if your conscience needs salving you can always give plenty of money to charity instead.

Net profits and losses, and use your exemption up

Most tax codes offer an annual tax free exemption from capital gains tax, and the ability to net off profits and losses. These are generous annual gifts from the tax authorities that should not be squandered or ignored. Normally when you're considering reweighting or substitution trades you'll have some which would generate capital gains, and others capital losses. With care you can match these trades up to minimise, or even eliminate, taxes.

Take tax into account when considering substitution

It's relatively simple to work out the effect of tax when you are considering a series of substitutions. Like switching costs, and unlike future returns, taxes are certain. All you need to do is include the tax that would be liable on a particular set of trades within your cost versus benefit analysis:

Benefit = (up front div. benefit) + 20 × (cost old fund − cost new fund)

Substitute the fund if: benefit > initial trading cost + tax due on switch

Consider the example I used earlier in the chapter: a $1,000 allocation to a single ETF for Australia and New Zealand, which we plan to replace with two ETFs for different countries. The switching cost was $4 (0.4% of $1,000), and the diversification benefit had a present value of $12 (1.2% of $1,000). Now suppose that the new fund has a management fee of 0.1% versus 0.5% in the old fund; but switching will incur $100 in capital gains tax when we sell the old fund (10% of $1,000).

Benefit = 1.2% + 20 × (0.5% − 0.1%) = 9.2%

Substitute the fund if: 9.2% > 0.4% + 10%

Clearly this trade will make no sense regardless of how much we pay in trading costs; the hefty tax bill has overwhelmed the potential savings in fund management fees and diversification benefits.

Don't forget to net off losses and profits, and calculate the tax at the marginal rate due after any annual exemption.

Warning: never let the tax tail wag the investment dog. Only consider trades that already make sense because they provide more diversification and/or a future saving in annual costs. Don't do trades purely for tax purposes that wouldn't otherwise provide any net benefit.

Take tax into account when reweighting

Unlike with substitutions, there is no simple cost benefit analysis method for potential reweighting trades. To be conservative you should assume that any tax payable will always exceed the benefits of reweighting. I recommend that you should **never do any reweighting trades that will generate a capital gains tax liability**.

Selling to fund tax free accounts

If you don't have enough spare cash to maximise your annual contribution to tax free accounts is it worth selling taxable assets to fund them? The benefits of this are obvious: not having to pay dividends and capital gains taxes in the future. Unfortunately it will involve paying right now in the form of trading costs and possibly capital gains tax if you sell positions that are showing a profit.

The future benefits of holding tax free investments are incredibly hard to quantify. They depend on the precise tax rules, your returns, and your strategy for buying and selling.

I've done some research on this subject and my conclusion is that it's fine to sell and rebuy to fund tax free accounts if you only have to pay transaction costs; as long as your trades are larger than my suggested minimum trade size[285] for rebalancing: £250 or $150. However, if you also have to pay any capital gains tax on your sales then I'm not confident you will be able to recoup this in future benefits.

Split up your investments

It's often more tax efficient to spread your investments around rather than keep them all in one place.[286] Obviously you should keep as many investments as possible in tax exempt wrappers, and gradually add to those over time to the maximum extent possible. If you still have some taxable investments then you should choose carefully what you put in your taxable, and tax exempt, accounts.

If there is a part of your portfolio that you're more likely to be actively trading then keep that inside your tax sheltered IRA or ISA. For example, if you have individual stocks which you've selected using the dividend yield model then it's better to keep those in a tax free account, since you'll be regularly rotating them as yields change. Choosing stocks by yield ranking tends to generate capital gains since it is biased towards selling stocks that have risen in price.[287]

Tax rules don't account for volatility – probably a good thing as they're complex enough already. More volatile instruments like stocks are more likely to generate larger taxable

---

285. As usual these values assume you are paying £6 or $1 as a minimum brokerage fee. If you are paying more the values should be multiplied by the ratio between your minimum fee and the figures I am using.

286. This also reduces potential losses if your broker bites the dust since there are normally limits on the compensation available when this occurs.

287. This assumes that you pay the same brokerage commissions inside an ISA or IRA. Brokers often charge more inside tax sheltered vehicles; however the tax savings from keeping stocks inside an ISA or IRA will probably be larger than the extra brokerage fees unless the minimum commissions are extremely steep – above $30 or £30 per trade.

gains when you rebalance. It's better to keep them inside taxable shelters if you can, with safer assets like bond ETFs and cash outside.[288]

Another strategy is to keep part of a given position in a tax sheltered account, and the rest in an ordinary taxable account. If you have to sell some of your holding, and this would realize a capital gain, then you sell out of the tax free account. On the other hand if the sale would crystallise a loss then sell the position in your taxable accounts. You can then use the tax loss to net against profits on other trades. This only makes sense for larger investors since smaller traders will want to avoid paying two sets of fixed trading costs for the same holding.

Splitting investments across you and your spouse, or other family members, is also a good way to minimise taxes if each has a separate tax free allowance. For example, a £15,000 profit on a sale of shares that would currently attract capital gains tax in the UK would become two separate gains of £7,500 if shared between spouses, which would be tax free assuming no other profits were made. You will also get more flexibility for netting profits and losses.

Splitting can also reduce taxes on dividends if each person has an annual tax free allowance for dividend payments. You can also reduce dividend taxes by putting higher yielding equities inside tax sheltered accounts, and leaving lower yielding assets like bonds outside.

Summary

Why do you need to rebalance	Rebalancing is necessary because of (a) price changes and other external events like takeovers, and (b) because you decide to change your Target Weights.
Reweighting trades	A **reweighting** trade is a partial change in position to get your portfolio weights closer to your Target Weight. Adjust your position so it is at the edge of the **No-Trade-Zone**, assuming the resulting trade is larger than the **Minimum-Trade-Size**. Set the No-Trade-Zone at half the average position size. Set the Minimum-Trade-Size at the larger of 0.1% of your portfolio and £250 or $150.*

288. This assumes that you pay the same tax on dividend payments as interest received on cash. This advice would be incorrect in a country with very perverse tax laws. For example let's assume a dividend yield of 5% and interest on cash of 1%, and also assume that the investor does not have to pay capital gains tax. If dividends were taxed at a marginal rate of 8% (0.4% a year as a proportion of investment value), and cash interest at 50% (0.5% a year), then it would make sense to keep cash inside an ISA or IRA, and leave stocks outside. But these tax rates are highly unrealistic. In real life it almost always makes sense to leave higher yielding assets inside tax shelters.

Substitution trades	**Substitutions** are the complete replacement of one asset with another. To see if they make sense compare the initial trading costs with the present value of the diversification benefit plus any effect on annual holding costs.
Taxation	The effects of tax can completely change the cost-benefit analysis of each set of potential rebalancing trades. You need to consider any tax implications when deciding which trades to do and when to do them.

* These values assume you are paying £6 or $1 as a minimum brokerage fee. If you are paying more the values should be multiplied by the ratio between your minimum fee and the figures I am using. For example if you're paying $5 commission you should use a minimum trade size of $150 × ($5 ÷ $1) = $750.

CHAPTER SEVENTEEN

Portfolio Maintenance

THE PROCESS OF REGULAR **PORTFOLIO MAINTENANCE** IS extremely important. Assets that are overweight need to be sold and underweight assets should be topped up.

In this chapter I show how to apply the theoretical methods from the last chapter in a practical way to keep your smart portfolio well maintained. I explain the process you should go through every month, quarter or year to decide what needs selling, and what should be bought.

Chapter overview

Annual review	Checks you should make on your portfolio every year.
Reacting to external events	Rebalancing decisions that have to be made in response to events happening in the market, such as takeovers.
Period portfolio reweighting	Regular checking of your portfolio weights to make sure they are in line. This could be done annually, monthly, weekly, or even daily.
Tax implications of portfolio maintenance	Deciding what trades to do and which to skip in light of any tax you might have to pay.
Portfolio maintenance example	An illustration of how to do annual portfolio maintenance.

The next chapter is about portfolio repair – a more drastic process than mere maintenance.

Annual review

There are some tasks that only need doing annually, regardless of how often you are rebalancing your portfolio.

Check for more diversifying collective funds

New ETFs come out all the time. It's worth checking periodically to see if you can utilise them to introduce more diversification into your portfolio. You may also see a new fund with a lower management charge than an existing product.

If there are one or more diversifying funds **entirely** replacing your existing fund then you should treat this as a potential **substitution**. Sometimes a more diversifying fund will be **partly** replacing an existing one. If that's the case then you need to modify your optimal portfolio weights. This is a potential portfolio **reweighting**.

Check for cheaper funds

Similarly you should check to see if a passive fund you own can be replaced with a cheaper version, charging lower fees for the same product. This is a potential **substitution**.

Use the techniques on page 416 to decide if the substitution is worth it.

Active fund monitoring

If you have active funds in your portfolio you need to make sure you're still happy with them. Rerun the statistical tests in chapter fifteen to see if their performance still justifies their inclusion. Similarly you might have a watch list of potential replacement funds whose performance you are monitoring.

Check for changes in stock selection

If you're selecting one or more stocks from each sector using my dividend yield model, or a similar valuation metric, then you need to periodically check to see if you still own the highest yielding stock. Follow the process on page 408 to see if it's worth **substituting** any current higher yielders for the stocks you already own.

Reacting to external events

The outside world won't wait patiently until you're ready to do a regular review of your portfolio. You have to react to events as they unfold.

Stock takeovers

If you own a firm which is taken over in exchange for stock in the acquirer you need to consider whether the new firm is one you'd still want to own. Use the method on page 410 to decide if you should hang on to the shares you'll end up with, or **substitute** them for something else.

Sometimes in a takeover you'll be given the option of taking cash or stock. If you're going to sell the acquirer's stock anyway, then taking the cash option will save you some commission. However, you should think carefully about the tax implications of each option: taking cash will generate an immediate capital gain, whilst being paid with stock will allow you to time the sale yourself and perhaps reduce the tax payable.

Cash takeovers, bankruptcies, fund delisting

If one of your holdings is taken over in exchange for cash this will leave you with an unbalanced portfolio: too much cash, and not enough of the missing stock. A fund delisting[289] will also result in an involuntary sale of part of your portfolio. Similarly a bankruptcy will also leave you with unbalanced portfolio weights, though without the consolation prize of surplus cash.

You should consider how to replace the missing stock or fund. This means finding the largest or highest yielding stock in a sector you don't currently own depending on your selection criteria, or the cheapest remaining fund that gives you the exposure you need.

In all cases you should consider bringing forward **a periodic reweighting** of your portfolio.

Periodic portfolio reweighting

On a periodic basis you should think about **reweighting** your portfolio.

Institutional investors usually rebalance monthly or quarterly after investment committee meetings. Larger investors with full-time portfolio managers may also want to rebalance monthly, weekly or even daily.

A daily rebalancing using these techniques doesn't mean you will actually do a trade every single day. But it means your average trade will be smaller. For institutional investors, doing many small trades intermittently throughout the month is a much better strategy than doing fewer large trades at the beginning of each month, especially when other funds will be trying to do the same.

---

289. Fund delistings tend to be predictable. An ETF where the AUM is low and falling may indicate an imminent fund closure – it isn't economic to manage very small funds due to fixed costs. Sometimes an ETF will start trading at a significant premium or a discount to the underlying assets. This is a sign that the ETF is an 'orphan' which is no longer being properly managed.

Retail investors should rebalance at least annually to avoid their weights drifting too far out of line, and ensure they can make best use of their annual tax allowances.[290] I'd avoid waiting until the very end of the tax year, since that is when everyone else will be trading for the same reasons; this will create weird distortions in prices. Instead choose a particular month in the middle of the year and stick to it.

It may also be worth doing an additional reweighting earlier in the year if it will generate a tax loss which will be useful later.

First, work out the Target Weights you would like to have (i.e. your optimal cash weights), and the Current Weights implied by your current holdings, share prices, and exchange rates.

Then compare your Target Weights and Current Weights. Remember you should only do a reweighting trade if it is outside the No-Trade-Zone.

You should normally trade to the edge of the zone. However, if you are doing more buying than selling then it makes sense to trade closer to the middle of the zone rather than be left with un-invested cash. The same applies if you are doing more selling than buying, and don't want to be short of money.

Finally, any reweighting trade must be greater than the Minimum-Trade-Size.

Tax implications of portfolio maintenance

You should now have a list of potential **substitution trades** (matched sells and buys) and a list of potential **reweighting trades** (sales and purchases that do not need to be matched). Each of these trades has already been justified with a cost-benefit analysis, without considering tax. If you are investing only through tax sheltered trusts or accounts like ISAs or 401(k)s, with no need to worry about capital gains or dividend tax, then you can go ahead and do all the trades that you like.

Otherwise you should follow the process in this section to do your trades in the most tax efficient way. I'm assuming here that you can net losses against gains, and that you have an annual tax free allowance for profits which you can accrue without incurring tax. Tax rules can be complex and idiosyncratic so make sure you fully understand the implications of any potential trades.

Do loss making sales or those without tax implications

Do all selling trades that generate a tax loss first, or which are inside tax-free accounts. It does not matter if these are substitution or reweighting sales.

---

290. It's sometimes possible to carry forward losses into future years, but this kind of accountancy trickery is way beyond my understanding and the scope of this book.

Because they generate a tax benefit it is worth making all your reweighting sales as large as possible, by trading to the far end of the No-Trade-Zone. You'd normally sell down to the closest upper edge of the zone but if this generates a tax loss then it's better to trade to the lower edge.

The best substitution sales that generate a profit, up to your tax free allowance

You now have to look at sales which will generate a taxable profit. Substitution trades have the largest benefit, so you should do these first. For each substitution trade you should already have worked out the net benefit after any initial trading costs. Do the trades with the largest net benefit first.

At this stage only do as many substitution trades as you can without generating net profits above your tax free allowance.

Remaining substitution sales, considering tax costs

If you can do all your substitutions without exhausting your tax free allowance then skip this step.

From now on any selling trade will penalise you with a tax liability. Work through the remaining list of sales in the substitution category, recalculating their net benefit but this time include the tax charge that would arise on each one. You should then do any substitution trades which still have a net positive benefit.

At this point you should have a list of successful substitution sales; and perhaps some sales that you have been unable to do. Make a list of the substitution buys that match each successful sale. Discard the buys which match sales you couldn't make; you won't be doing these trades.

If possible, any reweighting sales up to your tax free allowance

You should only do sales for the purposes of reweighting if you have some of your tax free allowance remaining. Do the largest reweighting sales first, since they will have the most impact on your portfolio. If you have some tax-free allowance left then it is okay to do a partial sale to use this up, assuming this trade still meets the minimum trade size requirement, even if this leaves you with a position that is still outside of the no trade zone.

Set aside target cash for withdrawals and fund tax efficient accounts

Before you begin buying you should ensure there is enough cash on hand to meet your cash target for any withdrawals that you have to make. If you don't have sufficient funds then go back and make extra sales that will generate the necessary extra cash. Do the sales that will generate the lowest tax impact and see if you can reduce your position whilst staying within the no trade zone around the new optimal cash weight. If this isn't possible then leave your final position as close as possible to the edge of the zone.

You should also ensure you can make best use of tax efficient accounts by funding them to their maximum annual limits. Do not do any additional selling purely to fund tax free accounts if this will generate a taxable gain; you are unlikely to get this money back in the form of lower future tax bills. Unless you are a very large investor it is better to sell out of entire positions rather than split them between taxable and tax-free accounts. Try and sell out of higher return assets like equities that are better held inside tax-free wrappers.

Do all necessary transfers of cash to tax-free accounts to fully utilise your annual allowances before making any purchases.

Buying within tax free accounts

You are now ready to start buying. Start by purchasing in your tax free account.

In a tax-free account you will ideally be buying higher volatility, higher yielding assets like equities (particularly emerging market equities) or riskier bonds. First you will need to do **transfer trades**, where you've sold a position in a taxable account to fund a purchase of the same position in a tax-free account. Do the largest trades first.

Next do any buying which matches **substitution** sales that you have completed, again largest first. Finally, do purchases for **reweighting** purposes.

It's okay to adjust the size of your buys, as long as your final position remains within the No-Trade-Zone. This could be necessary to make sure you have the right amount of cash after all your trading is completed. You should increase the size of your purchases if you would otherwise end up with excess cash, and reduce them if you would have end up with insufficient funds. However, make sure all trades are above the Minimum-Trade-Size.

Do not leave any residual cash in your tax free account.

Buying within taxable accounts

In accounts where you have to pay tax you should be buying low volatility, lower yielding, assets – like bonds. Focus first on large substitution buy trades where you've already done the matching sale, then on smaller matched substitution trades before moving on to reweighting trades; again doing the largest buys first.

Rebalancing example

Do you remember UK-based investor Patricia, from chapters thirteen and fourteen? She was a young banker who had £25,000 to invest. Below, I use her as an example of how to perform an annual portfolio maintenance example. US investors can still read this example, since the general procedure will be the same. Investors who don't have to worry about tax can skip all mentions of that unfortunate subject and focus on the rest of the rebalancing process.

Initial portfolio

I've reproduced Patricia's initial portfolio after applying forecasting model multipliers in table 75. I've also included the initial share prices of each ETF, and worked out the number of shares to buy.

TABLE 75: STARTING ALLOCATION FOR PORTFOLIO MAINTENANCE EXAMPLE USING FORECASTING MODEL

	Risk weight target	Vol.	Cash weight A	Cash value B = £25K × A	Account type	Share price C	FX rate D	Number of shares approx: B × (C × D)	Risk weight actual
US equities	6.9%	15%	5.8%	£1,450	Tax free	$200.5	0.82	9	5.9%
Canada equities	11.4%	15%	9.6%	£2,400	Tax free	£34.33	1	71	9.8%
UK equities	4.2%	15%	3.5%	£875	Taxable	£6.86	1	124	3.4%
Europe ex-UK	6.8%	15%	5.7%	£1,425	Tax free	€27.48	0.90	59	5.9%
Japan equities	10.5%	15%	8.8%	£2,200	Tax free	£23.70	1	94	8.9%
Asia ex-JP eq.	13.4%	15%	11.2%	£2,800	Tax free	£96.96	1	30	11.7%
EM equities	12.7%	23%	6.9%	£1,725	Tax free	$3.82	0.82	555	7.0%
Dev. govt. bonds	5.5%	6%	11.6%	£2,900	Taxable	$90.39	0.82	37	11.0%
Dev. corp. bonds	6.2%	6.5%	11.9%	£2,975	Taxable	$96.73	0.82	36	11.5%
Dev. HY bonds	3.5%	8%	5.6%	£1,400	Taxable	$96.40	0.82	17	5.4%
EM bonds	5.1%	8%	8%	£2,000	Taxable	$65.56	0.82	36	7.8%
Gold	13.7%	15%	11.5%	£2,875	Tax free	$25.09	0.82	143	11.8%

Table shows risk weights after applying forecasting model multipliers, and the calculation of cash weights and number of shares.

Like all UK investors Patricia has access to a tax-free ISA account[291] which is limited to £15,240 of new investment a year.[292] Remember from earlier in the chapter that ideally you should put high risk, high return assets into tax-free wrappers. There wasn't quite possible for Patricia since her total investment in equities and gold comes to £15,442. She has had to put her smallest equity allocation, for the UK, into a taxable account.

I've adjusted the number of shares slightly to ensure her full ISA allowance is used up, and to make sure there is no un-invested cash. The end result is that Patricia has £15,193 of investments plus just over £4 of cash in the ISA account, having paid £42 of commissions (seven trades at £6 each). In her taxable account she has £9,728 in ETFs and £2 in cash.

Annual checks and reaction to corporate actions

Patricia's first job is to check the market for better funds. She finds a new emerging market bond fund AEEM to replace the rather pricey SEML. Instead of 0.5% in management fees this costs just 0.25% a year. Multiplying the annual saving of 0.25% by 20 gives an up front value of 5%, or around £100 of the initial allocation of £2,000. Although Patricia's current holding will have a different value this still comfortably exceeds the up front cost of switching, which from table 72 comes in at around £7.

There have been no fund de-listings. Because Patricia has not bought any individual shares she doesn't have to review share rankings by dividend yield or other metric.

Periodic portfolio reweighting

Work out new optimal risk weights

Now it's time to begin the heavy lifting of working out the new Target Weights. Since the list of funds is basically unchanged the starting point will be the same handcrafted weights as in the initial example, except that Patricia is substituting the new emerging bonds fund for the original. I've reproduced the starting handcrafted weights from chapter 11 in table 76.

---

291. Patricia could use other tax free vehicles like a pension plan, but I'm ignoring these to make this example a bit simpler.
292. This figure is accurate at the time I'm writing this, but will change annually.

TABLE 76: STARTING ALLOCATION

	Asset class A	Emerging or developed B	Region or credit C	Within region D	Risk weight E = A×B×C×D	Volatility	Target Weight (cash)
US equities	80%	75%	33.3%	60%	12%	15%	11.5%
Canada equities	80%	75%	33.3%	40%	8%	15%	7.6%
UK equities	80%	75%	33.3%	20%	4%	15%	3.8%
Europe ex-UK eq.	80%	75%	33.3%	80%	16%	15%	15.3%
Japan equities	80%	75%	33.3%	40%	8%	15%	7.6%
Asia ex-JP Eq.	80%	75%	33.3%	60%	12%	15%	11.5%
EM equities	80%	25%			20%	23%	12.5%
Dev. govt. bonds	10%	75%	40%		3%	6%	7.2%
Dev. corp. bonds	10%	75%	30%		2.3%	6.5%	5%
Dev. HY bonds	10%	75%	30%		2.3%	8%	4%
EM bonds (AEEM)	10%	25%			2.5%	8%	4.5%
Gold	10%				10%	15%	9.6%

Table shows the calculation of portfolio weights. All weights shown are risk weights unless specified otherwise. Values shown are as a proportion of entire portfolio.

The next step is to recalculate the new adjustment factors from the two forecasting models that Patricia has been using: momentum and dividend yield. I won't show the lengthy calculations here since I already presented these in chapter fourteen. Table 77 has the new multipliers.

TABLE 77: NEW COMBINED MULTIPLIERS FROM BOTH MODELS

	Asset class A	Emerging or developed B	Region or credit C	Within region D
US equities	1.2	0.85	0.84	1.21
Canada equities	1.2	0.85	0.84	0.77
UK equities	1.2	0.85	1.14	1.10
Europe ex-UK eq.	1.2	0.85	1.14	0.9
Japan equities	1.2	0.85	0.92	0.68
Asia ex-JP eq.	1.2	0.85	0.92	1.39
EM equities	1.2	1.19		
Dev. govt. bonds	0.9	1.05	1.22	
Dev. corp. bonds	0.9	1.05	0.77	
Dev. HY bonds	0.9	1.05	1.12	
EM bonds	0.9	0.95		
Gold	1.05	1		

Table shows the multipliers to be applied to each asset, based on the yield and momentum forecasting model for each group.

Table 78 shows the allocation with the new multipliers included. Patricia is just using my default volatility figures, so these are unchanged in the Target Weight calculation. She does not need any cash left over after the rebalancing, so the target cash is zero, and the cash weights are set to add up to 100%.

TABLE 78: ALLOCATION WITH NEW MULTIPLIERS

	Asset class A	Emerging or developed B	Region or credit C	Within region D	Risk weight E = A×B×C×D	Volatility	Target Weight (cash weight)
US equities	83.1%	68.2%	29%	70%	11.5%	15%	11.5%
Canada equities	83.1%	68.2%	29%	30%	4.9%	15%	4.9%
UK equities	83.1%	68.2%	39.3%	23%	5.2%	15%	5.2%
Europe ex-UK eq.	83.1%	68.2%	39.3%	77%	17.1%	15%	17.1%
Japan equities	83.1%	68.2%	31.7%	25%	4.4%	15%	4.4%
Asia ex-JP eq.	83.1%	68.2%	31.7%	75%	13.6%	15%	13.6%
EM equities	83.1%	31.8%			26.4%	23%	17.3%
Dev. govt. bonds	7.8%	76.8%	46.3%		2.8%	6%	6.9%
Dev. corp. bonds	7.8%	76.8%	21.9%		1.3%	6.5%	3.0%
Dev. HY bonds	7.8%	76.8%	31.8%		1.9%	8%	3.6%
EM bonds (AEEM)	7.8%	23.2%			1.8%	8%	3.4%
Gold	9.1%				9.1%	15%	9.1%

Table shows the calculation of portfolio weights, original weights from table 76 with multipliers from table 77. All weights shown are risk weights unless specified otherwise. Values shown are as a proportion of entire portfolio.

Work out Current Holdings

The current state of Patricia's portfolio is shown in table 79. The number of shares held is the same as before, but share prices and exchange rates have changed. As well as the investments, she has received dividends in both the taxable and tax-free accounts.

Unfortunately Patricia has not had a good bonus this year. She only has an additional £2,000 of money to invest. This will only form part of her tax free ISA allowance of £15,240; ideally she'd like to generate the rest by selling taxable assets.

Her total portfolio value is now £29,742, including £2,740 in cash.

TABLE 79: CASH WEIGHTS AFTER FIRST YEAR, BUT BEFORE REBALANCING

	Number of shares A	Share price B	FX rate C	Value D = A×B×C	Status	Current Weight D / SUM(D)
US equities	9	$205	0.85	£1,568	Tax free	5.3%
Canada equities	71	£36	1	£2,556	Tax free	8.6%
UK equities	124	£6.50	1	£806	Taxable	2.7%
Europe ex-UK	59	€25.48	0.98	£1,473	Tax free	5.0%
Japan equities	94	£25.00	1	£2,350	Tax free	7.9%
Asia ex-JP eq.	30	£112.32	1	£3,370	Tax free	11.3%
EM equities	555	$3.90	0.85	£1,840	Tax free	6.2%
Dev. govt. bonds	37	$88.17	0.85	£2,773	Taxable	9.3%
Dev. corp. bonds	36	$96.15	0.85	£2,942	Taxable	9.9%
Dev. HY bonds	17	$97.40	0.85	£1,407	Taxable	4.7%
EM bonds	36	$66.00	0.85	£2,020	Taxable	6.8%
Gold	143	$32.06	0.85	£3,897	Tax free	13.1%
Cash tax free				£2,531	Tax free	8.5%
Cash taxable				£209	Taxable	0.7%

Table shows the calculation of current cash weights after new investment cash is paid into the tax-free account.

Calculate reweighting trades

It's now time to consider the reweighting trades. In chapter sixteen I suggested using a No-Trade-Zone width of half the average portfolio weight, and a Minimum-Trade-Size of £250. For Patricia's current portfolio that translates to a width of (100% ÷ 12) ÷ 2 = 4.2% and a minimum trade of 250 ÷ 29742 = 0.9% (rounded up). The resulting trades are shown in table 80.

TABLE 80: REWEIGHTING TRADES ANALYSIS

	Current Weight A	Target Weight B	No trade zone B + / − zone width	Weight at edge of zone C	Trade C − A
US equities	5.3%	11.5%	9.5% – 13.6%	9.5%	+4.3%
Canada equities	8.6%	4.9%	2.8% – 7%	7%	-1.6%
UK equities	2.7%	5.2%	3.1% – 7.3%	3.1%	Too small
Europe ex-UK eq.	5.0%	17.1%	15% – 19.2%	15%	+10%
Japan equities	7.9%	4.4%	2.3% – 6.5%	6.5%	−1.4%
Asia ex-JP eq.	11.3%	13.6%	11.5% – 15.7%	11.5%	Too small
EM equities	6.2%	17.3%	15.2% – 19.3%	15.2%	+9%
Dev. govt. bonds	9.3%	6.9%	4.8% – 9%	9%	Too small
Dev. corp. bonds	9.9%	3.0%	0.9% – 5.1%	5.1%	−4.8%
Dev. HY bonds	4.7%	3.6%	1.5% – 5.7%	4.7%	0%
Gold	13.1%	9.1%	7% – 11.2%	11.2%	−1.9%

All figures are cash weights. Current Weights from table 79. Target weights from table 78. Zone width of (100% ÷ 12) ÷ 2 = 4.2%. Minimum trade size of 250 ÷ 29742 = 0.9% (rounded up). We trade to the edge of the zone. The trade is the difference between the Current Weight and the Target Weight.

Tax and trading

Patricia benefits from a capital gains allowance of around £11,100. For any taxable gains beyond that she will pay 28%.

Do loss making sales or those without tax implications

The reweighting sales in table 81 are all tax exempt. There are no loss-making sales.

TABLE 81: FIRST TRANCHE OF SALES – NO TAX DUE

	Status	Trade £	Trade value
Canada equities	Tax free	−1.6%	£476
Japan equities	Tax free	−1.4%	£416
Gold	Tax free	−1.9%	£565

The best substitution sales that generate a profit, up to your tax free allowance

There is only one substitution sale, shown in table 82.

TABLE 82: SECOND TRANCHE OF SALES – SUBSTITUTIONS

	Status	Old value	New value	Taxable profit	Trade value
EM bonds (old: SEML)	Taxable	£1,935	£2,020	£85	£2,020

Taxable profit equal to difference in old and new values (entire amount sold).

Remaining substitution sales, considering tax costs

There are no more substitution sales.

If possible, any reweighting sales up to your tax free allowance

I said in chapter twelve that reweighting trades should only be done if there are no tax implications (page 418). Do the largest reweighting sales first.

TABLE 83: THIRD TRANCHE OF SALES – TAXABLE REWEIGHTING

	Status	Old value	New value	Taxable profit	Trade value
Dev. corp. bonds	Taxable	£2,855	£2,942	£42	£1,428

Taxable profit based on difference in old and new values, pro-rated by proportion sold (trade value divided by new value).

Set aside target cash for withdrawals and fund tax-efficient accounts

Patricia wants to ensure the best use of tax-efficient accounts by funding them to their maximum annual limits. So far she has put £2000 into her tax-free ISA. There is another £209 in dividends received in her taxable account, and the sales in that account have so far generated £3,436 (£2,020 from EM bonds plus £1,428 from developed corporate bonds, less £12 commissions). She could sell the rest of her taxable investments and still be well below the £15,240 annual investment limit.

This should only be done if there are no taxable implications, but fortunately even with these extra sales Patricia will still be well below the £11,100 capital gains limit, as table 84 shows.

TABLE 84: FOURTH TRANCHE OF SALES – TAXABLE REWEIGHTING

	Status	Old value	New value	Taxable profit	Trade value
UK equities	Taxable	£851	£806	−£45	£806
Dev. govt. bonds	Taxable	£2,742	£2,773	£31	£2,773
Dev. corp. bonds	Taxable	£2,855	£2,942	£87	£2,942
Dev. HY bonds	Taxable	£1,344	£1,407	£63	£1,407

Taxable profit equal to difference between old and new values (entire amount sold). The Developed Corporate bond trade replaces the earlier trade in table 83.

Patricia has now raised a total of £9,918 from sales in her taxable accounts (£2,020 from the substitution sale of EM bonds plus everything in table 83, less £30 commission from five trades), realising only £221 in taxable profits, well below her annual capital gains allowance. She transfers this to her tax-free ISA along with the £209 of accrued dividends in her taxable account. Along with the £2,000 she had originally transferred, she has put £12,127 into her ISA this year.

There it joins the residual cash of £6 from the original investment, £531 of dividends earned in her ISA, plus £1,457 realised from ISA sales in table 81 (less £18 of commission), for a grand total of £14,103 in cash.

Buying

Patricia is now ready to start buying. Since all her cash is in her tax-free account she won't need to distinguish between different assets. She takes a deep breath and quickly takes stock of her portfolio in table 85.

TABLE 85: CASH WEIGHTS AFTER SALES HAVE OCCURRED

	Value A	Status	Current Weight A / SUM(A)	Target Weight B	No trade zone B + / – zone width
US equities	£1,568	Tax free	5.3%	11.5%	9.5% – 13.6%
Canada equities	£2,080	Tax free	7%	4.9%	2.8% – 7%
UK equities	£0	Taxable	0%	5.2%	3.1% – 7.3%
Europe ex-UK	£1,473	Tax free	5.0%	17.1%	15% – 19.2%
Japan equities	£1,934	Tax free	6.5%	4.4%	2.3% – 6.5%
Asia ex-JP eq.	£3,370	Tax free	11.3%	13.6%	11.5% – 15.7%
EM equities	£1,840	Tax free	6.2%	17.3%	15.2% – 19.3%
Dev. govt. bonds	£0	Taxable	0%	6.9%	4.8% – 9%
Dev. corp. bonds	£0	Taxable	0%	3.0%	0.9% – 5.1%
Dev. HY bonds	£0	Taxable	0%	3.6%	1.5% – 5.7%
EM bonds	£0	Taxable	0%	8.5%	6.4% – 10.6%
Gold	£3,332	Tax free	11.2%	9.1%	7% – 11.2%
Cash tax free	£14,103	Tax free	47.5%		
Cash taxable	£0	Taxable	0%		

Values from table 79 after sales from tables 81, 82 and 84. Target Weights from table 78. Zone width of (100% ÷ 12) ÷ 2 = 4.2%.

Ideally Patricia would first replace the assets she only sold out of to fund her ISA transfer, then do her substitution sale. Both of these trades would ideally take her straight to the optimum new cash weight for the respective assets. She should then do her reweighting purchases, all of which would take her to the lower bound of the no trade zone. However this would need around £940 more in cash than she has available once commissions are paid.

It makes more sense on this occasion to slightly reduce the transfer and substitution trades, since they'll still remain within the No-Trade-Zone, and above the Minimum-Trade-Size. The final purchases are shown in table 86. I've not shown the actual amount of shares purchased; fractional rounding will mean the amounts will be slightly different from those shown here.

TABLE 86: PURCHASES AFTER ADJUSTING TO ENSURE PATRICIA DOES NOT RUN OUT OF CASH

	Current Weight A	Target Weight B	No trade zone B + / – zone width	Adjusted Weight C	Trade C - A
UK equities	0%	5.2%	3.1% – 7.3%	4.6%	£1,366
Dev. govt. bonds	0%	6.9%	4.8% – 9%	6.2%	£1,841
Dev. corp. bonds	0%	3.0%	0.9% – 5.1%	2.3%	£683
Dev. HY bonds	0%	3.6%	1.5% – 5.7%	3.0%	£891
EM bonds (AEEM)	0%	8.5%	6.4% – 10.6%	7.9%	£2,346
Europe ex-UK eq.	5.0%	17.1%	15% – 19.2%	15%	£2,969
EM equities	6.2%	17.3%	15.2% – 19.3%	15.2%	£2,672
US equities	5.3%	11.5%	9.5% – 13.6%	9.5%	£1,277

First four trades are transfer trades, replacing assets sold to fund taxable account. The final cash value is slightly below the optimum to reduce their cost. The next trade (EM bonds) is a substitution purchase, again reduced in size. The final three trades are reweighting trades which result in the cash weight reaching the lower end of the no trade zone. Total value spent £14,045 plus £48 commission equals £14,093. Optimal cash weights from table 78. Zone width of (100% ÷ 12) ÷ 2 = 4.2%.

Patricia's final portfolio is shown in table 87. All the actual cash weights are within the no trade zone, with the exception of Asia ex-Japan equities where the difference is well below the minimum trade size level.

TABLE 87: FINAL PORTFOLIO

	Value A	Final cash weight A / SUM(A)	Target Weight B	No trade zone B + / – zone width
US equities	£2,845	9.6%	11.5%	9.5% – 13.6%
Canada equities	£2,080	7.0%	4.9%	2.8% – 7%
UK equities	£1,366	4.6%	5.2%	3.1% – 7.3%
Europe ex-UK eq.	£4,442	15.0%	17.1%	15% – 19.2%
Japan equities	£1,934	6.5%	4.4%	2.3% – 6.5%
Asia ex-JP eq.	£3,370	11.4%	13.6%	11.5% – 15.7%
EM equities	£4,512	15.2%	17.3%	15.2% – 19.3%
Dev. govt. bonds	£1,841	6.2%	6.9%	4.8% – 9%
Dev. corp. bonds	£683	2.3%	3.0%	0.9% – 5.1%
Dev. HY bonds	£891	3.0%	3.6%	1.5% – 5.7%
EM bonds (AEEM)	£2,346	7.9%	8.5%	6.4% – 10.6%
Gold	£3,332	11.2%	9.1%	7% – 11.2%
Cash	£10		0%	

Values from table 85 plus purchases from table 86. Target Weights from table 78. Zone width of (100% ÷ 12) ÷ 2 = 4.2%.

Summary

Annual review	Check annually to see if there are more diversifying or cheaper funds newly available. Also check on the performance of any active funds. If you're selecting individual equities using dividend yield or another method then you should review these annually to see if there are better options.

Reacting to external events	Takeovers, bankruptcies and fund delistings; all mean you have to take action immediately. Decide whether you want to keep any acquiring firms. Perform a portfolio reweighting taking into account the assets and cash that you now hold.
Periodic reweighting	You should reweight your portfolio periodically: annually, quarterly or more frequently; and after a substitution has been made. Compare Target and Current weights to work out whether any reweighting trades are justified, using the No-Trade-Zone and Minimum-Trade-Size techniques.
Consider tax	If you're exposed to taxation in one or more of your trading accounts then follow the procedure from page 425 onwards to minimise the effect of tax on your portfolio returns.

CHAPTER EIGHTEEN

Portfolio Repair

T**HE PREVIOUS CHAPTER COVERED REGULAR MAINTENANCE OF A** portfolio that is in good working order. This chapter is about **repairing** portfolios that have gone badly wrong.

Chapter overview

What is portfolio repair?	What repair involves, and the techniques you need to do it properly.
A six-step plan for portfolio repair	The priorities when repairing damaged portfolios.
Some practical points on repair	A couple of things to watch out for when repairing.
Portfolio repair example	A worked example showing how to repair a portfolio.

What is portfolio repair?

The ideal reader of this book would have just found a large chunk of money lying around somewhere, having already learned the basics of investing in ETFs and equities, but had not yet got round to investing their cash. They'd be able to use my techniques to build the ideal smart portfolio from scratch.

I'm almost certain that the ideal reader of this book does not exist. If you have enough experience to have read and understood the last seventeen chapters you probably already own a selection of assets. It's also unlikely that these look exactly like the kind of portfolio

I've been advocating. Significant amounts of buying and selling will be required to whip your portfolio into shape.

This isn't the annual checkup of a relatively healthy portfolio requiring just some light maintenance as in the last chapter.

Typical symptoms of a portfolio in need of serious repair are the presence of costly active funds, misaligned asset allocation, and excessive home country bias. There may also be multiple small holdings of individual equities.

In this chapter I explain how to determine the priority of the various repairs needed to your portfolio, showing how to fix the most serious faults first, before gradually moving on to others.

This approach makes sense because it's unrealistic to try and fix all the problems you have by executing a mammoth series of trades in a single day. This could prove expensive for retail investors paying fixed commissions, and they could also end up incurring capital gains tax on assets which are outside of tax shelters. The market impact costs would also badly hurt institutional traders. Following a staged and gradual approach will substantially reduce the total cost of repairing your portfolio.

Portfolio repair effectively involves a series of substitutions in your portfolio. So it's worth rereading the section in chapter sixteen from page 411, where I explained how to work out if a substitution is worth doing given it's trading costs; particularly table 73.

You may also find it useful to look to figure 29 (chapter six, page 146) which shows the improvement in geometric mean when diversifying from individual shares, to industries, and then to countries and regions.

A six-step plan for portfolio repair

Priority one: Emergency diversification

In early 2000, during the final dying throes of the nineties tech bubble, I was working for an online stockbroker. This wasn't glamorous high finance. Instead I worked part-time answering the phones to fund a university degree in Economics.

When a call came in, the first job was to check the holdings in each client's account. At the time I was studying, amongst other things, the theory of portfolio diversification. It quickly became clear that none of the people calling up the brokerage firm had read the same books as I had. Many held only one stock. Others held half a dozen stocks; all UK or US-based dot-com technology stocks. It wasn't inconceivable that all the firms in a typical client's portfolio could simultaneously collapse in value. Many did, just a few months later.

Back to the present day, and I still know plenty of people who hold a single stock in their portfolio. Often this is the firm they work for, since they've acquired the shares through employee share purchase schemes and not got around to selling them. Others bought their single chunks of equity as part of government privatisations, or to show their support of a publicly listed sports team. But it doesn't matter how you ended up with such a concentrated portfolio: it's still incredibly dangerous.

From a theoretical point of view, the gains from selling out of a single stock are very high, as table 73 shows (page 412, row three, 58% breakeven initial cost); and selling out of a single sector or entire country is pretty worthwhile as well (rows four and five, 48% and 34% respectively). Even with an expensive broker and a small portfolio, these benefits massively outweigh the up front costs of switching out of an overly concentrated equity portfolio into a market cap weighted global equity passive fund.

Priority two: Cut costs

Get rid of expensive active managers

The only way to virtually guarantee higher returns is by cutting costs. If your portfolio is stuffed full of active managers, then getting rid of them will probably be the best thing you can do. You can easily save 1% or more a year in costs by switching from active to passive managers.

You might protest that your active managers have been carefully selected, and that they're all incredibly skilled and hard working. I suggest you reread the section in chapter fifteen on comparing active to passive managers, and then ask yourself if there is really enough evidence to justify paying these guys their monstrously high management fees, plus paying for the extra trading they're likely to do inside their funds.

To work out the up front benefits of switching just multiply the cost differential between funds using the normal rule of 20. Then compare this to the initial trading costs you'd pay to switch. Don't forget to account for any tax implications where relevant.

Ideally you'd do a proper cost calculation including the effect of higher turnover by the active manager, but the difference in management fees alone is normally large enough to justify switching. This will give active managers a slight advantage in any comparison; but then they need all the help they can get.

Except for the very tiniest portfolios, even saving just 0.1% (present value of 2%), is likely to give you significantly more future benefit than the immediate trading costs of switching out of an expensive fund and replacing it with a cheaper one; assuming there are no serious tax implications.

Reconsider not so cheap passive funds

High costs without higher returns isn't just the preserve of much maligned active fund managers. Most ETFs are cheap, but some aren't. There can be significant differences in charges between different providers for the same product. With new funds entering the market all the time there may be cheaper options which weren't available when you first put your portfolio together.

Again you should use the **rule of 20** to double check if it's worth switching from a slightly more expensive ETF to one that is cheaper. Multiply the difference in management fees by 20 and compare that to the initial cost.

Fancy smart beta ETFs usually charge more than plain vanilla market capitalisation trackers. They will also have higher turnover, making for a significantly higher total cost bill. As I pointed out in chapter fifteen, the benefits of these funds usually aren't large enough to compensate for the extra cost. You should seriously consider ditching them.

Priority three: Get your asset allocation right

Now you've pared your costs to the bone it's time to think about portfolio weights. You should follow a top-down process: exactly as you'd do if you were starting from scratch. As table 73 shows (page 412), there are diminishing returns as you move deeper into a portfolio and make more granular substitutions. So asset allocation should be where you start repairing your portfolio weights.

Priority four: Get your emerging/developed, regional and country allocation right

You can see in table 73 (page 412) that the benefit of further diversification inside asset classes isn't so dramatic. But rows six to eleven, and fourteen to fifteen, still show up front benefits of at least 0.4% for diversifying down to country level. You will probably be paying less than this in trading costs unless your portfolio is very small.

Priority five: Get your equity sector (and bond type and credit) allocation correct

With sufficient capital you may want to diversify within countries, and into individual sectors (for equities), and bond types or credits. The benefit of doing this is relatively small, but it may be worth doing if your account is large enough.

Priority six: Consider individual shares or funds

If you have enough money to justify it,[293] you might want to consider buying individual stocks, at least in your home country, and perhaps further afield if you have the capacity and desire to manage overseas equity holdings.

If you already own individual shares, but your portfolio is theoretically too small to contain them, then don't feel you must sell them all and buy country or regional ETFs

---

293. Refer to tables 37 and 38, from page 171, to check this.

instead. Evaluate the benefits (slightly more diversification) against the costs (paying management fees on ETFs and initial cost), before making a decision.

Some practical points on repair

Don't try and get to perfection

In chapter sixteen I pointed out that it's not worth doing very small trades, and I introduced the **No-Trade-Zone**. This is half the average portfolio weight in size, so for example with 20 assets it would be (100% ÷ 20) ÷ 2 = 2.5%: you shouldn't bother doing trades which are smaller than this.

Although this idea is mainly used in **portfolio reweighting**, it's also an important concept in portfolio repair. It's better to do a smaller number of trades that end up getting your portfolio weights fairly close enough to their optimal. Once your portfolio is roughly correct the cost of getting it perfect will probably outweigh the benefits.

Know where you are going – don't retrace your steps

I presented a simple consecutive process above, but reality is a little more complicated. If you always stick stubbornly to the order shown you'll probably end up doing a lot of unnecessary trading.

For example, suppose you are an investor who starts with a portfolio which was half in a US active equity manager, focusing on the technology sector, and half in Apple stock. If you robotically followed the process above you'd first sell your Apple stock (priority one – emergency diversification), then exchange your active fund for a passive US equity tech ETF (priority two – cut costs). Then you'd sell your passive tech fund and use all your cash to buy a global bond ETF, and a global equity ETF (priority three – asset allocation).

Then you would sell both those global ETFs to buy a diversified set of equity ETFs covering other countries (priority four – regional and country exposure). You then decide to get your US exposure via sector ETFs (priority five). So you'd sell your single US equity ETF, and buy a series of sector ETFs instead.

Looking at priority six you decide to take your exposure in each US sector by buying individual shares. You pick one stock from each sector, and sell your ETFs to buy them. Guess which stock you choose to cover the tech sector? You guessed right: Apple.

At the end of this your broker will be significantly richer, and you will feel pretty stupid when you buy back that Apple stock. Also some of these trades might not even happen: it's possible one or more of the incremental steps won't pass a cost benefit test, even if the total net benefit of all the portfolio changes is positive.

There is a better way. First decide what the final portfolio will look like. You then need to work your way towards that, fixing the high priority problems first, but always with the end goal in sight to avoid doubling back. More than one level of diversification might happen at each stage. When you're considering multiple levels of diversification the benefits can be added up.

Let's start again with the example I used a moment ago. Before you kick off your portfolio repair you have 50% in a US active equity tech fund, and 50% in Apple. In this situation you should sell Apple first since you have horrific concentration risk in equities, with all your eggs in Tim Cook's basket (priority one). But don't sell your entire Apple holding; instead retain what you would ultimately need to get exposure to the US tech sector.

You should then use the proceeds to buy bonds, thus fixing your asset allocation at the same time (priority three). However, rather than buy a single global bond ETF you should replace it with the set of bond ETF funds you want to end up owning (something like portfolio 60 on page 280).

At the end of this stage the asset allocation is right with just over half your portfolio in stocks, and half in bonds. But your entire equity holding is still in US tech stocks, including what's left of your Apple position. You should then start selling down the US active tech fund, since it is costing you money in extra charges (priority two) as well as being undiversified (priorities three and four).[294]

As you start to sell the equity tech fund you should be buying country equity ETFs, again keeping your final preferred allocation in mind. You should start with the countries which aren't so correlated to the US – first emerging markets, and developed markets outside of America. This will give you more diversification quicker. Once you have equity exposure to all the non-US countries you should sell the final tranche of the US tech fund, using the proceeds to buy your preferred individual shares in the other US sectors (not tech: since you already own Apple).

Now you're done. You have only had to execute one set of sales and purchases, without any re-buying or selling of funds you've only just sold or bought.

Portfolio repair example

In the spirit of the famous quote "Physician heal thyself", I am going to use one of my own portfolios as an example to illustrate the healing powers of portfolio repair. This is a portfolio which I manage for my mother, so "Physician heal thy mother" is more accurate. I set it up a number of years ago, before I developed any of the techniques in this book, and frankly it is a bit of a mess.

---

294. Alternatively you could deal with both problems simultaneously; selling both Apple and the tech fund, unless there are tax implications.

PORTFOLIO 87: MY MOTHER'S PORTFOLIO – BEFORE CHANGES

	Ticker	Asset class	Area	Country, region or type	Sector	Value
ETF: Global high yield bonds	IGHY	Bonds	Developed	High yield		£15,545
ETF: Developed corporate bonds (GBP denominated)	SLXX	Bonds	Developed	Corporate		£8,919
ETF: Asia Pacific equity dividend	IAPD	Equity	Developed	Asia		£3,582
Barratt Developments	BDEV	Equity	Developed	UK	Consumer discretionary	£6,513
Carillion	CLLN	Equity	Developed	UK	Industrials	£6,191
Drax	DRX	Equity	Developed	UK	Utilities	£1,872
Interserve	IRV	Equity	Developed	UK	Consumer discretionary	£6,454
Lloyds Bank	LLOY	Equity	Developed	UK	Financials	£812
ETF: European equities	XEMU	Equity	Developed	Europe ex-UK		£17,345
ETF: S&P 500	IUS	Equity	Developed	US		£6,476
ETF: Korean equity	IKOR	Equity	Emerging	Korea		£3,864
ETF: Global equities	VWRL	Equity	Global			£15,921
ETF: Developed property	IWDP	Property	Developed			£6,506

Portfolio 87 shows the starting point of my mother's portfolio. To avoid exposing my mother's private financial affairs I have adjusted all the values shown so that the total portfolio has an arbitrary worth of £100,000. It's entirely in a tax sheltered ISA so we don't need to worry about tax, and my mother pays £9 per trade (plus stamp duty of 0.5% on individual share purchases). This is half as much again than the £6 I pay myself, so I need to multiply per trade costs and minimum holdings by 1.5.

This means the minimum value for an ETF holding[295] will be £1,800 × 1.5 = £2,700. I've also modified table 72 (from chapter twelve) to reflect my mother's higher trading costs; this is shown in table 88.

TABLE 88: COST TABLE FOR A UK INVESTOR PAYING A MINIMUM OF £9 PER TRADE

	Direct	**ETF**
£100	£9.3	£9.1
£500	£11.25	£9.2
£1,000	£12	£9.5
£5,000	£24	£11.5

Total cost for a given trade size (average cost of buys and sells). All assumptions as per Appendix B, page 480.

Portfolio 88 analyses my mother's portfolio, calculating cash weights and risk weights within various groups of assets. Following the mantra of "know where you are going" I've also added the optimal risk weights which each part of the portfolio would ideally have if I was starting from scratch. My mother is a brave investor who is happy to hold a high risk portfolio with only 10% of the risk weight in bonds, and keep 10% of her portfolio in genuine alternatives.

Using the method in chapter sixteen, I calculated the no trade zone at half the average portfolio weight in size, or (100% ÷ 13) ÷ 2 = 3.8%. Because my mother is paying £9 rather than £6 commission I also need to multiply the default minimum trade size of £250 by 1.5; this gives me £375 as the minimum.

---

295. Remember I derived this value in chapter six, page 175.

PORTFOLIO 88: MY MOTHER'S PORTFOLIO EXPOSURE – BEFORE CHANGES

		Cash weight	Risk weight	Optimal risk weight
	Equities	75.5%	89%	85%
	Bonds	24.5%	11%	10%
	Genuine alternatives	0%	0%	5%
Equities	Traditional equities		91%	95%
	Equity-like alternatives		9%	5%
Traditional equities	Developed	92%	88.2%	75%
	Emerging	8%	11.8%	25%
Developed equities	North America		21.2%	33.3%
	Europe		69.5%	33.3%
	Asia		9.3%	33.3%
Emerging markets	Korea *		70%	6%
	All other emerging		30%	94%
European equities	UK		53%	20%
	Europe, ex-UK		47%	80%
North American equities	US		95%	60%
	Canada		5%	40%
UK equities	Consumer discretionary	59.4%	62.7%	9.1%
	Industrials	28.3%	24.7%	9.1%
	Utilities	8.6%	8.3%	9.1%
	Financials	3.7%	4.7%	9.1%
Traditional bonds	Developed		100%	75%
Developed bonds	Corporate **	63.5%	59%	30%
	High yield	36.5%	41%	30%

Optimal risk weights assume a high risk portfolio with 10% in alternatives. Property is an equity-like alternative. There are no genuine or bond-like alternatives in the portfolio. I have decomposed the exposure of the global equity fund VWRL to its constituent countries. * The optimal weight for Korea is based on a regional emerging Asian weight of 40%, and country weight within that of 15%. ** SLXX only covers GBP denominated corporate bonds, the optimal weight shown is for the entire developed corporate bond universe.

Priority one: Emergency diversification

For all its faults, this portfolio is no one-share wonder: the largest firm, UK house builder Barratt, only takes up 6.5% of the portfolio, so there is no need to pull the emergency cord and start selling out of highly concentrated equity positions.

Priority two: Cut costs

There are no expensive active funds here. However, some of the passive funds aren't that cheap either, as table 89 illustrates.

TABLE 89: FEES ON MY MOTHER'S ETFS

	Ticker	TER %	TER £
ETF: Global high yield bonds	IGHY	0.5%	£78
ETF: Developed corporate bonds	SLXX	0.2%	£18
ETF: Asia Pacific equity dividend	IAPD	0.59%	£21
ETF: European equity	XMEU	0.3%	£52
ETF: S&P 500	IUS	0.4%	£26
ETF: Korean equity	IKOR	0.74%	£29
ETF: Global equity	VWRL	0.25%	£40
ETF: Developed property	IWDP	0.59%	£38
Total			£302

IUS is an obviously expensive option; you can get a much cheaper fund for US exposure. IAPD is a single factor smart beta fund, using dividends. Ideally I'd switch this to something cheaper but it is the only option for Asian exposure in the UK.

I won't be taking any immediate decisions on which funds to dump or keep, but this will help inform my thinking as I move on to consider asset allocation.

Priority three: Asset allocation

In risk weighted terms this portfolio should be 80% in equities, 10% in bonds, and the final 10% in genuine alternatives. Instead my mother has 80.8% of her risk weighted assets in traditional equities, 11.5% in traditional bonds, and 7.6% in equity-like alternatives (property fund IWDP).

Getting closer to the target portfolio means selling IWDP (which costs around 0.34% a year) and buying a genuine alternative, like a gold ETF (SGLN is the cheapest, with an expense ratio of 0.25%).

This kind of comparison doesn't fall within the neat rows of table 73 (page 412). But after doing my own calculations I'm reasonably confident that the diversification benefit from doing this is around 0.08% a year. The reduction in costs adds another 0.09%. That's a total future benefit of 0.17% every year: after using the rule of 20 I still get a total initial benefit of 3.4%.

From table 88 the cost of doing this trade comes in at around £30, or 0.46%. So it's worth selling IWDP (property) and replacing it with SGLN (gold). This leaves my mother with the asset class exposure shown in portfolio 89.

PORTFOLIO 89: MY MOTHER'S PORTFOLIO EXPOSURE – AFTER SELLING IWDP AND BUYING SGLN

	Cash weight	Risk weight	Optimal risk weight
Equities	69%	80.9%	80%
Bonds	24.5%	11.5%	10%
Genuine alternatives	6.5%	7.6%	10%

Optimal risk weights assume a high risk portfolio with 10% in alternatives.

TRADES: SELL IWDP, BUY SGLN.

Priority four: Area, regional and country allocation (equities)

If you cast your eye over portfolio 88 the obvious problems are a large overweight in the UK, smaller overweights to the rest of Europe and Korea, a significant deficiency in the developed Asian weight, a general shortcoming in the non-Korean emerging markets, and a distinct lack of Canada.

The Korean fund (IKOR) is expensive and replacing it with a cheaper generic emerging market (EM) fund will improve diversification. AEEM is the fund I suggested using, which costs 0.20% versus the 0.74% a year for IKOR.

The up front value of the lower cost is 0.74% – 0.2% = 0.54%, which using the rule of 20 gives 10.8%. I don't need to include the diversification benefit or work out any likely saving in invisible trading costs: selling IKOR and buying AEEM makes perfect sense.

My mother still needs more emerging market exposure, and the obvious place to look for money to fund this is in UK stocks. She has two stocks in the consumer discretionary sector (Carillion CLLN and Interserve IRV), and zero in most other sectors, so it's crazy to keep both CLLN and IRV. These stocks were originally picked on a dividend-yield basis. Right now CLLN has a forecast yield of 6% and IRV comes in at 4.7%. Selling the lower yielding IRV will free up just over 6% of the entire portfolio in cash, or 9.1% as a proportion of equity risk weighting.

My mother can use this extra money to buy some more emerging market AEEM, bringing the emerging market risk weight up to 24.3% – almost on target. This will increase costs by 0.2% a year since owning a UK stock costs nothing but my mother has to pay management fees for the AEEM ETF. However, the diversification benefit is around five times that: 1%.[296] The net benefit will be 1% – 0.2% = 0.8% a year, or 16% after multiplying by 20. This is much higher than the up front cost of trading.

TRADES: SELL IKOR & IRV, BUY AEEM.

Portfolio 90 gives an update on my mother's asset class and equity exposure. She is still a little light on North America (specifically Canada) and developed Asia. It's time to start reducing Europe ex-UK. If I sell 30% of the XMEU holding that is enough to bring it down to my target level. XMEU costs 0.3% a year in management fee. With the proceeds my mother can buy some more Asia (IAPD with a management fee of 0.59%).

I'm confident that better diversification from this trade will improve the entire developed equity portfolio pre-cost geometric mean by around 0.04%.[297] That equates to 0.4% a year on the 10% of my portfolio I'm considering trading. The management fee is higher, costing an extra 0.29%, so the net annual benefit after cost comes in at 0.11%, or in up front terms once multiplied by 20 around 1.1%.

The trade value is around £5,200, which according to table 88 will cost 0.46% for a sell and rebuy. So this is worth doing.

TRADES: SELL £5,200 worth of XMEU, BUY IAPD.

---

296. Row 3 (Single stock to global MC portfolio) of table 73 (page 412) gives an annual benefit of 2.9%. The benefit of a single stock to a global emerging markets portfolio is slightly lower.
297. Assuming correlation between developed equity regions of 0.68; from Appendix B. Starting weights: 23.6% North America, Europe 66.1%, 10.3% Asia. Weights for comparison, buying IAPD: North America: 23.6%, Europe 56.9%, Asia 19.5%.

PORTFOLIO 90: MY MOTHER'S PORTFOLIO EXPOSURE – AFTER FIRST FEW TRADES

		Cash weight	Risk weight	Optimal risk weight
Traditional equities	Developed	83%	75.7%	75%
	Emerging	17%	24.3%	25%
Developed equities	North America		23.6%	33.3%
	Europe		66%	33.3%
	Asia		10.2%	33.3%
European equities	UK		45%	20%
	Europe, ex-UK		55%	80%
North American equities	US		95%	60%
	Canada		5%	40%
UK equities	Consumer discretionary	42.3%	45.8%	9.1%
	Industrials	40.2%	35.9%	9.1%
	Utilities	12.1%	12%	9.1%
	Financials	5.3%	6.2%	9.1%

Optimal risk weights assume a high risk portfolio with 10% in alternatives. I have broken down the exposure of the global equity fund VWRL to its constituent countries.

It's now time to confront the four remaining UK stocks. Without selling around four-fifths of their value I won't be able to fix the remaining problems: too much UK and hence Europe, versus too little Asia and North America. The best option is to sell the whole lot, and then use some of that to purchase a FTSE 100 tracker to get the right UK exposure. From figure 29 the benefit of going from exposure to four sectors to an entire country is around 0.9% a year in improved geometric mean.[298] The cheapest FTSE tracker, ISF, only costs 0.07% a year in TER plus an estimated 0.1% of turnover cost inside the fund. With 20 × (0.9% – 0.17%) = 14.6% of up front benefit this trade is a no brainer.

---

298. Actually the benefit here will be slightly higher than that because my mother owns one share in each sector, not the entire sector.

Of the £15,388 realised from selling the remaining UK stocks, around £8,000 should be invested in Asia, IAPD. My mother can use another £5,000 to buy a Canadian ETF, UC24. Both these trades make sense after comparing diversification versus higher management fee and initial trade cost. This leaves £2,388 to invest in ISF.

Finally my mother still has slightly too much in the US compared to Canada. She owns IUS, which with a management fee of 0.4% is a rather pricey way to get US exposure: a competitor fund IVV costs just 0.04. So I'd also suggest that my mother sells her £6,476 of IUS entirely, and buys £5,000 worth of IVV instead; the remaining cash going into the UC24 Canadian bucket.

TRADES: Sell BDEV, CLLN, DRX, LLOY, IUS. Buy £2,388 ISF, £8,000 IAPD, £6,476 UC24, £5,000 IVV.

Priority four and five: Area allocation (bonds) bond types and credits

Looking at the target allocation to bonds of just over £24,000, the right portfolio is something like portfolio 63 (from chapter twelve, page 284); I've copied it here as portfolio 91. I've also made one change; splitting the developed corporate bond allocation into a GBP and USD section to reflect the fact my mother already owns a GBP denominated developed corporate bond fund, SLXX.

PORTFOLIO 91: OPTIMAL BOND PORTFOLIO FOR MY MOTHER

Portfolio £100,000							
Bonds £24,464							
Developed 75%					Emerging 25%		
Normal 90%			Inflation 10%	Normal 55%		Foreign 45%	
Government 40% SAAA	Corporate 30%		High yield 30% IGHY TICK	Government 100% SGIL	Government 100% SEML	Govt. 40% LEMB	Corporate 60% EMCP
	USD 50% CRPS	GBP 50% SLXX					
27.0%	10.2%	10.2%	20.3%	7.5%	13.8%	4.5%	6.8%
(31.2%)	(10.8%)	(10.8%)	(17.5%)	(8.7%)	(11.9%)	(3.9%)	(5.2%)
£7,632	£2,642	£2,642	£4,218	£2,218	£2,911	£954	£1,272

Risk weightings are shown; Cash weightings in **(bold)**. Actual cash in bold. Final row shows weight within bonds sub-portfolio. Copy of portfolio 66 with SLXX exposure included.

My mother would need to do a lot of trading to end up with this portfolio. She needs to sell most of IGHY and about three-quarters of SLXX, and then buy everything else. Is this worth doing? Well the management fee of the original two bond funds comes in at an average of 0.39%. But portfolio 91 has a fee of just 0.32% a year. That's a 0.07% advantage, which has an initial value of 1.4% using the **rule of 20**. That's significantly more than the up front trading costs (eight trades at £9 each is £72 or 0.4% of the total value traded of £17,541), and I haven't even considered the diversification benefits.

TRADES: SELL £6,276 SLXX & £11,265 IGHY. BUY £7,732 SAAA, £2,642 CRPS, £2,128 SGIL, £2,911 SEML, £954 LEMB, £1,272 EMCP.

Priority five: Equity sector allocation, individual shares

I've already decided it was not worth getting UK sector exposure through individual stocks.

My mother's final portfolio

After all the trading the final version is shown in portfolio 92.

PORTFOLIO 92: MY MOTHER'S PORTFOLIO – FINAL

	Ticker	Asset class	Area	Country, region or type	Cash weight
ETF: Global high yield bonds	IGHY	Bonds	Developed	High yield	4.3%
ETF: Developed corporate bonds (GBP denominated)	SLXX	Bonds	Developed	Corporate, GBP	2.7%
ETF: Dev. govt. bond	SAAA	Bonds	Developed	Government	7.4%
ETF: Dev. corp bond USD	CRPS	Bonds	Developed	Corporate, USD	2.7%
ETF: Dev. Inflation bond	SGIL	Bonds	Developed	Inflation	2.1%
ETF: Emerging govt. domestic	SEML	Bonds	Emerging	Government, domestic	2.9%
ETF: Emerging govt. USD	LEMB	Bonds	Emerging	Government, USD	1%
ETF: Emerging corp. USD	EMCP	Bonds	Emerging	Corporate, USD	1.3%
ETF: Asia Pacific equity dividend	IAPD	Equity	Developed	Asia	18.1%
ETF: UK equity	ISF	Equity	Developed	UK	2.4%
ETF: Canadian equity	UC24	Equity	Developed	Canada	6.5%
ETF: Euro equity	XMEU	Equity	Developed	Europe ex-UK	10.9%
ETF: S&P 500	IVV	Equity	Developed	US	5%
ETF: Emerging equity	AEEM	Equity	Emerging		10.4%
ETF: Global equity	VWRL	Equity	Global		16%
ETF: Gold	SGLN	Gold	Developed		6.5%

Portfolio 93 is a repeat of the analysis I did earlier showing the exposures. This is much improved compared to the starting portfolio 93. As there are now 16 assets in the portfolio the new no trade zone is (100% ÷ 16) ÷ 2 = 3.1%. All the new weights are well within that range.[299]

PORTFOLIO 93: MY MOTHER'S PORTFOLIO EXPOSURE – AFTER ALL TRADES

		Cash weight	Risk weight	Optimal risk weight
	Equities (traditional only)	69%	80.9%	80%
	Bonds (traditional only)	24.5%	11.5%	10%
	Genuine alternatives	6.5%	7.6%	10%
Traditional equities	Developed	82.6%	75.6%	75%
	Emerging	17.4%	24.3%	25%
Developed equities	North America		32.4%	33.3%
	Europe		34.1%	33.3%
	Asia		33.4%	33.3%
European equities	UK		20.5%	20%
	Europe, ex-UK		79.5%	80%
North American equities	US		61.6%	60%
	Canada		38.4%	40%
Traditional bonds	Developed		75%	75%
	Emerging		25%	25%
Developed normal bonds	Corporate		30%	30%
	Government		40%	40%
	High yield		30%	30%

Optimal risk weights assume a high risk portfolio with 10% in alternatives. I have broken down the exposure of the global equity fund VWRL to its constituent countries. The exposure within developed and emerging bonds (not shown) is at optimal levels.

299. Strictly I should compare Current and Target cash weights, rather than risk weights as I've done here, but this would give the same results.

Table 90 is an updated analysis of the fees my mother is paying (compare to table 89).

TABLE 90: FEES ON MY MOTHER'S ETFS (AFTER)

	Ticker	TER %	TER £
ETF: Global high yield bonds	IGHY	0.5%	£21
ETF: Developed corporate bonds	SLXX	0.2%	£5
ETF: Dev. govt. bond	SAAA	0.2%	£15
ETF: Dev. Corp bond USD	CRPS	0.2%	£5
ETF: Dev. Inflation bond	SGIL	0.25%	£5
ETF: Emerging govt. domestic	SEML	0.5%	£15
ETF: Emerging govt. USD	LEMB	0.5%	£5
ETF: Emerging corp. USD	EMCP	0.5%	£7
ETF: Asia Pacific equity dividend	IAPD	0.59%	£107
ETF: Euro equity	XMEU	0.3%	£33
ETF: S&P 500	IVV	0.04%	£2
ETF: UK equity	ISF	0.07%	£2
ETF: Canada equity	UC24	0.28%	£18
ETF: Emerging equity	AEEM	0.20%	£21
ETF: Global equity	VWRL	0.25%	£40
ETF: Gold	SGLN	0.25%	£16
Total			£317

Total is sum of un-rounded values.

Fees are up by £15 a year, mainly due to a higher allocation to IAPD and removing the fee-free individual equities from the portfolio. I estimate that the 24 trades I've done on behalf of my mother cost around £340; lower than you might expect as there is no stamp duty on sales of individual equities or any trades in ETFs. Commissions of £9 per trade accounted for £216 of this, with market impact making up the rest. If I convert the one-off initial cost of £340 using the rule of 20 I get £17 a year.

The bottom line is an annual increase in costs from higher ongoing charges (£15) and initial trading (£17) of £15 + £17 = £32 a year. This is just 0.032% of the portfolio value. A very conservative estimate of the improvement in expected returns from extra diversification is around 0.3%; nearly ten times the extra cost. Hopefully I will stay on my mother's Christmas card list.

Summary

General advice	Analyse your existing portfolio, and decide what your optimal portfolio would look like.
	Know where you are going: avoid having to backtrack.
	You won't get to perfection: use the No-Trade-Zone and Minimum-Trade-Size concepts from chapter sixteen to avoid tiny adjustments that won't add any significant value.
	Weigh up changes in fees and diversification benefits (multiplied by 20 to get present value), versus up front costs.
Priority one	If you're holding just one or two shares you need to diversify fast.
Priority two	Cut out expensive active managers that can't justify themselves, and pricey passive funds where a cheaper alternative exists.
Priority three	Sort out your asset allocation before attacking the rest of your portfolio.
Priority four	Ensure your area, region, country, type and credit exposures are okay.
Priority five	Deal with sector concentration in equity markets.
Priority six	Consider investments in individual shares.

Epilogue

In the introduction I said that one of my favorite books on investment is *Simple But Not Easy* by Richard Oldfield. You'd probably hesitate to describe the book you have just read as **easy**! However, the last few hundred pages can be boiled down to a few **simple** principles of smart investing:

Don't try to predict the future	It's very hard to predict risk-adjusted returns.
	Be sceptical of others who think they can predict the future better than the market can, and be sceptical of your own ability to do so.
	Be highly sceptical of anyone that recommends extreme reweighting of your portfolio to reflect their predictions; they have way too much confidence in their forecasting ability.
	If you want to try to predict the future, then simple forecasting models can be used to tweak your portfolio weights.
Diversify, diversify, diversify	If you can't predict risk-adjusted returns then the only way to improve your expected return is by diversifying. Buy the maximum number of funds and shares you can given the amount of capital you have. Use the handcrafting method to spread your capital out in a diversified way.
Cut costs	You *might* be able to predict risk-adjusted returns. You'll *probably* earn a benefit from diversification. But you'll *definitely* have higher returns if you have lower costs. Avoid expensive funds; trade slowly and infrequently.
Stick to your guns	Sticking to a consistent portfolio allocation is more important than getting the allocation *right*. There is no *right* allocation but changing your portfolio in an arbitrary and unstructured way is definitely wrong.

Glossary

Terms in **bold** appear elsewhere in the glossary.

Absolute momentum	A variation of the **momentum** forecasting model, where you may not always be fully invested. As a result you will be holding extra cash in the portfolio if one or more assets are expected to fall in price. See page 330. Opposite of **relative momentum**.
Accumulating	A **collective fund** where dividends in the underlying investments are retained within the fund and not paid out to investors, resulting in the price increasing. Accumulating funds have a **dividend yield** of zero. Opposite of **distributing**.
Active fund, Active management	A **collective fund** where securities are bought and sold actively to try to outperform the general market. Normally more expensive than **passive funds**, as active fund managers think they can generate, and charge for, extra returns. As distinct from **passive funds** and **passive management**.
Agency bond	A kind of bond issued by a quasi-government agency such as Fannie Mae in the US or UK housing associations. Agency bonds usually have an implicit or explicit government guarantee. They are considered slightly riskier than government bonds issued by central or local government.
Alternative assets	A type of **asset class** that is different from equities or bonds. Examples of alternatives include commodities, gold and **hedge funds**. The three categories of alternative assets that I use are: **genuine alternatives**, **bond-like alternatives** and **equity-like alternatives**. See chapter nine.

Arithmetic mean	Usual way to get an average, e.g. of a series of returns. For example the arithmetic mean of +10%, +30%, and −10% is +10%. See **geometric mean**.
Asset class	Name for a general kind of investable security, e.g. equities, bonds, commodity futures and commercial property are all asset classes. See chapter eight.
Basis point (bp)	One hundredth of one percent, e.g. 0.01%.
Beta	Getting returns from being exposed to the overall market, without having any particular skill. Owning a **passive index fund,** such as an ETF linked to the French CAC 30 stock market, will give you **beta** returns for the relevant market. See also **smart beta**.
Bid-ask spread cost	Part of the **execution cost** of buying an asset. Given a spread in the market, e.g. 100 (bid) to 101 (ask), the bid-ask spread cost is the difference between the mid-price (100.5) and the price paid (if buying, 100; if selling 100). The bid-ask spread cost (0.5 in this case) is equal to half the bid-ask spread (half of 1.0). See page 127.
Bond-like alternatives	Any **alternative asset** which is highly **correlated** with bonds. See page 217.
Bootstrapping (portfolio optimisation)	A method of **portfolio optimisation** which takes into account the uncertainty in historical data. See page 496 in Appendix C.
Bootstrapping (statistical estimates)	A method of estimating the degree of **parameter uncertainty**. See page 44.
Bottom up	A method for building portfolios where you choose the assets you like (funds or equities) without regard to the overall exposure it gives you to different **asset classes**, countries, or industries. Opposite to **top-down**.
Cash weighting **Cash weights**	**Portfolio weighting** in cash terms. So if an asset has a weight of 10%, and you have $100,000, then you'd put $10,000 into that asset. See **risk weighting**.

Collective fund	A fund which buys you a share in a portfolio of securities. Types of collective fund include: **ETFs;** mutual funds in the US; or in the UK investment trusts and unit trusts. Collective funds can be **active** or **passive**.
Convertible bond	A bond which under certain conditions will be converted into equity in the issuing firm.
Corporate bonds	Bonds issued by companies. See **investment grade bonds**, **cross over bonds**, and **high yield bonds**.
Correlation, Correlated	A measure of how two things co-move; how similar their returns are. Normally used in relation to daily returns from different assets. A correlation of −1 indicates two things always move in opposite directions, +1 indicates they always move in the same direction and 0 means there is no linear relationship (uncorrelated). See page 52 and page 493.
Covered bond	Bonds backed by cash flows, e.g. from mortgages, or infrastructure like toll bridges and road tunnels.
Cross over bond	A bond with a credit rating just below **investment grade** but not quite as poor as **high yield**.
CTA	Commodity trading advisor: A type of **hedge fund** that usually runs a **managed futures** type strategy. AHL, my former employer, is an example of a CTA.
Currency hedging	Protecting yourself from a change in exchange rates when investing in a foreign currency. For example, a UK investor buying the US S&P 500 index will suffer if the USD falls against GBP, even if nothing happens to stock prices. By trading certain **derivatives** a fund manager can eliminate this exposure to GBP/USD rates. See page 27.
Current Weight	The portfolio **cash weight** implied by the number, price, and exchange rate of your current holdings. See page 387.
Derivative	A way of benefiting from an asset going up or down in price without actually owning it. Futures, spread-bets, options and contracts for difference are all examples of derivatives. Derivatives usually provide more **leverage** than the underlying assets.
Direct investment	Directly buying individual shares or bonds rather than using **collective funds**.

Distributing	A type of **collective fund** where all equity dividends and bond coupons in the underlying assets are passed on to the investors in the fund. The **dividend yield** on a distributing fund is a reasonable approximation for the equity dividend yield or bond **yield to maturity** in the underlying assets. See **accumulating.**
Distribution of returns	Pattern of historic or expected returns for an asset or portfolio of assets. A distribution can be summarised using a **statistical model**. See page 38.
Dividend yield	The percentage dividend on an equity or **ETF**. Equal to the annual cash dividend per share, divided by the current share price.
Duration	The sensitivity of a bond to changes in interest rates. Bonds with a long time to maturity have higher duration than those with a shorter maturity. See page 270.
Embarrassment	Worrying about underperforming peers or the market generally by deviating from the **market capitalisation weighted** consensus. **Tracking error** is a formal measure of potential **embarrassment**. See page 26 and page 112.
Equal weighting	Allocating **portfolio weights** equally across a group of assets.
Equity-like alternatives	A type of **alternative asset** which is highly correlated to equities. See page 212.
Exchange Traded Fund (ETF)	A type of **collective fund** which can be traded and owned like a normal equity.
Execution cost	The **invisible cost** of trading an **instrument**, because you have to pay more when you buy, and sell for less. Equal to the difference between the mid-price and the traded price. Made up of **bid-ask spread cost** and **market impact**. See page 127.
Fixed point expectation	A forecast which has absolutely no uncertainty; for example "The FTSE 100 will close the year at a level of 7015.76 precisely." See page 23.
Full optimisation	A type of **portfolio optimisation** which uses the full **statistical model** of past returns, including **Sharpe Ratios**, **correlations** and **standard deviations**. It is very unstable, and not recommended. See chapter three.

Fund of funds	A type of **collective fund** that invests in other funds.
Gaussian normal distribution	A statistical distribution which is shaped like a bell, and which is often used as a **statistical model** for returns. If your returns are Gaussian normal then you will see returns one **standard deviation** or less around the average about 68% of the time, and returns two standard deviations or less about 95% of the time. See page 40.
Genuine alternatives	Category of **alternative asset** which is genuinely uncorrelated to traditional assets like equities and bonds. The two subcategories of genuine alternative I use are **standalone assets** and **insurance-like assets**. See page 207.
Geometric mean	My preferred way to get an average, e.g. of a series of returns. The geometric mean is the consistent return required to get the correct final portfolio value. See **arithmetic mean**, page 20 and page 491.
Global macro	A type of **hedge fund** which makes bets on multiple asset classes based on macroeconomic and political forecasts. Famous examples include George Soros' Quantum fund, which bet on the exit of the pound from the ERM mechanism in 1992. Global macro funds are a type of **standalone alternative asset**, which is a subcategory of **genuine alternative assets**. See page 209.
Handcrafting	A method of **portfolio optimisation** where you set weights by hand, grouping similar assets together, and then set weights within each group (usually using **equal weighting**). See page 99.
Hedge fund	A type of **collective fund** which uses **leverage** and/or **short selling**.
High yield bonds	A type of **corporate bond** which is especially risky; also called **junk bonds**.
Holding cost	The annual cost of owning an investment, regardless of whether you do any further **rebalancing**. Types of holding cost include annual fund management charges and the **trading cost inside the fund**. See also **rebalancing cost** and **initial cost**, and page 123.
Home bias	The preference that investors have for investing in their own country.
Index tracker	See **passive fund**.

Inflation-linked bonds	Bonds which are protected against inflation and pay **real returns**.
Initial cost	The initial cost of setting up an investment portfolio. Initial costs include brokerage commissions, taxes and **execution costs**. See also **holding cost** and **rebalancing cost**, and page 123.
Institutional investor	A large investor, with at least £10 million or $10 million in investable assets.
Insurance-like asset	A type of **genuine alternative** asset which is expected to give a negative return over the long run, but which should provide protection against falls elsewhere in the portfolio. See page 208.
Insurance currencies	Currencies like the yen and US dollar which are expected to be **safe havens** in the event of market meltdown; a type of **insurance-like asset**, which is a subcategory of **genuine alternative assets**. See page 210.
Inverse ETF	An **ETF** which bets on the price of an asset falling.
Investment grade bonds	A type of **corporate bond** which is considered relatively safe. Investment grade bonds are issued by large blue chip firms.
Invisible cost	Costs of trading or holding investments which are not normally disclosed. See page 121.
Junk bonds	See **high yield bonds**.
Large capitalisation (large cap)	Firms with a large market capitalisation. Examples of large cap indices are the S&P 500 in the US and the FTSE 100 in the UK. See also **mid cap** and **small cap**.
Leverage	Borrowing to invest, either explicitly or by using a **derivative** such as a future or spread-bet where your exposure is greater than your initial cash payment.
Long volatility	A type of **hedge fund** strategy which involves using **derivatives** to bet on the market falling; this should protect the rest of your portfolio in a downturn, making it an **insurance-like asset**, which is a subcategory of **genuine alternative assets**. See page 208.

Managed futures	A **hedge fund** strategy which uses systematic trading rules to bet on futures; a type of **derivative**. Most managed futures strategies have historically made profits when the underlying markets and other strategies did badly. They are a type of **standalone alternative asset**, which is a subcategory of **genuine alternative assets**. See page 209.
Market capitalisation weighted	A type of **portfolio weighting** where weights are allocated in proportion to the value of the issued equity or bonds. Most market indices are formed with market cap weighting, which means it is also used by most **index trackers**.
Market impact	The extra cost that large investors have to pay because there aren't enough shares bid or offered in the market to meet their needs. Equal to the difference between the offer price if buying (bid price if selling) and the average price actually paid (or received, if selling). Part of the **execution cost**. See page 127.
Maturity (of a bond)	The time period before the proceeds of a bond issue have to be repaid.
Maximum diversification	A type of **portfolio optimisation**. See page 373.
Maximum geometric mean portfolio	A portfolio suitable for an investor with a high tolerance for risk which has a limited allocation to safe assets like bonds. See page 77.
Maximum Sharpe Ratio portfolio	A portfolio suitable for an investor with a low tolerance for risk which has no constraints on allocation to safe assets like bonds. See page 77.
Mid capitalisation (mid cap)	Medium sized firms. Examples of mid cap indices include the FTSE 250 in the UK and the Russell Midcap Index in the US. See **large cap** and **small cap**.
Minimum-Trade-Size	A technique for reducing trading costs when **reweighting** your portfolio. See page 402.
Minimum variance	A type of **portfolio optimisation**. See page 374.

Model uncertainty	The uncertainty we have about whether a **statistical model** of returns is correct. **Parameter uncertainty** is the most noteworthy form of **model uncertainty**. See page 43.
Momentum	A model for **forecasting** returns, and a **risk factor**. It assumes asset prices will continue to go up after previous rises; or go down after recent falls. See page 328.
Mortgage-backed security (MBS)	A type of bond which is backed by mortgages. MBS can be **corporate bonds** issued by financial institutions or **agency bonds**.
Municipal (Muni) bond	A type of government bond issued by a municipality (any sub-national government entity, like a city, state or county).
No-Trade-Zone	A technique for reducing trading costs when **reweighting** your portfolio. See page 401.
Nominal (bond)	Any bond which does not provide protection against inflation. See also **inflation-linked bonds**.
Nominal return	Returns which haven't been corrected for inflation. See page 26.
Parameter uncertainty	The inherent uncertainty around estimates of **parameters** in a **statistical model** of historic returns. My preferred term for this is **uncertainty of the past**. See page 44.
Parameters	Values used to specify a **statistical model** such as the **geometric mean, standard deviation, Sharpe Ratio** and **correlation** of returns. See page 23.
Passive fund, Passive index, Passive management	A type of **collective fund** which is invested and managed passively in a portfolio of securities according to some predefined weights. As distinct from **active funds**. Usually these funds are **index trackers** which follow indices such as the FTSE 100 or S&P 500. Passive funds are a cheap way to get broad market, or **beta**, exposure. More complex passive funds can give you exposure to **smart beta**.
Portfolio maintenance	The process of regular **rebalancing** of your portfolio to ensure the weights are as close as possible to what you currently require without incurring excessive costs. See chapter seventeen.

Portfolio optimisation	Finding the optimal (best) portfolio by deciding in which **portfolio weights** to hold your assets, depending on your expectations of **Sharpe Ratios**, **correlations** and **standard deviation** of returns. Useful methods of portfolio optimisation include simple **handcrafting,** plus more complex **bootstrapping** and **shrinkage**; I do not recommend **full optimisation**. See chapter three.
Portfolio repair	A serious portfolio **rebalancing** exercise when your investments need large scale changes. See chapter eighteen.
Portfolio weights	The weights that assets have in a portfolio: the proportion of your wealth that is invested in different assets. See **risk weighting** and **cash weighting.**
Real returns	Returns which have been corrected for inflation. Opposite of **nominal** returns. See page 26.
Rebalancing	Adjusting your portfolio weights after your initial investment. Types of rebalancing include **substitution** and **reweighting**. Regular rebalancing is **portfolio maintenance**; one off large-scale rebalancing is **portfolio repair**. See part four.
Rebalancing cost	Trading costs involved in **rebalancing** your portfolio after your initial investment. See also **holding cost** and **initial cost**, and page 123.
Relative momentum	A variation of the **momentum** forecasting model, which ensures you are fully invested at all times even if one or more assets are expected to fall in price. Opposite of **absolute momentum**.
Retail investor	Someone with a relatively small investment account. Opposite of **institutional investor**.
Reweighting	A type of portfolio **rebalancing** which involves adjusting portfolio weights but not completely **substituting** one asset entirely for another. See page 396.

Risk	Risk is the expected variation in the returns of assets or investment portfolios. I measure it using **standard deviation**. See page 24 and page 39.
Risk factors	In academic theory, exposure to different kinds of risk should be compensated for by higher returns. Risk factors include **yield** and **momentum**. See page 325.
Risk parity, **Risk parity fund**	A type of **portfolio optimisation**. See page 106 and page 373.
Risk weighting, **Risk weights**	A technique used in **portfolio optimisation** where all asset returns are first adjusted so they have the same **standard deviation**. The resulting optimal portfolio weights are **risk weights**; you then convert these into normal **cash weights** by dividing by the **volatility** of each asset and then normalising the weights to add up to 100%. See **cash weighting** and page 96.
Robo advisor	A fund manager who invests in a portfolio of passive funds like **ETFs** using mostly systematic methods to decide **portfolio weights**. See page 379.
Rule of 20	A way of converting a series of future annual costs or benefits into a single up front value; by multiplying them by 20. See page 124.
Safe haven asset	An asset expected to perform well in the event of general market carnage, such as: a government bond issued by a stable country, **insurance currency**, or gold.
Selective investment	Including only certain assets in your portfolio, and excluding others. For example, buying ten stocks out of the FTSE 100 equity index.
Sharpe Ratio (SR)	A measure of how profitable a trading strategy is, with returns adjusted for risk. Formally it is the mean return over some time period divided by the **standard deviation** of returns over the same time period. I normally measure the annualized Sharpe Ratio – annualised returns divided by annualized standard deviation. See page 50.
Short biased	A **hedge fund** strategy which finds overvalued firms and then uses **short selling** to profit when they fall in price. See page 208.

Short selling	A way of betting on share prices falling.
Shrinkage	A type of **portfolio optimisation** where Sharpe Ratios and correlations are adjusted to produce more robust results. See page 496.
Small capitalisation (small cap)	Firms which aren't very large. The FTSE and S&P SmallCap 600 are examples of small cap indices. Small cap firms tend to be riskier, less liquid, and more expensive to trade. See also **mid cap** and **large cap**.
Smart beta	**Passive indexing** using alternative portfolio allocation methods to **market cap weighting**. Smart beta weighting may also increase exposure to certain **risk factors** to improve returns. See page 372.
Standalone alternative asset	A type of **genuine alternative asset** which provides genuinely uncorrelated returns, but is also expected to earn positive returns. See page 209.
Standard deviation	A measure of how dispersed some data is around its average value. If our data points are x^1, x^2, ... x^n then the average $x^* = (x^1 + x^2 + ... x^n) \div n$. The standard deviation is $\sqrt{ (1 \div n) [(x^1 - x^*)^2 + (x^2 - x^*)^2 + ... (x^n - x^*)^2] }$ See page 39 and page 489.
Statistical model	Summarising historic or expected returns by describing the average outcome and the expected variation; using statistical **parameters** and assuming a **distribution of returns** such as the **Gaussian normal distribution.**
Substitution	A type of portfolio **rebalancing** where you completely replace one or more assets with different assets. See page 408.
Tail protect	A type of **hedge fund** strategy which bets on extreme falls in the market. Tail protect funds are a type of **insurance-like asset**, which is a subcategory of **genuine alternative assets**. See page 208.
Target weight	The desired portfolio **cash weight** given the optimal **risk weight** and **standard deviation** of each asset in the portfolio.
Ticker	The code used to identify a security on an exchange. For example MSFT is the ticker for Microsoft.

Top-down	A type of portfolio allocation where you choose your asset allocation, then your allocation within assets. **Handcrafting** is a top-down portfolio allocation method. Opposite to **bottom up**. See chapter seven.
Total return	Return from changes in price plus **dividend yield**.
Tracking error	A formal measure of how **embarrassed** you would be if you deviate too much from the consensus, **market cap weighted** portfolio. A simple measure of tracking error is the **standard deviation** of the difference between your returns and the market cap portfolio. See page 26.
Trading cost inside the fund	A type of **invisible cost**; the **holding cost** from trading done inside a **collective fund** such as ETFs by the fund managers. See page 129.
Turnover	A measure of how often you are **rebalancing** your portfolio. A turnover of 2 means you buy your entire portfolio, and then sell it again, in a single year.
Uncertainty of the past	My preferred informal term for **parameter uncertainty**.
Value	A style of model for forecasting returns, and a **risk factor**. Assets which are cheap, such as stocks with high dividend yields, outperform those which are expensive like low yielding stocks.
Visible cost	Costs that are publicised and easy to find; for example brokerage costs, purchase taxes, and fund management charges. See page 121.
Volatility	A shorthand term for **standard deviation**.
Volatility parity	A type of **portfolio optimisation**. See page 373.
Yield	A model for forecasting returns, and a subcategory of **value** models. You buy only high-yielding stocks (see **selective investment**), or give higher-yielding funds a larger weight in your portfolio. See **dividend yield** and **yield to maturity**, and page 331.
Yield to maturity	The yield on a bond which reflects the future coupons you will receive plus the final payment when the bond reaches maturity.

APPENDICES

Appendix A: Resources

Further reading

Exchange Traded Funds

FT Guide to Exchange Traded Funds and Index Funds	David Stevenson, 2012, Financial Times	ETF reference book for UK investors.
The ETF Book	Richard Ferri, 2009, Wiley	ETF reference book for US investors. Suitable for beginners.
The ETF Handbook	Dave Abner, 2010, Wiley	ETF reference book for US investors. More technical than *The ETF Book*.

Uncertainty

Fooled by Randomness	Nassim Taleb, 2001, Random House	Philosopher-trader Taleb is the unquestioned guru when it comes to uncertainty in financial returns, and the pitfalls of using statistical models. A non-technical but in places rather esoteric book.
The Black Swan	Nassim Taleb, 2007, Random House	More of the same.

Risk factors

Efficiently Inefficient	Lasse Pedersen, 2015, Princeton	A peek inside the world of hedge fund investing. Interesting blend of relatively technical material complete with mathematical formulas, and chatty interviews with fund managers.
Expected Returns	Anti Ilmanen, 2011, Wiley Finance	Comprehensive guide to the sources of returns, and risk premia.

Technical stuff

Robust Portfolio Optimization and Management	Frank Fabozzi, 2007, Wiley	Most people shouldn't bother with formal portfolio optimisation. If you insist, read this first (and page 496 onwards in Appendix C).
Portfolio Performance and Benchmarking	Jon Christopherson, David Carino and Wayne Ferson; 2009, McGraw-Hill	Must read if you want to formally measure your degree of embarrassment.

Miscellaneous

Capital Ideas	Peter Bernstein, 1991, Wiley	Excellent and accessible history of the development of portfolio theory.
Simple But Not Easy	Richard Oldfield, 2007, Doddington Publishing	A book which closely reflects my own principles of investment, but is considerably shorter and simpler than this one.
Beat the Dealer	Ed Thorp, 1966, Random House	If you think investing is too hard, then read this book to learn how to become a professional blackjack player.
Systematic Trading	Robert Carver, 2015, Harriman House	Necessary reading if you want to use leverage or more complex methods to forecast returns.

Websites

These links are correct at the time of writing, but may change or vanish entirely in the future.

www.systematicmoney.org/smart	The website for this book.
etfdb.com	My favourite site for researching US ETFs.
etf.com	Another site for finding US ETFs.
justetf.com/uk	Excellent site for screening UK ETFs.
financetoys.com/portfolio/portfolio.html	Good resource to explain portfolio optimisation.
fintools.com/resources/online-calculators/volatilitycalc	Volatility calculator. Works for any US-listed equity or ETF.
uk.finance.yahoo.com/q?s=CLLN.L	How to use Yahoo to get the price for funds or equities. This example is for London ('.L') listed firm Carillion CLLN.
www.bloomberg.com/quote/CLLN:LN	How to use Bloomberg to get prices.
msci.com/end-of-day-data-search	Data for MSCI equity indices.
interactivebrokers.com	The broker I used whilst writing this book. Their chief virtue is they are extremely cheap and allow you to trade a wide variety of markets. This is not a recommendation: please do your own research into alternative brokers.

Appendix B: Cost and Return Statistics

Trading costs

In this section I describe the assumptions I use to estimate trading costs, and explain where they come from. Platform and account management fees are ignored since these have to be paid regardless of the investment made and so don't affect any decisions.[300]

Trading costs

Taxes

Stamp duty is 0.5% in the UK on purchases only. On purchases over £10,000 a PTM levy of £1 has to be paid. No purchase taxes in US.

Commissions

For ETFs and direct equity investments, I used the rates from my own broker since these are extremely competitive, and they are available across multiple countries (I use Interactive Brokers). Rates are correct as of March 2017.

UK retail	£6 per trade under £50,000. 0.05% of value over £50,000 up to a maximum of £29.
US retail	$0.005 per share, with a minimum of $1 per order and a maximum of 0.5% of trade value. In the US I assume large cap shares cost $100, mid cap $50 and small cap $5.

---

300. There is some complexity around annual platform fees and rebates on fund charges for collective funds; but it's very hard to put these into simple formula. At best these slightly reduce the very poor value that active funds represent.

US institutional	$0.0035 per share.
UK institutional	0.015% per trade.

Spreads and market impact

I use the spreads in table 91 for direct investments in equities. These were based on averages across US, UK and European markets sampled during 2016.

TABLE 91: DIRECT INVESTMENT IN EQUITIES: SPREADS, INITIAL MARKET IMPACT AND TURNOVER IMPACT

	Spread	Initial impact	Turnover impact
Developed large cap	0.1%	0.3%	0.15%
Developed mid cap	0.5%	0.75%	0.4%
Developed small cap	1%	1.5%	0.8%
Emerging markets	5%	3%	1.5%

Spread is bid-offer (averages from author's own price sampling). There are small differences between markets, with the US a little cheaper. Initial impact is market impact when initial purchase is done in institutional size. Turnover impact is market impact when a trade 10% the size of the initial purchase is done. Impact figures inferred from sources referenced in table 92.

I assume no market impact for retail investors. This may be unrealistic for larger portfolio sizes, although the use of order smoothing should help. For institutional investors I used the figures in the second and third columns of table 91.

Costs of active funds

Active funds like UK unit trusts and US mutual funds have notoriously high annual management fees. But they also have many types of invisible costs. It's important to make sure that any performance figures you are using reflect all these fees.

Front end loads

This is a type of initial charge, which is effectively like a percentage brokerage commission. When doing analysis for my own portfolio I use a front end load of 0.90% for actively managed US mutual funds, and 4% for UK unit trusts. Based on my research across a number of different providers and industry publications these seem like reasonable averages.

These won't normally be deducted from fund performance figures. Divide the cost by 20 to get an equivalent annual cost.

Dual price spread/dilution levy

US mutual funds normally have a zero spread. UK unit trusts have two pricing structures. Dual pricing is equivalent to the bid/ask spread on investments in equities and ETFs; although the spreads are normally much larger. Single price funds do not have a bid-ask spread. But they will often charge a dilution levy which equates to the same thing. These charges will increase both initial and rebalancing costs.

For UK unit trusts I assume a 0.5% spread when I've done analysis for my own portfolio. Spreads vary considerably; but based on my research across a number of providers this is a reasonable average.

These won't normally be deducted from fund performance figures. Divide the cost by 20 to get an equivalent annual cost.

Management fees

Excessively high management fees make up the bulk of holding costs for active managers. For US equity mutual funds the industry average annual fee is around 0.85%. As this includes some passive funds the average for active funds is probably even higher. Similarly for actively managed UK equity unit trusts the average annual management charge is around 0.75%; plus 0.20% for other fees. You need to check they have been deducted from fund performance figures.

Sales loads/trailing commissions/administration costs/marketing costs

These are types of holding cost that aren't always included in the management fee. They are normally disclosed in the small print. You need to check they have been deducted from fund performance figures.

Turnover cost inside fund

This invisible holding cost is much higher for active than for passive funds. See table 93. Published performance figures should already reflect these costs.

Trading costs inside collective funds

Some research has been done on determining the cost of turnover inside collective funds,[301] which I summarise in table 92 (I also used this research in constructing table 91).

TABLE 92: SOME ESTIMATES OF EXECUTION COSTS IN COLLECTIVE FUND

	Fees	Bid-ask spread	Market impact	Total	Turnover	Implied CPT
UK passive large cap				0.2%	10%	2.0%
UK passive balanced				0.1%	10%	1.0%
UK passive global equities				0.2%	10%	2.0%
UK passive emerging markets				0.8%	10%	8.0%
UK active large cap				3.1%	100%	3.1%
UK active balance				1.9%	100%	1.9%
UK active global equities				3.0%	100%	3.0%
UK active emerging markets				11%	100%	11%
US passive, emerging markets	0.1%	0.4%	0.4%	0.9%	10%	9%
US active, emerging markets	1%	3%	3%	7%	100%	7%
All US large cap	0.18%	0.1%	0.33%	0.61%	130%	0.42%
All US mid cap	0.23%	0.19%	1.1%	1.44%	164%	0.90%
All US small cap	0.24%	0.41%	1.67%	2.32%	168%	1.49%
Global large cap			0.10%			
Global small cap			0.20%			

First four columns are the actual costs paid for trading inside funds, broken down by category where available. Fifth column is turnover, where not available I use 10% for passive and 100% for active funds. The final column is the implied cost per turnover. Turnover is the number of buys or sells in the portfolio each year.

---

301. UK figures from 'When is a TER not a TER' (Frontier Investment Management, 2007). US figures are based on *The Intelligent Asset Allocator* (W. Bernstein 2001) and 'Shedding Light on Invisible Costs' (Roger Edelen and co-authors, *Financial Analysts Journal*, 2013). Global figures from 'Trading Costs of Asset Pricing Anomalies' (Andrea Frazzini and co-authors, Chicago Booth Paper No. 14-05).

I used this research to construct my own figures in table 93.

TABLE 93: MY ESTIMATES OF INTERNAL TURNOVER COSTS FOR EQUITIES

	CPT	Turnover (passive)	Passive Cost	Turnover (active)	Active cost
US large cap	0.4%	10%	0.04%	100%	0.4%
US mid cap	0.9%	10%	0.09%	100%	0.9%
US small cap	1.5%	10%	0.15%	100%	1.5%
Other developed market large cap	1.0%	10%	0.10%	100%	1.0%
Emerging markets	8.0%	10%	0.80%	100%	8.0%

Internal turnover cost is cost per turnover (CPT) multiplied by turnover. Turnover is the number of buys or sells in the portfolio each year.

Turnover for other asset classes is in table 94, and for smart beta funds in table 95.

TABLE 94: MY ESTIMATES OF INTERNAL TURNOVER COSTS FOR BONDS AND ALTERNATIVES

	CPT	Turnover (passive)	Passive Cost	Turnover (active)	Active cost
Global bonds	0.5%	20%	0.1%	100%	0.5%
Alternatives	2.0%	10%	0.2%	100%	2.0%

Internal turnover cost is cost per turnover (CPT) multiplied by turnover.

TABLE 95: TURNOVER COSTS INSIDE FUND FOR SMART BETA

Size	Market cap	Equal weight	Single value factor	Multiple value factors	Single momentum factor	Value plus momentum
Small cap	0.15%	1%	1.2%	1.2%	1.6%	1.6%
Mid cap	0.09%	0.7%	0.9%	0.9%	1.3%	1.3%
Large cap	0.04%	0.34%	0.55%	0.55%	0.85%	0.85%

Figures are for US equities, but relative values would be similar elsewhere

Standard deviations

I used the following estimates for standard deviation of returns when writing this book.

TABLE 96: MY ESTIMATES OF ANNUAL STANDARD DEVIATIONS FOR ASSET CLASSES

	Std. Dev
Traditional bonds	6.1%
Traditional equities	15.2%
Bond-like alternatives	6.1%
Equity-like alternatives	15.2%
Genuine alternatives	15.2%

Figures are for market capitalisation weighted indices.

TABLE 97: MY ESTIMATES OF ANNUAL STANDARD DEVIATIONS FOR EQUITIES

	Developed	Emerging
Individual equities – large cap	27.0%	43.0%
Individual equities – mid cap	32.0%	
Individual equities – small cap	40.0%	
Industry	25.0%	40.0%
Country	22.2%	35.3%
Geographic region	17.5%	26.7%
All Developed or All Emerging	14.8%	23.2%
All global equities	15.2% (all)	

Except for individual equities, figures are for market capitalisation weighted indices.

TABLE 98: MY ESTIMATES OF ANNUAL STANDARD DEVIATIONS FOR EQUITY INDUSTRIES

	Developed	Emerging
Consumer discretionary	26.4%	42.2%
Consumer staples	16.0%	25.7%
Energy	19.5%	31.2%
Financials	28.6%	45.8%
Real estate	26.4%	42.2%
Health care	25.2%	40.3%
Industrials	21.8%	34.8%
Information technology	39%	62.3%
Materials	21.8%	34.8%
Telecom	26.4%	42.2%
Utilities	24.1%	38.5%

Figures are for market capitalisation weighted indices.

TABLE 99: MY ESTIMATES OF ANNUAL STANDARD DEVIATIONS FOR BONDS

	Developed	Emerging
Government	5.5%	7.3%
Corporate	6.0%	8.0%
High yield	7.3%	9.7%
All developed or all emerging	6.0%	8.0%
All global bonds	6.1% (all)	

Figures are for market capitalisation weighted indices. Assumes that the average duration of the bond index is around eight years.

Correlations

The following tables show the estimates of correlations that I use in the book (calculated at a 75% confidence interval).

TABLE 100: CORRELATION OF RETURNS FOR ASSET CLASSES

	Tr. bonds	Tr. equities	Bond-like alt.	Equity-like alt.	Genuine alt.
Traditional bonds	1				
Traditional equities	0.1	1			
Bond-like alternatives	0.5	0.1	1		
Equity-like alternatives	0.1	0.5	0.1	1	
Genuine alternatives	0	0	0	0	1

Key: Tr.: Traditional, Alt. Alternatives.

TABLE 101: MY ESTIMATES OF CORRELATIONS FOR EQUITIES

	Developed	Emerging
Individual equities, same country & industry	0.85	0.85
Industries, same country	0.75	0.75
Equities, same country, different industries	0.80	0.80
Countries, same region	0.56	0.44
Regions	0.6	0.75
All emerging and all developed	0.7	

TABLE 102: MY ESTIMATES OF CORRELATIONS FOR BONDS

	Developed and emerging
Same type and credit, different maturity	0.90*
Same type, different credit	0.8
Same credit, different type	0.7
Countries, same region	0.56
Regions	0.6
All emerging and all developed	0.7

Bond type: inflation, normal or foreign denominated. Bond credit: government, corporate or high yield. I use a pooled estimate for developed and emerging markets due to a lack of relevant data. * Closely related bonds with similar maturity will have much higher correlations than the value shown.

Appendix C: Technical Stuff

As the name suggests this Appendix is only for the technically minded who want to go beyond the basic techniques I use in the bulk of the book, or understand how I got certain results. There are many jargon-laden sentences here, which I do not explain.

Aggregate returns

Many times you will have to work out **aggregate returns** for a group of assets in your portfolio. So for example you might want to know the returns for the US equities you own.

The options for dealing with this are listed below, in order of preference (best first):

1. If you already own the assets add up the returns from the relevant part of your portfolio.

2. Work out a weighted average of the returns of each asset, using the desired portfolio weights within each group.

3. Use the returns from an index that is similar to the relevant group of assets (e.g. for US equities, the S&P 500).

4. Use the returns from an ETF which has a similar composition to the relevant group of assets (e.g. for US equities one of the many relevant ETFs).

5. Use the returns from a similar index or ETF. For example if you wanted the returns for Egyptian equities, but can't find an index or ETF, then it's reasonable to use an emerging market in the same region like Israel.

Standard deviation

Given a series of returns $r_0 \ldots r_N$ the standard deviation is: $\sqrt{[(1 \div N) \sum (r_t - r)^2]}$ where r is the arithmetic mean return.

The standard deviations for a series of returns applies to the time frequency of those returns; daily returns give a daily standard deviation, weekly returns give a weekly standard deviation and so on. To convert between frequencies you should multiply by the square root of the number of business days (this is an approximation which assumes there is no autocorrelation, and Gaussian returns, but is close enough for most purposes).

For example, if you have estimated a daily standard deviation of 1.5% and want the annualised standard deviation, then you should multiply by the square root of the number of business days in a year. This is around 256, so you should multiply $1.5\% \times \sqrt{256} = 1.5\% \times 16 = 24.0\%$.

All the figures in this book are for annual returns. However if possible you should use daily, weekly, or monthly returns to calculate annual standard deviations as this will give a more accurate answer.

I recommend that you use about one year of data to estimate standard deviations (roughly the last 256 business days). To do this in a spreadsheet package assuming that the column A contains daily prices, then you should populate column B with returns:

B2 = (A2 − A1)/A1, B3 = (A3 − A2)/A2, …

You can then calculate the standard deviation from row 257 onwards, using the last year of business days (256 returns), and multiplying by 16 to go from daily to annual returns:

C257 = STDEV(B2:B257) * 16, C252 = STDEV(B3:B257), …

If you have weekly returns you would replace 16 with the square root of 52 (7.211); with monthly returns you'd use the square root of 12 (3.464).

The alternative is to use an **exponentially weighted moving average of volatility**. This gives a smoother estimate. In general for some variable X if we have yesterday's EWMA Et-1 then today's EWMA given a smoothing parameter A is:

$$(A \times X_t) + [X_{t-1} \ (1 - A)]$$

First of all you need to decide on an A parameter. I suggest using A = 0.0054 for daily returns, A = 0.026 for weekly returns and 0.11 for monthly returns.[302]

Put the value of A in cell AA1. Then assuming the prices are in column A, and the returns are in column B; in column C you put the square returns:

C2 = B2 ^ 2, C3 = B3 ^ 2, …

You should set your first estimate of the variance equal to the first square return:

D2 = C2

After that you set the estimate recursively based on your smoothing parameter:

D3 = C3 * AA1 + ((1 − AA1) * D2)

---

302. This is set to give the same half life (128 days) as using all the returns in the last 256 days, equally weighted.

D4 = C4 * AA1 + ((1 – AA1) * D3) ...

Finally the actual volatility is the square root, annualised by multiplying by 16:

E2 = SQRT(D2)*16, E3 = SQRT(D3)*16, ...

Geometric means, standard deviations, and Sharpe Ratio

Mathematically the geometric mean is $[\sqrt[n]{(1+r_1)(1+r_2)....(1+r_T)}]-1$ where rt are each of T returns. Alternatively it's $\exp[(1 \div N) \sum \ln(1+r_r))] - 1$ where ln is the natural log, and exp is the exponent function.

If you don't have every return available, or you're just lazy, then you can approximate the geometric mean from the arithmetic mean and the standard deviation $\mu_g = \mu_a - 0.5\ \sigma^2$ where μ_g is the geometric mean, μ_a is the arithmetic mean and σ is the standard deviation of returns. I've used this approximation throughout the book.

Warning: This approximation will overestimate the geometric mean for fat tailed and negatively skewed return distributions.

The standard deviation of returns is extremely similar for both geometric and arithmetic returns. Hence an excellent approximation for the geometric Sharpe Ratio is $\mu_g = (\mu_a - 0.5\ \sigma^2) \div \sigma$. Notice this is equal to the arithmetic Sharpe Ratio ($\mu_a \div \sigma$), less a correction for risk: 0.5σ.

Is it correct to use geometric mean?

There has been considerable debate amongst academics and industry experts about whether finding the highest geometric mean is the correct strategy for maximising portfolio value.[303]

Have a look at table 103. Here I've taken the same analysis I did for table 10 (chapter four, page 80), but this time instead of looking at the distribution of geometric means I have looked at the distribution of final portfolio values. By design the 'All equities' and 'Maximum GM' portfolio have the same average geometric mean of returns.

---

303. 'The Limitations of Diversification Return' by Donald Chambers and John Zdanowicz (*Journal of Portfolio Management*, 2014).

TABLE 103: CHARACTERISTICS OF DISTRIBUTION OF FINAL PORTFOLIO VALUES, TWENTY YEAR RETURNS

	Mean	Median	Probability <100%
All equities	265%	184%	24.6%
Maximum GM	232%	184%	19.5%
Compromise	204%	177%	14.8%
Maximum SR	170%	158%	14.3%

Based on bootstrapping annual returns of US stocks and bonds from 1928–2015. First column: the mean of final portfolio values across all alternative histories (100% = zero growth). Second column: the median of final portfolio values across all alternative histories (100% = zero growth). Third column: the proportion of the time that a portfolio loses money over 20 years.

Notice that the **mean** of the distribution of final portfolio values is higher for the 'All equities' option than for the 'Maximum geometric mean (GM)' portfolio. If you are trying to maximise the expected final value of your portfolio because you are a risk neutral investor, and you believe that the mean of the distribution is the correct function to assess expectations, then you should be maximising arithmetic return and investing in all equities portfolio.

However, the **median** of the distribution of final portfolio values is identical for both 'All equities' and 'Maximum geometric mean' (which have equal geometric means). Equal geometric returns implies equal median final portfolio values. I personally believe that the median of the distribution is a better measure of expectations than the mean. For a longer discussion see my blog article:

qoppac.blogspot.com/2017/02/can-you-eat-geometric-returns.html

This is important when we consider the benefits of diversification, as I did in chapter six. Diversification of similar assets like stocks in the same country is unlikely to increase arithmetic return (if they have the same standard deviation and the same Sharpe Ratio). But it will increase costs and geometric return. You can only use the higher geometric return to pay higher diversification costs if you also believe the median of the distribution of final portfolio values is the best way to determine expectations.

Gaussian distributions

In chapter two, I worked out that the chances of a 0.5% loss or greater in the investment game (with an average return of 0.086% and a standard deviation of 0.322%) was 3.4%. How can you reproduce this result in a spreadsheet? First initialise the variables:

A1 = 0.086%

B1 = 0.322%

C1 = −0.5%

There are two methods you can use.

Method one: Showing all the working out involved in normalising the result.

D1 = C1 − A1 = 0.586%

E1 = D1 / B1 = 1.83125

F1 = NORMDIST(E1, 0, 1) = 0.03353

Method two: Skip the normalisation step and let your spreadsheet do it for you.

F1 = NORMDIST(C1, A1, B1) = 0.03353

Correlations

First get the percentage returns for the assets you are interested in. These can be for any time period, but I recommend weekly or monthly. Annual returns will give a less precise estimate, and daily returns may underestimate correlations particularly for assets that trade in different time zones. If you can find it, I recommend using at least five years of data to estimate correlations.

Next paste these into a spreadsheet package. If the returns for your two assets are in cells A1:A100 and B1:B100, then the correlation will be given by:

=CORREL(A1:A100, B1:B100)

Bootstrapping and sampling distributions

Sampling distributions of parameter estimates

Bootstrapping is the best way of working out the sampling distribution for parameter estimates within **statistical models**, like means, standard deviations, and correlations. You can use these to quantify the **uncertainty of the past** by looking at their **sampling distribution**.

Running a bootstrap is easy with the right computer software but more difficult if you only have a spreadsheet. There are some approximations you can use to avoid the lengthy process of bootstrapping.

The average of a distribution of means is the estimated mean of the sample. For a large enough number of points an approximation for the standard deviation of the distribution of means is the estimated standard deviation of the sample, divided by the square root of the number of returns or other data points. This is true regardless of the properties of the underlying distribution, thanks to the central limit theorem.

For example, in chapter two there was an example of 35 cards with an average of 0.0857% and a standard deviation of 0.322%. The sampling distribution of the mean has a standard deviation of 0.322% ÷ √35 = 0.0544%. If you wanted to work out the probability of the sample mean being positive, then you could use a spreadsheet function with the appropriate inputs:

F1 = NORMDIST(0, 0.0857%, 0.0544%) = 0.058

So 5.8% of the sampling mean distribution values are below zero. This means there is a 1 – 0.058 = 94.2% chance that the sampling mean is positive.

You can do similar calculations with the estimate of standard deviations. The average of the sampling distribution of standard deviations is equal to the standard deviation estimate of the sample. For a sample with more than 20 observations the standard deviation of the sampling distribution of standard deviations is approximately 0.72 multiplied by the standard deviation estimate of the original sample, divided by the square root of the sample size.

Again for the simple example in chapter two the distribution of the estimate for standard deviations will have a mean of 0.322%, and a standard deviation of (0.322% × 0.72) ÷ √35 = 0.0392%.

Sampling distributions of correlations are not symmetric and so there is no straightforward formula to approximate the standard deviation of the sampling distribution. I'd suggest using the **Fisher transformation**, details of which can be found in any decent statistics textbook or on the internet.

Sampling distributions of geometric means are not symmetric; because a geometric mean is the average of log returns the distribution will be log-normal, and positively skewed. The skew is relatively small however and you can use the same sampling uncertainty for the arithmetic mean as an approximation.

Sampling distributions of portfolio properties

It's also possible to get sampling distributions for estimates of portfolio performance, like the geometric mean, by bootstrapping. Here the underlying data are the historical returns for a particular portfolio.

Warning: bootstrapping portfolio returns will not account for time series correlation, unless you use block bootstrapping techniques where you randomly sample blocks of returns; for example one month of daily returns at a time.

Portfolio optimisation

Here is some more detail on the techniques of formal portfolio optimisation, and how I prefer to use them. This is a huge and complex subject, and before embarking on this route you ought to read Frank Fabozzi's book *Robust Portfolio Optimization and Management* (full details in Appendix A), or something similar.

Basic maths behind optimisation

Given a vector of portfolio weights w (w_1, w_2, ... w_N), with expected average returns r (r_1, r_2 ... r_N) and expected covariance matrix Σ

Expected portfolio return = w'r

Expected portfolio standard deviation = $\sqrt{(\text{w'} \Sigma \text{w})}$

Then, using the approximation for geometric mean earlier in Appendix C:

Expected portfolio geometric mean = w'r – 0.5 (w' Σ w)

Expected portfolio geometric Sharpe Ratio = [w'r ÷ $\sqrt{(\text{w'} \Sigma \text{w})}$] – 0.5 $\sqrt{(\text{w'} \Sigma \text{w})}$

Formal portfolio optimisation will normally involve (a) maximising the Sharpe Ratio or maximising the expected return subject to a constraint on maximum risk.[304] Additionally there are normally other constraints: no negative portfolio weights or borrowing (the sum of the weights can't be more than 100%).

Using the maths to work out expected benefits

Although I don't advocate using portfolio optimisation it is helpful to use the relevant formulae to work out the expected performance of different portfolio weights given some sensible assumptions about expected returns. For example, I did this in chapter six to test if diversification was worth doing given certain cost levels.

To do this I used the relevant correlation and standard deviation assumptions from appendix B. I then assumed that pre-cost risk-adjusted returns are equal for each asset, which allows me to work out the expected return. Then I plug these values into the usual formulas:

Expected portfolio geometric mean = w'r – 0.5 (w' Σ w)

---

304. As you'll know if you're an experienced optimiser it's usually easier to **minimise** the **negative** utility function (Sharpe Ratio or expected return).

Expected portfolio standard deviation = $\sqrt{(w' \Sigma w)}$

Other methods of portfolio optimisation

Handcrafting combined with risk weighting is my preferred technique for portfolio optimisation, but there are more respectable formal methods available. Warning: if you are using these you need to ensure you are using pure out of sample data. There is much more on this subject in chapters three and four of my first book, *Systematic Trading*.

Bootstrapping

It's possible to **bootstrap** optimal portfolio weights. As with other bootstrapping techniques, we generate alternative histories by randomly selecting periods in the past with replacement, to generate a series of asset returns the same length as the available data. For each of these alternative histories you then use the standard portfolio optimisation method to find the best portfolio weights for that particular alternative history.

The optimal portfolio weights are the average of the weights across all historical periods. Weights for each history tend to be extreme, but averaged weights are usually more reasonable. Bootstrapping has the nice property that it automatically corrects for the amount of information in the past history of returns: if certain portfolios have done consistently well then they will be over-represented in the averaging process, whereas if there are no consistently good portfolios then the final weights will be close to equal weighting.

However boot-strapping is time consuming, and requires the ability to program computer code for implementation. It also has difficulty dealing with constraints; if you constrain each individual optimisation then the final averaged weights will usually be far below the constraint, which is inefficient. There are ways round this, but they aren't easy to implement. Finally, bootstrapping doesn't produce intuitive results; it's very much a black box method.

Bootstrapping can be combined with risk weighting. You can also equalise the estimated means or Sharpe Ratios in each individual optimisation, so that the bootstrap is only taking into account the uncertainty of correlation estimates.

Shrinkage

Bootstrapping runs many optimisations; however with **shrinkage** we run just one optimisation but with altered estimates for statistical parameters. This is done by taking a weighted average of a **prior** estimate, and our actual estimate, of the means, standard deviations, and correlations you are planning to use. The degree of weighting is the **shrinkage**: full shrinkage (1.0) means we use only the prior; high shrinkage (0.5 to 1.0) implies more weight on the prior and less on the estimate; and zero shrinkage means we only use the estimated value and ignore the prior.

Priors should be chosen so that they produce a sensible portfolio with full shrinkage. So, for example, using equal means and equal standard deviations as priors would result in a portfolio which gave us maximum diversification. If there is enough information in the data to justify it then we'd tilt our actual portfolio away from this towards whatever the shrunken parameter estimates implied. This leads to quite intuitive results when using shrinkage.

Like bootstrapping, shrinkage can also be combined with risk weighting. But shrinkage has two large disadvantages. It requires you to know (a) what suitable priors to use, and (b) how much shrinkage to use.

A nice way of getting suitable priors is to use the technique developed by Fisher Black and Bob Litterman.[305] Here you start with a prior set of portfolio weights and then use an inverted version of the portfolio optimisation technique to derive values for prior estimates. Normally you'd assume your estimates for correlations and standard deviations were fine, and then use the inversion technique to derive a prior for the mean returns.

Common prior portfolio weights to use are: (a) the market cap weighted portfolio, and (b) equal weights. Ideally prior portfolios should use no forward looking information so that historical back tests are not over fitted. You can use a handcrafted portfolio as a prior, although arguably this could be forward looking since it requires some knowledge of how similar asset returns are in advance.

The correct amount of shrinkage will depend on the sampling distribution of the relevant estimate, therefore it's sensible to shrink means (or Sharpe Ratios if using risk weighting) more than correlations and standard deviations; and to shrink more if you don't have much data. As a rule of thumb I recommend using shrinkage parameters of 0.9 for Sharpe Ratios and 0.5 for correlations.

As with bootstrapping, constraints are tricky to implement when using shrinkage.

Formal method for dealing with different group sizes

Handcrafting assumes that the most appropriate weighting amongst groups is an equal weight to each group. But that isn't true if groups are of radically different sizes, or if they have different degrees of internal diversification.

The formal method for dealing with this is as follows:

Calculate the diversification multiplier within each group

Given N assets within each group, with a correlation matrix of returns ρ and risk weights $\mathbf{w}$ summing to 1, the diversification multiplier will be $1 \div [\sqrt{(\mathbf{w'} \rho \mathbf{w})}]$.

---

305. 'Global portfolio optimisation' (*Financial Analysts Journal*, September 1992).

You will get a higher diversification multiplier for larger groups, those with closer to equal weighting, and those with lower correlations. In a spreadsheet for a three-asset portfolio, if the correlation matrix is in cells A1:C3, and the weights are in cells F1:F3, then the diversification multiplier will be:

    1/SQRT(MMULT(TRANSPOSE(F1:F3), MMULT(A1:C3,F1:F3)))

Multiply each group weight by it's diversification multiplier

This will give certain types of group a larger relative weight: larger groups, groups with lower correlation, and groups that are closer to equal weighting.

Renormalise the weights

The sum of the weights for each group will now be much greater than 100%. Renormalise them so they add up to 100% by dividing them by the total weight across all groups.

Forecasting models

Creating your own forecasting model

A forecasting model can't predict returns precisely, but instead will give an idea of what the risk-adjusted returns will be, conditional on some information. For example, the momentum model that I explained in chapter fourteen gives you different expectations of future returns; if prices have gone up in the last 12 months they are more likely to go up subsequently, but there is no guarantee they will do so.

To build a systematic forecasting model you need to test your model by calculating the forecast values for some historic data: the more the better. Good variables to choose are those that use risk-adjusted returns. This means that you can pool data across different instruments when testing. You then need to calculate the **average absolute value of your forecasting variable**; using the median to calculate the average.

Here is a real example. I took the trailing 12-month Sharpe Ratio of returns for the 45 equity countries in my dataset as a forecasting variable (with monthly data going back to 1970 for some countries). Across all this data my forecasting variable (risk-adjusted trailing returns) has an average absolute value of 0.48. Let's call this value of 0.48 the **magic number**.

We don't want to bet on extreme forecasts, so we will be limiting our forecasting to a range: between minus two, and plus two, magic numbers. In this example that would be a range of 0.48 × 2 = –0.96, to 0.48 × 2 = +0.96. At the extremes we're going to vary our initial handcrafted weight by multiplying it by 0.6 (when the forecast is –0.96 or less; two or more magic numbers below zero) and 1.48 (when the forecast is 0.96; two or more magic numbers above zero).

I chose these multipliers (0.6 and 1.48) carefully to reflect the typical power of forecasting models.[306] Multiplying factors for intermediate values are shown in table 104.

TABLE 104: HOW MUCH SHOULD YOU ADJUST HANDCRAFTED WEIGHTS GIVEN A FORECAST?

Multiples of magic number	Adjustment factor
−2 or less	0.60
−1.6	0.66
−1.2	0.77
−0.8	0.85
−0.4	0.94
0	1.00
0.4	1.11
0.8	1.19
1.2	1.30
1.6	1.37
2 or more	1.48

The table shows the adjustment factor to use for handcrafted weights (second column) given a forecast, in multiples of magic number.

If I put the actual forecast values in for the momentum forecasting rule, rather than multiples of magic numbers, I get a table which is specific to this rule: table 105 (with some rounding). This should be recognisable as table 46 (page 329).

---

306. To be precise they are derived from examining the difference in portfolios with weights bootstrapped based on return distributions conditional on relatively high or low forecasts.

TABLE 105: HOW MUCH SHOULD YOU ADJUST HANDCRAFTED WEIGHTS GIVEN TRAILING RETURNS?

Trailing SR	Adjustment factor
−1.0 or less	0.60
−0.80	0.66
−0.60	0.77
−0.40	0.85
−0.20	0.94
0	1.00
0.20	1.11
0.40	1.19
0.60	1.30
0.80	1.37
1.0 or more	1.48

The table shows the adjustment factor to use for handcrafted weights (second column) given trailing Sharpe Ratio (SR).

If you are interested in this subject and would like more detail I suggest you read my first book, *Systematic Trading*.

Creating your own stock ranking system

In part three I described a stock ranking system, based mainly on dividend yield (with some suggested filters to produce a safer portfolio). There are two types of stock ranking system: quantitative and qualitative.

Quantitative model

A quantitative stock scoring system is one which can assign either an **annual**, or an **up front**, explicit value to the stock. So, for example, the dividend yield model I introduced in part three assigns an annual value to dividend payments.

But you can also calculate an up front value. One simple method is to use a dividend discount model. Here you add up the present value of the flow of annual dividends, discounted to reflect the fact you will receive them in the future. Earlier in the book I suggested using a factor of 20 to do this: the up front value of a stock will be 20 times the current dividend. But you can also use actual interest rates and discount each annual dividend using the appropriate rate.

Other models that produce an initial valuation are the Gordon growth model (which allows for dividends to grow) and book value growth model.[307]

Once you have an initial value you should compare this to the current share price, and work out the expected return that you'd get if the price appreciated to it's value. You then rank stocks by expected return, highest first, and select as many as your portfolio size dictates.

Let's take an example. I've already covered annual models with the dividend yield model I used in part three, so here I'm going to introduce an up front model which relies on trading closed end funds, which are known as investment trusts in the UK. A closed end fund is a kind of collective fund which owns some assets, and is listed on the stock exchange. To invest in the fund you just buy shares, like you would with an ETF.

But unlike an ETF the price of a closed end fund can deviate significantly from the underlying value of the assets (the **net asset value**, or NAV). A simple trading strategy is to buy closed end funds with steep discounts; effectively buying the underlying assets at a discount. The initial value of this trade is just the growth implied by comparing the NAV and the share price. For example, as I'm writing this the Dolphin Capital Investors fund is trading at £9.88 with a NAV of £29.09. This is a discount of (£29.09 – £9.88) ÷ £29.09 = 66%. If the discount narrows tomorrow then I'd make (£29.09 – £9.88) ÷ £9.88 = 194%.

Even if the discount takes a year to narrow then receiving 194% in a year's time is still going to be worth 188% (with current interest rates of 3%).

You might be sceptical of this high forecast return – I certainly am. There are probably good reasons why Dolphin is trading at such a massive discount. You can do some research to find out what is going on,[308] or you can use a better and slightly more complicated strategy.

The better strategy I'd recommend involves comparing the current discount to its historic average. If the historic average of Dolphin was a 20% discount then you'd expect the price to appreciate to £29.09 less 20%, or £23.27. If the discount narrowed to its average then you'd make (£23.27 – £9.88) ÷ £9.88 = 135%. Still pretty good, but not as much as you'd expect if you hadn't taken the historic average into account.

---

307. These and other models are described in more detail in Lasse Pedersen's book *Efficiently Inefficient*, details of which are in Appendix A.

308. In this case Dolphin Capital Investors is currently (January 2017) the subject of a regulatory warning in the UK: never a good sign. Plus the NAV of the fund has been falling: the discount also reflects the fact that the NAV is probably out of date and an updated NAV will be even lower.

Personally I'd still be suspicious of Dolphin Capital, and as with the dividend yield ranking model I'd probably add additional filters to this strategy before using it. Potential filters could include: NAV increased over the last year, positive dividend yield, and discount less than 40%.

Qualitative model

Not every stock valuation method can be neatly translated into financial terms. For example, you might want to look at a variety of different accounting ratios without combining them into a single valuation number. There are also qualitative factors such as quality of management that can't be easily converted into a number.

I suggest using a **scoring approach**. Take all the factors you are interested in and assign them a score out of 10. For example, you might want to score companies on three qualitative factors: quality of management, strength of brand name and barriers to entry. The scoring here will be complete subjective.

To this you can add five financial factors: dividend yield, price earnings ratio, price book ratio, return on equity and leverage. For each of these factors you need to translate the financial ratio into a score out of 10. So with dividend yield you might assign a score of 0 if the dividend yield is 0%, and 10 if the yield is 10%, interpolating other values appropriately. Since very high yields can be dangerous you should then assign a value of 9 for a yield of 11%, 8 for a yield of 11% and so on down to a yield of 20% which would get a score of zero. I'd advise you take a similar approach with other financial ratios.

Then add up the scores for each stock; in this example with eight factors this would give a score out of 80. Once you have a total score for each stock then you can rank them, highest score first. Finally you should choose as many of the top ranked stocks as you can fit in your portfolio.

Dealing with changes to stock rankings when rebalancing

Quantitative model

When I discussed rebalancing the dividend yield stock selection model in part four I showed you a straightforward way to calculate the benefit of switching to a higher yielding stock.

First you should calculate the yield pickup. For example, if the yield rises from 4.5% to 4.7% then that is a 0.2% pickup. On a $5,000 position that translates to $10 a year in additional dividends. Now you need to work out the value of expecting to receive an extra $10 a year, every year, for the rest of the time you'll be holding this stock.

In chapter five I said you should use a factor of 20 to translate any initial costs of purchasing stocks or funds into an annual rate. You can also do the reverse calculation: if you knew the future benefit with certainty then logically you should also multiply it by 20 to find its present value.

But the improvement in returns from a higher dividend yield isn't certain, so I suggested dividing by a factor of 5 to reflect the uncertainty involved. In this simple example you'd divide the expected yield improvement of $10 by 5 to reflect uncertainty, giving $2 a year. You should then multiply that by 20 to get an up front amount: $40. That can then be compared to the costs of selling the lower yielding stock you already own, and replacing it with a higher yielder.

You can easily adapt this process if you have your own method for ranking stocks. Any method that involves calculating the future cash flows of a stock can easily be adapted using the "rule of 5" to reflect uncertainty. Similarly where the intrinsic value of a stock is calculated you can also divide the implied profit from buying cheaper than this by 5.

Let's return to the simple example of buying closed end funds when they are at a significant discount to net asset value (NAV). Suppose, for example, a particular fund NewCo normally trades at a 5% discount to NAV, but is currently at a 10% discount. You already own a fund OldCo whose discount is at 2% compared to a historic average of 1%. Also suppose that you expect the discount to close reasonably soon: soon enough that you don't have to convert the expected profit into current monetary values.

If the NewCo is priced at £90 (10% discount), and is expected to move to £95 (5% discount), this will give you a return of £5 ÷ £90 = 5.6%. The existing fund OldCo, expected to go from £98 (2% discount) to £99 (1% discount), should return 1%. The extra return is 5.6% – 1% = 4.6%

Using the rule of five to account for uncertainty this is 4.6% ÷ 5 = 0.92% of expected benefit from switching to NewCo. Because it's a single one-off return rather than an annual benefit you shouldn't apply the rule of 20 in this case. You should then compare this benefit to the initial trading cost and any tax that is payable to see if it's worth switching.

Qualitative model

You can't use the method above for qualitative stock ranking models, as there is no monetary value for the expected return that can be compared to costs to see if a trade is worthwhile. Instead I suggest you use **a minimum score increase** to see if it's worth trading. I'd recommend using a minimum equal to 10% of your maximum score. For the example I described above with a maximum score of 80 the minimum score increase would be 8.

Suppose that you own one stock in the US health care sector, and it's currently Amgen Inc which you've scored at 68 out of 80. A year later Amgen's score has fallen to 62, and Gilead Sciences is now the best health care stock with a score of 69. But the potential score increase from trading of 69 – 62 = 7 is less than the minimum required. You wouldn't sell Amgen and buy Gilead until the gap between their scores increased to 8 or higher.

This is similar in spirit to the **no trade zone** technique that I described in chapter sixteen. One more thing: scores are partly subjective, so try not to massage scores to create a trade.

Acknowledgements

In the nearly two decades since I first came across the implausibly neat idea of portfolio optimisation I've learned an enormous amount from a large number of people. This book would not have been written without them. I don't want to name individuals, and remembering specific names is too taxing for my aging brain, but they include: the academics at the University of Manchester, and Birkbeck College, University of London; the research team at AHL and the Oxford Man institute; and numerous other people whose presentations, papers, and books have helped me think more deeply about this simple but difficult problem.

This book would have been written, eventually, without the help of my three reviewers: but it would have been considerably longer, incredibly badly written, and almost unintelligible.

Riccardo Ronco provided helpful feedback mainly in the form of "It is probably just my own ignorance, but I don't understand this part… or this part… or this part." It wasn't you Riccardo, it was my writing that was entirely at fault.

I wouldn't consider myself an expert in portfolio optimisation, but fortunately I did have an expert to make sure I got the technical stuff right: Tansu Demirbilek. Tansu's help was also invaluable when filling in the many gaping holes of my knowledge of the US ETF and taxation landscape.

My third reviewer was Thomas Smith who never held back with his constructive criticism: "Vacuous BS", "Adds nothing" and "This whole section is really boring" were some of the kinder comments he made. This is the second book I've written that he has done an excellent job of reviewing with no monetary remuneration. I hope I can return the favour one day, as he is a considerably better writer than I am so reading his work should be relatively enjoyable.

I'm often asked why I don't go down the route of self-publishing. One of the things you learn when studying Economics is the theory of comparative advantage. To summarise the theory: leave things to the experts. And the team at my publisher, Harriman House, are undoubtedly all experts. In particular I'd like to thank Stephen Eckett for rashly commissioning a second book, just weeks after the first was on the bookshop shelves. I'm also extremely grateful for the sterling work done by Craig Pearce who provided excellent strategic feedback on shaping the book for its target readership, whilst also patiently correcting my consistently poor grammar.

Finally I'd like to thank my family for putting up with the grumpy man who was either staring at a screen in disbelief at the gobbledegook he'd just typed; or staring into space and thinking about the next chapter. It's impossible to express in words how important your love and support has been.

Reference

This section includes copies of material and tables that are used throughout the book.

Investor types and recommended portfolios

See page 77 onwards.

Ultra safe (page 86)	Risk tolerance: very low. No access to leverage.
	Example: Closed pension plan with a high proportion of retired investors.
	Maximum Sharpe Ratio portfolio plus cash.
	No constraints on risk weights in bonds.
Careful (page 89)	Risk tolerance: low. No access to leverage.
	Example: Elderly retiree supplementing a modest pension.
	Maximum Sharpe Ratio portfolio.
	No constraints on risk weights in bonds.
Average (page 89)	Risk tolerance: medium. No access to leverage.
	Example: Middle-aged worker close to retirement with inadequate pension provision.
	Compromise portfolio.
	Constrain bonds to a 30% risk weight.
Brave (page 90)	Risk tolerance: high. No access to leverage.
	Example: Relatively young and well paid investor with no financial commitments or dependents.
	Maximum geometric return portfolio.
	Constrain bonds to a 10% risk weight.

Borrower **(page 90)**	Risk tolerance: medium to high. Can use leverage.	
	Example: Relatively young, well paid, and financially sophisticated investor; like a banker or stockbroker.	
	Maximum Sharpe Ratio portfolio plus leverage.	
	No constraints on risk weights in bonds.	

Costs

Main types of costs

	Visible	Invisible	Initial	Holding	Rebalancing	Variable %	Fixed %
Minimum brokerage commission	✓		✓		✓	✓	
Percentage or per share brokerage commission	✓		✓		✓		✓
Fixed taxes	✓		✓		✓	✓	
Percentage taxes	✓		✓		✓		✓
Bid-ask spread cost		✓	✓		✓		✓
Market impact		✓	✓		✓	✓*	✓*
Fund annual management fees		✓		✓			✓
Trading costs inside funds		✓		✓			✓

* Market impact is fixed at zero for retail traders, and increases in size for institutional traders

Cost formulas

bid-ask spread cost = (bid price − ask price) ÷ 2

execution cost = bid-ask spread cost + market impact

initial cost = commission + tax + execution cost

ETF holding cost = annual management cost + trading costs inside fund

total annual cost = (initial cost ÷ 20) + holding cost

ETF performance = benchmark return − ETF holding cost

Minimum investments

Exchange Traded Funds (ETFs)

WHAT'S THE MINIMUM VIABLE INVESTMENT PER FUND TO AVOID PAYING EXCESSIVE COSTS GIVEN THE MINIMUM BROKERAGE FEE? (COPY OF TABLE 40, PAGE 175)

Minimum fee	UK investors	US investors
Free		$300
1	£300	**$300**
2	£600	$600
5	£1,500	$1,500
6	**£1,800**	$1,800
10	£3,000	$3,000
15	£4,500	$4,500
20	£6,000	$6,000

Minimum investment per fund when deciding whether to split up an investment in a single fund into a more diversified portfolio. Each row shows the investment size given a minimum brokerage commission in the relevant currency. Columns are for investors in different countries. Values in bold are the defaults I will use in this book. Assumes that diversification benefit cancels out higher holding costs. All other assumptions as per Appendix B.

Individual shares – US

WHAT'S THE MINIMUM INVESTMENT TO MAKE DIRECT SHARE BUYING AND ADDITIONAL SHARES WORTHWHILE FOR US INVESTORS? (COPY OF TABLE 37 AND TABLE 39, STARTING ON PAGE 171)

Total investment breakeven	Minimum brokerage fee, $			
	$1	$2	$5	$10
ETF holding cost 0.1%	$15,000	$30,000	$65,000	$150,000
ETF holding cost 0.2%	$6,000	$12,000	$30,000	$60,000
ETF holding cost 0.3%	$4,000	$8,000	$20,000	$40,000
ETF holding cost 0.4%	$3,000	$6,000	$15,000	$30,000
ETF holding cost 0.5%	$2,350	$4,700	$12,000	$24,000
ETF holding cost 0.75%	$1,600	$3,200	$8,000	$16,000
ETF holding cost 1%	$1,200	$2,400	$6,000	$12,000
ETF holding cost 1.25%	$950	$1,900	$4,700	$9,500
ETF holding cost 1.5%	$800	$1,600	$4,000	$8,000
ETF holding cost 2.0%	$600	$1,200	$3,000	$6,000
Minimum per additional share	$2,000	$4,000	$10,000	$20,000

Bottom row: Minimum investment per share when deciding whether to buy additional shares in each sector for a given minimum brokerage fee, assuming you are already invested in one share per sector. Other rows: Breakeven point at which selective direct investment is cheaper than buying a market cap weighted ETF. Breakeven point based on geometric mean after costs. Direct investment: Assumes buying one share within each sector, equally weighted. Rebalancing costs assuming portfolio is turned over 10% a year. ETF: Holding cost is management fee plus trading cost within fund. All other assumptions as per Appendix B.

Individual shares – UK

WHAT'S THE MINIMUM INVESTMENT TO MAKE DIRECT SHARE BUYING AND ADDITIONAL SHARES WORTHWHILE FOR UK INVESTORS? (COPY OF TABLE 38 AND TABLE 39, STARTING ON PAGE 171)

Total investment breakeven	Minimum brokerage fee, £			
	£6	£10	£15	£20
ETF holding cost 0.1%	£120,000	£200,000	£300,000	£400,000
ETF holding cost 0.2%	£45,000	£80,000	£120,000	£160,000
ETF holding cost 0.3%	£27,000	£45,000	£65,000	£90,000
ETF holding cost 0.4%	£20,000	£32,000	£48,000	£65,000
ETF holding cost 0.5%	£15,000	£25,000	£37,000	£50,000
ETF holding cost 0.75%	£10,000	£17,000	£24,000	£34,000
ETF holding cost 1%	£7,500	£12,000	£18,000	£24,000
ETF holding cost 1.25%	£6,000	£10,000	£15,000	£20,000
ETF holding cost 1.5%	£4,700	£8,000	£12,000	£16,000
ETF holding cost 2.0%	£3,500	£6,000	£9,000	£12,000
Minimum per additional share	£10,000	£18,000	£27,000	£35,000

Bottom row: Minimum investment per share when deciding whether to buy additional shares in each sector for a given minimum brokerage fee, assuming you are already invested in one share per sector. Other rows: Breakeven point at which selective direct investment is cheaper than buying a market cap weighted ETF. Breakeven point based on geometric mean after costs. Direct investment: Assumes buying one share within each sector, equally weighted. Rebalancing costs assuming portfolio is turned over 10% a year. ETF: Holding cost is management fee plus trading cost within fund. All other assumptions as per Appendix B.

Rebalancing

MINIMUM TRADE SIZE AND NO TRADE ZONE WHEN REBALANCING

Fund size	Minimum trade size	No trade zone
UK investors		
Less than £250,000	£250	
£250,000 to £25 million	0.1% of portfolio value	Half average portfolio cash weight
More than £25 million	£25,000	
US investors		
Less than $150,000	$150	
$150,000 to $50 million	0.1% of portfolio value	Half average portfolio cash weight
More than $50 million	$50,000	

Assumes you are paying $1 or £6 in minimum brokerage commissions. If necessary multiply the minimum trade sizes shown by the ratio of your minimum to these levels.

MINIMUM PORTFOLIO SIZE WHEN USING FORECASTING MODELS

	Momentum model	Yield model
UK investors	£10,000	£7,500
US investors	$2,000	$1,500

Assumes you are paying $1 or £6 in minimum brokerage commissions. If necessary multiply the values shown by the ratio of your minimum to these levels.

Choosing ETFs

This section summarises the factors you need to consider when comparing competing ETFs that cover the same underlying assets.

Accumulating and distributing funds	Buy an accumulating fund if you are more concerned about dividend taxes, otherwise buy a distributing fund. See page 25.
Currency hedging	Avoid currency hedging if possible as it adds extra expense. See page 27.
Costs: management fee	You want to have the lowest possible annual management fee.
Costs: trading cost inside fund	You can calculate trading costs inside the fund by comparing the fund performance to a benchmark. See page 133.
Leveraged	Avoid leveraged ETFs – they are dangerous and expensive. See page 95.
Short or inverse ETFs	Avoid short ETFs (sometimes called inverse ETFs) that bet on the price falling. They share some bad characteristics with leveraged ETFs. Short volatility ETFs (like short VIX) are especially dangerous as they contain hidden leverage.
Short maturity bonds	Depends on investor type, see "Different investor types" on page 86. Careful, average and brave investors: Avoid short maturity bond funds (duration less than five years) as these are a waste of capital. Ultra safe investors: You can invest in these bonds, and reduce your cash holding to compensate for the lower return. Borrowing investors: You can invest in these bonds, and increase your leverage to compensate for the lower return.
Exchange Traded Notes, synthetic ETFs	Avoid these if possible as they have counterparty risk which a normal ETF does not. See page 130 and page 214.
Low assets under management	Small funds are expensive to run, so this could be a sign of an **orphan fund** which is in danger of being shut down. Avoid ETFs which don't manage very much money: anything less than $500 million in the US or £100 million in the UK.

Large discount or premium to asset value	Never buy an ETF at a significant premium to asset value. Conversely, a discount to asset value could, in theory, be a sign of an **orphan fund** (see 'Low assets under management' above).
Sector ETFs	Do not buy a suite of sector ETFs unless their management fee premium is less than 0.04% over the equivalent large cap ETF. See page 255.
Small and mid cap ETFs	Do not buy a mid cap fund unless the management fee premium is less than 0.2% over the equivalent fund. The maximum premium for a small cap fund is 0.35%. See page 257.
Smart beta: equal and capped weights	Do not buy an equal weight fund unless it is at least 0.3% cheaper in annual management fee than the equivalent market cap fund. See page 166. Do not buy a capped weight fund unless it is at least 0.1% cheaper in annual fee than the equivalent market cap fund. See page 168.
Smart beta: other weighting schemes	For example, maximum diversification, risk parity, volatility parity. Avoid these unless there is no other way to avoid excessive sector concentration, and they are at least 0.5% cheaper in annual management fee than the equivalent market cap fund. See page 372.
Smart beta: risk factors	Do not buy if the extra management fee is greater than the likely benefits, less any increase in trading costs inside the fund. See table 65, page 378.

Information for weighting

Reasons for deviating from equal weights

See chapter four, page 110, for more details.

1. When there is a large mismatch between group sizes.

2. When equal weights deviate too far from the market capitalisation weighted consensus, causing potential embarrassment.

3. When some assets are going to be more expensive to trade or hold than others.

4. When some assets have very unpredictable risk, or risk which deviates significantly from a Gaussian normal distribution.

Categories of alternative assets

Genuine alternatives	Standalone	Managed futures, and global macro hedge funds.
	Insurance-like	Long volatility, tail protect hedge funds, short biased hedge funds, insurance / safe haven currencies, gold and precious metals.
Equity-like alternatives		Private equity, venture capital, real estate, commodities (excluding precious metals), and most hedge fund strategies.
Bond-like alternatives		Private debt, peer-to-peer lending, infrastructure, real assets, asset-backed securities, long biased fixed income hedge funds.

Current MSCI Country classification

Developed	North America	US, Canada
	EMEA	UK, Ireland, Germany, Austria, Switzerland, Netherlands, Belgium, Sweden, Finland, Norway, France, Italy, Spain, Portugal, Israel
	Asia	Japan, Australia, New Zealand, Hong Kong, Singapore
Emerging	Latin America	Brazil, Mexico, Chile, Colombia, Peru
	EMEA	Russia, Poland, Hungary, Czech Republic, Greece, Turkey, Qatar, UAE, Egypt, South Africa
	Asia	China, India, Taiwan, South Korea, Malaysia, Indonesia, Thailand, Philippines

Current MSCI Equity sectors

Consumer discretionary	Consumer staples	Energy	Financials	Real estate	Health care
Industrials	Information technology	Materials	Telecom	Utilities	

Index

A note is indicated by 'n' and the footnote number following the page number. Glossary entries are indicated by the use of **bold** for the page number.